VISIONS OF INEQUALITY

VISIONS

OF

INEQUALITY

From the French Revolution to the

End of the Cold War

BRANKO MILANOVIC

The Belknap Press of Harvard University Press

Cambridge, Massachusetts London, England   2023

LIBRARY OF CONGRESS CATALOGING-IN-PUBLICATION DATA

Names: Milanović, Branko, author.
Title: Visions of inequality : from the French Revolution to the end of the
Cold War / Branko Milanovic.
Description: Cambridge, Massachusetts ; London, England : Belknap Press of
Harvard University Press, 2023. | Includes bibliographical references and index.
Identifiers: LCCN 2022062085 | ISBN 9780674264144 (cloth)
Subjects: LCSH: Income distribution—History. | Equality—Economic
aspects—History. | Economics—History.
Classification: LCC HB523 .M53 2023 | DDC 339.2—dc23/eng/20230428
LC record available at https://lccn.loc.gov/2022062085

CONTENTS

VISIONS OF INEQUALITY

Prologue

The objective of this book is to trace the evolution of thinking about economic inequality over the past two centuries, based on the works of some influential economists whose writings can be interpreted to deal, directly or indirectly, with income distribution and income inequality. They are François Quesnay, Adam Smith, David Ricardo, Karl Marx, Vilfredo Pareto, Simon Kuznets, and a group of economists from the second half of the twentieth century (the latter collectively influential even as they individually lack the iconic status of the prior six). It is a book about the history of thought in one important area that was formerly prominent, was then eclipsed, and has recently come back to the forefront of economic thinking.

In writing this book I have taken a certain approach that is not the usual one. Because knowing how I approached the task matters to understanding what follows, some paragraphs should be spent at the outset on the characteristics that make it distinctive. They are: its tight focus on income distribution; its attempt to present ideas from each thinker's own perspective; its chronological ordering of the concepts considered; its indifference to the various thinkers' normative views regarding inequality; and its use of a certain standard (of my own devising) to identify, out of the sea of inequality studies that have been conducted, the ones that are truly important. Let's consider these in turn.

Tight focus on income distribution. Each chapter here focuses on a thinker whose (often voluminous) writings cover many topics, but the objective here is to extract only their views on income distribution and to consider what concrete answers they provide to the essential questions of inequality. These are questions like: How are wages determined? Is there a conflict between profit and rent? As a given society develops, how will income distribution evolve? Will profits or wages tend to go up or down?

Naturally, this means that other subjects addressed by these thinkers are not discussed at all. Each of the authors produced a daunting body of work; one could easily be drawn in and spend an entire career engaging with it and the commentaries it has generated. If we simply look at their output, it is prodigious (with the exception of Ricardo, whose opus was relatively limited, if one does not include his letters, and who died young). Marx's work, as attested to by the continuing saga of the MEGA (*Marx-Engels Gesamtausgabe*) project, runs to about 120 planned volumes, scaled down from the earlier 164.[1] Pareto's collected works, in their many variants, are almost as huge, and even Adam Smith's ideas fill many volumes—despite the fact that his unpublished papers and correspondence were burned, on his orders, at his death—in part due to the publication of notes taken by his students (published as *Lectures on Jurisprudence*). Quesnay's case is also interesting in that his writing relationship with Mirabeau resembles the relationship between Marx and Engels: it is not easy to delineate where one author's contribution ends and the other's begins. Quesnay's own and jointly written works, especially if we include anonymous texts published by his "school," probably exceed two thousand pages. And Kuznets wrote for more than fifty years, over which time his contributions were extremely varied, ranging from the definition of national accounts to growth and income distribution, to demographics, and to economic development.

If a historian of thought were to engage with the writings of an Adam Smith, Marx, or Pareto—spanning political science, philosophy, sociology, epistemology, economics, anthropology, and even psychology—that historian would aim to deal with them in their totality, discussing all or most of these topics as a generalist. A historian of economic thought might focus on economic themes (as, for example, Schumpeter did), or more narrowly on economic themes as seen from the neoclassical angle, as Mark Blaug did by leaving out Pareto's sociological volumes or Marx's philosophy.[2] But I ignore all parts of an author's work—however important— that can be logically separated from what it has to offer on income distribution.

It is, for example, not relevant to Marx's writings about income distribution, the evolution of wages, and the tendency of the profit rate to fall that he also had a labor theory of value. The same views on these topics could be held by others with different theories of value (as indeed they were). Marx's labor theory of value is clearly important to understanding his concepts of surplus value, exploitation, and alienation. It influenced his many followers' views regarding the fairness of income distribution under capitalism. But, as I will explain below, I do not deal here with normative views of income inequality. His theory of value can be treated entirely distinctly (that is, left out) from the discussion of forces that, according to Marx, affect income distribution between classes.

There are thus many interesting economic topics that remain outside this book's purview. Pareto's extension of Walras's work (with some modifications) along the lines of general equilibrium, for example, has no discernible relationship to his theory of income distribution. (I do, however, link that theory with what it can be related to: his sociological view of the circulation of elites.) Likewise, the famous Pareto optimum is logically separable from his theory of income distribution. While it is indeed a statement regarding redistribution, and it is often adduced in discussions of redistribution via taxes and subsidies, it is an essentially normative statement (appearing, or masquerading, under the guise of positivism).

In short, the authors whose ideas fill this book might not have thought (actually, we know they did not think) that the study of the distribution of income among classes or individuals was the most important part of their work. Nor did they see income distribution the way we see it today. But all are included for the same reason: as well as having great overall influence on economics, they contributed to the understanding of income distribution.

Presentation from each author's own perspective. To present the ideas in these chapters, I adopt each thinker's own point of view (with one major exception, noted just below), and I engage in critical analysis only to the extent that such analysis is helpful to clarify their theories. I try to refrain from criticizing flaws and omissions that have only become evident with hindsight. My focus is on whether an approach is coherent in the context of the author's other views and not on, say, whether Quesnay forecast how the Revolution would change income distribution in France, or whether his work explains the level of US income inequality today. Such starkly absurd examples are useful to show how unreasonable it is to judge work from the perspective of the present: Quesnay never expected the Revolution to happen, much less the distribution of land to peasants, so to dismiss his views on income distribution in light of what happened thirty years after he wrote would be facile, unfair, and meaningless. Even more so would be to dismiss Quesnay's view of income distribution because it failed to anticipate the rising share of the top one percent of the US population in the twenty-first century.

My objective is almost to "be" the thinker in question, to see the world as much as possible from his perspective, and not to criticize him for problems or omissions in his writings (unless these omissions are logical errors or omissions *within* his own system) or to subject his predictions to detailed scrutiny. For sure, at times I do both, and I increasingly do so with thinkers closer to the present, as with Pareto and Kuznets. But I do it only when it is necessary to provide a sharper view of income distribution than perhaps an author did, or to highlight some contradiction in their thinking, or to offer possible multiple interpretations. One way to think about this book is to imagine that each of the authors reviewed here was asked to respond to the same question: What does your work reveal about income distribution as it exists in your own time, and how and why it might change?

The exception to this general approach of adopting the author's viewpoint is the critical stance take in Chapter 7, which reviews the state of inequality studies in socialist and capitalist countries between the mid-1960s and the early 1990s. The fact that Chapter 7 combines multiple authors reflects a judgment that no other individual of that time, as a student of inequality, approaches the stature of the earlier writers. Whereas other chapters present individual contributions, the objective in Chapter 7 is different: it is to explain why studies of income distribution went into retreat during the Cold War era. The tone is, compared to the rest of the book, more opinionated, and more critical of the type of economics that held sway, in both the East and the West, in the decades leading to the end of communism.

In short, this is a book on the history of economic thought in one area (income distribution) as it was approached by the thinkers themselves—as far as possible. While I occasionally read authors critically, and do so especially in Chapter 7, my main approach could simply be called "adhering closely to the sources," and I try to take their writings at face value.

Chronological ordering. The evolution of thinking about inequality considered here reflects authors' perceptions about the main cleavages influencing inequality in their times and locations. Considering these authors chronologically highlights the fact that the underlying conditions affecting inequality, and the thinking about it, were changing across two centuries.

The chronological approach, starting before the French Revolution and extending to the end of communism, has the further advantage of revealing to us that *inequality,* at different times and different places, meant very different things. The cleavages perceived to be most important between people, classes, genders, or ethnic groups were not always the same. One should be wary, however, of mistaking a chronological approach for a teleological view, implying a gradual advance toward ultimate truth. Generations before us have tried to reify the prejudices of their day into some eternal truth, and we should not repeat that error. On the contrary, taking a chronological approach should suggest to us that no concept of inequality exists outside its place and time. What we today regard as key factors causing inequality will surely be seen differently in the future.

The structures of the first six, author-focused chapters are similar: each opens with a section that focuses on some interesting aspects of the person's life or work (some of them perhaps not so well known, or reinterpreted here). These are not capsule biographies, which can be much more easily found on Wikipedia, but highlights of some relevant personal characteristics. A schematic timeline of authors' lives is shown in Table I.1.

Next comes a section presenting what is known today about inequality in countries where the author lived and which he studied, with the benefit of modern data. The objective is to situate their views on income distribution within the context of their times. In some ways, thanks to empirical studies conducted largely in the past two decades, that context is much better known to us than it was to them. This is true for all except Kuznets, who worked on US income distribution

Table I.1   Timeline of Authors Studied

	Born	Published main works		Died
François Quesnay (80)	1694	1763		1774 (Two years before American independence)
Adam Smith (67)	1723	1776 (American independence)		1790 (Just after the French Revolution)
David Ricardo (51)	1772	1817 (Just after the Napoleonic wars)		1823
Karl Marx (65)	1818 (Just after the Napoleonic wars)	1848 (Revolutions in Europe)	1867 (Meiji Restoration)	1883 (Just before the division of Africa conference)
Vilfredo Pareto (75)	1848 (Revolutions in Europe)	1896		1923 (Mussolini in power)
Simon Kuznets (84)	1901	1955 (Cold War)		1985 (Gorbachev in power)

directly. But although our knowledge of income inequality in, say, England in the nineteenth century is better than Ricardo's and Marx's, they must have been aware of the main trends—their work testifies to that. Even if Quesnay did not know empirically the level of inequality in prerevolutionary France, and could not calculate its Gini coefficient (a measure invented some 150 years later), he was quite conscious of the main types of French inequality and of the country's social structure—and even tried to describe it in numbers.

While writing this book, I unexpectedly encountered a similar structure in Leszek Kolakowski's *Main Currents of Marxism*.[3] This discovery, which turned out to influence my writing on various levels, was simply due to my reading (or in this case, rereading) different authors writing about Marx. Kolakowski's book is excellent in many respects, but what attracted me, structurally, was that Kolakowski was able to present the evolution of Marxist thought through discussion of individual contributions in an interconnected way. The chain that takes us from the early socialist writers preceding Marx all the way to Marcuse and Mao is almost uninterrupted. Yet *Main Currents* is not organized around its various thinkers in the way that, for example, Robert Heilbroner's *The Worldly Philosophers* is.[4] In Kolakowski, there is an organic unity between the authors' contributions and evolving ideology. Of course, Kolakowski benefited from the fact that his book was a study of a single ideology, which made it easier to connect different authors and their views. When we study economists' approach to income distribution and inequality, the difficulties are much greater because the authors do not necessarily belong to the same school of thought. I do try, though, to bring out influences and inheritances of ideas as much as it is reasonable to do: it is indeed the aim of the book to chart the intellectual history of thinking about inequality and not simply to present a roundup of different economists' ideas.

Indifference to normative views regarding inequality. The authors studied here had varying philosophical and ethical opinions regarding income distribution and whether certain sources of income and levels of income inequality were justified—but this book is indifferent to such views. This is a consciously instrumental approach which, while it always adopts the author's point of view, ignores all normative or quasi-normative statements on income distribution and focuses on the actual distributions the authors highlight, what they see as determining the actual incomes of individuals and classes, and how they think the distribution is likely to change as society advances. I do note ways in which ideology appears to have influenced a thinker's conclusions—for example, arguing that Quesnay's physiocracy and view of agriculture as the only source of economic surplus made him more inclined to justify incomes of nobility, and that, by contrast, Ricardo's framing of rent as monopoly income served a desire to defend capitalists against landlords. And I do present political implications of the authors' views. But I do not engage in normative debate. I also largely ignore what might be called tacit or unexamined normative judgments about matters such as who counted for the purpose of analysis. Most of these authors focused on inequality among males, or families, in their own nations and did not concern themselves with others. Not all were explicitly concerned with the status of women or disadvantaged groups, though some were.

This book's indifference to normative views also helps to explain my selection of authors to profile. If I were concerned with normative theories or, somewhat less ambitiously, normative views of income distribution, then philosophers such as Plato, Aristotle, Confucius, and Rousseau—and in modern times, Rawls, Hayek, and Sen—would be given their place. But since none of them described how income distribution across individuals and classes was actually shaped, much less how that shape would evolve, they are not included in the book. This can be perhaps best illustrated by Rawls. His contribution in *A Theory of Justice* has been highly influential on modern thinking about income redistribution. He advocates, for example, both taxation of inheritances and increased public spending on education on the grounds that they level the generational playing field for people who do not start out with familial advantages.[5] Still, he expresses no view about what income distribution in contemporary capitalism looks like, or how it might change. The same

8

is true for Sen, who has written a lot about income distribution (both regarding methodology and underlying theory) but nothing about the actual forces that shape it.[6] One would search in vain in Rawls or Sen trying to discover either's view on, for example, whether skilled workers save enough to become capitalists, or what sources of income enrich the top one percent.

Finally, given the instrumental approach I am taking to these authors' thinking on inequality, a special comment about Marx is in order. To read Marx without regard for his normative positions might sound impossible, but it should be noted that Marx was generally uninterested in questions of inequality in the way that we pose them now. His view, shared by most Marxists, was that unless the background institutions of capitalism—namely, private ownership of means of production and hired labor—were swept away, any political struggles to reduce inequality could at best lead to reformism, trade unionism, and what Lenin later called "opportunism." Inequality was thus a derivative, secondary issue, barely addressed in Marx's writings. Descriptions of poverty and inequality fill the pages of *Capital,* especially its first volume. But they are there to show the reality of the capitalist society and the need to end the system of wage-labor. They are not there to advocate reductions of inequality and poverty within the existing system. Marx was not a meliorist. Trade-unionist struggle for reduced inequality could at best be justified, as Shlomo Avineri writes, as a means to bring about among workers the feelings of solidarity and conviviality. It is, in other words, just a useful practice for a new society that would emerge after antagonistic social classes had been abolished.[7]

Marx also rejected the idea that his critique of capitalism was based on moral grounds, and wrote rather dismissively of many who criticized capitalism from that point of view. Exploitation (appropriation of the surplus value by the capitalists) was to him a technical and not a normative concept. It reflected the nature of the system: a worker is not paid less than the value of his or her labor power, so there is no unfair exchange but there is exploitation. Consequently, the normative aspect, even if present indirectly in Marx's discussion of the condition of the working class (especially in the first volume of *Capital* and some other political and didactic writings), does not influence his theory. An instrumental approach to Marx's view on inequality, and disregard of the normative, is thus not only possible but fully consistent with Marx's own thinking.

Some traces of normative thinking on distribution appear in Marx's discussion of incomes under socialism and communism, but these comments are very few and tentative. As Marx himself said, he did not want to deal with the "recipes for the cook-shops of the future."[8] And, obviously, they do not refer to capitalism, with which I am concerned in the chapter on Marx (Chapter 4). I do include these comments in my Chapter 7 discussion of income distribution studies under socialism. Even there, however, I follow the instrumental approach, looking at the real forces that influenced both distribution under socialism and the thinking about that distribution, and not at the kinds of normative statements that party ideologues have always liked to pluck from Marx and Engels.

A standard of what constitutes important work. In the selection of these authors, and assessment of their work, did I also use some definable criteria for judging what ways of studying income distribution are better than others? Yes, I did. And it is important to be very explicit about this—especially because it will clarify my critique of Cold War era inequality studies in Chapter 7.

In my opinion, the best income distribution studies combine three elements: narrative, theory, and empirics. Only when all three are in place do we get the valuable result I call an *integrative study* of income distribution.

An inequality *narrative* is an author's account of how an income distribution takes shape through the interaction of particular forces. It is important to give coherence to the theory and to explain to the reader what empirical evidence is being privileged by the author. The eighteenth- and nineteenth-century authors in this book, for example, fashioned their narratives around the class structure of society, while Kuznets's story of inequality centered on the effects of modernization (urbanization, with the development of manufacturing). Other narratives describe struggles between organized labor and employers over shares of net product, or monopolists "swallowing up" smaller producers, or wars and epidemics affecting income distribution.

There is no reason other than convenience to name this element first. The other two elements are not subordinate to it. One's narrative can be the product of, or influenced by, empirics just as it can be informed by one's apprehension of larger historical processes or whatever else. But a narrative must exist if we plan to convince others of our view of the world, and not to succumb to the shallowest empiricism where equations are run simply based on the availability of data.

Theory is what gives the narrative a stronger logical scaffolding. If we want to tell a persuasive story of class struggle, for example, we need to develop theories of relative power structures and conflicts over income shares between the classes. A theory about the key forces shaping income distribution can be expressed mathematically or verbally. It can be an economic, political, sociological, or other flavor of theory. But without a theoretical part, the narrative alone is too vague. And finally, to bring the data that can give rise to, support, undermine, or revise the claims of narrative and theory requires *empirics*. This is an absolutely indispensable part. Data equip the writer trying to convince the reader, but also allow the reader to check if the evidence being used to advance a theory is faulty. All three elements matter equally, and if any is lacking, an approach to income distribution can only be called incomplete.

Possible omissions. There are arguably two notable omissions from the book's coverage of the history of inequality studies. The first is its omission of pre-Quesnay writers, and in particular the mercantilists. This, however, is not an important omission given the focus of the book. It was Quesnay, after all, who was the founder of political economy and the first to introduce social classes explicitly in his analysis and to define the economic surplus. Both concepts would play enormous roles in the later development of political economy and economics. Mercantilists were concerned with inequality between countries, of course, as caused by unequal gains from trade. Studying their views on within-county inequality, to the extent that they had them, may be an interesting niche topic. But it is not, in my opinion, more than that.

The second omission is more serious, but is a partial one: the absence of the Latin American structuralists and the *dependencia* school. As Chapter 7 will note, the Cold War economics practiced in capitalist and socialist countries roughly from the 1960s to the early 1990s was largely barren ground for serious research on income distribution. The exception was the work of the structuralists, most of them from Latin America, and those associated with the neo-Marxist dependency school. The fact that Latin America produced the most interesting work on income distribution during this period was not an accident. Because of its political position that was neither pro-Soviet nor uncritically pro-American, and because Latin American societies are glaringly class-based, the topic of inequality was approached differently in the region, and much more creatively than in Europe (whether western or eastern) or the United States. I do acknowledge in Chapter 7 the contribution of the dependency school and specifically Samir Amin, whose work I have followed for several decades. But, unfortunately, my knowledge of work by Raúl Prebisch, Celso Furtado, Octavio Rodriguez, and others is not sufficient for me to confidently discuss them. A more knowledgeable commentator would have devoted more space in Chapter 7, if not an additional chapter, to discussing these (and possibly other Latin American) authors and their contributions.

Competing Visions of Inequality

It might also be useful to the reader to have, at the outset of the book, a brief sketch of how the authors' visions of inequality differ and overlap. The first four—Quesnay, Smith, Ricardo, and Marx—see inequality as essentially a class phenomenon. The rest see things differently. In the case of Pareto, the key cleavage is between the elite and the rest of the population. In Kuznets's view, inequality is caused by the differences in incomes between rural and urban areas, or between agriculture and industry. For the authors of the last three decades of the twentieth century, inequality is a marginal phenomenon.

But even among the first four authors, views of class-based inequality differ. For Quesnay, classes are legally defined. This is most obvious in his use of owners, a class that includes clergy, aristocracy, and state administrators and that, by law, receives the surplus. Quesnay's classification reflects the actual state of affairs before the Revolution, when the French population was made up of legally separate "estates." The same legal separation continued to exist until almost the end of the nineteenth century in societies that were based on serfdom, cast, or forced labor (like tsarist Russia, India, and the countries of Central Europe) and in societies that maintained slavery (such as the United States, Brazil, and the Caribbean colonies). In such societies, it made quite a lot of sense to think of class differences not only as economically based but as differences in legal positions, which were then translated into material and income differences.

With Smith, and especially with Ricardo and Marx, class-based differences become entirely grounded in the ownership of different types of "assets": land, capital, and labor. There were no longer formal legal distinctions between classes and individuals, but in the economic sphere, the assets one possessed mattered greatly. Inequality was seen through the lens of what is today called functional inequality—that is, inequality in incomes derived from different factors of production. This is why the discussion of inequality in Smith's, Ricardo's, and Marx's writings boils down to varying shares of land rent, profits from capital, and wages from labor. It is tacitly assumed that people receive all or most of their income from only one factor of production, and that classes are "ranked." This means that practically all workers are assumed to be poorer than all capitalists, and all capitalists to be poorer than all landlords. This is, for sure, a very simplified description of our authors' more abstract or theoretical work. When they, and this is especially true of Marx, study concrete historical instances of income inequality, the classification becomes much more detailed and nuanced (as indeed will be shown in Chapter 4).

With Pareto we enter a different world: classes disappear and individuals, or elite versus the rest, take over. Why did this happen? Although, in purely empirical or measurable terms, inequality in the societies with which Pareto was familiar (Italy and France at the turn of the twentieth century) was close to the level of inequality in Great Britain at the peak of industrial capitalism, class distinctions in Italy and France were probably less salient, and social mobility was greater. Italy and France also had less wealth inequality.[9] Another reason for the occultation of class analysis can be found in Pareto's sociological theory—in his belief that the most important distinction in society was between the elite and the rest of the population. In a capitalist society, the elite can indeed be composed of owners of capital. But this is merely a specific illustration of a general elite-based principle. In a socialist society, the elite would be composed of government bureaucrats. In other words, the basis on which the elite is built may vary, but the elite versus the population split remains. Elites just take different sociological forms in different societies.

Simon Kuznets worked and lived in the United States of the 1950s and the 1960s, in an entirely different environment from the other authors considered here. Inequality in the country had by then substantially decreased from its early twentieth-century peak, the United States was by far the richest nation of the world, and its class cleavage was seen (in part because class differences were objectively lower than elsewhere, and partly due to the Horatio Alger myth) as largely irrelevant. Changes in income distribution were thought to be caused by shifts in the relative incomes of urban versus rural areas and of agricultural versus manufacturing activities. This was a new view of inequality, very closely related to the theory of modernization that was popular at the same rime.

In the period after Kuznets—an era when studies of income distribution declined in importance, in both socialist and capitalist countries—there was no organizing principle, be it class- or group- or elite-based, spurring on new work. There were "objective" reasons for this: inequality of income was on the decline both in socialist economies, which had experienced revolutions and expropriations of private capital, and in capitalist economies, which had created the welfare state. The eclipse of inequality studies was, however, largely politically motivated. But it also came about because of the very changed environment of the 1970s to the 1990s, in which the economists featured in Chapter 7 lived and worked.

Finally, the recent revival of inequality studies that I discuss in the Epilogue has come with the discovery and documentation of a trend that had been advancing under the radar during the neoliberal ascendence: very high inequality levels had been reached, which had been effectively concealed by an environment of easy borrowing by the middle and lower-middle classes. When this easy borrowing ebbed, debts had to be repaid, and the underlying low growth of middle-class income and high inequality were revealed. This helped studies of income distribution make a strong comeback.

But that comeback occurs under very different conditions, and today's attention is being paid to cleavages that (while hardly new) have been largely ignored for the past two centuries. These are racial and gender cleavages. To be fair to the nineteenth-century authors whose work is reviewed here, none would have disputed the relevance of race and gender to income disparities in their times, but neither were these issues integral to their work. Racial exploitation is mentioned by both Smith and Marx. Smith, thoroughly critical of the institution of slavery, thought its elimination impossible because the slaveholders with political power would never vote in favor of losing their property.[10] Marx was an active supporter of the North, and particularly of Lincoln, during the American Civil War. He saw the war as a way in which history, through the use of violence when needed, replaces a less efficient social formation (like a slaveholding society) with a more progressive (such as a capitalist) one.[11] And although Marx, toward the end of his life, paid much more attention to extra-European affairs, including colonialism, serfdom, and slavery, those considerations have remained peripheral in the dominant (and not unreasonable) interpretation of Marx as a Western thinker.[12] Gender inequalities were even less integrated in income distribution work until rather recently. The implicit reasons for ignoring them were, first, that inequality was a matter of differences in family incomes, and second, that women either partook of income and wealth of family, or were "invisible." Today, both gender and racial differences are given a much greater role in inequality studies than in the past.

There is also much greater interest today in studying intergenerational transmissions of income and wealth and how they exacerbate inequality. This is due in part to greater availability of data, and in part to a growing recognition of the advantages that are routinely conveyed across families and generations—and how they undermine a modern society formally dedicated to the idea that birthright privileges should be eliminated or at least minimized.

Tracing Threads of Influence

There are various connections among the authors included in this book. The book opens with François Quesnay, the founder of the physiocratic doctrine and also the founder of political economy. Adam Smith met Quesnay during his two-year trip to France in 1764–1766. We do not know how often they met, how much they conversed, and what influence Smith might have had on Quesnay, but we do know that Quesnay's influence on Smith was perceptible, even if Smith tended to downplay it (as discussed in Chapter 2). It seems unlikely that Smith exerted much influence on Quesnay given the difference in their age and social status. Quesnay was on his home ground, sixty-one years of age, and at the peak of his political influence in France, while Smith, almost thirty years his junior, was just a visitor in a foreign country, not known for his own work but accepted thanks to David Hume's recommendations. They met on Quesnay's turf: in Parisian salons, where Quesnay was idolized by his cultish followers and Smith was included most likely only to listen. It is not clear how Smith, whose French was halting, could have contributed much, with so many around him speaking at once in an idiom he only imperfectly understood.[13] As difficult as this is to envisage—so high is Smith's reputation today—Smith might not have spoken in the salons at all.

Ricardo began writing about political economy while reading Smith and making notes on *The Wealth of Nations.* Throughout his life he remained influenced by Smith; it could be even said that he wrote *The Principles* with the idea to correct Smith where the latter was wrong. In turn, Marx's notes from and on Ricardo's *Principles* are similarly copious. In his *Theories of Surplus Value,* which is the fourth volume of *Capital,* ten out of twenty-two chapters, or more than seven hundred pages, are dedicated to Ricardo and the Ricardian socialists. In fact, Ricardo's presence is felt throughout *Capital.* It is not an overstatement to say that no economist influenced the development of Marx's thought more than David Ricardo.

Then there was Pareto, whose first book on political economy, *Les systèmes socialistes,* was written to criticize social democrats of the time and to disagree with some of Marx's basic ideas.[14] Pareto, however, was not as anti-Marxist as he is sometimes portrayed. He was, at times, very laudatory of Marx, and agreed with Marx that class struggle was a major, and perhaps even the main, driver of economic and political history. But he disagreed with Marx on many other points, including Marx's labor theory of value and Marx's belief that under socialism society would be classless.

A clear thread, then, can be traced through the first five authors I treat, starting with Quesnay in the middle of the eighteenth century and ending with Pareto in the early twentieth. The sixth author marks a break in the lineage. Perhaps too much time—time that included two world wars—elapsed between Pareto and Simon Kuznets. Kuznets's work was strongly empirical, and he did not have much (or almost anything) in common with Ricardo or Marx. Nor did he and Pareto share much beyond their concerns with interpersonal rather than class inequality and reliance on empirical methods. Kuznets's theory of income distribution was an intuitive and inductive theory that owed little to his predecessors in political economy. The theory of modernization and structural change that underpins Kuznets's work can only be vaguely connected to Smith's or Marx's stadial theories of development. Kuznets's view of change was much more economistic than social or political.

Different Voices, Different Styles

Each of the authors studied here also had a distinctive style of writing and way of approaching the topics at hand. Here in the Prologue is a good place to do what isn't done in individual chapters: set these different talents and mannerisms side by side for comparison and contrast.

Quesnay's style is murky and made all the more difficult by his many numerical errors. His readers are often left feeling somewhat frustrated as he raises a question to which the answer appears to be tantalizingly close, only to delay the arrival of it time after time with some complex numerical example or bizarre (from today's perspective) digression. One has a sense of traversing an attractive intellectual landscape yet having the enjoyment of it spoiled by repetitions, contradictions, errors, and ellipses. Grimm thought that Quesnay's writings were intentionally obscure: "Mr. Quesnay is not only obscure by nature; he is obscure systematically, and he believes that the truth must never be said clearly."[15] In the end, the journey becomes a long, hard slog. Unusual connections between the phenomena and the facts are revealed, some of them extraordinarily prescient and modern-sounding, only to be "canceled out" by other statements, surprisingly old-fashioned and coming straight from the eighteenth century's arsenal of *idées reçues*. One can easily go down the rabbit hole of Quesnay's work (and many have), trying to figure out the logic of his arguments while hacking through a thicket of technical mistakes. I have always thought that Quesnay must attract a special group of masochistic economists who grow obsessed with correcting his errors, one day making a step forward in understanding this complicated man and his followers, only to fall back the next day by almost as much. If they ever arrive at their destination, it is only after many years of travel and travail.

Adam Smith's style is entirely different. The contrast between the complex, brilliant, and at times confusing mind of Quesnay and the acerbic, sharp-witted, and commonsensical mind of Adam Smith is striking. These were the only two writers among the six in this book who met in person, but one wonders how the two of them communicated. As I said, probably not too much. It has been stated by many others that Smith's influence in economics and social sciences owes much to his skill as a writer—which allows even errors of logic and contradictory statements to be missed on first reading. Admittedly, *The Wealth of Nations* is badly organized and does have its very tedious and repetitive parts (including a very long chapter on land rent in Book I, an extensive discussion of financial manipulations in Book II, and a section devoted to the minutiae of British custom rules in Book IV). In the main, despite its ungainly organization, it is a very well written book, and the fact that Smith is so often cited in so many different contexts is not an accident.[16] It is a testimony to his style, his startling analogies, and the versatility of his knowledge.

The rampant quotation of choice lines from *The Wealth of Nations* does, however, come at the cost of understanding. Not infrequently, a sentence from Smith is quoted with one objective in mind (which seems perfectly consistent with the sentence itself), but anyone reading the sentence in its original context would see that Smith meant something very different. Understanding or misunderstanding Adam Smith, and using an isolated quote to back one's position, has acquired the status of a cottage industry; it began almost immediately after his death. I take sides in some of the relevant disputes by arguing that *The Theory of Moral Sentiments* and *The Wealth of Nations* are not to be distinguished by the time when they were written, but by the objective and the audience that Smith had in mind.[17] (I do not claim that this is an original position, but it is hard to have an original position when it comes to Smith.) This argument is not of mere antiquarian interest—it has important implications for how we see Adam Smith as an economist of inequality.

Ricardo's style is yet different. It is mathematics written without mathematical symbols. His was an arid style, the original case of what Schumpeter famously called "the Ricardian vice."[18] But that arid and dispassionate style has aroused passions for two centuries since the publication of *The Principles of Political Economy and Taxation*.[19] One is both repelled by the dryness of writing and awed by the logical consistency pushed (at times) to its frigid extremes. While Adam Smith is mostly fun to read, and Quesnay alternately fascinating and frustrating, Ricardo is nobody's idea of an attractive author. Even Ricardo himself expressed a rather low opinion of his writing and speaking talents, writing to James Mill: "I have difficulties in composition—in clothing my thoughts in words, in a degree that I seldom witness in others."[20] It is hard to tell how much he believed this and how much of it was simply the self-deprecatory affectation common to the British epistolary genre of the nineteenth century. Ricardo's historical examples (*excursi*) are very few, and the examples he does provide appear to function simply as illustrations and reveal nothing of depth about actual countries and their histories. The contrast with Smith is strong, especially considering that Ricardo's interest in economics started with his careful and annotated readings of *The Wealth of Nations*. Smith's knowledge of and curiosity about economic matters around the world—and across history, ranging from the Roman and Aztec Empires to China and Scotland—set him apart from Ricardo.

But if one concentrates on the issue at hand in Ricardo, and follows the argument sentence by sentence, the gains are huge. I would single out the famous Chapter XXXI, "On Machinery," as the best example of Ricardo's writing: it is a big topic, the argumentation is tight and comprehensible, and Ricardo is entirely honest about having abandoned his earlier belief that the introduction of machinery could not hurt workers' interests (Marx praised him for displaying his "good faith").[21] The chapter thus combines Ricardo the man, in search of knowledge wherever it takes him, and Ricardo, the first-rate thinker.

Ricardo's and Marx's numerical examples are a story of their own, not least because of their frequent use of fractiles and of the obsolete pound-shilling-pence system. I wonder how many dissertations have been devoted to working out the meaning and accuracy of Ricardo's and Marx's numerical examples. There are certainly enough of them to occupy years of work. Marx's examples often contain arithmetic errors; some of them were corrected by Engels, and others took a hundred years or more and the joint work of translators and editors to be caught. Some errors, in the case of Marx, still lead to confusion, as I have noticed (not intentionally, but out of sheer necessity) in comparing Penguin's editions of Marx's *Capital* with the extremely useful, but at times error-strewn, electronic versions of Marx's writings available on Marxists.org. Given the quasi-religious status that Marx's writing have acquired, there is also the issue of translation of his key terms into English and other languages. Although the English translations of such important terms and concepts as alienation, surplus value, primitive accumulation (although in some cases also *primary* accumulation), and the tendency of the profit rate to fall are now standard, there are still differences that crop up from one publication to another. Because I do not speak German, Marx is the only author here I have not read in the original, instead relying on a mix of English, French, and Serbian translations. Luckily for me, and for other economists, there are fewer terminological issues in Marx's economic writings than in his philosophical ones. For example, Martin Milligan, the translator of one version of *Economic and Philosophic Manuscripts of 1844,* opens the book with a four-page note on the translation of several key terms, including an explanation of why *estranged* is closer to the German original than the more commonly used *alienated.*[22]

Marx's aim in writing the first volume of *Capital* was, as he said, to write a work of art and not merely a book of political economy, or even a critique of political economy (as the subtitle says). He met that standard by bringing together philosophy, literature, history, and political economy. He was helped throughout by his vast knowledge of Greek and Roman philosophy and literature. (Marx's dissertation was on Democritus's and Epicurus's philosophies of nature.) Marx's use of irony is exceptional; as just one example, consider his assessment of Louis Napoleon: "As a fatalist he lives devoted to the conviction that there are certain higher powers, whom man, particularly the soldier, cannot resist. First among those powers he numbers cigars and champagne, cold poultry and garlic sausage."[23] His easily recognizable style of repetitions of antitheses, especially in his political and historical writings, is similarly brilliant and quotable—although perhaps he resorts to it too often and at times it gets overly formulaic. One nice example is his mockery of British nineteenth-century liberals: "the British Whigs must turn out to be . . . money-mongers with feudal prejudices, aristocrats without point of honour, bourgeois without industrial activity, finality-men with progressive phrases, progressists with fanatical Conservatism, traffickers in homeopathic fractions of reforms, fosters of family nepotism, Grand Masters of corruption, hypocrites of religion, Tartuffes of politics."[24]

Not everyone, however, has been entranced by Marx's style, as shown by Benedetto Croce's harsh (but not entirely off-the-mark) critique of the first volume of *Capital*:

Account must be taken of the strange composition of the book, a mixture of general theory, of bitter controversy and satire, and of historical illustrations or digressions, and so arranged that only [Achille Loria, an Italian economist known for his own disorderly prose] can declare *Das Kapital* to be the finest and most symmetrical of existing books; it being, in reality, unsymmetrical, badly arranged and out of proportion, sinning against all the laws of good taste; resembling in some particulars Vico's *Scienza nuova*. Then too there is the Hegelian phraseology beloved by Marx, of which the tradition is now lost, and which, even within that tradition he adapted with a freedom that at times seems not to lack an element of mockery. Hence it is not surprising that *Das Kapital* has been regarded, at one time or another, as an economic treatise, as a philosophy of history, as a collection of sociological laws . . . as a moral and political book of reference, and even, by some, as a bit of narrative history.[25]

The second and third volumes of *Capital* were never finished, of course, and were edited by Engels, who used what we might call today the cut-and-paste method. Their unfinished state has both advantages and disadvantages. Some important parts (like the discussion of the tendency of the profit rate to fall) are clearly unfinished. Some parts of the third volume are just long citations from the interminable discussions held in various Westminster parliamentary committees. But the advantage in their not having been finished is that, in some parts, we can see and admire a brilliant mind at work at the peak of its power and inspiration. Some passages (and the same holds for *Grundrisse*) are true diamonds in the rough—I believe they were never reread or corrected by Marx. They seem to have been published as they were written, in one go and in the grip of inspiration on whatever day it was, in Marx's cluttered room in London or at the desk he claimed as his own at the British Museum.

Marx's enormous thirst for knowledge, covering everything from journalistic writings to politics to economics to philosophy, has not surprisingly led to thousands of people spending in total millions of hours of work, and some of them their entire lives, poring over his writings. (Some people, of course, even died for Marx, or because of him—which cannot be said for any other writer studied in this book.) In a recent article commenting on the publication of new volumes of collected works, Heinz Kurz writes about the relative sterility of Marx's latter years, which he explains by describing Marx's insatiable appetite for learning. Marx burrowed into the literatures of not only all parts of human social existence—including learning new languages such as Russian—but also of mathematics, chemistry (in his ripe age), geology, and other natural sciences.[26] One gets the impression that, if a covenant could be made that the world should be stopped in its tracks just as it was in 1870, and that Marx should be given two centuries to analyze it, he could not complete the task. Marx's ambition to soak up the world's knowledge got in the way of his finishing many parts of his writings. Had it not been for his unexpected fame—triggered by becoming, after the October

Revolution, not a mere founder of a republic or a monarchy, but the founder of a new social order destined to spread to the entire Earth—many of his writings would never have reached the public. (For example, his 1844 manuscripts, *Grundrisse,* and most of his correspondence would not likely have been published in book form, beyond perhaps some very specialized editions.[27]) As it is, his collected works, many of them mere notes or scribbles, are still in print a century and a half after his death.

Pareto's writings are imbued by the author's love of the paradox, his search for controversy, and his desire to *épater le bourgeois,* even if in most of his writings he was defending their bourgeois virtues. Pareto's mechanistic writings, excessively ordered into sections such as "3.2A.4" (without much apparent reason), and his nonintuitive terminology make his work difficult to read; it requires a high level of commitment and patience from the reader and often cries out for elucidation. The best parts of Pareto are when he forgets his usual desire to shock by stating paradoxes, or to discipline with engineering-like divisions of the text, or to impress by creating Greek neologisms, and allows his opinions to be expressed in a more "natural" way. Despite their flaws, Pareto's writings do hold a certain perverse attraction. It is unfortunate that he is so little read today, although he might not think so. As a lover of paradoxes, with an aristocratic bent of mind, he might take some pride in a lack of popularity and appeal to the masses.

Kuznets's writing style is probably the least interesting of the six authors studied in this book. In part, it mirrors the man himself—careful, measured, boring—and in part it reflects the evolution of economics as it gradually changed from a broad social science to a narrow field examining just part of human existence. Kuznets did have strong interests in demographics, and often acknowledged the importance of politics, social factors, and even psychology, but did not write in these fields. Perhaps to maintain a seemingly more scientific affect, he expressed his complex ideas in sentences full of caveats and qualifications, complicating them even more. It was not uncommon for Kuznets to start a sentence seemingly arguing in favor of *A*, but by the end of it pile up so many problems faced by *A* that the reader begins to believe that *A* must be wrong and *B* more correct. Pareto's and Kuznets's styles represent the antipodes, with one provocative and the other, trying to be the least provocative possible. Both were careful, however, as they addressed matters of inequality and income distribution, not to overstate their cases. This is especially notable for Pareto, who was more prone to make strong statements only to retract them later, at least partially.

Uneven Integrations of Narrative, Theory, and Empirics

Earlier, I outlined my own standard for what constitutes substantial work on inequality: it features a compelling narrative, well-developed theory, and empirical evidence. When we look across all our authors with this standard in mind, we might argue that Quesnay, Smith, and Ricardo all had very strong and clear narratives, and a good connection between the narratives and theory (this is probably clearest in Ricardo's case), but little in the way of empirics. The absence of empirics was due to the simple fact that most of the data they needed did not exist at their time. This is why Ricardo had to resort almost entirely to illustrative calculations and numerical examples. Some data on rents, profits, and wages did exist, but the sources were fragmentary and dispersed—even in the works of authors like Malthus who were more interested in empirical evidence than Ricardo, and who were scouting for data in practically any publication they could find. There was a dearth of empirics compared to what we expect today.

In Marx's work, and even more so in Pareto's, all three parts are present. Marx's use of data and facts marked a dramatic improvement upon Ricardo and Smith. Pareto would take this to a new level because of his access to the fiscal data on income distribution. (As Chapter 4 will show, Marx, too, cited fiscal data on English and Irish income distributions—the same type of data that three decades later would provide the empirical core of Pareto's claims.) Both Marx and Pareto also had clear narratives and theories. And the same is true for Kuznets: all three components of the "good" approach are present.

But with the Cold War, and economics as practiced at the time in socialist and capitalist countries, things were different. This was not immediately clear to me as I faced the problem of how to explain the sudden eclipse of income distribution studies after approximately 1960 in the West. That eclipse had occurred even earlier in the East, but for the latter, an explanation could be found in the belief that social classes had been abolished, and in the political pressure not to allow studies that might challenge this (imposed) belief. But as for the West, was there something in neoclassical economics and the political climate induced by the Cold War that turned its economists against studying inequality in their capitalist and democratic countries?

The puzzle was solved when I realized that the discipline of economics, as it was taught and studied between 1960 and 1990 in the West, was really designed for the period of the Cold War. Political elements were not the only relevant elements, though; there was an objective element in it, too, as the period saw a significant decline in inequality. Inequality seemed like a problem that was going away, and this reduced interest in studying it. There were also the abstract turn in economics and the funding of research by the rich to blame—but the political climate was perhaps the most important determinant. In the type of economics favored during the Cold War in the West, there was no place for class inequality research, and thus for any serious study of income distribution—at least, as long as communist countries on the other side of the Iron Curtain were claiming to have abolished classes. Each side had to insist that it was more equal and less class-based than the other.

The evisceration of social or class gradation during the Cold War is evident when we look at the historical evolution undergone by income distribution studies themselves. Quesnay, Smith, Ricardo, and Marx used social classes as a way to organize their thinking about economics. Classes were the natural concepts around which income distribution was "built." Pareto moved to interpersonal inequality but did not forget about the social structure. The elite (the upper income class) and the rest of the population took the place of social classes—or more exactly, depending on the political system, different social classes could become elites. Capitalists in one system, bureaucrats in another. It was only with Kuznets that social classes and the elites both disappeared, and the focus shifted to individuals who were socially differentiated by their location (rural versus urban), by their occupations (agriculture, industry, or services), and by their education (skilled versus unskilled). But none of these groupings represented a social class in the way the classics saw it—playing a distinct role in the process of production—and none constituted an elite. The trend toward demoting social markers as primary categories through which we comprehend inequality commenced with Kuznets and continued after him even more strongly and is, in my view, one of the reasons that income distribution studies regressed in the second half of the twentieth century.

There were other reasons, too, that income distribution studies went backward under the aegis of Cold War economics. This is the subject of Chapter 7. It is worth mentioning here, however, that the desirable tripartite structure fell apart. Purely empirical studies (which were numerous) became unrelated to a narrative, whether political, class-based, or international. Most often, there was no narrative at all. Or, where there was a narrative, as in the "world systems theory," there was very little in the way of empirics. Theoretical studies, meanwhile, became excessively simplistic and unrealistic in their assumptions—as well as teleological, because the assumptions themselves dictated the eventual results. Such theoretical studies dispensed with both the narrative and the empirical part. Things fell apart also because of excessive specialization in the work on income distribution, where none of many strands was able to incorporate all three dimensions.

A version of Cold War economics existed in socialist countries, too. That version was simplified dogmatic Marxism shorn of its class analysis when applied to socialist societies. As in Western economics, inequality and its causes were ignored. The narrative and theory parts were supplanted by normative views of income distribution, while empirical studies (unlike in the West) were few in number due to the lack of data and, when the data existed, the secrecy in which they were shrouded. Studies of income distribution in socialist countries thus had, at best, some, often weak, empirical content but almost no narrative or theory.

The situation was better in some parts of the Third World, notably in Latin America. For a long time, Latin American authors produced empirical studies of income inequality in their countries. But their main advantage compared to the Western Cold War economics was in their ability to anchor these studies to the structuralist narrative that linked the international economic and political position of these countries with an analysis of their internal (class) structures. The theory was thus much richer than in Cold War, neoclassical economics.

How about the researchers? Keynes famously wrote of the "rare combination of gifts" a great economist must have.[28] In my opinion, scholars of income inequality need to know intimately the politics and relevant histories of the societies they study, and they must be good in mathematics and empirical techniques. They must also have a broad "vision" regarding the topic they are studying, and familiarity with the economic history of foreign countries, including their economic literature. Such characteristics, combined in one author, were in short supply, perhaps because of an education system that placed undue emphasis on division of labor and unreasonable specialization.

Gaining Perspective on Our Own Visions

One advantage of the approach taken here is that it gives us insight not only into the authors studied but into our own biases when we look at inequality today. It also makes us better appreciate the historic specificity of our current concerns with inequality. Our own views do not have a universal relevance but are the expression of what we see today as the most important forces that determine inequality. The "historicity" should help us realize that the forces shaping inequality may be different in different societies and in different times.

Having said this, I must also admit that in this book I will occasionally refer to an observed effect as a law—for example, mentioning Marx's law by which the profit rate tends to fall, or Pareto's law, or the law implied by Kuznets's inverted U curve. In all these cases, the truth is that these are hypotheses and, at best, when they seem to be confirmed, tendencies. The term *law* is taken from the natural sciences and used for convenience but claims too much; clearly, social phenomena do not lend themselves to equally predictive statements.

Each generation focuses on what it considers to be the salient features of inequality, or the main causes of it. By looking at how the most important economists thought about it in the past, we learn about history and indirectly question—or rather note—that our own approach is limited both by our conception of contemporary society and by what we today think are key markers of inequality.

Eighteenth- and nineteenth-century authors (as noted above) were scarcely concerned with racial and gender inequalities, and with how they overlapped and influenced overall inequality. Both are mentioned only incidentally. Even inequality among nations, of which they were obviously aware (and which increasingly played a role in Marx's thinking), did not nearly have the place it has today. During most of the eighteenth and nineteenth centuries, equality under the law was at most an aspirational objective.

While almost all of the writers discussed here personally faced legal inequality, it did not play a substantial role in their work. Quesnay took it as self-evident that legal equality of social classes cannot exist; Smith did not have the right to vote in Scotland; Ricardo did not shy away from buying a seat in Parliament and apparently never visited his constituency; Marx's father had to convert to Protestantism to continue working as a lawyer; Pareto could not marry a woman whom he loved until, almost at the end of his life, he managed to find a place in Italian-ruled Istria where divorcées were allowed to remarry; Kuznets was a migrant who originally, after arriving to the United States, thought it prudent to change his name from the Russian Kuznets to the English Smith (the two being semantically the same).

The larger point is that perception of inequality changes over time, and each author considered in these pages was influenced by the conditions of a time and place. Appreciating this allows us to grasp the important truth that every inequality is a historical phenomenon; its drivers vary between societies and ages, and perceptions of inequality differ in function of ideologies that we hold. We cannot thus speak of inequality in general or abstract terms; we can only speak of specific features of each inequality.

An objective of this book is to tease out these time- and place-specific features and to enable readers to recognize how our own views of inequality are influenced by the key features of our societies. Accepting that our own conception of inequality is shaped by our historical and place-defined context might improve our ability to think forward, toward the issues that the future will bring.

CHAPTER ONE

François Quesnay: Social Classes in a "Rich Agricultural Kingdom"

François Quesnay and the physiocrats may rightly be considered the founders of political economy. They were a group of scholars, among whom Quesnay and Mirabeau *père* are best known, who were initially called "les économistes"—the first time such a label was used. Only later did they become known as the physiocrats, a term probably coined by Quesnay himself and referring (as the subtitle of his book indicates) to "the natural laws of governance most advantageous to the human kind": respect of liberty and private property founded on the wealth-creating power of agriculture.[1]

The physiocrats' contribution is important in three respects. First, they were (and Quesnay in particular was) the first to see the economic process as a circular flow and subject to regular rhythms. Second, they were the first to see that surpluses are created within the economic process and not from commerce, as mercantilists argued.[2] While it is true that they saw a surplus arising only in agriculture, where the forces of nature ("the inexhaustible powers of the soil," to quote Adam Smith) combine with workers' labor to produce output, their essential idea that surplus is created through production proved crucial and still holds today in our modern concepts of value-added and gross domestic product. In fact, some economists see in the physiocrats' work the precursor of modern national accounting.[3]

Third, and this is what interests us here the most, the physiocrats created *Le Tableau économique,* which displays numerical relations in the economy and defines social classes and their incomes in a way that gives us today an empirical basis to study income inequality in prerevolutionary France. Theirs was the first clear definition of social classes in economics, and probably the first definition of class conflict.[4]

Inequality in France at the Time of Quesnay

Quesnay was the personal physician of Madame de Pompadour in the court of Louis XV at the time when France was the most populous country in Europe. France was a large agricultural kingdom with the king at the top and a formal legal distinction between its three estates: clergy, nobility, and *le tiers état.* The latter included everybody else: bourgeoisie, workers, farmers, paupers, and vagrants. This formalized class structure influenced, as will be argued below, Quesnay's own view of class differences.

Income inequality in France, as we can gauge based on tax data and social tables, was very high. French inequality was considered to be greater than inequality in England. The Gini coefficient for France, calculated from contemporary sources including data provided by Quesnay himself, ranges between 49 and 55, compared to an English Gini estimated to have been under or around 50 at the time.[5] The level of inequality indicated by a Gini above 50 is, of course, not unknown today; it is the level of inequality we find in Latin American countries such as Colombia, Nicaragua, Honduras, and Brazil. As these modern examples suggest, it is a very high level of inequality. Morrisson and Snyder, in a detailed study of French inequality over two centuries, estimate the income share of the top decile in 1760–1790 to have been 56 percent (see also Chapter 5 below).[6] Since wealth is typically more unequally distributed than income, the people in the top decile by wealth might have owned as much as 70 percent of national wealth.[7]

Moreover, the mean income of prerevolutionary France was much lower than that of modern Latin American societies, and thus the prerevolutionary "real" inequality was much greater. A given Gini in a poorer society vis-à-vis a richer one means that the elite is able to push actual inequality much closer to the maximum feasible inequality.[8] ("Maximum feasible inequality" is defined as inequality such that all but a tiny, and at the limit, infinitesimal, elite live at the subsistence level.) This makes a poorer society with the same Gini more "exploitative." The "inequality extraction ratio," which is the ratio of a society's actual inequality level to what is considered its maximum feasible level, is estimated to have reached 70 percent in prerevolutionary France.[9] The same Gini in today's Brazil implies an inequality extraction ratio of around 55 percent. In other words, the French ruling elite pushed inequality as high as it could—for sure, not as close to the 100 percent mark as was the case in many colonies, but not very far from it either.[10]

French income levels were lower than English levels. French mean income is estimated (based on the same sources as used for inequality estimates) to have been between 3.3 and 3.8 times the subsistence level.[11] The English mean income at the same time was about six times the subsistence level.[12] Similarly, the Maddison Project, the main source of historical national accounts data, estimates in its 2020 update that English GDP per capita in the year 1760 was around $3,000 (in international dollars), while French GDP per capita was $1,700.[13] This is in line with Quesnay's perception: "The level of prosperity which we suppose [for France] is much below what is a reality for a nation of which we just spoke [England]."[14] The difference in incomes is nicely captured by François-René de Chateaubriand's impressions on his return to France in 1800, after a period of exile in England:

I was struck by the look of poverty in the country: barely a few masts were visible in the port. . . . On the road, hardly any men could be seen; women . . . their skin tanned dark, their feet bare, their heads uncovered or only wrapped in handkerchiefs, were plowing the fields: one could mistake them for slaves.[15]

The contrast is also observed on many occasions by the British writer Arthur Young, who traveled through French cities, towns, and countryside in the years immediately preceding the Revolution. Young's impressions of France are perhaps excessively negative but nevertheless paint a consistent picture of poverty coexisting with huge wealth, as in this quote (which rather amusingly concerns Chateaubriand's own ancestral castle in Normandy):

> I told M. de la Bourdonaye that his province of Bretagne seemed to me to have nothing in it but privileges and poverty, he smiled, and gave me some explanations that are important; but no nobleman can ever probe this evil as it ought to be done, resulting as it does from the privileges going to themselves, and the poverty to the people.[16]

It is interesting to note that, only two generations later, the tables would turn. While England continued to be seen as a leader in industrial progress and even in political developments and was admired for this by many French thinkers, including Alexis de Tocqueville, a puzzle emerged. England, while economically more advanced, also had much deeper poverty than France. Thus, Tocqueville was in 1835 tasked by the Academy of Cherbourg to travel to England and study British poverty. He wrote a short draft, *Mémoire sur le pauperisme*, but never completed the essay; it was delivered to the Academy and published only after his death (in French in 1911, and in English only in 1968).[17] While Tocqueville failed to give a fully satisfactory explanation of why English poverty was so deep and pervasive (perhaps explaining why the essay was not formally published during his lifetime), it is clear he believed the situation was principally due to the movement of labor from agriculture into industry: people who had previously farmed their own land and enjoyed a modicum of welfare (including ample food) had been displaced from the countryside and squeezed into the new industrial centers. Primogeniture, entails, and the "improvident" behavior of a new proletariat deprived of possessions, were, according to Tocqueville, the main causes of poverty.[18]

The plight of the British proletariat during the Industrial Revolution impressed many observers, including, of course, Friedrich Engels, who published his famous pamphlet on the subject in 1845.[19] Likewise, it affected Karl Marx and his own views of deepening class polarization and the pauperization of workers during the Industrial Revolution (a topic that will be taken up in Chapter 4). By contrast, the French yeoman peasantry who obtained land after the Revolution now looked relatively prosperous, and the British proletariat impoverished and overworked.

But that was not the case in the mid-eighteenth century, when the physiocrats' main objective was to influence economic policy and help France become a "rich agricultural kingdom" and catch up with England. Their first motivation was not to create a new science but to influence policy, although they did see themselves as "scientists" and their approach as scientific.[20] They argued in favor of "laissez-faire, laissez-passer," an expression coined by Quesnay. Laissez-faire meant, like today, freedom of enterprise without government interference. Laissez-passer meant freedom from internal tariffs that limited the movement of goods and in particular grain within France.

The physiocrats, in a break with tradition, also regarded the wealth of the poor classes as the best indicator of the wealth of a country, and were concerned about underconsumption if incomes of the poor were too low. This appears as Quesnay's Maxime XX (one of thirty in his list of "maxims of economic government"): "Let the welfare [*aisance*] of the lowest classes of citizens not be diminished, because reducing their consumption of the nation's products would reduce the reproduction and revenue of the nation."[21] Concern with the *aisance* of the lower classes was a novel idea and a marked departure from the previous mercantilist view whereby the wealth of the top class, or the wealth of the state, expressed in stocks of gold and positive trade balances, was the barometer of economic success. The physiocrats' view, which we shall see expressed even more forcefully by Adam Smith, was that the living conditions of the majority of the population represented the key indicator of the wealth of a country and of the soundness of its economic policies.

The physiocrats were much influenced by the idea of China (as China was understood in Europe at that time) for reasons that are easy to understand: like France, it was an agricultural kingdom ruled by an absolute ruler who, in principle, was benevolent and interested in the well-being of his subjects. This emperor, moreover, was understood to maintain a body of noble scholars to implement policies in the public interest, who not only advised him but collectively, to some extent, limited his autocratic powers.[22] Not surprisingly, the physiocrats imagined for themselves the same role as that of the Chinese mandarinate.[23] In a monograph entitled "Le despotisme de la Chine," Quesnay devoted eight chapters to topics ranging from religion to accountability for public expenditures in China, and criticized Montesquieu and others who had claimed that China's despotism was antinomic to progress.[24]

Not everybody agreed with what the physiocrats sought to accomplish. In *The Ancient Regime and the French Revolution*, published some sixty years after the French Revolution, Tocqueville was very critical of the physiocrats. He despised their dogmatism and desire to refashion every institution of society and impose their own way of thinking on everyone else, indifferent to political freedom: "According to the Economists [physiocrats] the function of the state was not merely one of ruling the nation, but also that of recasting it in a given mold, of shaping the mentality of the population as a whole in accordance with a predetermined model and instilling the ideas and sentiments they thought to be desirable into the minds of all."[25] Most important, the ideologically liberal Tocqueville, an admirer of the British system, saw the physiocrats as intellectually "imprisoned" within the traditional and hierarchical monarchical system. Note the heavy dose of sarcasm in Tocqueville's description of the physiocrats' admiration of China, whose system held no particular attraction for him:

They went into ecstasies over a land whose ruler, absolute but free from prejudices, paid homage to the utilitarian arts by plowing a field once a year; where candidates for government posts have to pass a competitive examination in literature; where philosophy does duty for religion and the only aristocracy consists of men of letters.[26]

Apart from his interest in China, Quesnay found support for the importance of agriculture, and the harmfulness of high inequality and ostentatious urban consumption, in the historical experience of the decline and fall of the Roman Republic. The preeminence of agriculture and small peasant holdings had been the glory of the Roman Republic and the basis of its power. But when wealth accumulated and the large landowners left the countryside to congregate in Rome and spend their money on "the arts of luxury and works of an ingenious industry" (instead of investing in agriculture), they left the conquered lands to be cultivated by hired laborers and slaves, and harvests suffered. As Rome began to depend on shipments of grain from abroad, and agricultural knowledge and customs were forgotten, the decline was inevitable:

Such was the fruitful origin of the Roman Republic, which was composed at first of robbers and malefactors, a worse than unproductive class, but which soon by necessity transformed itself and was dedicated solely to the work of agriculture; thanks to the products of agriculture, always held in high esteem, and thanks to being protected at home for more than five hundred years, it saw its population and its glory increase continually, and grew to be the happiest, richest, and most powerful state of the known world. . . . But when the great landowners congregated in Rome and spent their incomes there, when the provinces were abandoned to the tyranny of tax-farmers, and the work of agriculture left in the hands of slaves; when it was necessary to call upon the corn of Egypt to feed the capital, which was thus reduced to reliance on a merchant navy; when the arts of luxury and the labors of an ingenious industry had made the townspeople important and the *capita censi* [the lowest class] into valuable men, when this multitude of causes had, by departing from the natural order of things, brought about the destruction of morals, the state, weakened on all fronts, just waited for—and could not and should not but wait for—devastation and enslavement.[27]

Consistent with their concerns about agriculture, the physiocrats displayed a strong anti-urban bias, mixed at times with barely concealed contempt for urban philistines. It was a somewhat strange attitude given that their writings were directed at the urban *literati* or the court, the elite of the French society (although some of its members might have liked to imagine themselves "rural," with Versailles serving as a Disneyland-like version of the French countryside).

Social Classes and Their Sources of Income

In the class structure introduced by the physiocrats we see for the first time in economics a very clear delineation of the principal economic classes. Table 1.1 shows the summary of the factoral income distribution that appears in *La philosophie rurale,* published in 1763. The book was written mostly by Mirabeau, but its seventh chapter, dealing with income distribution, was authored by Quesnay.[28] Unlike *Le Tableau Économique,* where the quantities were merely illustrative, here the objective was to depict the real situation of the French economy. Mirabeau and Quesnay, before settling on the final title of the book, thought of calling it *Le Grand Tableau Économique.* The book itself was an ambitious project, perhaps the most ambitious ever undertaken by the *économistes.* It was "an exposition, pure and simple, magisterial and complete, of a . . . superior truth, whose principles are to apply to all countries and all times."[29] It was to be the Pentateuque of the future sect.[30]

The physiocrats define four sources of income—wages, profit, interest, and net surplus—and (at least) four social classes (see Table 1.1). If we break the ruling elite into its component parts (landlords, gov-

Table 1.1   Summary of Class Structure in *La philosophie rurale*

Social class	More detailed social groups	Income in terms of overall mean	Population share (in %)
Workers	Agricultural laborers	0.5	48
	Manufacturing low-skill workers (*gagistes inférieurs*)	0.6	22
Self-employed	Self-employed in viticulture	0.8	6
	Artisans and craftsmen in manufacturing (*gagistes supérieurs*)	2.3	4
Capitalists	Capitalists (tenant-farmers)	2.7	8
The Elite	Propriétaires (landlords, clergy, government administrators)	2.3	12
	Total	1	100

Note: Categories and values represent the distribution of earners (people with positive net income), not of the entire population.

ernment officials, and clergy), we get a total of six social classes.[31] The working class is composed of agricultural laborers and low-skilled workers outside agriculture (*gagistes inférieurs*) who together account for 70 percent of the active population. Their incomes are around half to 60 percent of the overall mean. Next are the self-employed, who make up 10 percent of the population and come from two groups. Some are agricultural workers, with Quesnay assuming that all wine producers own their land and use their own capital.* The others are manufacturing workers, artisans, and craftsmen (*gagistes supérieurs*).† The viticulturers in the former group are not much better off than ordinary workers, but the artisans of the latter group are much richer, with an average income

---

* It is never explained why it is only in viticulture that this particular ownership structure holds.

† As with many terms in Quesnay (perhaps because they were new), there are some ambiguities that require redefinitions. One example is that artisans and craftsmen, who are mostly self-employed, are both called *gagistes supérieurs*— a term whose "gage" has the same etymological origin as the English "wage," leading one to think these must be hired workers, which they were not.

2.3 times the mean. Capitalists or tenant-farmers, who receive compensation for management of the farm (that is, profit) and interest on the capital they advance to workers, are all engaged in agriculture. They have the highest income of all classes (2.7 times the mean) and make up 8 percent of the population.

It is important to note that the only capitalists in the physiocratic system are the tenant-farmers who rent land from landlords.* The class conflict takes place, as in Ricardo (see Chapter 3), between tenant-farmers and landlords. Workers do not participate in that conflict because their wages are assumed to be equal or close to the subsistence regardless of how the distribution between the landlord's rent and tenant-farmers' profits goes. As Vaggi writes, Quesnay tended at first to take the side of tenant-farmers, because he saw their activity as crucial for the expansion of agricultural production.[32] He advocated longer-term land leases and greater stability in the relationship between the two classes—because, obviously, if tenant-farmers could not expect to see returns on their investments, they were not likely to undertake any. He even thought of tenant-farmers and nobility as co-owners of the land: "in agriculture the possessor of the land and the possessor of the advances necessary for cultivation are both equally proprietors, and on that account there is equal dignity on each side."[33] It was nothing less than a call for a change in the French legal system, which had drawn a sharp distinction of clergy and nobility versus everybody else. This could not please the powerful aristocracy, among whom Quesnay himself moved, or the king, and gradually Quesnay's advocacy of capitalists became more muted.[34]

It is notable that capitalists outside of agriculture do not exist in this world. Existing outside agriculture are only the self-employed artisans and craftsmen and, of course, hired workers. As Weulersse writes:

The Physiocrats, who consider industry as "the wage earner" [salarié] of agriculture, do not imagine that this order of things can

---

* Tenant-farmers bring the plow, animals, seeds, and so forth (that is, the capital) on which they expect a return.

be reversed; that the manufacturing entrepreneurs come to realize a real net profit, while the farmers, and the propriétaires themselves, are reduced to a condition closer to wage labor than to their former economic primacy. The hypothesis of a society where it would be the rich manufacturers who would sustain agriculture seems to them implausible and, so to speak, monstrous, at least in a country having a vast and fertile territory like France.[35]

The three classes that were not directly involved in the process of production (landlords, government officials, and the clergy) are jointly called "propriétaires" by Quesnay. They broadly overlap with *le premier* and *le deuxième état*—formally, the two top social classes in France. The propriétaires receive their income out of the surplus: landlords receive rent, government officials are paid out of taxes, and the clergy are paid through another tax (tithes). There are quite a few of the propriétaires (amounting to 12 percent of the population) and on average their income is 2.3 times the mean. As can be easily seen, the class structure as defined by the physiocrats closely matched the official classification of classes that existed in prerevolutionary France.

Let us now consider in more detail the composition and income levels of each class, beginning with workers. There are three types of workers: hired workers in agriculture; female agricultural labor (*servantes de basse cour*), whose very low wages are only one-fourth of the unskilled workers'; and unskilled workers in the manufacturing sector.* We may suppose that the latter's wages are at the subsistence level, although this is never clearly stated. Ambiguity regarding subsistence is a feature that, as we shall see, is shared by many classical authors. Subsistence must be understood, of course, as Robert Allen has argued in his many papers, not as subsistence just for the worker, but subsistence for the worker *and* the worker's family.

---

* It is implicitly assumed that female servants do not have families to maintain. Their average wage of 125 *livres* is therefore, on a per-capita basis, in line with the 500 *livres* received by the agricultural hired worker who has, on average, a family of four.

Capitalists or tenant-farmers, in Quesnay's *Tableau,* own varying amounts of capital, so there is differentiation in income that comes straight from their differences in wealth. They receive income by virtue of both the capital they own (interest) and the fruits of their management (profit). Capitalists also apply capital in different branches of production, but they receive everywhere the same rate of return of 10 percent per year. We should not take that specific rate of return too seriously; the point to note is the equalization of the profit rate, which applies not only to diverse areas of agriculture but also to commerce and manufacturing. Capital, in other words, is mobile.

In principle, lots of income inequality may come from variations within the capitalist class (tenant-farmers). Figure 1.1 presents a more detailed picture of income inequality that distinguishes among different capitalists. As shown, the richest class are the capitalists who invest in grain production, forestry, and commerce; their income is, on average, about 3.8 times the mean. Since we have already accepted the assumption that the rate of return is the same across areas of investment, the higher income of these capitalists simply results from the greater amounts of capital invested in grain production, forestry, and commerce. Presumably, Quesnay had judged these branches to be more capital-intensive than others.

Propriétaires' incomes are all the same. This lack of income differentiation among the three top classes (leaving aside the income differentiation *within* each of these classes, which must also have been substantial) is probably Quesnay's greatest and most unfortunate simplification. The top class, which includes very rich aristocrats but also rather modest or even poor bureaucrats and priests, was heterogeneous. In this lumping together of the "elite" we see the main source of Quesnay's overall underestimation of French income inequality.

Taking all classes shown in Figure 1.1, the income difference between the richest and the poorest is more than seven to one. But although the classes are, broadly speaking, ranked by their income levels—with workers at the bottom, capitalists in the middle, and propriétaires at the top—that ranking, when we look more closely,

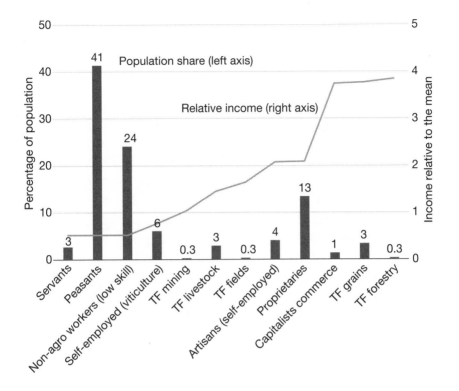

Figure 1.1. More detailed social structure (twelve classes)

Note: TF stands for tenant-farmers, or land capitalists. Classes are ranked from left to right according to income. Population shares are shown by the bars. Relative income (to the mean) is shown by the line. This is the distribution of the entire population, so class shares are not necessarily the same as in Table 1.1. For example, servants and peasants represent 44 percent of *total population* in Figure 1.1 but 48 percent of *all earners* in Table 1.1.

Data source: Mirabeau and Quesnay, *Philosophie Rurale.*

does not always hold. Capitalists can have either greater or smaller incomes than propriétaires, and the self-employed in manufacturing (artisans), who do quite well for themselves, earn more than several groups of capitalists. There are also within-class inequalities: capitalists, as we have seen, earn different amounts depending on how much capital they invest, and among the workers (if we include female servants) some are paid more than others.

Incomes within agriculture are differentiated, but outside of that realm, the class structure is pretty rudimentary. The non-agricultural realm is considered "sterile" because it does not generate surplus for the three top classes. It is assumed that non-agricultural production does not yield taxes, rent, or tithes for the clergy; it simply covers the costs of labor and the average rate of return on capital. There are no residual claimants—that is, landlords, government officials, or clergy drawing on the surplus. Alternatively, and perhaps more accurately, one could say that what mattered was not the inherent productivity of agriculture (land working together with the laborer, to paraphrase Quesnay) but the fact that in manufacturing there was no institutionalized hierarchical relationship that would allow anyone not directly involved in production to receive an income from it. We can simply imagine that manufacturing in Quesnay's world pays zero taxes (and indeed Quesnay argued in favor of a single tax on land), and is free from any institutionalized force above it forcing it to transfer part of its income to people not directly involved in production.[36]

The Importance of the Surplus

It is important to realize that, for Quesnay, the objective of economic activity was production of surplus (as it is today) but that *surplus* was much more narrowly defined than today's *value-added,* because it excluded wages and return to capital. This seems strange from today's perspective, but it wasn't from Quesnay's: wages and interest can be regarded as simply necessary costs of production (given that no legally free worker supplies labor without a wage, and no capitalist lends money or advances capital without compensation). But for Quesnay this was not sufficient. For a society to exist and flourish, it had to generate a surplus sufficient to sustain its ruling classes, whose members, although not directly involved in production—that is, neither working nor advancing capital—played indispensable roles in the society's functioning. For without sufficient surplus, there could be no activities beyond hand-to-mouth production: no administration of justice, no defense or protection of property, no ideology (religion) to maintain the entire structure. The surplus may be considered a precondition for the existence of a civilized society, not any differently than taxes are thought of today.*

The three top classes here play the same role, as Marx noticed, that the capitalist class plays in Ricardo.[37] They are residual income claimants and their income is vital to the economy. For Ricardo, the net income of capitalists is needed for investments and ultimately for growth.† For Quesnay, the net income of the propriétaires is needed for the economy and for society to continue functioning: to provide for law and order, and the spiritual sustenance presumably contributed by the clergy. A society unable to pay propriétaires for their functions would dissolve, cease to exist, and descend into a kind of Hobbesian anarchy and chaos.

Growth, never very explicitly discussed by the physiocrats as the goal of the economy, would come from the return on capital received by capitalists, which would then be reinvested. This presumption, however, is not unanimously accepted. Isaac Rubin, for example, argues that Quesnay in reality had in mind only a stationary economy (a system of simple, not expanded, reproduction) and that the return to capital was merely a compensation for depreciation.[38]

Similarly, Quesnay did not imagine that the surplus could be used either to increase wages above subsistence, or to pay higher profit to capitalists. He saw it by definition accruing to the top classes: landowners, government officials (like Quesnay himself), and priests. "In order to get an income from land," he wrote, "agricultural work must produce a net income above the wages paid to workers [and interest paid to tenant-farmers], for it is this net product that allows other classes to exist."[39]

---

* It does, however, have some similarities with the mercantilist view that it is the income and power of the top classes that matters.

† In Ricardo, capitalists receive their income only after rent is taken by landlords and wages have been paid to workers. (Technically, in Quesnay, wages are paid even earlier, as an advance.)

45

Quesnay gives us only a static, one-shot picture of the class structure in a predominantly traditional society before the Industrial Revolution. He offers no predictions of how that class structure might be affected by economic development, or how the incomes of the classes might change. This is one of the major shortcomings of the static image of inequality we have inherited from the physiocrats. Was it simply that physiocrats were not interested in a dynamic analysis? Or perhaps they did not recognize the importance of charting the evolution of social classes as a society becomes richer?

More likely, I think, it was because the objective of all their work was to lead the reader to a prior conclusion they had established. The structure of the society they describe, and the income numbers they provide, represent a somewhat embellished version of the French economy at the time. This is because the concealed objective of the physiocrats throughout their studies was to illustrate to the rulers—that is, to the king and the people around him—the prosperity that could be France's were the right policies adopted. The right policies were, of course, those advocated by the physiocrats. Thus, the physiocrats tacitly conveyed the social structure of the ideal society. It was the one they were precisely sketching: a rich, and perhaps stationary, agricultural kingdom. If the ideal is reached, there is no need for dynamics.

CHAPTER TWO

Adam Smith: "Progress of Opulence" and an Implicit Theory of Income Distribution

In today's terms, Adam Smith could be considered a development economist. His objective in *The Wealth of Nations* was to describe and argue for government policies that would lead to the maximum "opulence" for a population. He was among the first to develop a stadial theory of development, proposing that societies evolve from a primitive state ("rude state of society") to a pastoral, then an agricultural or feudal, and eventually a commercial state.[1] Similarly, he divided societies into those advancing, stationary, and declining in wealth. In his own time, northern Europe and North America belonged to the first group, the rest of the world to the second, and perhaps only China to the third.[2]

Book I of *The Wealth of Nations* (roughly 340 pages out of 1,200 in the edition I am using) deals with improvements in productive forces—that is, with the subject of growth. Book II (130 pages) addresses the accumulation of capital. Book III (fewer than 60 pages) relates the history of how different societies, from the Roman era up to Adam Smith's times, have had their economies organized.[3] In these three broad topics, today's development economists easily recognize their own field. It is not difficult to understand why Adam Smith's interests were similar to those of today's development economists: England and Scotland at his time were developing economies. Indeed, they were (together with the Netherlands) ahead of that long peloton of countries that would try to develop their economies in the next two centuries. Their problems—finding the right mix between individual initiative and government policy, finding the proper balance between capital and labor, increasing investment to accelerate "opulence"—were the same ones development economists faced in Africa, Latin America, and Asia in the 1960s and later. Smith's stadial theory of economic development was replicated, in different forms, by others, from Marx, Rudolf Hilferding, and Lenin down to Walt W. Rostow and his modernization theory of stages of economic growth.

Smith begins with the statement of what he believes we all desire. It is wealth as a means for improving our lives: "An augmentation of fortune is the means by which the greater part of men propose and wish to better their condition."[4] He felt fortunate to have discovered that the system of "natural liberty" is the one that maximizes economic wealth—that is, best satisfies human passion. That, in turn, meant there was a natural coincidence between human freedom and economic growth.

Smith has often been interpreted too narrowly as opposing almost any government interference in economic matters. This is not true: Smith himself gives many instances where the government's involvement is necessary (in matters of national security like the Navigation Act, protection of infant industry, prevention of monopoly, limiting the exploitation of labor, introducing financial regulation, and enacting anti-collusion policies, especially regarding employers scheming together against workers).[5] But other than in these specific cases, Smith was in favor of getting the government "out of the hair" of the participants in economic life. This famous quote captures the main idea:

> Little else is requisite to carry a state to the highest degree of opulence from the lowest barbarism, but peace, easy taxes, and a tolerable administration of justice; all the rest being brought about by the natural course of things. All governments which thwart this natural course, which force things into another channel, or

which endeavour to arrest the progress of society at a particular point, are unnatural, and to support themselves are obliged to be oppressive and tyrannical.[6]

Another quote, putting the arrogance and the conceit of the government in its place, makes his view even clearer:

It is the highest impertinence and presumption, therefore, in kings and ministers, to pretend to watch over the economy of private people, and to restrain their expense, either by sumptuary laws, or by prohibiting the importation of foreign luxuries. They are themselves always, and without any exception, the greatest spendthrifts in the society. Let them look well after their own expense, and they may safely trust private people with theirs. If their own extravagance does not ruin the state, that of their subjects never will."[7]

The Wealth of Nations (much more than *The Theory of Moral Sentiments*) abounds with references to the rest of the world (that is, beyond the British Isles). It is, I think, his historical knowledge of other countries and epochs that enabled Smith to create a stadial theory of economic development, and to provide examples of it ranging from ancient Greece and Rome to China, Holland, Poland, the Ottoman Empire, Indostan, Bengal, Angola, North America, Spain, Portugal, Russia, Peru, the Aztec Empire, and many other lands. He was a witness to—and participant in, given his position as commissioner of Scottish customs (1778–1790)—Scotland's brilliant economic development in the eighteenth century.[8] Moving between England and Scotland, he was able to contrast the rules in the two parts of the kingdom (for example, on guilds, corporations, and free movement of workers in Scotland versus limits on between-parish movements in England) and relate them to differences in outcomes. France, too, played a special role in forming Smith's view of the world, not least because of his travel there from 1764 to 1766 (at the age of forty-one to forty-three) as a tutor to the young (eight- to ten-year-old) Duke of Buccleuch. It was there that he was acquainted with the theories of the physiocrats and met François Quesnay.

Smith's worldwide interests included colonial management and mismanagement, and it is not surprising, since his objective was to find the "secret to economic growth," that he was especially scathing on the topic of merchant companies governing colonies, because merchants' fates were not just divorced from those of the citizens of the "unfortunate countries" they oversaw but ran distinctly in the opposite direction: "It is a very singular government in which every member of the administration wishes to get out of the country, and consequently to have done with the government as soon as he can, and to whose interest, the day after he has left it and carried his whole fortune with him, it is perfectly indifferent though the whole country was swallowed up by an earthquake."[9] The discussion of European colonial practices covers more than a hundred pages in Book IV of *The Wealth of Nations* (this is about 8 percent of the entire volume), and is almost uniformly negative, except for a few instances where Smith argues that colonists should be allowed to do as they please (as in continental North America)—that is, where they are not considered as default villains. It is worth underscoring (especially because it is often ignored) that Smith's view of imperialism—including his view of the Crusades, engineered, according to Smith, by those archvillains the merchant republics of Venice, Genoa, and Pisa—is almost entirely negative. In some ways he was more critical of imperialism than Marx, who portrayed it at times, especially in his writings on India, as a handmaiden of capitalist development and thus ultimately of socialism.

One practice, surprisingly, that Smith does not manage to explicitly condemn is slavery. In several instances he expresses implicit or indirect condemnation of it, but he never takes a direct stand. One can speculate that he refrained from doing so because it would have put him squarely at odds with the interests of many powerful people who owned slaves—not least, many members of the Scottish aristocracy. This is all the more interesting because, in many instances, he did not exactly manage his words regarding the rich and the powerful.[10]

Given the broad historical and geographical interests evinced by *The Wealth of Nations,* it is fitting, although it was accidental, that the book was published in 1776, with the parts dealing with North America probably completed in 1775. Smith devotes the last pages of the book to discussing the demands of the insurrectionists (whom Smith generally did not support).* *The Wealth of Nations* ends with a prophetic note:

> If any of the provinces of the British empire can't be made to contribute toward the support of the whole empire, it is surely time that Great Britain should free herself from the expense of defending the provinces in time of war, and of supporting any part of their civil or military establishment in time of peace, and endeavor to accommodate her future views and designs to the real mediocrity of her circumstances.[11]

Smith's interests, like the best development economists' research, spanned the entire globe, and it is useful to sort the countries he mentions into several broad categories according to his perception of their wealth and level of development. This is done in the first two columns of Table 2.1. The Netherlands is at the top because it was often treated by Smith as the most advanced commercial society, even if, based on wage levels alone, one might be tempted to put the North American colonies ahead of any other contemporary society. (Smith made multiple references to high wage rates there.) Smith's ranking of other countries is more or less clear, with peripheral European countries like Portugal and Poland considered the least developed in Europe. He is also rather dismissive of the Spanish-speaking Americas, and even more so of the pre-Colombian civilizations: "All the ancient arts of Mexico and Peru have never furnished one single manufacture to Europe."[12] India is discussed frequently, but

---

* To be more exact, one could summarize Smith's position by saying that he did not think that the American colonists had an economic case for secession (despite many metropole-imposed limits on their trade, with which Smith disagreed), but also did not believe there was a moral or ethical case *against* secession.

mostly in the context of mismanagement by the British East India Company, one of Smith's *bêtes noire,* and as for China, even if Smith is unsure whether it is merely a stationary society or going backward, it is far from being the exemplary kingdom Quesnay considered it. In one of his most damning passages about the country, Smith writes: "The poverty of the lower ranks of people in China far surpasses that of the most beggarly nations in Europe. In the neighborhood of Canton, many hundred, it is commonly said, many thousand families have no habitation on the land, but live constantly in little fishing-boats upon the rivers and canals. The subsistence which they find there is so scanty, that they are eager to fish up the nastiest garbage thrown overboard from any European ship."[13]

Finally, at the bottom of the development league are the African interior and "Tartary," which includes today's Siberia and Central Asia. These are deemed "barbarous." This tour du monde misses only Japan and the Ottoman Empire, the latter of which is discussed in many instances but only with regard to trade. This makes it difficult to gauge its level of development, although Smith notes that, as in Indostan, people there have to bury treasure to make sure it is safe from government and brigands, implying that he does not rate its level of development as high.

As the third column of Table 2.1, I added (*after* ranking countries according to my reading of Smith) the most recent data from the Maddison Project, which provides comparable GDPs per capita for most parts of the world.[14] The data used for comparison are for 1775–1776, and in a few instances for the closest year. As the comparison shows, Smith's rankings are very close to the income levels that we today, with some confidence, estimate for these countries. Smith's "rich" countries were indeed richer than the others, and the only misclassification is Portugal, which Smith placed in the underdeveloped category. He might also have overestimated the income of Poland, which according to statistics known today was not better off than China.[15] Smith's group compositions are very close to the modern data, implying that people of the time were aware of the development levels of different countries and Smith

Table 2.1 Various Countries' Levels of Development at the Time of *The Wealth of Nations*

Smith's classification (inferred)	Smith's ranking of countries (inferred and approximate)	GDP per capita around 1776
Rich	The Netherlands	4,431
	North America	2,419
	England	2,962
	Scotland	—
	France	1,728
Underdeveloped	Germany	1,572
	Nordics (Sweden)	1,562
	Spain	1,447
	Portugal	1,929
	Poland	995
Poor	Russia	—
	Mexico	1,446
	Peru	1,278
Destitute	Indostan (India)	1,068
	Java (Indonesia)	795
	China	981
"Barbarous" (Smith's term)	Africa	—
	Tartary (Siberia/Central Asia)	—

Data sources: Data in the first and second columns reflect author's reading of Smith. Data in the third column are from the Maddison Project, 2020. Most countries' GDP data are for 1775–1776; the exceptions are Germany (1800), Indostan (1750), Java (1815), and China (1780). Smith distinguishes between England and Scotland, placing England ahead, but here both are assigned GDP data for the UK generally.

had sufficient access to this knowledge, as well as the common sense, to correctly identify the positions of various parts of the world. In terms of global interest and knowledge, Smith (together with Marx) certainly rates above other economists studied in this book. His achievement is even more impressive given the paucity of data in the second half of the eighteenth century as compared to a century or two later.

Regarding the man as a person, there are three "Adam Smith puzzles" worth mentioning here: his approach to citations of other authors, the lack of insight into aspects of his personal life, and the mystery of the disposition of his wealth.

That Adam Smith was stingy with citations is well known. As Marx wrote, "with meticulous care he . . . keeps the sources secret to which he is indebted."[16] A search for all the authors mentioned, not even cited verbatim, in a book of 380,000 words (*The Wealth of Nations*) yields this list: Plato, six times; Aristotle and Hume, five times each; Montesquieu, four times; Colbert, four times; Quesnay, three times; and Cantillon and Mirabeau, one citation each. Another example: although the "mercantile" system (or approach or theory) is mentioned, mostly critically, ninety-nine times, its great exponent James Steuart is not named once. By no stretch of the imagination is such meager quotation of other authors acceptable. The most notable "undercitations" involve the contributions of Hume, in whose company and intimate friendship Smith spent more than half of his life, and Quesnay, who was a significant intellectual influence on Smith when they met in France.[17] Why would this be the case? One possibility is that Smith was jealously guarding his own influence and did not want to share it with others. Another explanation might be that he was loath to enter into polemics, and his reluctance to cite by name those with whom he disagreed also kept him very "economical" in revealing those from whom he learned and with whom he agreed. Quesnay falls into both categories. That Smith did not want to get into an argument with the physiocrats is obvious from the opening phrase of one sentence: "But without entering into the disagreeable discussion of the metaphysical arguments by which they support their very ingenious theory . . ."[18] Yet he also failed to cite Quesnay on topics where they agreed, and where the case could be made that Quesnay influenced Smith, including the system of natural liberty, the freedom of domestic and foreign commerce, the distribution of incomes between the classes, and the importance of the largest class's welfare as an indicator of national well-being and as a worthy objective of government policies.[19]

When it comes to citations and relations with his predecessors and contemporaries, Smith, especially if we compare him with the next authors in this book (Ricardo, Marx, and Pareto), appears much more restrained and cold. We seem to see Smith always through a dim glass. His virtues were loudly proclaimed by his friends at his death and afterward, yet phrased in the template-like fashion of so many other conventional encomia in eighteenth-century England and Scotland. Not much is really learned from the repetition of such qualities as "serenity" and "gaiety," or from references to the "inexpressible charm [of] his conversation" and so forth.[20] Samuel Johnson offered the less generic observations that "Smith was as dull a dog as he had ever met with," and was "a most disagreeable fellow after he had drank some wine."[21] These are (characteristically, for Johnson) brutal quips, but give us perhaps more insight into a possibly cantankerous Adam Smith, especially if under the influence of some alcohol.

Adding to the dimness of the profile—again, in contrast to Ricardo, Marx, and Pareto, whose lives, thanks to their vast correspondences, can be reconstructed almost down to their every day—is the fact that there are several "blank spots" in Adam Smith's life. We do not know of a single romantic connection of his; we are left to speculate why he lived almost the whole decade of his forties with his mother and a cousin, why he seemingly never had an interest in marriage, children, and the like. None of these choices in itself is strange (he might have lived with his mother because he liked her, or because it was more comfortable for a bachelor writing a book to have his food cooked by his mother than to frequent taverns), but together they make us wonder about Smith as a person. His decision to ask that all his manuscripts and correspondence be burned just before his death in front of himself, so that he could be assured that they were destroyed (no Max Brod for Smith!), adds another layer of mystery.

The final puzzle has to do with Adam Smith's wealth. After the publication of *The Wealth of Nations,* he was paid a £600 annual salary as commissioner for Scottish customs, still received an annual pension of £300 from the Duke of Buccleuch, and earned royalties from his books, making his income as high as £1,500 per year.[22] He was thus easily among the top one percent of the British income distribution. Joseph Massie's 1759 social table for England and Wales (which we shall use again below) gives the per-capita income of the highest class among the almost sixty classes it includes as just under £700. Smith's income was more than twice as much. If we express Smith's income with respect to the average earnings at the time (about £28 per year according to Massie), the ratio is 53 to 1.[23] If we then use the same ratio to translate Smith's annual income into present-day terms (using 2020 data for British full-time and part-time earners, whose average earnings were about £25,000 that year), we find it equivalent to about £1.3 million. His income as a younger man, even if not at that level, was quite high, too. But Smith's estate at his death was relatively modest.[24] Dugald Stewart's speculation is that Smith might have engaged through most of his life in acts of "secret charity," acquired "a small but excellent library," and provided "a simple, though hospitable table, where . . . he was always happy to receive friends."[25] The latter two expenses cannot explain the discrepancy, and the first is a mere guess.[26] We could propose various hypotheses, but they are all devoid of evidence; something does not fully match, but we are unable to put a finger on it.

Inequality in England and Scotland at the Time of Adam Smith

England's social structure around the time of Adam Smith's 1776 *Wealth of Nations* can be best apprehended from the almost contemporary social table Massie compiled for the year 1759.[27] As restructured recently by Robert Allen, it shows the English population to be made up of 56 percent non-agricultural workers (inclusive of servants and soldiers), almost 20 percent farmers, and almost 10 percent shopkeepers.[28] (See Figure 2.1.) Among the roughly 15 percent remaining, most were what today would be called "homeless." Only 4 percent were capitalists and just 1.5 percent were landed gentry and aristocracy. To translate this social table into a simplified, visual hierarchy, picture a tripartite pyramid based on factor income and class, with a top consisting of the 1.5 percent of the population that owned land, a next layer representing the

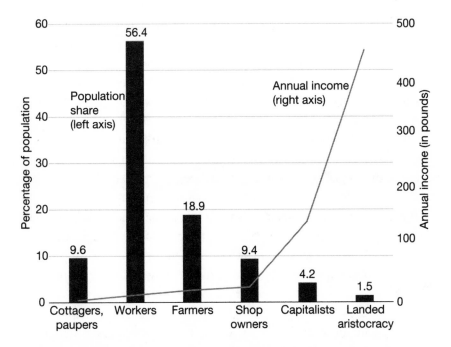

Figure 2.1. Class structure of England and Wales around 1759: population shares and annual incomes

Note: Classes are ranked from the poorest to the richest from left to right, with the line highlighting differences in their average annual per-capita incomes. The bars show the population shares of these classes (in percents adding up to 100).

Data source: Robert C. Allen, "Class Structure and Inequality during the Industrial Revolution: Lessons from England's Social Tables, 1688–1867," *Economic History Review,* 72:1 (2019): 88–125.

4 percent who were capitalists, and a base of the roughly 95 percent of the population who were farmers, hired workers, self-employed earners, and paupers.

What were the relative incomes of the main classes? Landlords' families, according to Massie's table as reworked by Allen, had an average per-capita income of £450 per year, capitalists £145 per year, and workers £14 per year. In between the capitalists and workers, there were shop owners and farmers with, respectively, £27 and £22 per year; and, at the very bottom of the social pyramid, cottagers and paupers with less than £3 per year. The ratio of landlords' to capitalists' incomes was about 3 to 1, and that of capitalists to workers was 10 to 1. This makes the advantage of landlords over workers a huge 30 to 1. One's position in society was by and large determined by which of the three basic types of factor income—rent, wage, or profit—one received. Landlords were most unlikely to be poor, and workers very unlikely to be among the rich.

Was interpersonal inequality rising in Smith's time or not? Here we have several studies, all based on the same set of social tables.[29] Despite differences in how they "translate" Massie's numbers (for example, adjusting for household size or not, consolidating certain social groups or not), all seem to show that at the time of Adam Smith inequality in England was very high. In terms of the Gini index's 0 to 100 scale, the estimates put it in the range of 45 to 51 Gini points.* This is the level of inequality that exists in today's Chile or Dominican Republic. It is high but not out of the range of modern experience. We do not see a clear increase in English inequality between 1688, when Gregory King produced the first social table, and 1759, for which we have Massie's social table. As discussed in Chapter 3, it seems that the sustained increase in English (and very likely British) inequality began only in the first part of the nineteenth century, two or three decades after the publication of *The Wealth of Nations*.

Social Classes in Smith, Ricardo, and Marx

What views of the world, regarding matters of inequality and class, are shared by Smith, Ricardo, and Marx? It is worth mentioning these similarities now before we engage with the authors individually. First, all three hold that functional income distribution determines one's position in interpersonal income distribution—in other words, that functional income distribution, practically alone, is what matters. Interpersonal income distribution is subsumed within it, or rather determined by it.

---

* Recall that this is less than the inequality in France at the same time, as noted in Chapter 1.

Second, none saw the three "functional" classes as just random assortments of individuals: they implied a clear ranking that went from landlords or aristocracy at the top through industrial and financial capitalists in the middle, down to the self-employed, peasants, and workers (most likely in that order). A large number, adding up to about 10 percent of the English population, according to Massie, were "vagrants, cottagers and paupers." They should not be forgotten. Their existence was the product of, on the one hand, the end of feudal attachment to land and the legal obligation to work, and on the other hand, the not yet fully developed industrial system.

At the time of Smith's writing, England and Scotland were more advanced than other European countries. Both probably had a lower percentage than France of the self-employed—that is, yeoman farmers working their own land. What was a typical British land arrangement (and indeed very different from the arrangements that prevailed in continental Europe, North America, and China) was already in place: a triple class division with landowners renting land to tenant-farmers, and tenant-farmers hiring wage laborers to work on it. The degree to which this local British land arrangement influenced the intellectual history of political economy is best appreciated when one reflects that, elsewhere, other arrangements were far more common: in France and other parts of continental Europe, as well as in most of China, peasants toiled on land they owned; in India, the land's output was shared by landlord and farmer; in Central and Eastern Europe, land was worked by people who were legally obliged to provide to the owner a given number of days of work free of charge; and in Russia, the Caribbean, and southern parts of North America, this forced work was done by serfs and slaves. In none of these other arrangements do we see capitalist-farmers—the people who, as Chapter 3 will show, played such a fundamental role in early British writings on economics and influenced our views of class structure up to the present.

Third, Smith, Ricardo, and Marx accept as self-evident a simplified model of class incomes by which "everybody" from a higher class has a higher income than anyone belonging to a lower class.

This is to say, in contemporary methodological terms, that there is *no overlap* of the different classes' incomes. This is obviously a simplification: in the social tables, as well as in reality, there are workers and self-employed earners (including, for example, self-employed merchants) with incomes higher than some capitalists' incomes. It was nevertheless reasonable to employ this simplification because it was true for the most part: incomes of different classes seldom overlapped, and a person's income often consisted entirely of one type, whether it came from capital or labor or land. (Think, for example, of Jane Austen's novels, where the rich—who populate all of her books—have incomes entirely derived from ownership of land or capital, and the poor, seldom seen, depend wholly on their labors.) Few landlords were also industrial capitalists, and probably even fewer industrial capitalists worked as hired employees. There was double stratification: between the classes that were hierarchically ordered, and between different income types that were seldom mixed within the same person.

The simplification was especially true for workers and peasants, who were unlikely to be better off than merchants, and certainly even less likely to be better off than capitalists. By contrast, shopkeepers' and traders' incomes span quite a range: in Massie's social table, the richest merchants are part of the top one percent while the poor merchants are around the mean of income distribution.

In stratified societies, functional distribution translates directly into interpersonal distribution. This is probably the principal reason why none of these authors addresses interpersonal distribution as a separate topic. It is striking how rarely Smith, Ricardo, and Marx mention inequality in the modern sense of the term. As we shall see later, the term practically does not appear in Marx, even though Marx was (obviously) critical of capitalism and concerned—or rather happy, because it presaged the end of capitalism—with what he, in some writings, held to be increasing immiseration of the working class. Singling out inequality among persons must have seemed redundant to the author of *Capital*, given that class stratification so clearly entailed different levels of incomes. The same was true for Ricardo.

What Is a Prosperous Society?

The Wealth of Nations was published only thirteen years after Mirabeau and Quesnay's *Philosophie rurale,* but it presents us with a very different picture of the economy, and to some extent of the world. Unlike in Quesnay, where agriculture is center stage, here industry takes that place. From *Philosophie rurale's* introduction of the typical classes of an agricultural society, based on legally defined estates, we move to Smith's workers, capitalists, and landowners—the clear tripartite class structure we still use today for developing countries—and to the binary structure (workers and capitalists) that, since Marx, is common for more advanced capitalist economies. Yet, as Wesley Mitchell writes, "Adam Smith's theory of distribution is an incidental rather than a cardinal part of his system."[30] Certainly, Smith's theory of distribution was derived in a rather casual way. He was mainly interested in the three components that make up a commodity's "natural price" (rent, profit, and wages), and his theory of distribution and the attendant class structure emerged as the subproduct of price formation.[31] As incidental as this theory may have been, however, its development still represented for Smith—and for later economists perhaps even more—an important beginning. It introduced the three essential classes of Western capitalism.*

This introduction of classes also allowed Smith to propound a radical view, the importance of which cannot be overestimated: that the opulence of a country is indistinguishable from the living conditions of its largest class, its workers. This represented a major break with the mercantilist position, which considered only the wealth of the governing classes and the wealth of the state to matter. This new point of view had been adumbrated by Quesnay and the physiocrats, as seen in Chapter 1, but not stated as forcefully by them as by Smith,

---

* On the negative side, it could be argued, especially in a Marxist context, that the reification of the Western, and even more narrowly of the British, class structure of the eighteenth and nineteenth century limited the ability to look at other, non-Western societies without always trying to find in them the tripartite class structure defined by Smith, Ricardo, and Marx.

partly because of the physiocrats' elliptic style of writing and partly because they linked the prosperity of the largest class to their underconsumptionist concerns. It was not always clear if they viewed greater prosperity of workers and farmers as a good thing in itself, as a sign of a prosperous society, or simply as something needed to avoid falling into an underconsumption trap.

In Smith, for the first time in the history of political economy, we encounter the idea that it is the welfare of the largest group that is important: "The high price of labor is to be considered not merely as a proof of the general opulence of society which can afford to pay well all those whom it employs; it is to be regarded as what constitutes the very essence of public opulence, or as the very thing in which public opulence properly consists." Noting that "servants, labourers and workmen of different kinds, make up the far greater part of every great political society," Smith added that "what improves the circumstance of the greater part can never be regarded as an inconveniency to the whole. No society can surely be flourishing and happy, of which the far greater part of the members are poor and miserable."[32] It was a truly revolutionary idea and it remains so, even if it has acquired the status of common sense by now.

Attitude toward the Rich in The Theory of Moral Sentiments and The Wealth of Nations

The Theory of Moral Sentiments and The Wealth of Nations are very different books, covering different topics and with different audiences in mind. The attention of economists is naturally directed toward The Wealth of Nations, yet The Theory of Moral Sentiments has of late become more widely read and is often quoted by them, too. The substantial differences between the two works begin with the fact that The Theory of Moral Sentiments is about our relations with those closest to us (our families, friends, and peers), whereas The Wealth of Nations deals with our relationship with, and behavior in, the larger world: our relations with people with whom we interact for economic reasons.[33] The difference in focus is obvious from the titles (though we might have become so used to them that we pay little attention to their meanings). In one case, Smith deals with *moral* sentiments, and in the other, with attainment of *wealth*—two very different things.

Smith in *The Theory of Moral Sentiments* is a moral philosopher and the book, in a view recently propagated by Amartya Sen, can be seen as "softer" in some ways than *The Wealth of Nations*, which George Stigler memorably called "a stupendous palace erected upon the granite of self-interest."[34] *The Theory of Moral Sentiments* places great emphasis on our ability to understand others. The "impartial spectator" that Smith introduces in its pages is endowed with empathy and the ability to understand the motivations and behaviors of others. The narrative use of such an empathetic onlooker is highlighted by Sen as a major advantage over dry, "contractarian" theories like Rawls's, which do not allow any external observer to have a say and thus, according to Sen, exclude the possibility of participants in the contract being judged themselves by an external source. Rawls's idea that impartiality requires decision-makers to adopt a "veil of ignorance" regarding their own interests, Sen says, "abstains from invoking the scrutiny of (in Smith's language) 'the eyes of the rest of mankind.'"[35] By contrast, empathy is not much present in *The Wealth of Nations,* where being guided by self-interest and reason and assuming that others are guided by these, too, is sufficient.

When it comes to Smith's attitude toward inequality and class society, however, the alleged "softness" of *The Theory of Moral Sentiments* does not translate into a more egalitarian stance. On the contrary, in matters of distribution, *The Theory of Moral Sentiments* is much harsher and more unyielding. The book is largely moralistic and religious in tone and substance, and features many deprecatory remarks about the moral deficiencies of the rich, but it accepts an immutable class structure. The top classes may be subject to expressions of derision in *The Theory of Moral Sentiments,* but their right to be on top is never questioned, nor are the origins of their fortunes ever examined. The quasi-religious acceptance of a hierarchy of wealth is strikingly illustrated in the passage where, for the first time in his work, Smith mentions the workings of the invisible hand in the economy.[36] Referring to the consumption habits of the vain and rapacious rich, he writes:

> They are led by an invisible hand to make nearly the same distribution of the necessaries of life, which would have been made, had the earth been divided into equal portions among all its inhabitants, and thus without intending it, without knowing it, advance the interest of the society, and afford means to the multiplication of the species. When Providence divided the earth among a few lordly masters, it neither forgot nor abandoned those who seemed to have been left out in partition.[37]

What is remarkable here is that a social order shaped by the existence of large income differences is accepted and even applauded because the rich, being desirous of goods and services provided by the poor, will necessarily spend some of their own earnings. By the identical reasoning, any income distribution, however inequitable, could be declared acceptable and even praised, since we all know the rich cannot live by eating their gold and sleeping on it. They need others to produce what is needed to sustain them, and must pay the others for that work. But that fact cannot, in any reasonable sense, be taken as a justification of their higher incomes or make the distribution acceptable.[38] The arguments for either have to be sought elsewhere. Particularly striking is the last, very Panglossian, sentence of the quoted passage suggesting that everything in this world of inequity turns out to be ideally arranged for the best possible outcome. The logic of this can likewise be expanded at will, to claim, for example, that even an income distribution in which all income is received by an infinitesimal minority is part of God's design. Recourse to providence (when everything else fails) is not unusual in *The Theory of Moral Sentiments,* but taking it to underwrite a visibly unjust social order is rare.

It is indeed trivial to show that, from the point of view of the poor, having one's own plot of land to work is far from the same as having

64

to depend on the willingness of the rich to hire one's services—whether we measure "the same" in terms of income, individual agency, power, or happiness. Smith's passage is exceedingly reactionary and one can even notice a certain cynical quality to its assertion that the rich, through their spending, "make nearly the same distribution of the necessaries of life, which would have been made, had the earth been divided into equal portions among all its inhabitants," and further that they "consume little more than the poor." One is taken aback by such statements: read literally, they imply that any distribution, however unequal and unjust, is no worse than another, and that in all of them the rich and the poor come away with about the same shares. (One wonders, then, why are the rich called the "rich"?) No similar argument will appear in *The Wealth of Nations*, where notably the only people criticized regarding the *origins* of their fortunes are the rich.

To further discount the relevance of unequal riches, in *The Theory of Moral Sentiments* Smith describes a pervasive self-deception: we are naturally impelled by our imaginations to seek finer things believing they will make us happy. This leads us to work hard and take risks to increase our wealth and greatness, often in ways that advance human industry and progress more broadly. It is thus a positive force. But that greater wealth does not bring us happiness, and "the beggar who suns himself by the side of the highway possesses that security which kings are fighting for."[39] This, in turn, means that the real inequality in happiness among people is much less than the apparent inequality measured in material goods. While wealth gaps may be large, happiness gaps are much smaller, and perhaps nonexistent. By that circuitous route, the importance of actual inequality of income is minimized and the wealthy are left in peace to hire the poor and consume their riches which, according to Smith, scarcely make them happy.

A marked distinction between the two works can be seen in their different uses of the language that is the "bread and butter" of a religiously inclined moral philosopher—namely, references to *God*, the *Divine, Providence,* and the *Great Maker.* These four terms appear 149 times in *The Theory of Moral Sentiments* but only six times in *The Wealth of Nations*. This despite the fact that the latter work is almost three times as long. To put it differently, the frequency with which Smith invokes terms for the divinity in *The Theory of Moral Sentiments* is almost fifty times greater than in *The Wealth of Nations*. This is not at all surprising in light of what we have said before: *The Theory of Moral Sentiments* is written by a theistic moral philosopher and, one could even say, a preacher.[40] *The Wealth of Nations* is written by a deeply skeptical, even chastened, observer of economic life and social mores.[41] The essayist Nirad Chaudhuri once described human life as having a fourth, and last, stage of "stern, almost exultant despair."[42] This applies quite well to the author of *The Wealth of Nations*. It does not describe the author of *The Theory of Moral Sentiments*.[43]

In *The Theory of Moral Sentiments,* the rich are derided for their behavior (for the "fatuity of wealth accumulation") and for their spending patterns, but their status and wealth are not questioned. It is a perspective similar to Thorstein Veblen's in *The Theory of the Leisure Class* (written a century and a half after *The Theory of Moral Sentiments*), as both make fun of those who are wealthier, more fortunate, and higher in social hierarchy but never deny their right to be there—and never envisage a situation where no such hierarchy exists.[44] Despite this mocking-of-the-rich affect (or perhaps because of it, as it dodges any deeper inquiry into the origins of rich people's power), Smith often appears in *The Theory of Moral Sentiments* to be not merely conservative but outright reactionary.

If one were, then, to summarize Smith's outlook in *The Theory of Moral Sentiments*, it would be fair to say that he believed the poor should accept their position because it was ordained by divine will and this is how all societies were structured, but also that he viewed the rich as not necessarily virtuous. Still, he thought the origins of the rich's wealth should not be scrutinized too closely. As for the poor, although the argument that they might be compensated for their poverty in the "world beyond" is never made explicitly, it often appears under a thin theological guise. None of this quasi-religious explanation of inequality will be made, as we shall see presently, in *The Wealth of Nations*.

Questioning Incomes of the Rich

When we move from *The Theory of Moral Sentiments* to *The Wealth of Nations,* we enter the realm of stern realism and self-interest; we move to the world of economic interactions that are by definition relations with strangers. We also move from organic communities, where our behavior is colored by empathy and even altruism (or, as we have just seen, acceptance of manifest injustice), to the world of mechanical communities, where the rules are different. Indeed, for *The Wealth of Nations* to stand firm and tall, self-interest is enough; Smith in that respect displays a praiseworthy economy of assumptions. We do not need too many assumptions to explain the behavior of people in the Great Society. It is sufficient to take it that they follow their own interest and are rational.

But—and this is a big difference in attitude toward the rich— where *The Theory of Moral Sentiments* is acquiescent to hierarchy, *The Wealth of Nations* is realistic and severe. It openly criticizes the rich, how they have acquired their wealth, and how they use it to further enrich and empower themselves. In some of their behavior, Smith sees only sanctimonious posturing: "I have never known much good done by those who affected to trade for the public good. It is an affectation, indeed, not very common among merchants, and very few words need be employed in dissuading them from it."[45] In some passages he treats them with scathing sarcasm: "The late resolution of the Quakers in Pennsylvania to set at liberty all their negro slaves, may satisfy us that their number cannot be very great."[46]

Even religion, as practiced by the people, is brought down to Earth and not spared ridicule (a thing unimaginable in *The Theory of Moral Sentiments*):

The laws concerning corn may everywhere be compared to the laws concerning religion. The people feel themselves so much interested in what relates either to their subsistence in this life, or to their happiness in a life to come, that government must yield to their prejudices, and, in order to preserve the public tranquility, establish that system which they approve of. It is upon this account, perhaps, that we so seldom find a reasonable system established with regard to either of those two capital objects.[47]

As well as being more realistic and "harsher," *The Wealth of Nations* is much more "leftist" when it comes to inequality than *The Theory of Moral Sentiments*. It does not accept the ethical validity of the hierarchy between the classes: incomes of the rich are often unjustly acquired. The rich may well be at the top of the pyramid, but that does not mean that they are worthy of it, or that their incomes and the way they got to the top should be left unstudied and uncriticized. A high income is indeed often a product of collusion, monopoly, plunder, or use of political influence. On collusion, Smith writes:

People of the same trade seldom meet together, even for merriment and diversion, but the conversation ends in a conspiracy against the public, or in some contrivance to raise prices. It is impossible indeed to prevent such meetings, by any law which either could be executed, or would be consistent with liberty and justice. But though the law cannot hinder people of the same trade from sometimes assembling together, it ought to do nothing to facilitate such assemblies; much less to render them necessary.[48]

And on monopoly:

In the spice islands the Dutch are said to burn all the spices which a fertile season produces beyond what they expect to dispose of in Europe with such a profit as they think sufficient. . . . By different arts of oppression [the Dutch] have reduced the population of several of the Moluccas nearly to the number which is sufficient to supply with fresh provisions and other necessities of life their own . . . garrisons.[49]

As the text suggests obliquely, the search for monopoly profits has led Dutch colonists not only to oppress members of the local population but to kill them, so that their numbers become "optimal" from the point of view of the production of spices and the servicing of foreigners.

On plunder, merchant companies (the British East India Company and its Dutch equivalent, the Vereenigde Oostindische Compagnie, or VOC) and the merchant republics are targeted for particular opprobrium because their profits are the result of a barefaced plunder:

The government of an exclusive company of merchants is, perhaps, the worst of all governments for any country whatever.[50]

And further on plunder:

The great armies which marched from all parts to the conquest of the Holy Land gave extraordinary encouragement to the shipping of Venice, Genoa, and Pisa, sometimes in transporting them thither, and always in supplying them with provisions. They were the commissaries, if one may say so, of those armies; and the most destructive frenzy that ever befell the European nations was a source of opulence to those republics."[51]

Finally, on political influence:

The Member of Parliament who supports every proposal for strengthening this monopoly [on foreign trade] is sure to acquire not only the reputation of understanding trade, but great popularity and influence with an order of men whose numbers and wealth render them of great importance. If he opposes them, on the contrary, and still more if he has authority enough to be able to thwart them, neither the most acknowledged probity, nor the highest rank, nor the greatest public services can protect him from the most infamous abuse and detraction, from personal insults, nor sometimes from real danger, arising from the insolent outrage of furious and disappointed monopolists.[52]

The skeptical view that pervades *The Wealth of Nations* does not apply only to capitalists and merchants. It extends to nobility:

> Entails [prohibiting great estates from being broken up] are thought necessary for maintaining this exclusive privilege of the nobility to the great offices and honours of their country; and that order having usurped one unjust advantage over the rest of their fellow-citizens, lest their poverty should render it ridiculous, it is thought reasonable that they should have another.[53]

Not only are the rich deprived of their claim to moral superiority but, as the origin of their wealth is subjected to scrutiny, the wealth gap may be seen to be the product of an unfair social order, or of an unjust commercial society. This is a point to which I will return below.

Wages, Rents, and Return to Capital as Society Develops

What is Adam Smith's view of labor incomes? A realistic or critical view of the top classes' incomes in *The Wealth of Nations* is accompanied by an emphasis on the lower classes' welfare: an advanced society cannot be a society where workers are badly paid. The success of a society is judged by how well the largest class in that society fares. Smith draws an unfavorable contrast between, on the one side, Spain and Portugal, whose small ruling classes exhibit high wealth while everybody else is poor, and on the other side, the Netherlands, widely held to be the most prosperous country at the time, with its high wages and low rate of interest.[54] According to Smith, high wages and a low rate of interest are the most desirable features of any society that wishes to advance economically and to maintain reasonable justice. "The rate of profit does not, like rent and wages, rise with the prosperity and fall with the declension of the society," he writes. "On the contrary, it is naturally low in rich, and high in poor countries, and it is always highest in the countries which are going fastest to ruin."[55]

It is not only that high interest is a mark of stagnant societies with insecure property rights (here Smith mentions the Ottoman Empire, India, and China) but that a low interest rate has the advantage of making it difficult for people to live off their wealth without working: "In a country which had acquired its full complement of riches, where, in every particular branch of business, there was the greatest quantity of stock that could be employed . . . the rate of interest . . . would be low [enough] as to render it impossible for any but the wealthiest people to live upon the interest of their money."[56] Thus, by a happy coincidence, what seems economically advantageous, and what is associated with more advanced societies and with lower inequality, is also judged to be ethically preferable.

When the welfare of the majority, which essentially means high wages for workers, becomes the criterion to judge how well a society is doing, we are in the presence of a new and very modern view of what the good society is. Smith coins the term *comeattibleness,* meaning the degree to which laboring classes can afford what they need: "That state is opulent where the necessaries and conveniencies of life are easily come at . . . and nothing else can deserve the name of opulence but this comeattibleness."[57] This identification of a state's advancement with the well-being of its largest class might be uncontroversial today, but was not embraced in Smith's time, when the misery of the working classes was often thought to be their inevitable fate, or even desirable because only threats of hunger and destitution would compel the poor to work.* Only six years before the publication of *The Wealth of Nations,* Arthur Young famously wrote that "everyone but an idiot knows that the lower classes must be kept poor or they will never be industrious."[58]

---

* As noted in Chapter 1, Quesnay similarly criticized the view that the poor will work only if driven by hunger. On this point, as on many others, Quesnay and Smith were in agreement.

It is therefore understandable that Smith did not believe that wages would, regardless of the system and the state of society, remain at the subsistence level, sufficient only for physical survival. Moreover, what constituted subsistence, Smith indicated, was not a constant of the human condition but could vary across time and place. He recognized as necessities "not only those things that nature, but those things which the established rules of decency, have rendered necessary to the lowest ranks of people."[59]

Necessities are not to be taken as a fixed bundle of goods and services given once and forever. This, of course, opens up the possibility of a rising real wage as society advances—a statement Smith makes explicitly. As more advanced societies also have lower rates of interest, that particular combination of factoral incomes (higher wages, lower interest) implies a society with less interpersonal inequality. We thus see in Smith the creation of an implicit theory of income distribution such that inequality between capitalists and workers, and probably between individuals in the society overall, diminishes as the economy develops.

We also, however, have to take into account the third factor of production: land, and its return, rent. The situation now gets more complicated because real rent is also supposed to rise as society advances, and not only in absolute amount, but in proportion to overall output.[60] This is so because societal progress brings with it increased demand for a number of goods (in addition to food) that are either grown on land (like cotton) or obtained from it through mining.[61] As a richer population demands more of such products, the value of land goes up and its owners earn higher rent. Therefore, the interests of workers and landlords are aligned with the interest of the public, as both workers' and landlords' positions improve with the advance of society. The class whose income is adversely affected by development is the capitalist class (employers or masters in Smith's terminology), because the rate of profit or interest, which constitutes its income, is bound to decrease.[62]

Smith's implicit theory of income distribution thus becomes more complex because the incomes of those at the top and the bottom are supposed to go up as society advances, and the incomes of those in the middle are to be reduced. Probably it is true that the advancement would result in an overall decrease in inequality, on account of the sheer size of the beneficiaries (as we have seen, 80 percent of the English/British population in Smith's time were workers and peasants), but one might also expect more polarization of the society as the top class (landlords, 1.5 percent of the population) grows increasingly wealthy. It could be said that, in Smith's view, development results in less income inequality (as we would measure it today using common synthetic measures of inequality like the Gini coefficient), but possibly also results in more polarization, and an even greater share for the top one percent, who are likely mostly landlords.

Finally, it is notable that in one of Smith's very few comments dealing with inequality as such (of which there are perhaps, with the most generous interpretation, only half a dozen), he compares inequality levels in North America and France. Despite the fact that France is a richer country, Smith observes, "on account of the more unequal distribution of riches, there is much more poverty and beggary" there than in America.[63] Even slaves in America are, by implication, thought to be better off than the poor in France.

Real Wage and Relative Wages in an Advanced Society

The difference in the real wage is used by Smith to distinguish among advancing, stationary, and declining societies. This may be regarded as part of a stadial view of history—especially when read together with Book III of The Wealth of Nations, which discusses the "natural progress of opulence" since Roman times—but it is also a fair description of societies in Smith's own time. As already mentioned, he finds real wages in different countries not to be the same, starting with the fact that they are much higher in Europe than in China or India.[64] Smith also uses wages to rank countries in Europe: Dutch real wages are the highest and the Netherlands is thus considered the most advanced country, followed by England, then Scotland,

France, and, much farther below, Poland and Russia.[65] (Smith's 1765–1766 European travels, as well as his work at the customs board, must have provided him with some evidence for the ranking.)

While nowadays we tend to think that the level of GDP per capita and the level of real wages are correlated, for Smith, a high wage level was related to the country's *growth rate*. Smith repeats on a number of occasions that it is the country's high growth rate that determines its level of wages. He obviously thought it important enough to insist on it.[66] Today, this might strike us as baffling: China's high growth rate in the twenty-first century does not make Chinese wages higher than American wages. There is, however, a possible explanation. Although he doesn't say it explicitly, Smith appears to assume that, until fairly recently (that is, before the Commercial Revolution), all countries were about equally poor and wages in all of them were close to supporting mere physiological subsistence. Only as some countries took off did real wages rise. It is in that sense, I believe, that we can see an economy's growth rate determining the real wage: the higher-growth countries in Smith's time would have been the ones that escaped the Malthusian trap (a term that, of course, did not exist at the time) and saw real wages increase. The colonial North American states, cited toward the end of *The Wealth of Nations* for their high wages, provide an example.[67]

When it comes to relative wages among workers (engaged in different kinds of work), these are argued to differ more than profit rates differ among capitalists (investing in different trades). This is because workers work in very different occupations, and in some of them (whether because they put workers in hazardous or dirty conditions, or are disreputable, or require long, expensive education) the compensatory component of wages is high.[68] The profit rate, meanwhile, does not differ as much across diverse uses of capital, because capital is more amorphous and can move much more easily than labor across occupations to equalize the returns.[69]

After a lengthy investigation at the end of Book I and in Book II of *The Wealth of Nations,* Smith concludes that relative wages and relative profits—that is, the ranges of wages and of rates of return—are not affected by the advanced or declining state of society. All wages go up or down together without changing relative to each other, and the same is true for profits:

> The proportion between the different rates both of wages and profit in the different employments of labor and stock, seems not to be much affected . . . by the riches or poverty, the advancing, stationary, or declining state of the society. Such revolutions in the public welfare, though they affect the general rates both of wages and profit, must in the end affect them equally in all different employments. The proportion between them, therefore, must remain the same, and cannot well be altered, at least for any considerable time, by any such revolutions.[70]

This is perhaps not the most satisfactory part of *The Wealth of Nations,* because one might have expected that technological change, or even the increased division of labor introduced in the very beginning of the book, would have varying impacts on the wages of different occupations, and on the wages of workers of different skills. The entire topic of technological change and its impact on labor (which, as we shall see, caused some headaches for Ricardo) is simply side-stepped by Smith. The incomes of the three main factors of production may move differently as society develops, but within each of them, relativities are not affected.

Implicit Theory of Income Distribution and Distrust of Capitalists

Smith's implicit theory of income distribution is intimately related to his distrust of capitalists as influencers of economic policy. This is because, in Smith's view, the higher incomes of workers and landlords that come as the result of societal advance align interests of these two classes with those of the society as a whole. For capitalists, the situation is the reverse. More advanced societies are associated with greater abundance of capital and lower rates of profit. (The profit rates go down because more abundant capital makes for tougher competition among capitalists.) The fact that capitalists have only to lose from development makes them a very suspect group to proffer advice on economic policy. This is even more true because, in Smith's view, neither landlords nor workers are apt to make a compelling case for the policies that benefit them (and in turn, society), given the landlords' indolence and the workers' lack of education and laziness.[71] Capitalists, by contrast, are very skillful in matters of political persuasion and advocacy. But their view of the world is narrow and their advice, because their interests do not run parallel with those of the society, should not be trusted:

> The proposal of any new law or regulation of commerce which comes from this order [of employers] ought always to be listened to with great precaution, and ought never to be adopted till after having been long and carefully examined, not only with the most scrupulous, but with the most suspicious attention. It comes from an order of men whose interest is never exactly the same with that of the public, who have generally an interest to deceive and even to oppress the public, and who accordingly have, upon many occasions, both deceived and oppressed it.[72]

The shades of Gramsci's theory of "hegemony" lurk from behind. And lest it be thought an isolated statement, it nearly repeats another one: "The interest of the dealers, however, in any particular branch of trade or manufactures, is always in some respects different from, and even opposite to, that of the public."[73]

Smith's theory of income distribution is thus at the origin of his skepticism about the political role of capitalists. Their advice would only retard economic development, because they themselves have nothing to gain from a more advanced society. In a famous passage, Smith contrasts "the genius of the British constitution which protects and governs North America, and that of the mercantile company which oppresses and domineers in the East Indies."[74] And

Table 2.2 Aligned and Unaligned Class Interests

	Landlords	Capitalists	Workers
With "improvement of society," the class . . .	Gains (as rents increase)	Loses (as profits drop)	Gains (as real wages rise)
The class's ability to persuade policy-makers is . . .	Low (due to indolence)	High (due to sophistry)	Low (due to lack of education)
Vis-à-vis the general public interest, the class's own interests are . . .	Aligned	Opposite	Aligned

in the clearest rejection of a policy role for owners of capital, Smith writes:

> But the mean rapacity, the monopolizing spirit of merchants and manufacturers, who neither are, nor ought to be the rulers of mankind, though it cannot perhaps be corrected, may very easily be prevented from disturbing the tranquillity of any body but themselves.[75]

Smith's view of income distribution is laid out with admirable clarity in the conclusion of the last ("very long," in Smith's own words) chapter of Book I of *The Wealth of Nations*. We can summarize it as in the table above.

While self-interest is the basis of *The Wealth of Nations*, it is also true that the self-interest of some may work against broader societal objectives or social "betterment." We clearly see from this discussion that not every self-interest is equally to be respected. The self-interest of large monopolists, government officials, and state-protected industries is deeply pernicious for the society as a whole and has to be kept in check. The main point of contrast with *The Theory of Moral Sentiments*, as well as with some later economic historians who overlook Smith's acerbic comments on the ruling classes, is Smith's questioning of the justice of some high incomes, and his arguing that the interests of capitalists often run counter to social interest. These two particular critiques are never directed at workers and peasants in *The Wealth of Nations*. Workers and peasants are exempt from criticism, one may think, not because Smith believes them to be morally better but because they lack the wealth and political power to impose their own self-interest. Wealth is not seen as necessarily morally bad, but it is seen as giving its holders the wherewithal to advance narrow interests without regard for what is socially desirable. Further, workers' interests are, according to Smith, more consistent with those of society.

It is important to underline that Smith's critique of capitalists' role in policy-making is not based on specific instances of monopolistic behavior, collusion, and the like, but on his more general view that capitalists' interests do not align with social interests because their source of income (profit) is bound to decline with the "general progress of opulence."

The argument outlined here can be interpreted to say that Smith presents two versions of capitalist or commercial society: the competitive one, which is a system of "natural liberty" where incomes are justly acquired, and another one based on cronyism or political capitalism, where incomes are the product of swindling, monopoly, or plunder. There is, in my opinion, little doubt that Smith sees the latter as the "actually existing capitalism," and that he holds up fully competitive capitalism as a society whose attainment should be the objective of the philosopher or the policy-maker. The moral, and at times mocking, critique of the rich in *The Theory of Moral Sentiments* becomes in *The Wealth of Nations* a critique based upon political economy. Why? Because incomes obtained by political power, monopoly, or furthering of particular interests are not only unjust; they also, by retarding development, undermine economic efficiency.

Thus two important critiques of unjustly gained wealth come together in *The Wealth of Nations*: one condemning it on philosophical or moral grounds and the other exposing its nefarious effect on economic growth. The latter is, of course, an instrumental critique of inequality. But it is a critique that makes sense only in the world of *The Wealth of Nations,* whose author's main objective was to uncover the principles that lead to materially richer lives.*

One begins to glean a possible unity of purpose behind *The Theory of Moral Sentiments* and *The Wealth of Nations.* In the long run, the world of empathy is not possible without the achievement of sufficient material wealth. The world of *The Wealth of Nations* then "naturally" comes first: it lays the material foundation for the world of *The Theory of Moral Sentiments.* Perhaps one can even say that it is justified, if the material bases of prosperity are widely shared, that only ridicule is meted out to the rich in *The Theory of Moral Sentiments.* We do not need to insist too much upon the injustice of rich people's incomes if we are all reasonably well-off; we can let our guards down, and just smile at the follies of billionaires.

Conclusions

What key points from Smith's *Wealth of Nations* interest us here? There are six. First, the prosperity of the largest class (workers and peasant) is an indicator of the state's economic success. Second, advanced societies have high wages and low returns on capital. Third, many high incomes are acquired fraudulently and, on account on that, the rich cannot claim moral superiority. Fourth, the conditions that ensure economic prosperity are the same as the conditions that ensure fairness of incomes. Fifth, there is an implicit theory of income distribution whereby rent and wages increase as society progresses, while profit and interest rates fall, so that overall inequality is probably diminished, albeit at the cost of greater income concentration at the top (landlords getting richer). Sixth, and very important, as the outcome of Smith's specific theory of income distribution,

---

* We see here the same alignment of moral arguments and economic efficiency that was noticeable in the critique of high rates of interest: high interest is bad not only because it allows the very rich to live without working but also because it is a feature of a backward society.

capitalists must not be allowed to rule the state, because their economic interests are opposite to those of the public.

Before bringing this chapter to its close, it is also, I think, important to highlight three aspects of Adam Smith's outlook that go far beyond the views of income distribution being investigated in this book, but that help to explain how his work is used today. Given that this will not be a feature of chapters to come, why offer this more expansive view of Smith? Simply because, of all the authors here, Adam Smith's influence on economics has been the greatest, and that influence comes from many parts of his work, not only from those that are related to the evolution of wages, profits, and rents.

The first aspect to emphasize is Smith's critical attitude toward the rich and the way they have gained their wealth, and especially his frequently expressed opinion that the interests of businessmen run so counter to those of the society that they must not be allowed to impose their narrow and peculiar interest on the rest. This is not merely a "left-of-center" Adam Smith, whose many quotes could easily be reprised by Bernie Sanders without many people's realizing that they come from one of the founders of political economy. This is an Adam Smith who comes very close to what is termed a "socialist" critique of capitalism in today's United States.

Second, however, while Smith was skeptical of the rich, he was equally skeptical of big government. His belief in the system of natural liberty made him suspect the motives of those who, under the cloak of general interest, would try to pass over their own interests. Adam Smith was thus in favor of a minimalist government that he limited to three functions: protection from external aggression, administration of justice, and public works and public education (to raise the general level of knowledge and ultimately improve the economy). He added other individual instances where government should act, but almost all of them were of a regulatory nature, intended to limit collusion and monopoly power. Smith's government functions are drastically less than those of any modern capitalist state. Broadly speaking, his government functions might have required expenditures of around 10 percent of GDP—that is, approximately a third or a fourth of what today's governments in developed capitalist countries spend. They would consequently have required much more limited, albeit mildly progressive (as suggested by Smith), personal taxation. This is the Smith often cited by free market economists and the media. It is indeed a true Smith, but it is only part of Smith. The right-wing economists seldom mention the anti-capitalist and left-wing Smith.

The third aspect of Smith's work important to underline here is that, even as he believed that a system of natural liberty and free competition was the best system for the advancement of human welfare, his clear-eyed assessment was that such a system was unlikely ever to be achieved in practice. An ideal state of natural liberty and free competition might be used as a yardstick for measuring the real world's achievements, but it was not rational to expect it to materialize. This realistic Adam Smith would, I think, have had little patience with or interest in abstract economic schemes, including general equilibrium analysis and many of the fairly recondite implications of such analyses. At best, Smith might have found them to be useful theoretical exercises, but more likely they would fall into the category of (to use his terms) "ornamental" but not "useful" knowledge, not meriting much of economists' and policy-makers' attention.

It is these three equally important but complex Smiths that make the inclusion of his work in today's political and economic discourse difficult. In a society that is ideologically divided and very conscious of these divisions, acknowledging contributions from a thinker who, from today's perspective, can be construed as left-wing, right-wing, or very pragmatic becomes difficult, and perhaps even impossible. This is the reason that Smith is both cited and used selectively.

CHAPTER THREE

The Ricardian Windfall: David Ricardo and the Absence of the Equity–Efficiency Trade-off

"Ecce homo," exclaimed Thomas De Quincey as he was reading the first chapter of *The Principles of Political Economy*.[1] Innumerable economists across the next two centuries had, as they read the slender and elegant volume, essentially the same reaction. There is a sort of fascination that Ricardo continues to exert long after the publication of the *Principles*, and it is likely to remain for a long time. The fascination stems from the simple, powerful, and elegant model that Ricardo created. It is essentially a mathematical model, but described in words and explained with clarity (although not fully free of contradictions). The mind behind the model is logically consistent and mathematical. This is the aspect of the *Principles* that attracted economists, especially after economics became highly mathematicized in the late nineteenth century.

Ricardo elevated the local problems of England to universal significance. The Corn Laws, against which his volume was directed, were an attempt at economic protection which raised the cost of living by placing tariffs on imported food. But in discussing this local problem Ricardo created the foundation for a theory of international trade and defined more sharply than anybody before him the three principal social classes that would feature so powerfully in economics for another two centuries. Smith had divided society into three classes, but Ricardo gave that class division a much more salient place in his system, and put the distributional conflict between the classes at center stage. A conflict which was real, but whose full implications were not drawn out by Smith, here became explicit.

Ricardo's class structure also reflected the state of development of England at the time. It is not surprising that the three classes that played such a big role in Ricardo would, within the next half century, coalesce, in Marx's writings, into only two: capitalists and workers. Landed proprietors became numerically and financially less important as industrialists proliferated. Land became just another form of capital. Landlords were thus eventually subsumed by Marx under the landowning capitalists *tout court*. In Ricardo's England, however, they played a big political and social role, so they were rightly considered separate from capitalists.

Yet the elegance of Ricardo's approach also sowed the seeds of a problem that later beset many parts of economics: a high level of abstraction and simplification of the actors and their interests and motivations. This tended to obscure real-world behavior, and to lead economics into an excessively abstract direction. The method attracted critics as soon as *Principles* was published, among them Jean-Baptiste Say:

> It is perhaps a well-founded objection to Mr. Ricardo that he sometimes reasons upon abstract principles to which he gives too great a generalization. When once fixed in an hypothesis which cannot be assailed, from its being founded upon observations not called in question, he pushes his reasoning to their remotest consequences, without comparing their results with those of actual experience.[2]

The same tendency would later be criticized by Joseph Schumpeter, who termed it the "Ricardian vice."

> He . . . piled one simplifying assumption upon another until, having really settled everything by these assumptions, he was left with only a few aggregate variables between which, given these

assumptions, he set up simpler one-way relations so that, in the end, the desired results emerged almost as tautologies."[3]

Ricardo remains a presence in today's economics both methodologically and through his insights in many areas, but principally so in international trade, fiscal policy, and the role of technological progress. He was also, as I will argue, the first person who unified the topics of distribution and economic growth. For Ricardo saw distribution, or more exactly the "correct" distribution of income among the classes, as the prerequisite for economic growth.

Unlike Smith's, Ricardo's travels and interest in the world were limited. He never lived as an adult for any duration of time abroad—a life experience entirely different from that of Marx, the permanent exile. Ricardo barely traveled anywhere outside of England and a couple of continental European countries, nor did he evince much interest in the rest of the world, at least beyond the purely pragmatic interest in foreign affairs and foreign bourses that helped him become immensely rich as a stockjobber. There are not many references to other places in his work. France appears in it, as does Holland (the country from which his father emigrated, and to which he was sent at age eleven to live with relatives for two years).[4] America, Spain, Russia, Poland, and Portugal (wherefrom the family, on his father's side, emigrated) are mentioned, but merely as convenient exemplars of points Ricardo wanted to make, not because he was particularly interested in them or conversant with their problems. In most of his mentions of foreign countries, their names could be replaced by letters—A, B, and C—and little would be lost. When he did travel, it was in grand style, for toward the end of his life he could afford to visit Europe with his extensive family like one of the old seigneurs. He died suddenly and exceptionally young, at fifty-one, from a seemingly minor but neglected ailment.

Ricardo's interests were also limited to England, where he bought himself a seat in Parliament in 1819, participated in numerous political discussions, began his interest in political economy by reading and commenting on Smith, penned several pamphlets, and was much admired and liked by all who met him. He acquired an enormous fortune during his life through successful trading and investments, including, by his own admission, during the interlude between Napoleon's escape from Elba and his final defeat at Waterloo, when English government securities fluctuated widely.[5] Perhaps Ricardo himself, though never vain or self-aggrandizing, described best the power that he commanded on the market:

> One said, not infrequently, to another—Mr. Ricardo has purchased this and that article or stock, and, depend upon it, you cannot do better. In this state of things, it must be manifest that I may often have created that very demand which enabled me to dispose of the article purchased, with a small profit, only a very short time afterwards. At length, such had my reputation as a successful speculator become, that I have sometimes thought it possible for me to have gone into the market and purchased at random, no matter what, with a good prospect of advantage to be gained by selling out again promptly.[6]

The comment is a nice articulation of a dynamic George Soros would later call "reflexivity."[7]

When Ricardo died in 1823, his assets amounted to £615,000, a sum that, to use one of Adam Smith's definitions of wealth—that a person is rich "according to the quantity of labor which he can command"—equaled the annual wages of some fourteen thousand skilled laborers.[8] His wealth easily placed him among the top one percent of the English population. Translated into current British terms, and using the same yardstick (average wage), his estate would be equivalent to about 350 million pounds.* Ricardo might thus have been the richest economist ever, as well as being one of the most influential.[9]

In Wesley Mitchell's understanding of Ricardo, both the style of his writing and his view of humans as being driven in business,

---

* I use the average 2020 gross wage of £25,000.

politics, and morals by self-interest owed much to his experience as a stockbroker, "where the purified, abstract quality of money-making is at its most obvious."[10] This is quite possible even if Ricardo's predilection for severely abstract thinking was already in place at an earlier age. But it was perhaps his intellectually curious and honest nature, and innate politeness, that made him popular and liked by economists from opposite ends of the political spectrum, who were often at loggerheads with each other. He maintained cordial, even friendly, relations with Malthus despite their disagreeing on many issues. He was the most respected of the classical economists by Marx.[11] And he was included by Alfred Marshall in his genealogy of economics, which became the standard way economists thought about the development of their science.

Even though he opposed the Poor Laws and the universal franchise, he was admired by contemporary progressives, and his work set the basis for the Ricardian socialists who appeared not long after his death—and then for the Neo-Ricardians, who challenged the neoclassical orthodoxy a century later.[12] Thus, this most "capitalist" of economists, perhaps precisely because he took social classes as a fundamental economic datum, continued to be influential not only among the "bourgeois" and neoclassical variants of economics but also among the left-wing and Marxist alternatives. He became the Juan Perón of economics: claimed by the left, the center, and the right. He thus occupies a unique place—not shared even by Adam Smith. Although his entire writings on economics (not counting his voluminous correspondence with Malthus, Mill, Say, and a few others) may fill at most two or three volumes, he has remained remarkably "alive" for more than two centuries after his untimely death.

Income Inequality in England at the Time of the Napoleonic Wars

Ricardo wrote in the time when Britain was becoming the predominant world power and British capitalism had greatly matured since the time of Adam Smith: some forty years separate the *Wealth of*

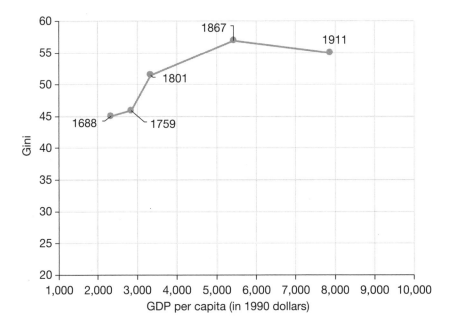

Figure 3.1. England/United Kingdom, 1688–1911: Gini and GDP per capita

Data sources: Calculated from social tables produced by Gregory King (1688), Joseph Massie (1759), Patrick Colquhoun (1801), Dudley Baxter (1867), and Arthur L. Bowley (1911), as reworked by Peter H. Lindert and Jeffrey G. Williamson, "Revising England's Social Tables 1688–1812," *Explorations in Economic History* 19 (1982): 385–408; Branko Milanovic, Peter Lindert, and Jeffrey Williamson "Pre-industrial Inequality," *Economic Journal,* 121:1 (2011): 255–272; Maddison Project Database, 2020.

Nations and the *Principles.* It was also the time when Britain and Europe went through the tumultuous and bloody period of the Napoleonic wars. *Principles* itself was published just two years after Waterloo and a year after the conclusion of the Congress of Vienna.

Inequality in England, calculated from contemporary social tables (see Figure 3.1), increased significantly between 1759, when Adam Smith was in his late thirties, and the early nineteenth century. According to the social tables, which underestimate inequality (since, for lack of precise information, we have to assume that everybody within a given social class had the same income), English inequality in

1801 stood at about 52 Gini points. This is equal to today's inequality levels in many South American countries, and almost 20 Gini points above current British inequality. Inequality between 1759 and 1801 grew by at least 7 Gini points. Again, a modern comparison is useful: that increase was just slightly less than what the UK witnessed (9 Gini points) between Margaret Thatcher's rise to power in 1979 and the peak of UK inequality almost thirty years later.

Principles was written not just at a time of large increases of inequality in income and wealth, but also at a time of relatively high growth. The most remarkable features revealed in Table 3.1 are, first, a dramatic increase in capitalists' incomes in the second half of the eighteenth century (these increased almost twice as much as the incomes of the next most successful group), and second, the concentration of that growth into fewer hands as the percentage of capitalist families dropped from about 4 to 3 percent of the population. At the same time, workers' nominal incomes increased at a below-average rate while their numbers expanded: from 56 percent of the population to 61 percent.

Keeping in mind the three main classes, or *personae dramatis*, of Ricardo's *Principles* (landlords, capitalists, and workers), we can conclude that the upper classes (landed aristocracy and capitalists) both declined in relative size, but that the capitalists' income growth far outstripped the aristocracy's. The income gap between the two was halved, from a ratio of 3 to 1 to a ratio of less than 1.5 to 1. Ricardo's own prosperity, as we have seen, bears witness to that of his class.

Workers, on the other hand, became more numerous and their relative position with respect to capitalists deteriorated. But the numbers we have today on the English situation in the early nineteenth century were not known at the time, and might have been only dimly perceived by Ricardo. It is not hard to imagine that he not only discerned a relationship between capitalists' prosperity and overall growth conceptually, in the sense that the high incomes of capitalists were needed to generate the savings and investments required to propel the economy forward, but also saw it empirically confirmed. Indeed, British cumulative per-capita real growth between 1759 and

Table 3.1 Size and Relative Income of Social Classes in England and Wales

	Percentage of families		Income (in nominal £ per year)		Income increase (in %)
	1759	1801	1759	1801	
Landed aristocracy	1.5	1.3	453	756	67
Capitalists	4.2	3.2	145	525	261
Shopkeepers	9.4	8.6	27	65	138
Peasants	18.9	10.8	22	49	126
Workers	56.4	61.1	14	23	67
Paupers	9.6	14.9	4	4	1
Total/mean	*100*	*100*	*28*	*52*	*88*
Real GDP per capita (in 1990 dollars)			*2,850*	*3,351*	*18*

Note: High inflation during the period is reflected in the large gap between the nominal and the real increase in total per-capita income (compare the data in the last two cells of "Income increase" column). Income is annual except for last row.

Data sources: Summarized and harmonized social tables by Robert Allen, "Revising England's Social Tables Once Again," Oxford Economic and Social History Working Paper 146, tables 11 and 12. GDP per capita from the Maddison Project 2020 version (in real 1990 PPP dollars).

1801 was, according to the Maddison Project's recent estimates, 18 percent (see the last line in Table 3.1).[13] This yields an average annual growth rate of 0.4 percent per person, a rate deemed low by current standards but high for Ricardo's time.[14] Also note that British population growth over the same period was 0.7 percent per annum.[15] Adding this, we get an economy expanding at above one percent annually for more than two generations.

It was the threat to that growth, and consequently, in Ricardo's view, the threat to the improving position of capitalists, that his *Principles* set out to explore—and to counter with suggested interventions. The issues of growth and distribution thus became intimately linked for Ricardo from the very beginning—and he treated them very differently than they would later be treated by neoclassical economists, who regarded production and distribution as governed by very different forces, with production obeying physical and economic laws, and distribution obeying social laws.

Income Distribution and Economic Growth

The functional income distribution, the conflict over net income, and the three main classes that participate in that conflict—workers, capitalists, and landlords—are at center stage in the *Principles*.[16] Like other classical writers, Ricardo never developed what happened in personal income distribution because it was self-evident, unnecessary to explain because individuals were defined by their class incomes. Workers' incomes were at a subsistence level and landlords' incomes were determined by the cost of production of corn on the worst parcel of land that yielded "reasonable" profit to the capitalist tenant (on top of, obviously, paying the wages of farm workers).* Distribution across classes determined distribution across individuals. Peter Lindert, in his study of English inequality in the nineteenth century, concludes:

> The titled and merchant classes, already far richer than the rest of society, widened their advantage across the Industrial Revolution century, in the way Malthus, Ricardo, Mill, and Marx deplored. Just how closely the economic ranks were tied to the three classic factors of production [can be seen from the fact that] . . . nearly all land was owned by the top income decile, which also got far more of its income from capital, and far less from labor, than the rest of society. In such a world, one could well offer explanations of movements in the size distribution of income or wealth in terms of rent, profits, and wages.[17]

Here, then, one just needs to recall the oft-quoted declaration in the preface to the *Principles:* "To determine the laws which regulate this distribution [among proprietors of land, owners of capital, and laborers] is the principal problem in Political Economy."

For Ricardo, unlike Smith, improving the incomes of the largest class was not the goal of economic activity.[18] Distribution was just a

---

* The worst land yields no rent in Ricardo, but that could be modified without introducing any substantial change, as Marx did by bringing in the concept of absolute rent.

tool to accelerate growth.* The principal objective of Ricardo's work, despite this prefatory statement, was to speed up growth. It was the stationary economy that he dreaded. In Marx's words:

> Ricardo championed bourgeois production in so far as it [signified] the most unrestricted development of the social productive forces, unconcerned for the fate of those who participate in production, be they capitalists or workers. He insisted upon the *historical* justification and necessity of this stage of development. His very lack of a historical sense of the past meant that he regarded everything from the historical standpoint of his time.[19]

And thus, Marx concludes elsewhere:

> Ricardo's ruthlessness was not only *scientifically honest* but also a *scientific necessity* from his point of view. But because of this it is also quite immaterial to him whether the advance of the productive forces slays landed property or workers. If this progress devalues the capital of the industrial bourgeoisie it is equally welcome to him. If the development of the productive power of labour halves the value of the *existing* fixed capital, what does it matter, says Ricardo. The productivity of human labour has doubled. Thus here is *scientific honesty*. Ricardo's conception is, on the whole, in the interests of the *industrial bourgeoisie,* only because, and *in so far as* their interests coincide with that of production or the productive development of human labour. Where the bourgeoisie comes into

---

* This is not to say that Ricardo denied the value of raising living standards among this largest class. He also wrote: "The friends of humanity cannot but wish that in all countries the laboring classes should have a taste for comforts and enjoyments. And that they should be stimulated by all legal means in their exertions to procure them. There cannot be a better security against a superabundant population." Ricardo, *Principles of Political Economy and Taxation*, ch. V, 57. Note, however, the implied problem with laboring classes that they lack the "taste" for enjoyment, and the treatment here of higher income not as an objective as such but something justified because it will provide a negative check to the growth of population.

conflict with this, he is just as *ruthless* towards it as he is at other times towards the proletariat and the aristocracy.[20]

Ricardo's goal was increased production: he would support whichever social class had interests most aligned with higher output. In this interpretation of Ricardo, there is but one step to supporting the rise of the proletariat if its interests can be shown to coincide with faster economic growth. Ricardo, of course, never entertained such an idea, because capitalists were the agents of progress—but logically, his analysis allows for it. We can even see the shadows of Ricardian analysis behind a five-year plan.

By casting income distribution merely as an instrument for higher economic growth, Ricardo produced the first integration of distribution and growth. In Smith, distribution appears on the stage because the price of any commodity resolves into three components (wages, profit, and rent), one of which belongs to workers, another to capitalists, and the third to landlords. For Ricardo it is different: the value of a commodity is determined by the amount of labor required to produce it. It includes labor of two kinds: the living labor of workers, and the "congealed" or "objectified" labor embodied in the tools. But while the value is given, the distribution of that value among different factors of production is not determined. The three classes fight over their shares: "When wages rise, it is always at the expense of profits, and when they fall, profits always rise."[21] To put it differently, we have an equation with three unknowns: wage + profit + rent = value. At first, only the value is known. But the solution becomes straightforward with the assumption of a constant real wage, at the subsistence level, and the knowledge of the cost of production of wage goods (in Ricardo's case, corn). Once the cost of production of corn on the marginal land is known, so is the rent, and the system is solved.

Ricardo's *Principles* (in the part that concerns us) can be seen as having been written to show that how the distribution among wage, profit, and rent is decided has a substantial effect on an economy's rate of growth. If profits are squeezed, growth falters. We are in the presence of a dynamic view of the economy: today's distribution determines by how much income will grow tomorrow. Distribution determines production. Or to put it one step closer to Marx: relations of production determine forces of production.

Thus, the main idea in Ricardo is a modeler's dream. Its simple clarity is one of the reasons for the sustained intellectual success of the *Principles*. The book, as mentioned, was conceived as a pamphlet against the Corn Laws. But to show how detrimental these laws were to English growth, Ricardo created the first and possibly the most influential model in economic science.

Before we proceed, a terminological clarification is necessary. I use certain terms in their current meaning, not as Ricardo defined them. Thus, "real wage" expresses the actual physical amount of commodities that workers can purchase with their nominal wage. In Ricardo's terminology, "real wage" was what we today call the labor share, the proportion of the net income received by the worker. Another terminological clarification is that, in current usage, "net income" and "net value added" include the incomes of labor and capital. For Ricardo, that was "gross produce" and, in keeping with his view of the capitalist as the only active agent, "net product" or "net produce" consisted of profit only. (As for the physiocrats, "net income" meant only the income of the proprietaires.)

The Evolution of Wages, Profits, and Rent

The object of the Corn Laws was to regulate the amount of food imports in function of the domestic price and output of crops, reducing tariffs only when domestic production was insufficient. The argument against them can be quickly summarized: If the Corn Laws are maintained, and the population of England keeps rising, corn will have to be cultivated on ever less fertile soils. This means that costs of production of the marginal unit of corn, which determine its price, will become higher. As corn becomes more expensive, all other portions of the land (the more fertile, inframarginal plots) will yield higher rent. Thus, with rising population and continuation of the Corn Laws, rent will go up.

But the rising cost of subsistence will also increase the nominal wage. The cost of subsistence goes up because corn is now more expensive, and to receive the same physical amount of it (assuming that the wage is in any case at the subsistence level) the worker's nominal wage must rise. The nominal wage in turn governs the distribution of the net product between the capitalist and the worker. As the workers' nominal wage goes up, a smaller proportion of net income remains for the capitalist. The bottom line is that a higher price of corn reduces the amount of profits and the rate of profit.

The main idea can be presented graphically as shown in Figure 3.2. The point at which the production of food stops is determined by the size of the population (and workforce). Suppose this to be point B. The marginal cost of production is, for simplicity, supposed to increase linearly from very low at point A, which represents the most fertile land, to D on the last cultivated portion. This is the marginal parcel of land whose cost of production determines the amount of rent received by all infra-marginal parcels (that is, area ADC). So the total rent is determined. What needs to be decided next is the distribution of the area ABC between capital and labor. This is done by taking from that triangle whatever is the cost of labor, equal to the subsistence wage times the number of laborers. What remains is profit. The profit rate is, in this simple one-sector economy, given by the ratio of profit to wages, because wages advanced by capitalist-tenants are the only type of (circulating) capital supposed to exist.*

To go back to our equation, wage+profit+rent=value, the three unknowns are therefore solved as follows. If the real wage (in today's terminology) and the number of workers are given, then the amount of food to be produced is given, too; that, in turn, determines the last (marginal) portion of land that needs to be cultivated to produce that necessary amount of food. All infra-marginal lands receive rent; thus

---

* Notice a further detail. Since capital is the amount of advanced wages, as nominal wage increases, so does the amount of capital the capitalist advances. Thus, the profit rate goes down both because total profits (as the numerator) decrease and because capital (as the denominator) increases.

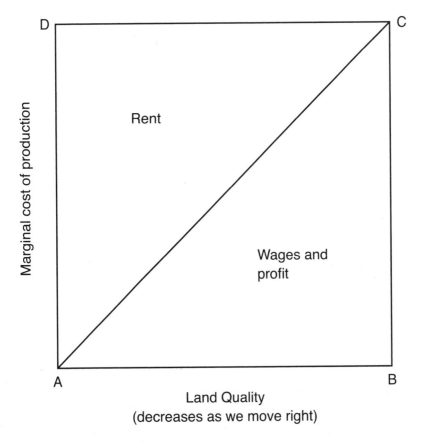

Figure 3.2. Ricardian model of distribution

Adapted from Maurice Dobb, *Theories of Value and Distribution since Adam Smith: Ideology and Economic Theory* (Cambridge University Press, 1973), 87n.

the total amount of rent is determined as well. And whatever remains goes to profits. Obviously, the more workers there are, the greater will be the necessary production of food and the poorer will be the land included on the margin—so the larger will be the portion of value going to rent, and the smaller will be the portion going to profit.*

---

* For simplicity, it is better to treat all expansion of production as taking place over the extensive margin (that is, including new and so-far-unused land). But clearly the same argument holds if we have in mind the intensive margin—that is, expansion of production on the already exploited land.

If the rate of profit goes down, there are simply less savings and investments: the growth rate of the economy slows down. Ricardo's greatest fear was that the wage would eventually become so high (not because the real wage was becoming higher but simply because of the increasing cost of food) that wages might exhaust the entire net income, leaving nothing, or almost nothing, for profit. And as the profit rate fell to zero, capitalists would cease to invest, and the economy would grind to a halt. Ricardo summarized it well, and clearly:

> It has been my endeavour to show throughout this work that the rate of profits can never be increased but by a fall in wages, and that there can be no permanent fall of wages but in consequence of a fall of the necessaries on which wages are expended. If, therefore, by the extension of foreign trade, or by improvements in machinery, the food and necessaries of the labourer can be brought to market, at a reduced price, profits will rise. If, instead of growing our own corn, or manufacturing the clothing and other necessaries of the labourer, we discover a new market from which we can supply ourselves with these commodities at a cheaper price, wages will fall and profits rise; but if the commodities obtained at a cheaper rate, by the extension of foreign commerce, or by the improvement of machinery, be exclusively the commodities consumed by the rich, no alteration will take place in the rate of profits. The rate of wages would not be affected, although wine, velvets, silks, and other expensive commodities should fall 50 per cent., and consequently profits would continue unaltered.[22]

Or, as he emphatically phrased it in a letter to Malthus: "All that I mean to contend for is that profits depend on wages, wages under common circumstances on the price of food and necessaries, and the price of food and necessaries on the fertility of the last cultivated land."[23] We can write it schematically:

High price of food → high rents → high nominal wage → low profit → low investment → slow growth

Ricardo's passage highlights two ways in which this process can be stopped. The first is through the import of food. Elsewhere he writes that if "in the progress of countries in wealth and population, new portions of fertile land could be added to such countries, with every increase in capital, profits would never fall, nor rents rise."[24] The second way is through technological progress that would make production of food cheaper.

Ricardo's view of the rate of profit is thus very different from Smith's and, as we shall see, from Marx's, too. For him, it is entirely embedded in the distribution. While for Smith the rate of profit is driven down by competition of capitals (that is, by having more capital around), for Ricardo "there is . . . no limit to the employment of capital while it yields any profit, and . . . however abundant capital may become, there is no adequate reason for a fall in profit but a rise in wages."[25] The threat to profit, accumulation, and growth thus comes entirely from rising cost of food production, via the higher nominal wage it dictates.*

The issue identified by Ricardo had long-term geopolitical implications. Almost thirty years later, the idea that England needed imports of food to continue her industrial growth led to the repeal of the Corn Laws, and then to the dependence on what Kenneth Pomeranz in *The Great Divergence* calls "ghost acreage"—that is, foreign land (mostly in the United States and Russia) that produced food and cotton exported to England.[26] But dependence on ghost acreage necessitates, as Avner Offer argues, control of the seas, lest the flow of vital commodities be interrupted by war, subjecting a nation to famine. Hungry workers could hardly be expected to fight, so the war would be lost. This understanding made British war planners emphasize control of the seas. The fleet became the substitute for tariffs.[27] German war planners made the same calculation (hence the naval

---

* Ricardo seems to imply that any profit at all is sufficient to keep capitalists producing and investing. Obviously, the lower the profit, the less there is to invest and the lower the growth rate, but the incentive for capitalist production remains as long as profit is not zero. This will be further examined in Chapter 4.

arms race before World War I), but their navy was much smaller and was, because of the British naval blockade, bottled up in the North Sea during the war. This forced the Germans to resort to submarine warfare to prevent food supplies from reaching Britain. The stakes were upped when Germany resumed unrestricted submarine warfare in early 1917. That brought the United States into the war and determined its course, although (to leave no doubt about the final outcome) the British naval blockade continued after the Armistice, until German morale was entirely broken. The Ricardian mechanism, devised after the Napoleonic wars, thus cast a very long shadow over the next century, all the way through the First World War.

The conclusion that Ricardo drew and that motivated his writing in the first place—for *Principles* was written backward, or "reverse engineered," from the desired conclusion to the model—was policy-oriented. The Corn Laws needed to be abolished lest rent skyrocket, an increasing labor share reduce profits to zero, and growth stop. Here we see clearly the integration of the theory of distribution and the theory of growth. A broader implication of Ricardo's model is that distribution determines growth; it represents a strong claim about their interconnectedness.

Table 3.2 summarizes the two states of England as Ricardo sees them: with and without the Corn Laws. We can easily contrast the improving state of England if the Corn Laws are abolished with the desolate or stationary state of the economy if the Corn Laws are kept. The real wage is assumed to be constant throughout. In the rest of the *Principles,* Ricardo does acknowledge that the wage can vary among countries and can even increase within an individual country, but for the purposes of his model—which, we may assume, holds over the short to medium term—the wage is taken as fixed.[28] This is best seen in his statement that a tax on wages is a tax on profit.[29] The claim is true because the tax will not affect the real wage rate, which is fixed at subsistence plus whatever the customs of a land allow, but will be entirely borne by the capitalist.[30] Ricardo's attitude toward wages can also be explained by his Malthusianism, as he holds that any increase in real wages is simply bound to bring

Table 3.2   The Two States of England

	Import of corn and growing economy	Corn Laws and stationary economy
Rents	Decreasing	Increasing
Real wages	Fixed	Fixed
Profits	Increasing	Decreasing
Rent share	Decreasing	Increasing
Wage share	Decreasing	Increasing
Profit rate	Increasing	Decreasing
Investments	Increasing	Decreasing
Growth rate	Higher	Lower, possibly zero

forth a higher population, making the wage ultimately go down to its previous level.[31] It has to be acknowledged, however, that Ricardo's treatment of wages is not consistent in the book. The best we can do to make it consistent is to argue that Ricardo foresaw an increase in real wage over the long term as society became richer, but for the purposes of his analysis, and as a practical matter, he preferred to assume that real wages were constant.

In the struggle between landlords and capitalists, in the case of the maintenance of the Corn Laws, the share of profits must decrease as it is squeezed from both ends: from the increasing wage share and from rising rents. Rent share most likely goes up, although, as a somewhat technical point, while the total amount of rent must increase as less fertile lands are brought under cultivation, the share of rent in total output need not. It will all depend on the cost curve of food production. Suppose that the new land that needs to be brought into use has only slightly lower productivity than the previous marginal land; that slightly lower productivity can be approximated by saying that the cost of production increases by an infinitesimal amount. Then the total amount of rent would also increase by very little, while the total production of food might increase much more. Thus, the rent share might decline.[32] But this extreme case—the ability to expand production to new areas at almost the same cost *without* using land from foreign countries—represents the situation Ricardo believed to be most unlikely.

Class Conflict

Principles presents a very stark picture of class struggle over net product among three classes. The main class conflict, however, is not so much between capitalists and workers (because workers are simply supposed to live on a subsistence wage which is fixed) as between landlords and capitalists. "The interest of the landlord is always opposed to the interest of every other class in the community," wrote Ricardo in his *Essay on the Influence of a Low Price of Corn*, published two years before *Principles* (but covering, regarding the issues discussed here, the same ground).[33] Contrast that with Smith's contention that the interests of *capitalists* are opposed to the interests of every other class.

Note that Ricardo, for simplicity, presents Smith's two conflicts (capitalists versus landlords, and then capitalists versus workers) as fundamentally just one: after the price of food is determined in the class struggle between capitalists and landlords, that price determines the shares of capital and labor in the net product, and thus the rate of profit. If Ricardo had wanted to make his model more realistic, and more complicated, he would have allowed the real wage rate to vary, which would then leave the shares of capital and labor indeterminate and let them emerge as a result of relative political power and bargaining between workers (often united in trade unions) and employers' associations. This was the step that many neo-Ricardians took more than a century after Ricardo's book was published.

Regarding the evolution of wages as society progresses, Ricardo somewhat reversed himself in his famous Chapter XXXI, which he added in the third edition of *Principles*. Its main point was to recant his previous opinion that introduction of new machinery could not be injurious to workers; now, he showed how more capital-intensive production could, in the short term, reduce demand for labor and presumably decrease the wage. Yet Ricardo still held that, over the longer term, machinery would, by increasing the quantity of commodities, improve workers' standard of living. Since we are here concerned chiefly with Ricardo's view of the longer-term evolution of income distribution, it should be clear that the temporary effects of increased capital intensity of production should be left aside. Moreover, even if labor-substituting technological changes were to keep occurring at short intervals, each of them depressing demand for labor, they would still inflict their effects along a curve of rising overall production and constant real wage. Thus the longer-term stickiness of the real wage, despite short-term fluctuations.

The picture of the economy and distribution offered by Ricardo is very different from that drawn by Adam Smith, who, as we have seen, believed that the prosperity of the most numerous class, workers, was synonymous with overall prosperity. In Ricardo, however, it is growth that is the most important goal, and consequently the income of capitalists that matters. Capitalists are the only active agents. They differ from landlords, who simply collect rent through no contribution of their own (because rent is determined by price, and does not determine the price). And they differ from workers, who are also not active agents, because they cannot invest (their wages being too low) and because their incomes are "passive," in the sense that they are always at the customary subsistence level.

Thus, to ensure growth, profits are necessary. High profits are a sign of progress. This is also very different from Smith, who saw low profits as a sign of prosperity and held up Holland as the example of an advanced economy with a low interest rate and low profits. Interestingly, Ricardo addresses Smith's point on Dutch prosperity and low interest, but does so by pointing out that its profits (and interest) are low because Holland, which imports all of its food, imposes heavy taxes on it.[34] This increases the nominal wage and squeezes out profits. Low profits in Holland are thus for Ricardo not a sign of mature prosperity, but are due to high food costs and thus undesirable.[35]

For Smith, high interest is a sign of lack of security of private property and of a backward economy. In stark contrast, Ricardo sees high profits as a sign of a dynamic and growing economy.

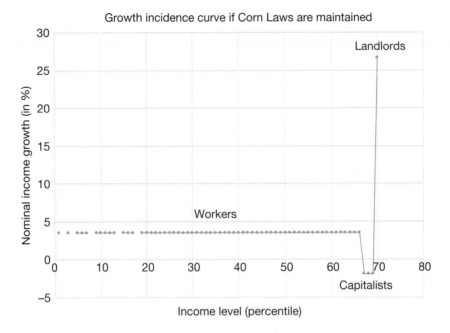

Figure 3.3. Growth incidence curves with and without the Corn Laws

Note: Left panel shows the scenario if Corn Laws are maintained, right panel if they are abolished.

The Ricardian Windfall

We have already seen that, in Ricardo's work, the link between income distribution and growth is very clear. The two societies he compares—the stationary society under the Corn Laws and the dynamic society without them—differ in their levels of income inequality, too. The stationary society is the one with high inequality: it has super-rich landlords, impoverished capitalists (whose rate of profit, Ricardo feared, might go down to zero), and workers earning subsistence-level wages.

The growing economy, despite the rising profits of capitalists, has lower inequality. Landlords' incomes are reduced and converge down toward capitalists' incomes, which rise (as indeed happened, as we saw above, in England in Ricardo's time). The two upper classes tend to become more similar than in the case of a stationary economy.

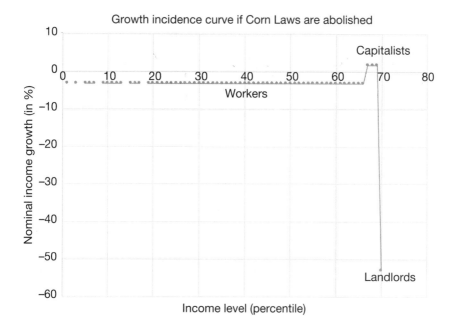

Figure 3.3. (continued)

Wages do not play much of a role, simply because they are supposed to be fixed in either a stationary or a growing economy. A growing economy is characterized by lower inequality due to the reduction of the incomes of the richest class (landlords), or what we may today call the top one percent.

If we now translate this "class-based" outcome into a personal income distribution, where all workers are at the bottom of the pyramid, all capitalists are in the middle, and all landlords are at the top, we can derive a growth incidence curve (which charts for different percentiles of income earners how their real incomes change over time). To make the figure more realistic, we can use the approximate population shares of the three groups (in Table 3.1) from Colquhoun's 1801 social table for England and Wales, as recently harmonized by Robert Allen.[36] We can then use Ricardo's own numerical example of what happens to the incomes of the three classes when, from a given position, corn prices increase or decrease. We take as the base price one of the five corn prices, with their distributional scenarios, given by Ricardo—namely, 4 pounds and 10 shillings—and consider first its increase to 4 pounds and 16 shillings (an almost 7 percent increase), and then its decrease to 4 pounds, 4 shillings, and 8 pence (a decrease of 6 percent).[37] The former shift, of course, reflects the continuation of the Corn Laws, and the latter shift reflects their abolition. Figure 3.3 (in its left and right panels) shows what happens to nominal incomes of workers, capitalists, and landlords under the two scenarios.

Workers' nominal incomes marginally increase when corn prices go up and decrease when corn prices go down—in both cases just enough to keep the real wage approximately constant.[38] In the left panel, capitalists' incomes go down by about 3 percent, and landlords' incomes increase by a whopping 27 percent. With the continuation of the Corn Laws, not only will functional income distribution move in favor of the rich landlords but personal income distribution will get worse as the richest class gains most.

In the right panel, when cheaper corn is brought in, the outcome is exactly the reverse: landlords' incomes are halved and capitalists' incomes increase (although, in this example, quite modestly by 2 percent). To capitalists, workers become "cheaper" as, for the same quantity of food production, a smaller portion of Ricardo's gross income is required to pay them, and therefore profits increase. Since profits are used for investments, the economy grows. The growth incidence curve shows that the top loses, the middle gains, and the bottom is unchanged (in real terms). Income concentration becomes less. Therefore, lower interpersonal inequality is associated with faster growth.

Arthur Okun claimed that there is always a trade-off between equality and efficiency, or, to put it slightly differently, between reducing income inequality and promoting economic growth.[39] For David Ricardo, the very opposite is true: lower interpersonal inequality leads to faster economic growth. It wasn't until thirty years after *Principles* that the Corn Laws in England were rescinded, but one can easily see the attractiveness of the sketch of development

Ricardo presented to his readers: it promised both to deliver faster growth and to reduce inequality.[40]

In conclusion, Ricardo created the first integration of income distribution and economic growth, linked a growing economy with high capitalist incomes, and argued that capitalists could play their role of active agents only if their profits were sufficiently high. But he did not see class conflict as primarily between capital and labor. Rather, reflecting the state of development in early nineteenth-century England, he considered the principal conflict to be between capitalists and landlords—between profit and rent. The more advanced state of society that would come through economic growth would be characterized by more income equality, because of the reduction of its highest incomes, those received by landlords. Adopting Ricardo's prescription would thus bring a windfall: along with higher incomes would also come lower inequality.

CHAPTER FOUR

Karl Marx: The Decreasing Rate of Profit but Constant Pressure on Labor Incomes

Leszek Kolakowski opens his monumental three-volume *Main Currents of Marxism* with this sentence: "Karl Marx was a German philosopher."[1] (It was modeled after the words Jules Michelet always used to begin his course of lectures on English history: "L'Angleterre est une île.") It seems an obvious way to think of Marx. It links him to the Hegelian and generally German nineteenth-century philosophical background that in many ways marked his youth, and perhaps his entire life and work.

But is it true? Does it define Marx accurately, even in the narrow terms of his German background? Things are, I think, more complicated. Michael Heinrich's excellent biography reveals many details that are either new or cast a new light on Marx's youth. Although the main contours of those early years were quite well known, Heinrich highlights a background rendered more complex and even "cosmopolitan" by cleavages along at least three important lines: national, religious, and political.[2]

A national cleavage. We all know that Marx, as Kolakowski wrote, was a German philosopher. But had he been born three years earlier, he would have been born a French citizen. He might have gone to study in Paris rather than Berlin. Heinrich brings out the complicated history of Marx's birthplace, the city of Trier. It was conquered by the French in 1794 and remained in French hands until the final defeat of Napoleon in 1815. The French at first introduced many progressive reforms, including full citizenship rights for the Jewish population, but gradually, as the fortunes of war changed, French rule grew more oppressive, taxes went up, and young men were conscripted to fight. Thus, Trier's bourgeoisie, who were fully Francophone and initially well disposed toward the French, grew increasingly disenchanted with Napoleon's rule. The Prussian administration in Berlin after 1815 was not much liked, either, and in return it did not see the Rhenish population as fully "reliable." A number of public offices previously headquartered in Trier were moved to Koblenz and Cologne. The heavy Prussian hand of monarchic prerogatives, stifling conformism, and pomposity proved oppressive. The Francophile spirit, largely coterminous with the idea of bourgeois liberalism and the ideals of the French Revolution, returned to the limitrophe province. Heinrich points to many instances of Trier's mixed Franco-German character—with the rather distant Berlin and Prussia looming in the background. The distance from Trier to Berlin, 722 kilometers, is about 300 kilometers more than from Trier to Paris. When Marx studied in Berlin, it took him between five and seven days to get there, crossing multiple German state borders in the process.[3] Today, the eight-hour train trip to Berlin is twice the four hours to Paris.

There was a linguistic issue, too. Marx's mother, Henriette Presburg, was raised speaking Dutch, and moved to Trier only after marrying in her mid-twenties. According to what Marx told his daughter Eleanor, Henriette never fully mastered the German language.[4] This is also evident in her letters to Karl. Her German remained rather limited even though she used it to communicate with her son and the rest of the family. Marx's own linguistic "cosmopolitanism" would later in his life be expressed in his command of several languages. It is estimated that 60 percent of Marx's writings were in German, 30 percent in English, 5 percent in French, and the remaining 5 percent in Russian, Spanish, and Latin.[5]

A religious and cultural cleavage. There was also a cleavage between Jewish and Christian traditions in Marx's young life. Both of his parents were born and raised as Jews. After moving to Trier, sometime between 1817 and the end of 1819, Marx's father, Heinrich, converted to Christianity, and chose Protestantism rather than the city's more common Catholicism.[6] Karl Marx was born in 1818, so his father's conversion was either a bit before or just after his birth. The reason behind it was in itself interesting. As Michael Heinrich explains, the discriminatory anti-Jewish laws that had been abolished when Trier became part of the Napoleonic Confederation of the Rhine were reintroduced, together with a raft of other regressive measures in 1808, as Napoleon's power waned and his rule "worsened." The discriminatory edicts were then taken over by the new Prussian administration. They excluded Jews from a number of occupations, including government administration. Marx's father was a lawyer, and lawyers were state officials. Therefore, a reasonably prosperous—even affluent—professional was presented with an invidious choice: to lose his job and start an entirely different career (at almost forty years of age) or to convert.[7] After trying to postpone the inevitable, he chose to convert, and within a few years had young Karl baptized (making him a Christian, as it were, "directly").[8] Making these choices must have affected the older Marx (a scion of a long line of rabbis) as well as Karl's mother, who postponed her own conversion until her mother died, perhaps to spare her a source of grief.

The religious conversion enabled the family to keep its high-income position and social reputation, as can be seen from the data in Table 4.1 for 1831–1832 (when Karl Marx was thirteen to fourteen years old). Heinrich Marx's income of 1,500 thalers placed the family in the top income decile, and likely even in the top 5 percent of Trier's population.

His family's original Judaism does not seem to have played much of a role in Marx's life.[9] His essay "On the Jewish Question," which he wrote at twenty-six, has even been described by some as anti-Semitic. Marx's innumerable citations of the Bible in his books, articles, and private letters reflect knowledge he acquired at elementary and middle school and at university in Berlin, where his

Table 4.1   Estimated Income Distribution of Trier in 1831–1832

Household total income in thalers	Percentage of population
Under 200	80
Between 200 and 400	10
Between 400 and 2,500	8.8
Above 2,500	1.2

Data source: Heinrich, *Karl Marx and the Birth of Modern Society*, 45.

philosophical career began with a critique of religion.[10] Thus, the educational system rather than the family was the source of Marx's religious knowledge. And, as with the Franco-Prussian cleavage discussed above, the Jewish-Christian cleavage probably heightened Marx's awareness that what is regarded as truth from one point of view may appear very different when looked at from an alternative angle.

A political cleavage. Heinrich Marx was, by all accounts and as far as we can see from his correspondence with Karl, a secularist, enlightenment-influenced liberal. But under the pressure of Prussian bureaucracy and spies, he had to hide such views. Michael Heinrich gives an excellent example of this in the speech made by Marx's father in 1834 at a celebratory banquet for local deputies to the Rhenish provincial diet. While sounding many "politically correct" notes in his speech, including praise for the monarch, Heinrich Marx's brief comments also carried a subversive tone that was not lost on the enforcers of Berlin's rule. For example, by commending the elected deputies for representing their constituents' perspectives at the diet, Heinrich Marx portrayed them as holding some power to decide political matters—which they most emphatically did not have, since the diet was merely a consultative body of the emperor. This was an advisory assembly, not a decision-making body similar to Great Britain's parliament.[11] Thus Heinrich Marx was employing "Aesopian language," communicating support for liberalism while camouflaging that with praises for the king. As Michael Heinrich points out, the king was thanked second, after the representatives, not first.[12] (It is somewhat ironic that many people, living later under regimes that claimed Karl Marx as their intellectual founder, have had to resort to the same subterfuge as his father: ostensibly praising a regime for its democracy in a way that actually conveys that it is not democratic.)

Marx's family background, although seemingly limited to a small slice of Western Europe, was thus in reality much richer, full of national, linguistic, religious, and political contradictions.

Wealth and Income Inequality in the UK and Germany at the Time of Karl Marx

Wealth inequality in the UK increased throughout most of the eighteenth and nineteenth centuries before peaking just on the eve of the First World War (Figure 4.1). At the time that Marx was writing *Capital*, wealth inequality in the UK was not only rising but exceptionally high: the top one percent of wealth-holders owned around 60 percent of the country's wealth. That was something unknown probably before and certainly afterward. In the United States, which nowadays has, among rich countries, an unusually high wealth inequality, those in the top percentile own about 35 percent of all wealth.[13] In the UK today, the top one percent own about 20 percent of all wealth.

Income inequality was very high, too, as noted in Chapter 3, and most likely increasing until around the 1870s. Baxter's social table for 1867, the same year that *Capital* was published, shows the peak of British nineteenth-century inequality (see Figure 3.1). Robert Allen's social tables, in a slightly different rearrangement, have the peak occurring in 1846.[14]

The relative incomes of the three main classes also changed (see Table 4.2). At the time of *The Wealth of Nations*, the average income of capitalists was eleven times, and that of landlords thirty-three times, greater than the average income of workers. At the time of *Capital*—about a century later—the workers' position was even worse vis-à-vis the capitalists (who now made fifteen times more) but it improved vis-à-vis landlords (who now made twenty-one times more). The data in Table 4.2 illustrate the declining position of

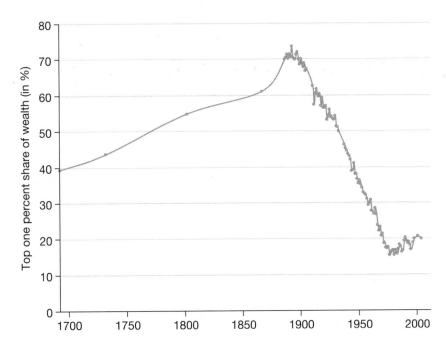

Figure 4.1. Wealth share of the richest one percent in England, 1670–2010

Data sources: Facundo Alvaredo, Anthony B. Atkinson, and Salvatore Morelli, "Top Wealth Shares in the UK over More Than a Century," *INET Oxford Working Paper* 2017–01 (2016); Peter Lindert, "Unequal British Wealth since 1867," *Journal of Political Economy* 94, no. 6 (1986): 1127–1162.

Table 4.2   Relative Incomes of Three Principal Classes in the UK

	Around 1776 (time of *Wealth of Nations* publication)	Around 1867 (time of *Capital* publication)
Landlords (aristocracy)	33	21
Capitalists	11	15
Workers	1	1

Note: workers' income = 1.

Data source: Calculated from Robert Allen's reworking of English social tables: Allen, "Revising England's Social Tables Once Again"; and Allen, "Class Structure and Inequality during the Industrial Revolution," tables 10 and 11.

the top class (the landlords) and the improving position of capitalists (trends already noted in Chapter 3 that were reinforced between Ricardo's *Principles* and Marx's *Capital*).

How about real wages? Here we have the data from Gregory Clark's and Charles Feinstein's estimations of English wages (Figure 4.2). According to Clark, wages were practically unchanged in real terms until the early nineteenth century, but after the Napoleonic wars they began to rise and, despite periods of sharp decreases during the slumps and depressions in the late 1840s and the global financial crisis in 1857, they trended unmistakably upward. According to Feinstein (who is more pessimistic), the increase was slower and it began a bit later. Yet according to both authors, real wages around the time of the publication of Marx's *Capital* were substantially higher than in 1820, the time of Ricardo's *Principles*. According to Clark, the real wage was 50 percent higher than in 1820 (which translates to a rate of growth averaging almost one percent per year, a huge number by the standards of the time) and, according to Feinstein, it was about 30 percent higher.[15]

This is something that Marx and Engels had noticed by the late 1850s. Engels writes in an 1858 letter to Marx that "the English proletariat is actually becoming more and more bourgeois, so that this most bourgeois of all nations is ultimately aiming at the possession of a bourgeois aristocracy and a bourgeois proletariat alongside the bourgeoisie. For a nation that exploits the whole world this is of course to a certain extent justifiable."[16] There was also—according to Engels—income differentiation among workers and the creation of what later became known as the "labor aristocracy." The embourgeoisement of workers required an explanation; one preferred by Engels was that higher real wages were made possible thanks to unrequited transfers from colonies (or, to put it less delicately, plunder). England, the largest colonial power, was able to transfer some of the resources from the colonies and, in Engels's words, gave its workers "a share in the benefits of the monopoly," even if the benefits were very unevenly distributed among workers.[17] That particular explanation would have quite a lot of resonance and influence in the early

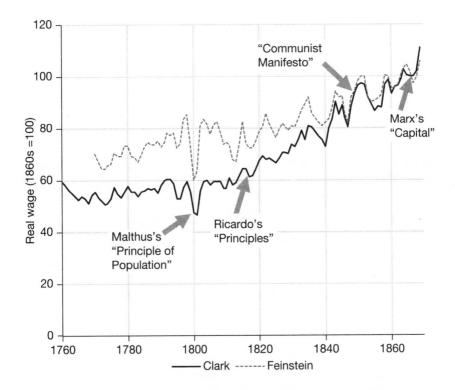

Figure 4.2. English real wages, 1760–1870

Reformatted and reprinted with permission of the author from Gregory Clark, "The Condition of the Working Class in England, 1209–2004," *Journal of Political Economy* 113 no. 6 (2005): 1307–1340, figure 8; Charles Feinstein, "Pessimism Perpetuated: Real Wages and the Standard of Living in Britain during and after the Industrial Revolution," *Journal of Economic History* 58, no. 3 (1998): 625–658.

twentieth century when it became the favorite explanation used by the left wing of the social-democratic movement, and especially by Lenin, for the more pragmatic, or revisionist, stance of the mainstream of social-democratic parties. If workers were getting better off under the capitalist system, what was the point of the violent overthrow of the system? Lenin and others ascribed, not wholly unreasonably, this "conciliatory" attitude to the "revisionists."

Marx also mentions various topics related to income and wealth inequality himself, and makes use of data that would subsequently be used by others (several decades and even a century later) to get a much better grasp of English/British contemporary inequality. To illustrate the rising share of capital incomes, Marx gives the data on taxable profits between 1853 and 1864 and contrasts their increase of more than 50 percent over that period with a much lower increase of wages (around 20 percent).[18] He then argues that real wages might not have risen at all, given that the costs of essential products consumed by workers had also gone up.[19] Marx also showed several income tax schedules for England and Wales and (separately) for Ireland for 1864 and 1865. These are of the same kind that Pareto would later use, at the turn of the century (as noted in a section below).

Finally, and rather strangely, the biggest controversy regarding Marx's citations—and Marx cited literally hundreds of writers and speakers—was stirred up in 1863 when he quoted a line uttered by William Gladstone on the subject of income inequality. Gladstone at the time was chancellor of the Exchequer (he would later become prime minister), and in a budget speech to Parliament might or might not have expressed the sentiment that Marx attributed to him. The subsequent fight over whether Marx had misrepresented Gladstone's meaning was so intense that, even decades later, Engels would devote almost the entire preface to the fourth German edition of *Capital* (some five to six pages) to rebutting the charges. (For more on this bizarre episode, see the Appendix to this chapter.)

It should also be mentioned that, in the second half of the nineteenth century, there was a significant expansion of British social legislation and of the electoral franchise. The Factory Act, which limited the duration of the working day to twelve hours in the textile industry, was passed in 1833, and in 1867 it was extended to all sectors. In the same year, voting rights were granted to a part of the urban working class, and in 1884, the franchise was further broadened to include about 60 percent of adult males. In 1875, strikes were allowed, and in 1880 there was a ban on child labor.

Robert Allen has recently reworked British social tables and estimated factor (capital and labor) shares.[20] Allen finds a noticeable decline in labor's share despite an increase in real wage. The capitalists' share increased significantly, from around 20 percent of national income in the late eighteenth century to 50 percent a hundred years later. This expansion of the capitalists' share came at the expense of both labor's and landlords' shares. Here we see another development that would be noticed by Marx—namely, that there was simultaneously an increase in the real wage and a declining labor share. This, I will argue below, influenced Marx's view of the world.

We can also look at the evolution of income inequality and income concentration in Germany. England was, of course, the country Marx ultimately took most interest in, living there most of his life and studying it as the paragon of capitalism and "demiurge of the bourgeois cosmos."[21] But Germany was at the same time undergoing dramatic economic developments and Marx was also interested in it—and not just because he was German. He had participated in political life there very actively before and during the 1848 revolution, and remained engaged afterward through his involvement with German social democracy. Germany also offered important lessons about long-term capitalist developments. Inequality data on Germany were unknown to Marx, as were most of the English data that we have just reviewed. This information is available to us now because economists have recently worked with data produced in the past but not previously published or analyzed in the modern fashion. Not even the methodology to study such data existed in the nineteenth century. The recent analysis by Bartels, Kersting, and Wolf shows the very interesting developments that were going on in Germany. Figure 4.3 displays the changes in income inequality from 1870 to 1914 in different areas of the country, with the areas being defined by how much of their total employment was made up of agricultural employment.

Every area—from the heavily agricultural to the moderately agricultural to the predominantly industrial—saw an increase in income inequality.[22] This is the kind of change that, by the mid-twentieth century, would be described as an "upward swing of the Kuznets curve," meaning that the early industrial development was associated with rising income inequality. (See Chapter 6.) In Figure 4.3 we

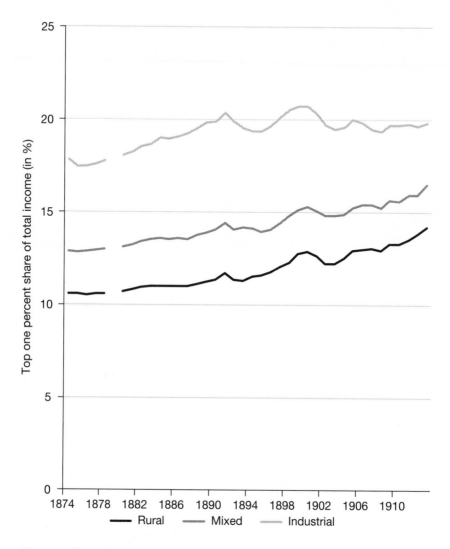

Figure 4.3. Top one percent income share in Germany, 1870–1914, in areas with different shares of agricultural employment

Note: Chart shows share of total income going to the top one percent of earners in three types of districts: rural (with more than 50 percent of workers employed in agriculture); industrial (less than 40 percent); and mixed (40 to 50 percent).

Data source: Charlotte Bartels, Felix Kersting, and Nickolaus Wolf, "Testing Marx: Income Inequality, Concentration, and Socialism in Late 19th Century Germany," Stone Center on Socio-Economic Inequality Working Paper 32, March 2021, figure 1.

see it in a very striking fashion because the increase in inequality took place in all three parts of Germany, regardless of their initial levels of agricultural or industrial development, and regardless of their initial levels of income inequality. So we can conclude that, in the case of Germany, the late nineteenth century (and, we may surmise, the entire second half of the nineteenth century) was characterized by increasing income inequality.

Clearing Decks: Key Marxist Concepts

We cannot discuss distribution of income in Marx the way we discuss it for other writers. This is because we need first to explain his view of the "unity," or interdependence, of production and distribution (and the attendant lack of importance of income inequality as such), his theory of exploitation and centrality of class struggle, and his historical definition of capital. These are all new moments, not present in Ricardo.

Production and distribution as historical categories. The unity of production and distribution may be best explained by contrasting Marx's views with some that came before him. Specifically, John Stuart Mill and then the neoclassical economists saw production as logically preceding distribution (things must be created before they can be distributed) and regarded economics as a science that aims, given existing constraints, to maximize production. While distribution is accepted as a historical category that can in principle be altered, production is taken to be determined by physical or mechanical laws, and relations of production among the participants are taken to be determined by the immutable laws of human nature.[23] As Marx writes critically in *Capital*:

A more developed and critical awareness [such as Mill's] concedes the historically developed character of these relations of distribution, but holds all the more firmly to the supposedly constant character of the relations of production themselves, as arising from human nature and hence independent of historical development.[24]

The truth of the matter, he goes on to explain, is that the "relations into which men enter in their social life-process . . . have a specific, historical and transitory character; and . . . the relations of distribution are essentially identical with these relations of production . . . as the two things share the same historically transitory character." A few pages on, he sums up: "The specific relations of distribution thus simply express the historically-determined relations of production."[25] And several years later he would state the point even more emphatically:

> Any distribution whatever of the means of consumption is only a consequence of the distribution of the conditions of production themselves. The latter distribution, however, is a feature of the mode of production itself. The capitalist mode of production, for example, rests on the fact that the material conditions of production are in the hands of nonworkers in the form of property in capital and land, while the masses are only owners of the personal condition of production, of labor power. If the elements of production are so distributed, then the present-day distribution of the means of consumption results automatically.[26]

What about the neoclassicists? The absence of history (explaining, for example, how capitalists became capitalists) and the symmetrical treatment of capital and labor in their work are probably their two most important differences with Marx. For them, output is distributed in accordance with participants' endowments of capital and skill, and according to factor prices generated within the process of production. Through political decisions, output can be further redistributed to help those who are poor and who receive insufficient income from production itself. Endowments, in such a view of the world, are seen as lying outside economics. This is clearly enunciated by Paul Samuelson in his *Economics*, as shown by Eli Cook.[27] Economists appear modest in their claims. Like the engineers of societal production, they are in charge of output maximization under conditions of given endowments and technology. Markets generate incomes and economists leave the task of further redistribution to those more qualified than them: the politicians.[28] Production and market-determined prices are technical, not historical, categories. This is akin to the situation in linear programming: there are resources, there is demand, there is an optimal output mix—and then there is distribution of what has been produced, with factor rewards just another set of prices.

For Marx, as we have seen, the laws of production and the laws of distribution are the same laws, just expressed under different forms. They are the laws specific to a given mode of production. The capitalist mode of production results in a given distribution of income.[29] It does not make logical sense—nor would it make any practical difference in real life—to focus on a change in *income* distribution when *endowments* are distributed unequally, and given that some endowments (namely, capital) allow those who have them to hire labor and appropriate the surplus value.* This is the origin of Marx's oft-stated rejection of the idea that socialism can be reduced to matters of income distribution: "Vulgar socialism . . . has taken over from the bourgeois economists the consideration and treatment of distribution as independent of the mode of production and hence the presentation of socialism as turning principally on distribution."[30]

Endowments, exogenous in the neoclassical world, are of key importance to Marx. They depend on the previous and current exercise of power. "Primitive accumulation" is part and parcel of the system, not an accessory. If endowments were differently distributed, the structure of production would be different, and so would be the power of various classes. To put it in reverse, were the power of various classes different, the distribution of endowments, and everything else, including the output mix and relative prices, would be different, too. Under different modes of production, the structure

---

* Marx did not think the state could play such a significant redistributory role that, beyond shifting income distribution, it could alter the distribution of endowments, so that capitalism would then "endogenously" produce less unequal distribution. The classes would obviously still remain.

of production, relative prices, and individual incomes are all different.

This emphasis on the powerful effects of endowments (privately owned capital), combined with the laws that protect the endowments, gives rise to Marxists' insistence that, under different historical ways of organizing production, the law of value takes different forms. If the dominant mode of production is small-scale commodity producers working with their own means of production, there will be no general tendency toward equalization of profit rates, and the structure of relative prices will not be what it is under capitalism.[31] And because relative prices will differ under the two systems, so will the output mix and the returns to the factors of production. This feature of Marx's economics had, as we shall see in Chapter 7, a strong influence on the economics of income distribution under socialism. Many discussions and fights focused on how the law of value was manifested in socialism (and even whether it could exist in socialism at all) and, in turn, on how to arrive at the "normal price" of a good, and thus the "normal" distribution among the factors of production.

Relative unimportance of income inequality. Marx's understanding of the unity of production and distribution has implications for his treatment of inequality. If income distribution cannot be dissociated from the underlying mode of production, then any notion that Marx's critique of capitalism turns on the question of distribution, and thus can be addressed within the capitalist system, is fundamentally flawed. Distribution cannot be changed in any material way until the system is changed. The issue is the abolition of classes, not marginal alteration of income inequality. It makes sense to speak of income distribution only after the establishment of "just" background institutions—namely, ones that transcend the antagonistic relationship between owners of capital and workers. "To clamor for equal or even equitable remuneration on the basis of the wages system," Marx writes, "is the same as to clamor for freedom on the basis of the slavery system."[32] For Marx, as Allen W. Wood nicely summarizes, "equality is properly speaking only a political notion, and even a specifically bourgeois political notion;

and . . . the real meaning of the proletarian demand for equality . . . is the demand for the abolition of classes."[33]

Engels's opinions on this topic were the same as Marx's, as seen from his introduction to Marx's "Critique of the Gotha Program" attacking a policy platform put forward in 1875 by the German Social Democratic Party. In a letter to August Bebel, he makes the point explicitly, writing that the program document's call for "'the elimination of all social and political inequality' rather than 'the abolition of class distinctions,' is similarly a most dubious expression. As between one country, one province and even one place and another, living conditions will always evince a *certain* inequality which may be reduced to a minimum but never wholly eliminated."[34]

Exploitation. Marx's theory of exploitation is an integral part of his theory of distribution. Only in the extreme case when the entire newly created value belongs to labor—that is, when the labor share is 100 percent—does his theory of exploitation (under capitalism) cease to apply.[35] In all other cases, no matter how pro-labor the distribution of net product may be, there is exploitation. The theory of exploitation is based on the assumption that the entire net product is produced by labor. The implication is that means of production— that is, the raw materials and tools that Marx calls the "constant capital"—simply transmit their value to the final product. The higher value of that final product is therefore wholly due to the contribution of labor, with only depreciation of the constant capital entering into the gross value-added. Seen in this light, the distribution between capital and labor is no longer simply an issue of distribution between the two factors of production; it becomes an issue of exploitation. Labor gets less than what it has contributed to the value-added under any scenario where profits are positive. Only if the rate of profit is zero does it get the entire net product—and if the rate of profit is zero, capitalism cannot function and it ends. Thus, exploitation is an indispensable feature of capitalism.[36]

How could Marx assert that labor gets less than what it contributes, while also maintaining that the law of value was valid? He explained this apparent contradiction by drawing a distinction between labor and labor-power. The capitalist buys (or rather rents) labor-power at its value, which is equal to the value of the goods necessary for the reproduction of labor-power. (We could think of this as the fundamental cost of living—the amount required to sustain the laborer's productive activity.) The value of labor-power might differ across countries and time periods (as will be discussed *infra*) but, whatever that value is, the specific feature of labor is that it creates a value that exceeds the value of labor-power. Returning workers to the same state of welfare that they had at the beginning of the process of production (and ensuring the long-term reproduction of this type of labor) costs less than the value they contribute during the process of production—this is the gap between the value of labor-power and the new value created by labor. If one hour of labor creates ten units of value, but the expenditure of muscular, intellectual, and other effort over that one hour of labor (the "necessary labor") requires goods and services worth only six units of value to fully replenish the worker, then the remaining four units (the "surplus labor") is value appropriated by the capitalist. Thus, as Marx emphasized, the exchange is based fully on the law of value: the workers are not treated unfairly, nor are they paid less than the value of their labor-power. Exploitation comes from this specific feature of labor: its ability to produce value greater than the value of goods and services expended in that effort and therefore necessary to compensate it. From the theory of exploitation comes also the conclusion that profit is the surplus value in another guise. The rate of exploitation, or the rate of surplus value, is then simply surplus s (received by the capitalist) divided by value of variable capital (v), the latter being the wages the capitalist pays to workers.[37]

Centrality of class struggle. Another major contribution of Marx was to make class struggle—which, as Chapter 3 made clear, played an important role in Ricardo—the centerpiece of human history. It is not only present in capitalism; in fact, capitalism is only one example of class struggle and of class society. Although *class* was never formally defined by Marx, and although the third volume of *Capital* ends with a tantalizingly short chapter called "Classes," something close to a definition can actually be found in *The Eighteenth Brumaire:* "In so far as millions of families live under economic conditions that separate their mode of life, their interests and their culture from those of the other classes, and that place them in an attitude hostile toward the latter, they constitute a class."[38] While one could argue that class conflict is an engine of growth in Ricardo, the class struggle becomes in Marx the engine of global history, and the very definition of class includes an element of "hostility" or conflict.

The role played by classes and their struggle over distribution is much more important, and more general, in Marx than it ever was in Ricardo—however sharply displayed it was in the latter's analysis. The class struggle not only concerns the distribution of the net product but also encompasses issues like the length of the working day, trade union rights, working conditions, and even workers' feelings of alienation.[39] Labor is separated from the object of its activity (its product). It lacks agency. It is treated purely as "variable capital" by the capitalist and consequently its relationship to the products it creates becomes remote and "alien": "Since his own labor has been alienated from himself by the sale of his labor-power, has been appropriated by the capitalist and incorporated with capital it must be . . . realized in a product that does not belong to him."[40]

Capital as a relation of production. Finally, we come to Marx's definition of *capital.* In all the preceding writers' work, capital was essentially considered as interchangeable with the tools of production or machines, or with money in the case of financial capital. For Marx, however, the situation is a bit different. In capitalist societies, tools acquire the form of capital when they are used by capitalists (who monopolize the ownership of such tools) to hire labor to work with them, and to appropriate the surplus value. In small-scale or petty commodity production, a tool is not capital but simply a tool—a machine we use for our own production is not capital. Thus capital becomes a social relationship or social form which, as Marx writes, is acquired by means of production when they are used to hire labor. In a famous quote, "capital is not a thing, it is a definite social relation of production, pertaining to a particular historical social formation, which simply takes the form of a thing and gives this thing a specific social character."[41] In other words, capital is a historical category. This is an important point because it links the existence of capital to the existence of wage labor. The two go together. In a less guarded, maybe less Marxist, way of speaking, people today often use the term *capital* when they simply mean the machinery or means of production. But in a more accurate Marxist terminology, capital is a means of production when it is used to hire labor and generate profit for the owner of the means of production.

Class Structure

As in Ricardo, there are three principal classes in Marx: land-lords, workers, and capitalists. As in Ricardo, too, it is class position that determines a person's position in the income distribution. Kola-kowski, in noting Marx's rejection of the utopian-socialist classifi-cation of people, rightly observes that "utopian division according to wealth is quite alien to Marx's thought."[42] But Marx, having studied the historical evolution of capitalism much more closely and empirically than Ricardo, and having written historical works and pamphlets, has a more nuanced view of class structure. Ricardo, aiming for clarity of exposition, treats it in a very simplified way (and with a level of historical knowledge that is very hard to divine based on his writings).

The three principal classes can be decomposed into several sub-classes. Table 4.3 compares the class structures as they appear in Marx's *Class Struggles in France* and *Eighteenth Brumaire of Louis Napoleon* with the structure in *Capital,* vol. III. They are almost identical. The capitalists are divided into industrial and financial (commercial) capitalists. While their interests are aligned in holding down wages, they diverge as soon as the surplus product has to be divided: the industrial bourgeoisie's "interest is indubitably reduc-tion of the costs of production, therefore reduction of taxes . . . therefore reduction of the state debts, the interest on which enters into the taxes" and provides a source of income for the financial

Table 4.3   Class Structure of Capitalist Societies

	As outlined in *Class Struggles in France* and *The Eighteenth Brumaire*	As outlined in *Capital* vol. III (source of income)
Capitalists	Financial bourgeoisie Industrial bourgeoisie	Financial capitalists (profit) Industrial capitalists (profit) Bankers (interest) Land capitalists (rent)
Self-employed	Petty bourgeoisie (includes landowning peasantry)	Petty bourgeoisie (profit and wage)
Workers (proletariat)	Landless or poor peasants Workers	Peasants (wage) Workers (wage)
Déclassés	Lumpenproletariat	Lumpenproletariat

Data sources: Marx, *Class Struggles in France;* Marx, *Eighteenth Brumaire;* Marx, *Capital,* vol. III, chap. 52 (the last and unfinished chapter).

bourgeoisie.[43] Bankers are introduced, as well; they are close to but technically not part of the financial or commercial bourgeoisie: their income is interest on capital lent and thus different from the profits received by owners. Landowners are simply treated as part of the general capitalist class. This is important because it shows that, in a more developed state of capitalism, landlords as a distinct class vanish: they become merely another type of capitalist whose *differentia specifica* is that their capital is invested in land. In other words, with development, Ricardian aristocratic landlords have been converted into mere landowning capitalists: "large landed property, despite its feudal coquetry and pride of race, has become completely bourgeois through the development of modern society."[44]

The second large class in Marx is made up of the self-employed or the petty bourgeoisie. They played quite an important role in many countries, including France (as we have seen in Quesnay), and they are present in both agriculture and industry. They do not appear in Ricardo, because Ricardo was concerned with the main conflict—the conflict between landlords, capitalists, and workers. In every historical analysis, however, whether Quesnay's or Marx's, they do have a role. The self-employed, owing to their contradictory class nature (being both capitalists and laborers) often vacillate between support for the proletariat and support for capitalists. This is brought out very clearly in *Class Struggles in France*, where the self-employed make common cause with the urban proletariat in the beginning, only to gradually change sides and join the forces of reaction.[45] In an 1846 letter to Pavel Annenkov, Marx defines the *petty bourgeois* as a man who is "dazzled by the magnificence of the big bourgeoisie and sympathizes with the sufferings of the people. He is at once a bourgeois and a man of the people. . . . [He] deifies *contradiction,* because contradiction is the basis of his existence. He himself is nothing but social contradiction, put in action."[46]

Next come laborers or workers who are divided into two groups: landless peasants (or, at least, peasants who are sufficiently poor that they need to offer their labor for hire) and proletarians (or urban workers, the "hired hands" of industry and services). Again, we see here the division already present in Quesnay, not something new.

The interests of workers, as is well known, are according to Marx identical to the interests of all humanity. This is because, being the exploited class (the last one in the history of class societies), their freedom from wage-slavery depends on a condition in which everybody else is liberated from it, too. Thus, workers, although they may in practice be interested in higher wages, have a historical aim (*telos*) of abolition of all exploitation, and no particular class interest of their own.[47] This distinguishes them, according to Marx, from the bourgeoisie, who also have a freedom-driven agenda (elimination of various legal estates), but whose objectives end at that point. Marx's own experiences with the Parisian urban proletariat, in both 1848 and 1871, convinced him of their egalitarianism, which could be interpreted precisely along the lines sketched above. French egalitarianism was indeed something on which writers opposed to the revolutions, like Chateaubriand and Tocqueville, did agree with Marx. But they did not consider such egalitarianism desirable.[48]

Peasantry is, according to Marx, a class with contradictory interests: it is not composed only of landless farmers and hired labor, but also of small and even moderately prosperous owners. Marx does not evince much sympathy for peasantry, which he calls, in *Class Struggles in France,* "a class that represents barbarism within civilisation," and in *Capital,* Vol. III, "a class of barbarians standing half outside society."[49] He treats it simply as a "class by itself," unable to coalesce and assert its own interests. In the famous paragraph where he describes the peasant class to be "constituted by the simple addition of equal magnitudes—much as a bag with potatoes constitutes a potato-bag," Marx also writes of the "allotment farmers," meaning those who got their holdings after feudal lands were distributed following the French Revolution, as "an immense mass, whose individual members live in identical conditions, without, however, entering into manifold relations with one another." He elaborates:

> Their method of production isolates them from one another, instead of drawing them into mutual intercourse. This isolation is promoted by the poor means of communication in France, together with the poverty of the farmers themselves. Their field of production, the small allotment of land that each cultivates, allows no room for a division of labor, and no opportunity for the application of science; in other words, it shuts out manifoldness of development, diversity of talent, and the luxury of social relations.[50]

This distinction within peasantry, according to the size of land owned, will reappear many times in communist regimes, especially in the Soviet Union and China, whether it was used for the good (land reform), or the bad (oppression of the *kulaks,* collectivization, and the creation of the communes).

The final class, which we might call declassés, are people who are in some sense outside of the proper class structure: they are the *lumpenproletariat,* as Marx labeled them, but differently we can see them as the "chronically unemployed, beggars, or vagrants" as tallied in English nineteenth-century social tables. They are not directly involved in the process of production. In Marx, this last social (or perhaps "nonsocial") class plays a role when the conditions are right and the demand for labor is strong. At that point, its members are drawn into the process of production and their role is to dampen the increase in the wage rates that would otherwise occur. They become "the reserve army of labor," the normally unemployed who are called forth by capital to exert pressure on wages when the economy is (in today's parlance) overheated. This same idea—that unemployment is used by capitalists as a tool to prevent a substantial increase in real wages and to discipline labor—is a theme on which both Kalecki and Leijonhufvud would later elaborate.[51]

Marx's definition of the lumpenproletariat recognizes it as an urban phenomenon, and is not very flattering: "Lumpenproletariat . . . in all towns form a mass strictly differentiated from the industrial proletariat, a recruiting ground for thieves and criminals of all kinds, living on the crumbs of society, people without definite trade, vagabonds, *gens sans feu et sans aveu* [people lacking hearths and faith]."[52] They can also be readily hired to support the high bourgeoisie or aristocracy when the rulers need mobs to impose "order."* Marx mercilessly describes the supporters of Louis Bonaparte as "dismissed soldiers, discharged convicts, runaway galley slaves, sharpers, jugglers, lazzaroni, pickpockets, sleight of hand performers, gamblers, procurers, keepers of disorderly houses, porters, literati, organ grinders, rag pickers, scissor grinders, tinkers, beggars—in short, that whole undefined, dissolute, kicked-about mass that the Frenchman style 'la Bohème.'"[53]

It is useful to contrast Marx's sociopolitical structure (developed in part with specifically French conditions in mind) with the social table for France in 1831 constructed from many nineteenth-century sources by Morrisson and Snyder. Table 4.4 shows Morrisson and Snyder's social table with class sizes and relative incomes, and maps their classes to the corresponding groups in Marx's classification.[54] Within both tables, the industrial and land capitalists have the top

---

* There are many modern examples of such uses of the lumpenproletariat. One of the most bloody and overt uses of it was Chiang Kai-shek's collaboration with the criminal Green Gang in putting down strikes and decimating the Communist Party of China in Shanghai in April 1927.

Table 4.4   Social Table for 1831 France

Morrisson-Snyder class (ranked by income)	Employment (percent of total)	Average income (expressed relative to overall mean)	Marx class most closely equivalent
Employers	3.4	8.6	Industrial capitalists
Large farmers	5.1	3.0	Land capitalists
High-level civil servants	1.1	1.8	[State]
Blue-collar employees	13.9	1.0	Workers
White-collar employees	2.0	0.9	
Self-employed	13.4	0.7	Petty bourgeoisie
Low-level civil servants	1.1	0.6	[State]
Small farmers	31.4	0.5	Peasants
Agricultural workers and servants	28.5	0.45	
Total	100	1	

Note: "State" denotes government employees not clearly separated as a class by Marx.

Data source: Employment and income figures are calculated based on data in Morrisson and Snyder, "Income Inequality of France," table 7, 73.

incomes, workers (accounting for almost 16 percent of employment) are in the middle, the petty bourgeoise (with 13.4 percent of employment, and income below the average) come next, and peasants (by far the largest class) are at the bottom, whether they own their land or work as hired agricultural labor. We get, more or less, an inverted pyramid whereby classes with fewer members tend to be richer.

The table highlights the contradictory nature of the self-employed or the petty bourgeoisie. By its income level, this class is close to workers and, according to the social table, even poorer on average than they are; yet the fact that it owns property puts it in opposition to workers, who have none. The same contradiction arises in the case of the landowning peasantry. It was very well described by Tocqueville, whose memoirs of the 1848 revolution include the observation that all those who owned property, however small it was, formed a common front against the urban proletariat:

A certain demagogic agitation reigned among the city workers, it is true, but in the countryside, the property-owners, whatever was their origin, their antecedents, their education, their very property [*biens*], became closer to each other. . . . Property, among all those who enjoyed it, became a kind of fraternity. The richest were like older cousins, the less rich like younger cousins; but they all considered each other like brothers, having all the same interest in defending their inheritance. Because the French Revolution [of 1789] has extended the possession of land to infinity, the entire [rural] population seemed to be included in that huge family.[55]

Absent from Marx's classification are state or government employees (the high- and low-level civil servants in Morrisson and Snyder's classification), a group that covers everybody from service-sector workers (such as mail carriers) to the highest government and military officials (ministers and generals). In fact, Marx by his own family background would belong to this class.

Marx's discussion of the main tendencies in the evolution of capitalist economies, and of income distribution in capitalism, is in some sense a simplified Ricardian analysis, as it deals with only with two classes (workers and capitalists) and their sources of income (wages for the workers, and for the capitalists, all property incomes derived from surplus value: profit, interest, and rent). While in his political writings Marx paid special attention to the "contradictory" social classes, such as the petty bourgeoisie or the self-employed, in his analytical writings the world was much simplified. It was an ideal-typical capitalism he described, as pointed out by early Marx critic Benedetto Croce.[56] In the same simplified way, the discussion of income distribution that follows will zero in on labor and capital incomes, and how their interplay determines what happens to inequality.

Labor and Wages

Turning to Marx's explanation of wages, there are two questions that need to be answered. First, do wages differ between different types of workers? If *yes*, we thereby introduce automatically a significant source of income inequality, since most people are workers. Second, does the average wage (or, in a different formulation, the minimum wage) differ between societies in function of their economic development? If *yes*, then economic development and average welfare for the majority are correlated. Therefore, if the answer is *yes* to both questions, the reductionist view of Marx—the view that holds that all workers must have more or less the same wage, and that the wage is at the subsistence regardless of the level of development—is shown to be wrong.

Complex and simple labor. Whether wages must be at the subsistence level, and whether there will be a variability of wages (at a given point of development of productive forces), are matters that are very simple to settle if one starts from Marx's fundamental principles. Labor (or more exactly labor-power) is a commodity like any other commodity. Thus, the laws governing its long-run price (value) must be the same laws as those governing the price formation of every other commodity. The long-run price of any commodity is determined by the amount of past and current labor needed to produce that commodity. The long-run price of labor-power is, then, equal to the value of goods and services needed to produce (or reproduce) it. If different amounts of goods and services are needed to produce different types of labor (because of differences in training costs and duration of training), then there must be differences in wages.[57] There cannot be a single wage for different types of labor-power any more than there can be a single price for different commodities. The simplest type of labor, requiring only a bundle of commodities that merely afford physiological subsistence, can be produced most cheaply, and other, more complex, types of labor must carry a higher price (wage). We thus easily establish three conclusions. First, only the lowest type of labor can command a subsistence wage. Second, there must be variability in workers' incomes. Third, if "subsistence" has a historical component in addition to a merely physiological one, then the lowest wage can rise above the minimum necessary for survival, and the entire real-wage distribution will move upward. Whether that general rise affects relative wages between different types of labor will depend on changes in the prices of commodities that enter into the cost of production of that particular type of labor-power. One could expect, for example, that if relative costs of higher levels of education went up, wage differentials would increase.*

In Marx, as in other writers' work, the level and evolution of wages is a topic of great importance. The key questions are whether wages tend to stay at the same level or not, whether that level is subsistence or not, whether wages differ by skill, and whether wages differ across countries. Marx was of course only too familiar with Ferdinand Lassalle's "iron law of wages," which dictates that wages under capitalism can never durably exceed subsistence.[58] It has been argued quite forcefully by Roman Rosdolsky and Ernest Mandel, however, that in Marx's writings there are no quotes that can be interpreted to imply that Marx accepted this as a law, or believed that wages under capitalism would necessarily be reduced to subsistence.[59] It is, in fact, quite common in Marx to see references to the differentials in wages among different categories of workers and among different countries.

Real wages at a given point in time and in a given country. Any claim that Marx thought that most (or all) workers would have a subsistence wage is easily refuted by the fact that Marx defines at least two types of labor: complex (or composite) labor and simple labor. The complex labor requiring more investment (such as education) is more expensive to reproduce and must be paid more. This has a very clear implication for inequality among workers because we can no longer, even at the first approximation, overlook inequality among workers and consider all workers as earning the same wage. The wage is the function of workers' reproduction costs.[60] Of course, it is not merely because it costs more to produce more skilled workers that the capitalist will be ready to pay them more. A more skilled

---

* It is therefore very easy to see why, within the purely Marxist framework, free education must result in a narrow wage gap. We shall encounter this again when discussing wage inequality under socialism, in Chapter 7.

worker must also be more productive—which we may assume to be the case by virtue of greater education.[61]

Similarity with neoclassical economics. Marx writes: "All labor of a higher or more complicated character than average labor is . . . labor-power whose production has cost more labor time and which therefore has a higher value than unskilled or simple labor."[62] The view that types of labor differ by the costs of producing them is similar, or even identical, to Jacob Mincer's theory of human capital, and indeed goes back to Adam Smith.[63] According to the Mincerian view, differences in wages are simply compensatory: they make up for the investment required during the period of training and for a shorter working life (due to the fact that more years are spent training, and assuming that retirement from all kinds of labor takes place at approximately the same age).[64] There are strong similarities between Marx and the neoclassicists here. The element that is specifically Marxist is the "reserve army of labor," which, as we have seen, is supposed to keep wages down. But even that army can be, in a neoclassical framework, approximated by the increasing attraction of employment at the time of expansion, when many discouraged workers who would normally stay at home (including female labor) rejoin the labor force. Bringing them into the realm of paid labor reduces wage pressure on capitalists.

Real wage and development. As for wage differences among countries, and thus the wage growth that accompanies the process of development, they are clearly acknowledged: "the more productive is one country relative to another in the world market, the higher will be its wages, compared to another."[65] In a note in *Capital*, volume III, Marx shows the difference in the nominal wages between the UK, France, Prussia, Austria, and Russia (see Table 4.5). The ratio of nominal wages in the UK, which is at the top, to Russia, at the bottom, is 5 to 1. To be sure, consumption goods were cheaper in Russia than in England, so the real wage gap might not have been that great, but still the ratio would have been perhaps 3 (or 2.5) to 1—a sizable difference. And assuming that wages in Russia were at the subsistence level (they could hardly have been below subsistence,

Table 4.5 Nominal Wages in Different Countries around 1848

Country	Annual wages (in thalers)
UK	150
France	80
Prussia and Austria	60
Russia	30

Note: The data are actually shown as the value of human capital, with wages capitalized at the rate of 4 percent per annum. From those figures, however, we can easily calculate the implicit annual wages.

Data sources: Capital, vol. III, ch. 29, 596n1. Marx's data are from Friedrich Wilhelm Freiherr von Reden, *Vergleichende Kultur-Statistik der Gebiets-und Bevölkerungsverhältnisse der Gross-Staaten Europa's* (Berlin: A. Duncker, 1848), 434.

since workers had to survive), wages in England must have been substantially above subsistence. This is an important point because it clearly shows that Marx could not have agreed with Lassalle's iron law of wages, and that he allowed, as Smith did, for the increase of wages in the process of development.

Marx argues, moreover, that the very concept of what is the minimal acceptable wage is historical.[66] And indeed, it would be hard to imagine Marx, for whom all economic categories are historical, not applying the same logic to labor-power. In lower or more primitive stages of development, when human needs are elementary, the "necessary labor" to produce goods for these limited needs (that is, the wage) will also be small. The reason that necessary labor is small is not because labor is productive.* It is, Marx writes, because needs are limited.[67] (The statement that needs are historically determined, and not innate or absolute, is an important point both in its own right and because it underlies wage determination.) In the unfinished manuscript published later as *Grundrisse der Kritik der Politischen Ökonomie (Foundations of a Critique of Political Economy)*, Marx writes:

---

* Technically, if productivity were high, reproduction of labor-power would take only a fraction of the workday; "necessary labor" would be low. But necessary labor depends on both labor productivity and the needs to be satisfied (which expand with development). Over time, productivity and needs work against each other, with rising productivity reducing necessary labor and new needs increasing it.

In production resting on capital, the existence of *necessary* labour time [to "produce" sufficient wage for the worker] is conditional on the creation of *superfluous* labour time [that is, labour time appropriated by the capitalist]. In the lowest stages of production . . . few human needs have yet been produced, and thus few [have] to be satisfied. Necessary labour is therefore restricted, not because labour is productive, but because it is not very necessary.[68]

We thus have a sequence: limited needs lead to low necessary labor, which leads to low real wage.

An obvious implication of needs being a function of the level of development is that the real wage rises with the level of development. With higher development, the needs become broader and more diversified; they extend to new goods and services, and consequently the necessary labor to satisfy these needs becomes greater (unless it is more than offset by increased productivity). The real wage must be higher, as well.[69] This is what Marx terms the "historical and moral component of the labor-power."[70] The same point, introducing in addition the climate-driven wage differentiation, is made again in volume III of *Capital*: "The actual value of labour-power diverges from the physical minimum; it differs according to climate and the level of social development; it depends not only on the physical needs but also on historically-developed social needs."[71]

Real wage, relative wage, and needs. This does not mean that the labor share must increase as the real wage increases. Actually, the reverse may be true: Marx argues that, while real wages are higher in more capitalistically advanced economies, the labor share ("the relative wage") is lower.[72] This is exactly as seen in Robert Allen's nineteenth-century data.[73] Marx drives this point especially strongly (repeating it several times) in *Wage Labor and Capital*, the text of his propagandistic 1847 lectures delivered to the German Workingmen's Club in Brussels. He emphasizes that the higher capital share—regardless of what happens to the real wage—increases the power of capital over labor. Thus, "real wages may remain the same, they may even rise, nevertheless the relative wages [the labor share] may fall. . . . The power of the capitalist class over the working class has grown, the social position of the worker has become worse," and also if "capital grows rapidly, wages may rise, but the profit of capital rises disproportionately faster. The material position of the worker has improved, but at the cost of his social position. The social chasm that separates him from the capitalist has widened."[74]

The contrast between the material position and the social position of the worker, the latter obviously a relative concept, is drawn strongly and repeatedly. It is consistent with Marx's view that both inequality and needs are relative, whether measured, as in the case of inequality, in relation to others, or, in the case of needs, in relation to others and to time. On inequality, Marx observes:

> A house may be large or small; as long as the neighboring houses are likewise small, it satisfies all social requirement for a residence. But let there arise next to the little house a palace, and the little house shrinks to a hut. The little house now makes it clear that its inmate has no social position at all to maintain, or but a very insignificant one.

And on needs, he explains:

> Our wants and pleasures have their origin in society; we therefore measure them in relation to society; we do not measure them in relation to the objects which serve for their gratification. Since they are of a social nature, they are of a relative nature.[75]

Needs are thus doubly relative: at a given in point in time, they develop in reaction to what others have, and historically, in comparison to what was habitual in the past. Both relativities were, as we have seen, present already in Smith's definition of minimum needs, or what in today's language would be called the poverty line. But Marx considers needs more philosophically, seeing them not merely as evolving mechanically as society develops but as being created by man's own activity. As Shlomo Avineri writes: "Marx denies that each generation's consciousness of its own needs is a mechanistic, automatic response of the human consciousness to merely material stimuli. Man's consciousness of his own needs is a product of his historical development and attests to the cultural values achieved by preceding generations."[76]

Rosa Luxemburg took Marx's distinction between real wage and relative wage further by arguing that labor share tends to shrink with the development of capitalism. She proposed the "law of the tendential fall of relative wages."[77] Luxemburg's stress on labor share has the advantage of leading to the study of the social relationship between capital and labor. This is also very similar to Ricardo, whose entire analysis was couched in terms of the differing shares of capital and labor. The fact that an increasing real wage can be accompanied by a lower labor share (which is something that we observe today, as well) means that the rate of exploitation (most likely) goes up. As we have seen, the rate of exploitation (s^*) is the ratio of the surplus value (s) or profit to the value of variable capital (v), which is the wage bill. But a question remains: What happens over time if the quantity of capital increases faster than labor? That is, what if the ratio between constant capital (c) and variable capital (v)—or as Marx calls this ratio in *Capital*, volume I, the "*organic composition* of capital"—goes up?

Before we consider this issue—which is important because it concerns the dynamics of distribution between capital and labor, and also marks the intersection of the Marxist approach and neoclassical theory of growth—we should clarify some Marxist terminology. Constant capital (c) is the cost of machinery and materials used in production. Variable capital (v) is the money spent on wages. For both c and v, Marx, like most classical authors, assumes the capitalist has the money needed on hand. If we disregard raw materials, then capital (K) from the neoclassical production function is equivalent to Marx's c.[78] Similarly, for a given wage rate, Marx's v moves parallel to the neoclassical labor force (L). Thus we can approximate

Marx's increase in the organic composition of capital—the increase in the c/v ratio—with an increase in the neoclassical K/L ratio.[79] We can speak interchangeably of the increase in the capital-to-labor ratio and of the increase in the organic composition of capital. What is always implied is that, with a *given* technology and given prices, there are more machines per worker.

Marx held that the rising organic composition of capital is one of the regularities of capitalist production: replacing labor by machines tends to cheapen production and thus to provide extra profit for the capitalists who first introduce machinery. The same action is then repeated by all other capitalists. This ultimately raises the overall K/L ratio.[80] This has several effects. First, the rising K/L ratio may reduce the rate of profit.* In Marx, this happens because only labor produces surplus value, and since there are fewer workers per unit of capital, assuming that the rate of surplus value (the rate of exploitation) does not increase or does not increase sufficiently, the profit rate must go down. (In neoclassical economics, the same thing happens because the marginal product of the more abundant capital is less.) Second, higher productivity implies the cheapening of the wage goods that enter into wage determination. The rate of surplus value (s^*) may thus move up.[81] (In neoclassical terms, for the labor share to be reduced, capital-deepening must not depress the rate of profit to the same proportional extent.[82])

We thus note four important points that can be pieced together from Marx's various writings to inform our interpretation of how income distribution will evolve in advanced capitalist societies. First, the real wage is likely to increase with development. Second, the rate of exploitation may go either way. Third, the labor share will tend to go down, and consequently the capital share will go up. And fourth, a point discussed next, the rising capital share may mean

---

* Here I will use Marx's definition of the rate of profit, as the surplus value over the sum of the capitalist's advances for capital both constant and variable: $s / (c+v)$. Unlike the neoclassical model, Marx's approach sees the capitalist as advancing money payment to workers for wages (or wage goods) *before* production begins.

not an increase in the rate of profit but rather its decline. This is because the amount of capital might increase faster than income from capital, in which case the profit rate, equal to $s/(c+v)$, would decrease. This fourth development, termed by Marx "the law of the tendential fall in the rate of profit," is one of the most famous of his constructs—even though it is discussed only in a rather fragmentary fashion in some sixty pages in three chapters of *Capital* volume III.[83] It also plays one of the most important and controversial roles in Marx's discussion of income distribution in capitalism, as well as in the ultimate fate of the capitalist mode of production. We turn to this next.

Capital and the Tendency of the Rate of Profit to Fall

The workings of the law. There are four great areas of discussion and disagreement related to Marx's economics: the labor theory of value; the transformation of values into prices of production (the transformation problem); the dynamic equilibrium between sectors that produce means of production and sectors that produce means of consumption; and the law of the tendential fall in the rate of profit.[84] The first two topics have to do with the application of the law of value in different historical formations, and the third one relates to the model of balanced and unbalanced growth. But the last one is the one that concerns us here, for two reasons. First, if the profit rate has a historical tendency to go down, this has clear and immediate significance for how we can expect inequality in incomes to change as capitalism develops. Second, and politically more important, if the rate of profit eventually drops to zero, capitalism cannot function. (The same view was held, as we have seen, by Ricardo.) If capitalism cannot function, then an alternative system (socialism, in Marx's belief) can replace it. Thus, the law of the tendential fall in the rate of profit became closely associated with the theory of the breakdown of capitalism—its terminal disease and death. This is why the law has attracted so much attention since it was published in 1895, in volume III of *Capital*.

For our purposes, however, the law matters because it reveals what Marx thought about income distribution in advanced capitalism, not because of its implications for the end of capitalism. This is a point worth underlining because of the exaggerated importance that the law has acquired in Marxist exegesis (to the extent it is often abbreviated as simply "The Law"). It has been used by proponents and opponents alike as either the proof of an eventual collapse of capitalism, or as proof of Marx's own uncertainty about the law's logical validity. But here it matters only in the very ordinary sense of reflecting Marx's view that, in the long run, capitalists' incomes are likely to become smaller, and inequality among classes (as least as far as income from capital is concerned) is likely to shrink.

The logic underpinning the law is quite standard. Marx believed, together with many economists, that progress consists of the substitution of living labor by machines (embodied labor). Greater productivity and greater profits require, for each individual capitalist, the application of more capital-intensive processes (in Marx's formulation, greater organic composition of capital). As all capitalists independently replace labor with capital to improve their individual positions and collect profit above the ruling average rate, the capital-to-labor ratio in the economy increases. As there are fewer workers compared to the capital stock, there is a relative decrease in the surplus value produced—assuming, that is, that the rate of exploitation does not sufficiently increase. Hence, and this is key, the ratio between profits and capital must decrease—that is, the rate of profit must go down. Marx is very clear: "The rate of profit falls, although the rate of surplus value remains the same or rises, because the proportion of variable capital to constant capital decreases with the development of the productive power of labor."[85] The rate of profit gets smaller and smaller, and eventually we can imagine it going down close to zero. If we want to put Marx's reasoning in a neoclassical garb, we can do so and obtain the same result: the greater abundance of capital compared to labor means that the marginal product of

capital must be less, so again the profit rate decreases.[86] The only
solution to this tendency of the profit rate to fall, in the neoclassical
system, is technological progress, which in discrete steps improves
the marginal productivity of capital and maintains the rate of profit.
The only solution in Marx's system is an increasing exploitation of
labor—plus the countervailing (or, more exactly, the retarding) tendencies discussed below.

It is worth stopping here for a moment because, as Heinrich emphasizes, the situation is a bit more complex.[87] When capitalists introduce more constant capital, either to replace labor or to make a
given number of laborers work with more machines, they are doing
so to improve productivity. The improved productivity, with a *given*
real wage, implies an increase in the rate of surplus values (s/v). Thus
the rate of profit that is by definition

$$p = \frac{s}{c+v} = \frac{s/v}{\dfrac{c}{v}+1} = \frac{rate\ of\ surplus\ value}{organic\ composition\ of\ capital + 1} \tag{1}$$

changes as both its numerator and denominator are increased. The
denominator clearly goes up as c/v increases. And meanwhile,
because of greater productivity that is not reflected in higher real
wages, s/v increases, as well. This is the same as stating that more
capital-intensive processes lead to greater output per worker, and
since the real wage is given, the surplus must increase. Therefore it
is not obvious that the rate of profit must decrease, since both the
numerator and the denominator go up. It all boils down to whether
the increase in c/v is greater than the increase in s/v.

The problem is an old one, first noticed by Ladislaus Bortkie-
wicz in 1907 and later formulated by many others. Here, for example, is Paul Sweezy: "If both the organic composition of capital
and the rate of surplus value are assumed variable . . . then the direction in which the rate of profit will change becomes indeterminate.
All we can say is that the rate of profit will fall if the percentage increase
in the rate of surplus value is less than the percentage [increase in the

organic composition of capital]."[88] To see why this is likely to be the case, suppose that the number of workers in relationship (1) is fixed, and that capitalists introduce more capital-intensive processes, thus raising c/v. As we have just said, s/v must go up simply because the more capital-intensive processes are supposed to be more productive, including in the production of wage-goods, and consequently the expense on the variable capital will be less even if the real wage is unchanged. (This is identical to Ricardo, where the lower cost of wage-goods drives the nominal wage down, and keeps the real wage unchanged.) Thus, Heinrich is right to state that the increase in s/v is not a force that counteracts the law; it is rather the condition under which the law occurs, or rather, the law itself makes s/v increase.[89]

Still, is it not true that s/v might tend to rise less than c/v? There are various possibilities. First, the real wage may go up, checking the increase in the surplus. Second, the increase in s/v is bounded from above, whether for historical reasons (legal limit on the length of the working day) or physiological reasons (work effort cannot be increased without limit), whereas the increase in the organic composition of capital has no bounds. Third, higher productivity may encourage or embolden workers to demand shorter working time, which would also check the increase in s.[90] Essentially, for any given s/v, we can always find an organic composition of capital that will drive the profit rate down.[91]

We are thus back to Marx's original, and crucial, contention that the profit rate will decline with greater capital intensity of production unless the effect of that change is offset by greater exploitation of labor. We simultaneously have three conditions holding:

(1) a rising real wage (as some of the productivity gains are shared with workers), and thus $dv > 0$

(2) a decreasing rate of profit, and thus $d\left(\dfrac{s}{c+v}\right) < 0$

(3) a decreasing labor share, and thus $d\left(\dfrac{v}{c+s}\right) < 0$

Circumstances under which these conditions hold and a simple numerical example are given in the footnotes below.* †

The meaning of the law. We saw in Chapter 2 that Adam Smith likewise held that, with economic development, the rate of profit tends to decrease. Marx's law is therefore hardly unique. Nor is his view that, with the profit rate being zero, capitalism cannot function. The same opinion was held by Ricardo—and indeed it was the principal reason why he undertook to write his book. Jevons, in *The Theory of Political Economy,* published only four years after *Capital,* likewise writes:

> It is one of the favorite doctrines of economists since the time of Adam Smith, that as society progresses and capital accumulates, the rate of profit . . . tends to fall. . . . The rate will ultimately sink so low . . . that the inducement to further accumulation will cease. . . . Our formula for the rate of interest shows that unless there be constant progress in the arts, the rate must sink toward zero, supposing accumulation of capital to go on.[92]

---

* The conditions that can be easily derived are:

$$\frac{ds}{s} < \frac{dc+dv}{c+v}$$

$$\frac{dv}{v} < \frac{dc+dv}{c+v}$$

They show that the percentage increase in total capital (c + v) must be greater both than the percentage increase in variable capital (which guarantees increase in the organic composition of capital) and also than the percentage increase in the surplus value (which ensures that the rate of profit must decrease).

† Take the following simple example. Let $c = 50$, $v = 50$, and $s = 50$. The rate of profit is $s/(c+v) = 50/100 = 50$ percent; the rate of exploitation (s/v) is $50/50 = 100$ percent; and the labor share in total gross value added is $v/(c+s+v) = 50/150 = 33$ percent. Suppose now that capitalists invest more in machines, so that they add 10 units to c. Assume further that they also increase the wage bill by 1 unit (which means that the real wage increases, because the amount of labor is by assumption fixed). If the rate of exploitation remains the same, the additional s is 1. The new rate of profit is $51/111 = 46$ percent, and the new labor share is $51/162 = 32$ percent. We conclude that the real wage increased, and both the rate of profit and the labor share went down.

The view that a capitalist economy may eventually become stationary has been, in one way or another, held by many other economists, including Joseph Schumpeter, Alvin Hansen, and more recently, Larry Summers. The law of the tendential fall of the rate of profit, in Marx's formulation, made so much ink flow not because it was so different from what other classical or neoclassical economists wrote (neither in its underlying logic nor in the statement that zero-profit capitalism is an impossibility) but because of its implications: that it sounds the death knell of capitalism. The law, in that interpretation, is the long-term force that works against capitalism. The short-term forces that break capitalism apart are the crises of overproduction. It is the joint or rather simultaneous action of the two—the coincidence of the secular low profits and economic crises—that will spell the end of capitalism. So capitalism will atrophy and wither away.

It is worth mentioning that many Marxists did not agree that a profit rate close to zero would spell the end of capitalism. Luxemburg and Kautsky (while not aligned on much else) both argued that the absolute amount of profit might still increase (simply because there would be much more of capital). But their logic is faulty. Capitalists are incentivized by high returns; if the rate of profit becomes, say, 0.1 percent, but, given large capital stock, it still produces large absolute profits, then the incentive to keep on investing and organizing production for such a meager (relative) return will be much diminished. Investments would be low and the economy would become stationary. To take a very simple example, if the average profit rate became 0.1 percent, with the capital-to-income ratio being around 5, as it is in the advanced economies today, then profit/income (or profit/GDP) would equal only 0.5 percent. Even if all profits were reinvested, the investment rate would be just 0.5 percent of GDP, a small fraction of what modern economies invest.[93] This, in turn, would imply a growth rate close to zero. But the situation would get worse: with close to zero long-term profits and close to zero long-term growth, the fundamental question would be raised: What incentive is there for capitalists to continue fulfilling the entrepreneurial function if the average return is essentially nil? For sure, since the rate of profit is a random variable with the assumed mean close to zero, there would still be some making positive returns, but they would be offset by those with negative returns who eventually go bankrupt.[94] Thus, as Schumpeter rightly argued, a stationary capitalist economy is an impossibility: to endure as a capitalist system, it must generate positive returns to capitalist-entrepreneurs; if it fails to do so, there is simply no incentive to continue with production.[95] Technically, such an economy would have to be taken over by the state or by "associated producers" to continue functioning.[96]

The law and income distribution. But, as noted above, this particular dynamic is not at the center of our interest here. What *is* at the center of our interest is what the law implies for Marx's view regarding the evolution of income distribution in advanced capitalism. It is obvious that, if the rate of profit decreases (and all else remains the same), capitalists will be less rich and income inequality will likely be reduced. If we add to that Marx's argument that the lowest (subsistence) wage includes a moral-historical dimension, then we can readily argue that Marx must have implicitly held that income inequality between the two principal classes would be lessened in advanced capitalism. This is not very dissimilar from the conclusion reached by Smith, who also viewed development as leading to higher wages and lower profits.

Yet this fairly bright interpretation regarding the future of inequality in capitalism is contradicted by other statements found in Marx. These fall into three categories. First, there are statements about the forces that slow or counteract the action of the law. Second, there are statements about the rising concentration of capital ownership. Third, there are statements about the growing role of the reserve army of labor that keeps wages in check. Any of these factors might slow the convergence between capitalists' and workers' incomes, or even reverse it. Thus we might end up with higher, not lower, inequality as capitalism develops. Each of these three categories deserves fuller discussion.

Counteracting the law. The forces that counteract the decrease in the profit rate are straightforward and they are listed explicitly by Marx.[97] There are six of them. First, there could be greater exploitation of labor (in other terms, an increase in the s/v ratio—say, by the lengthening of the workday or greater intensity of work); and second, there could be an attempt to drive the wage below its value. I think we can dismiss these two forces because they cannot operate in the long term (driving the wage below its value is possible only temporarily, as with any other commodity), or be extended without limit (because, as discussed above, the s/v ratio has its limits). Neither are they very well motivated. One could even argue that they are contradictory to the spirit of Marx's own system, a key claim of which is that capitalist developments should not be explained by recourse to ad hoc explanations, but be based on the assumption that market mechanisms will operate in a clear and unfettered fashion.

Another factor that, according to Marx, retards the action of the law is greater employment in the less capital-intensive sectors that produce more of the surplus value. If such employment increases, the total amount of profit is greater than it would be otherwise. This explanation cannot be entirely dismissed. There may be reasons why the distribution of labor in a more advanced capitalist economy would feature more people employed in less capital-intensive sectors. For example, if technological progress is highest in more capital-intensive sectors, those sectors would be the ones to release labor, leaving those workers to find employment in less capital-intensive sectors—as we observe today with the rise of employment in services. Thus, a shift in employment composition might indeed change the total amount of surplus produced and delay the action of the law.

While the three factors discussed above all have to do with labor, the remaining three do not. The fourth factor is due to the cheapening of (constant) capital brought about by crises. If crises make a significant portion of capital obsolescent, if it becomes mostly scrap, then the value of capital must go down, and the profit-to-capital ratio can very well be maintained at its earlier (higher) level. This is a very sophisticated argument, similar to Schumpeter's concept of creative destruction. The destruction of capital today keeps the profit rate high and makes production more profitable tomorrow. In Schumpeter's analysis, the reliable feature of a capitalist system, revolutionary changes (or, as we would say, crises) that "occur in discrete rushes which are separated from each other by spans of comparative quiet," is the mechanism that makes capitalist production sustainable over the long term.

The fifth factor is expansion of foreign trade. Here, a delay in the decline in the rate of profit can be predicted only if profits are assumed to be higher in foreign trade than in domestic trade. This is an area that was later developed by Rosa Luxemburg, who argued that capitalism remains viable only so long as it expands geographically to new areas, and swallows up, as it were, realms that had been less productive under earlier, pre-capitalist modes of production.[98] The explanation, as advanced by Marx, is questionable: it is not obvious that foreign trade profits are always, or even usually, higher than profits from domestic production and trade. If they were so over any given period, that would simply attract additional capital until the profit rate was equalized. Obviously, too, territorial expansion is limited, and the more that capitalism "invades" other pre-capitalist modes of production, the fewer opportunities to continue doing so remain. The explanation can be made more compelling, however, if we consider that, while the expansion of capitalism is necessary for its survival, this expansion need not be geographical. It can involve new ways to organize production, the introduction of new products, or the creation of entirely new markets (such as, for example, the short-term home-rental market, or the sale of one's own name as a brand, to name just two markets that have emerged recently). Seen in these terms, expansion opportunities are endless and the dynamics of capitalism can help keep the profit rate high.

The last factor identified by Marx is the spread of shareholding. The shareholders receive only dividends, which are, on average, less than profit. Accordingly, capitalists who are both owners and managers receive more than they would otherwise (dividends plus an aliquot share of undistributed operational profit). This slows the decrease in the rate of profit. The argument here rests on dividing capitalists into two groups: those who get dividends only and therefore make it possible for the others to get a higher π/K. This is a questionable argument: if we do not do the division into two rather arbitrary groups of capitalists—which runs counter to the spirit of Marx's work—then that particular factor cannot be operative in curbing the fall in the rate of profit.

We are thus left with only two significant forces that can slow the decrease in the rate of profit: the cheapening of constant capital, and the expansion to new areas and fields of production. It is a matter of judgment and empirics whether they would be sufficiently strong to overturn the forces of the more capital-intensive production that drive the rate of profit down.

Effects of increased concentration of capital on the law. But there are other forces. The rising concentration of capital ownership that would push the rate of profit and income inequality up is treated principally in the much-cited Chapter 25 of *Capital* (vol. I), "The General Law of Capitalist Accumulation." The topic is, in the light of the importance it has later received, treated rather cursorily by Marx. For even there, before discussing the concentration of capital, Marx writes: "The laws of this centralization of capital . . . cannot be developed here. A brief hint at a few facts must suffice." Elsewhere the concentration of capital is mostly mentioned as an obiter dictum and is often simply asserted. How does it occur? Greater concentration and centralization of capital, Marx holds, is brought about by technological progress that is embodied in more capital-intensive processes and hence favors large companies.[99] It is also driven by the increasing minimum size required to conduct business operations (what may be called today the entry costs). Higher entry costs imply economies of scale and thus also favor larger companies. Marx's view of technological progress, in short, assumed capital-biased technical change and economies of scale. Marx summarized these forces thus:

The battle of competition is fought by cheapening of commodities. The cheapness of commodities depends, *caeteris paribus,* on the productiveness of labour, and this in turn on the scale of production. Therefore, the larger capitals beat the smaller. It will further be remembered that, with the development of the capitalist mode of production, there is an increase in the minimum amount of individual capital necessary to carry on a business under its normal conditions.[100]

Marx's statement can be interpreted to mean that, within individual industrial branches of production, the rate of profit systematically diverges between companies by virtue of their size. In addition, economic crises tend to liquidate smaller capitalist firms. When the size necessary for the survival of the firm becomes too great, owners of smaller companies go bankrupt and join the working class.[101] We therefore have here together the forces that would make large-scale capitalist firms more capable of technological progress, producing at lower unit costs, and better able to survive crises. This in turn leaves capitalists fewer in numbers, and concomitantly renders a few of them extraordinarily rich.[102]

Although this is not an argument to be readily used in our context (since our objective is to discern what Marx thought inequality in the future might be, not necessarily to look at what actually happened), it is still worth pointing out that, in advanced capitalist economies, there is an increasing number of people who have both high capital and labor incomes, not the strong segregation that Marx posited. It is a development that I have termed *homoploutia*, defined as wealth in terms of both "human" and financial capital.[103] There is little doubt that, as individuals in advanced capitalist economies exhibit less stratification in factoral (capital versus labor) incomes, the split between people who are receiving only capital incomes and those receiving only labor incomes is not as sharp as it was in Ricardo's and Marx's time.

Effects of the reserve army of labor on the law. The last important element that slows the decrease of the rate of profit is the wage-checking role of the reserve army of labor. We have discussed it above. It suffices here to mention that the broadening of the capitalists' field of operation may bring many into the labor force who were normally left out. That would dampen the increase in wages; it would also increase the rate of exploitation, and might (temporarily) prevent the profit rate from falling. It is important to realize, though, that the reserve army of labor, however important in the short run, cannot be legitimately used as a *deus ex machina* to explain why the profit rate does not fall. The reserve army is limited in size by the working-age population. Thus, if one wants to argue against the tendency of the rate of profit to fall, one must invoke some inherent features of the system, not just the number of people left in the reserve army.

We may consider, however, that with globalization the domestic reserve army is no longer relevant; so long as there are internationally enough people to be brought into the realm of global capitalist production, the wage-checking role of that additional labor will remain. But here we are introducing arguments that were not present in Marx. While his treatment of globalization is much more thorough than Ricardo's (for whom globalization is limited to the trade in goods), it still falls short of what we experience today.

Marx's Overall View of the Evolution of Inequality: Brighter Than Usually Supposed

On underconsumption. As we turn to the topic of underconsumption, it must immediately be noted that the discussion here of the evolution of inequality is concerned only with long-term or secular forces—not with crisis situations. First, I am not discussing Marx's view of the short-term changes in wages versus profits that precede or follow crises, or his identification of underconsumption as the cause of crises. The objective is not to discuss the so-called breakdown hypothesis but to understand how (according to Marx) long-term forces drive the evolution of incomes under capitalism. Second, while it may be that crises of underconsumption can be caused by high inequality (or "maldistribution," to use Hobson's term), our focus here is not on the consequences of inequality but on how inequality evolves. In other words, inequality here is a dependent, not causal, variable. Third, Marx's own views on underconsumption as the cause of crises are not entirely consistent. In *Capital,* volume III, Marx very strongly endorses the underconsumptionist view:

> The ultimate reason for all real crises always remains the poverty and restricted consumption of the masses, in the face of the drive of capitalist production to develop the productive forces as if only the absolute consumption capacity of society set a limit to them.[104]

But in volume II, he equally strongly dismisses such a view and writes that crises cannot be due to wages being too low because wages are often at their peak just before the outbreak of the crisis.

> It is a pure tautology to say that crises are provoked by a lack of effective demand or effective consumption. . . . If the attempt is made to give this tautology the semblance of greater profundity, by the statement that the working class receives too small a portion of its own product, and that the evil would be remedied of it received a bigger share, i.e. if its wages rose, we need only note that crises are always prepared by a period in which wages generally rise, and the working class actually does receive a greater share in the part of the annual produce destined for consumption. From the standpoint of these advocates of sound and 'simple'(!) common sense, such periods should rather avert the crisis. It thus appears that capitalist production involves certain conditions independent of people's good or bad intentions, which permit the relative prosperity of the working class only temporarily, and moreover always as a harbinger of crisis.[105]

I think that Ernest Mandel is right in arguing that Marx saw crises not as caused by maldistribution of income but as the result of the unbalanced growth of Department I (means of production) and Department II (consumption goods).[106] Thus, to study crises we have to look at how balanced or unbalanced economic growth is—that is, look at the "anarchy" of capitalist production—rather than look at the distribution of income.[107] We thus dismiss the topic of under-consumption and return to the distribution.

Forces driving income distribution. Although Marx never summarized or fully explained his view about the evolution of inequality in advanced capitalism, putting all the pieces together, we can create an overall picture of the expected changes in inequality. It is much brighter than normally assumed. The key components of this picture are the following.

The tendency of the profit rate to fall must reduce inequality because capitalists (together with landlords who are treated just as a subgroup of capitalists) are the richest class. Clearly, if the top class's incomes do not rise, or even decline, we may expect an improvement in distribution. This may be true even if there is an increased concentration of capitalists' incomes and some capitalists become very rich while others go bankrupt and join workers.[108]

On the side of labor, Marx's unambiguous view that the minimum wage includes a historical component, linked to the level of country's real income, means that with the advancement of society, the minimum wage would rise, and with it the entire chain of other wages. There is certainly no persuasive argument made for the "immiseration" of labor in Marx, a point that is also stated (as discussed above) by Mandel and Rosdolsky. Even chapter 25 of *Capital*, volume I, which is the most significant part of Marx's writings to deal with the dynamic forces of accumulation of capital and its effect on wages, begins with the discussion of wages *rising* as the demand (driven by accumulation of capital) outstrips the supply of labor. Moreover, we have noted above that the tendency of the rate of profit to fall is associated, or is even dependent in the long run, on a fixed or only slowly increasing s/v ratio, which, under conditions of technological progress, implies an increasing real wage. Joan Robinson was thus right to say that Marx "seems to have overlooked . . . when he is discussing the falling tendency of profits [to make a] reference to the rising tendency of real wages which it entails."[109] In other words, the argument for an increasing real wage in Marx is supported also by his argument regarding the "law" of tendential fall in the rate of profit.

But there are also forces, both on the side of capital and on the side of labor, working in the opposite direction, pushing inequality up by keeping profits high and squeezing wages (Table 4.6). On the side of capital, these are the concentration and centralization of production caused by the lower unit costs of larger (more capital-intensive) companies; economic crises, which while detrimental to capital over the short term, maintain the profit rate at a higher level over the longer term; and expansions of capitalist production to new areas which keep the rate of profit up.

The situation on the labor side with the industrial reserve army of labor is even more important. It plays the role of a wage-regulator, especially at the time of economic prosperity when the demand for labor increases:

> we have seen, too, how this antagonism between the technical necessities of modern industry, and the social character inherent in its capitalistic form . . . vents its rage in the creation of that monstrosity, an industrial reserve army, kept in misery in order to be always at the disposal of capital.[110]

And very importantly and clearly:

> the general movements of wages are exclusively regulated by the expansion and contraction of the industrial reserve army, and this in turn corresponds to the periodic alternations of the industrial cycle.[111]

As mentioned above, the industrial reserve army of labor can be approximated (under today's conditions) by tallying all those who are tempted to move into the labor market only when the demand for labor becomes tight, either because they become more optimistic about getting a job, or because their reservation wage is high. (For example, a person taking care of a young family might not take a

Table 4.6   Factors Affecting Inequality

	Inequality-Reducing	Inequality-Increasing
Capital	Profit rate tendency to fall	Crises
		Expansion of production to new areas
		Increased concentration of capital
Labor	Increased real wage	Reserve army of labor

job unless its wage sufficiently compensated for the alternate care-giving they would have to procure.) At the time of Marx, however, the reserve army was composed of parts of the lumpenproletariat and of what Marx calls the "nomad population." Of the latter group, he writes: "They are the light infantry of capital, thrown by it, according to its needs, now to this point, now to that. When they are not on the march, they 'camp.'"[112] Another part of the reserve army might be women who could move into or outside of the labor force depending on their family situations, and who indeed played an important role in the industrial labor force in Western Europe. The "reserve army" presents a permanent threat to the position of labor, a threat that becomes activated when labor starts to get, as capitalists might put it, uppity or too big for its boots.

When the forces increasing inequality become particularly strong and dominant, the situation can be rather bleak. Indeed, it is *only* the action of these inequality-augmenting factors that is addressed in the famous statement where Marx in *Capital,* volume I, combines greater concentration of capital on the one hand with increasing class polarization on the other:

Along with the constantly diminishing number of the magnates of capital, who usurp and monopolise all advantages of this process of transformation, grows the mass of misery, oppression, slavery, degradation, exploitation; but with this too grows the revolt of the working class, a class always increasing in numbers, and disciplined, united, organised by the very mechanism of the process of capitalist production itself. . . . Centralisation of the means of production and socialisation of labour at last reach a point where they become incompatible with their capitalist integument. This integument is burst asunder. The knell of capitalist private property sounds. The expropriators are expropriated.[113]

A similar sentence occurs in volume I, chapter 25.[114] Reading these two sentences, where only inequality-augmenting factors are at play, many commentators have concluded they represent Marx's complete view of the matter. But careful study of Marx's full writings suggests these malign forces may be only temporary forces. Over the longer term, the more benign forces of economic development may have effects on profits and real wages similar to what Adam Smith expected: profits will be reduced, and real wages will be increased. The overall picture that emerges from Marx's writings is certainly less sanguine than Smith's, but it is far from the simplified state of society that many Marxists saw: an ever-deeper split between a small group of immensely rich capitalists and masses of impoverished workers. This may be true only if the inequality-increasing forces operate *both* in the realm of capital and labor. Differently, one can see inequality-increasing forces working on the capital side, but being checked by inequality-reducing forces on the labor side (such as secularly rising wages), or with both a reduced rate of profit and higher industrial wages working to reduce inequality. There are four possibilities, as shown in Table 4.7.[115] The bleakest is just one of four potential scenarios. Focusing only on inequality-augmenting forces seems excessively limiting; there is no factual and logical basis in Marx's writings to entertain *exclusively* such a view.

A note on the politicization of Marx's views on income distribution. No opinion of the authors studied in this book on the future developments of income distribution has been as politicized as one possible set of Marx's expectations. As mentioned, the immiseration of the working class, with concentration of capital ownership into ever fewer hands, is just one of the four possible scenarios. It has, however, held a special attraction, first for Marxists and then for anti-Marxists.

Table 4.7 Four Possible Evolutions of Income Distribution in Marx

Optimistic scenario	Regressing society scenario
Secular increase in real wage	"Immiseration of labor"
Secular decline in the profit rate	Secular decline in the profit rate
(Possible modern equivalent: Western Europe)	(Possible modern equivalent: some Latin American societies)
Polarized society scenario	Breakdown scenario
Secular increase in real wage	"Immiseration of labor"
Increasing concentration of capital	Increasing concentration of capital
(Possible modern equivalent: United States)	(Possible modern equivalent: South Africa)

To regard incomes in the future as increasingly polarized between, on the one hand, a proletariat with fixed or even decreasing real wages and under constant pressure from nomadic workers and the lumpenproletariat, and, on the other hand, an ever-increasing concentration of capital incomes, held obviously a special attraction for those who believed in the ever-rising contradictors of capitalism and its eventual downfall. The immiseration of the labor force went together, according to this reading of Marx, with the deskilling of labor as many of the more skilled functions were mechanized. Technological progress was seen as low-skill biased, in contrast to the opposite view today. It might reduce income differentiation among workers, while widening the average gap between workers and capitalists. At the other end of the spectrum, the tendency of the profit rate to fall would not affect the incomes of the richest capitalists since lower rate of profit was, according to this reading of Marx, accompanied by concentration of capital ownership, and the increased wealth of the few. The outcome was therefore a deep polarization of the population, increasing inequality, and—it was reasonable to suppose—ever more likely revolution spelling the end of capitalist relations of production.

The expectation of the declining average profit rate added to the gloom, as it indicated the inability of capitalism to expand and grow. Thus, the two aspects, polarization of incomes and deceleration of growth (or even stagnation), presaged the end of capitalism.

It is quite understandable why such a reading of Marx was privileged by social-democratic, and later communist, parties in the first half of the twentieth century. It seemed based on a scientific analysis in Marx. It showed significant resemblance to what was happening in reality (including centralization of capital, and the rising role of trusts and monopolies), and it imbued Communist Party members with optimism regarding the future.

As developments in the advanced capitalist countries in the second half of the twentieth century went in the opposite direction (with rising wage rates, reduction in the overall income inequality, increased skill levels of the labor force, and reduced class-based polarization), Marx's immiseration and concentration theory became propagated by anti-Marxists to show how far from reality Marx's prognostications were, and how, accordingly, the rest of his work must be equally defective.

As argued here, this particular evolution of income distribution (capital concentration cum immiseration of labor) is just one of the four scenarios that can be legitimately defended, based on close reading of Marx. Its polar opposite is the scenario where wages, which Marx contended had a historical and social component, increase in step with the increasing GDP of capitalist economies, and returns to capital go down. That scenario leads to an exactly opposite conclusion from that of immiseration and concentration: in effect, income inequality is likely to go down, wages to go up, and profits to be reduced.

There are also two intermediate scenarios that combine elements from the polar cases (increase of the real wage combined with greater concentration of capital incomes, and stagnation or decrease of the real wage combined with a lower rate of profit). My contention is that Marx himself was not sure which of the four possible scenarios was the most likely. His writings on the issue, many of them never completed, thus allow for all four possible interpretations. Whether because of lack of time, or the complexity of the matter, or simply because of the fact that his writings were so dispersed and responded to different needs (political, historical study, propaganda, economic analysis), Marx probably never came to firmly set or determined views on the evolution of income inequality under capitalism. Marx's theory of income distribution is thus fundamentally indeterminate.

The interpretation offered here rejects the view that Marx was a high-Victorian determinist when it comes to the evolution of income distribution in capitalism. The four possibilities suggest a much more probabilistic view where tendencies matter, but they are just that—tendencies, and not the irreversible unfolding of history. Additionally, there may not be just one scenario for all capitalist societies. We can readily envisage—as the simple contemporary examples given in Table 4.7 suggest—that different capitalist societies may follow different income distribution paths. Thus, at any given point in time, we may observe more than one scenario.[116]

The only part of modern capitalist developments that is entirely unexpected (and thus never discussed) by Marx is homoploutia, the recent trend among the richest income groups to be both labor-income and capital-income rich, to receive high wages in return for their high-skill labor and also high profits from their ownership of assets. In their own personae, they "overcome" the antagonistic relationship between capital and labor. Marx, like all classical authors, thought it self-evident that the richest people would rely on capital incomes only and would not double up as wage-laborers. This development is, I think, the only one *fundamentally* alien to Marx's way of thinking and to the ideas expressed in *Capital* and elsewhere. For all other, or almost all other, developments in modern capitalism, a reasonably relevant discussion can be found in Marx's writings.

Moving On to Pareto and Interpersonal Income Inequality

In the same chapter just discussed, "The General Law of Capitalist Accumulation" (*Capital,* volume I, chapter 25), where Marx writes about the concentration of capital ownership and income, he illustrates it with 1865 income tax data from England and Wales.[117]

The tax data used are from the so-called Schedule D, which included profits from businesses, concerns, professions, and employments. In 1865, such tax was paid by approximately 1.5 percent of households in England. (In most countries, including the United States, direct taxes did not exist at all in those days.) Marx displays the published data on cumulative income and the cumulative number of taxpayers by income tranche. In the lowest tranche of people paying the tax, the average income per taxpayer was £133 (the tax threshold was £60), and this tranche included some 308,000 out of the total of 332,000 taxpayers. (In other words, it included more than 90 percent of taxpayers.) In the top tranche were just the 107 richest taxpayers, whose average per-capita income was £103,526. This group, representing about 0.03 percent of the taxpayers in England and Wales, earned more than 10 percent of the total taxable income. Such dramatic concentration of income or wealth at the top will be, as we shall see in the next chapter, exactly what would attract Pareto's attention only about a decade after Marx's death.[118] It would lead Pareto to define the eponymous income distribution function still much used today, and, more importantly for our purpose here, it would lead him toward his distinct view of the evolution of interpersonal income inequality—a view in many ways opposite that of Marx.

Had Marx decided to transform the tax data that he shows in *Capital* in the same way that Pareto would soon do, he could have drawn a nice straight line linking the (log) income levels of various tranches and the (log) inverse cumulative distribution of taxpayers. He would have obtained the graph shown in Figure 4.4, which yields a Pareto coefficient of 1.2, very much in line with Pareto's own results based on similar tax data from late nineteenth-century Western European cities and states. The coefficient of 1.2 implies (as will become clear in the next chapter) a very thick right-end tail of income distribution, and a very high Gini coefficient (another methodological innovation for which we shall have to wait until the 1920s) of seventy-one among the English and Welsh taxpayers.

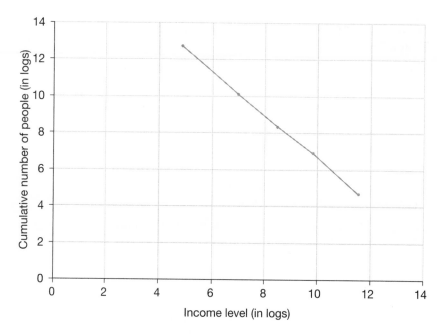

Figure 4.4. Distribution of income among the English and Welsh taxpayers, 1865

Note: The horizontal axis shows the average taxable income level in pounds (in logs), and the vertical axis shows the cumulative number of people (in logs) who receive income at least equal to the income level shown on the horizontal axis.

Data source: Karl Marx, *Capital,* vol. I (New York: Penguin Books, 1977), chapter 25.

Appendix: The Gladstone Squabble

The greatest controversy regarding Marx's citations had to do with income inequality in Britain as it was described by William Ewart Gladstone, then chancellor of the Exchequer, in his 1843 and 1863 budget speeches to the British Parliament.

Gladstone's 1843 speech was cited by Marx as follows: "It is one of the most melancholy features in the social state of this country . . . that while there was a decrease in the consuming power of the people, and while there was an increase in the privations and distress of the labouring class and operatives, there was at the same time a constant accumulation of wealth in the upper classes, and a constant increase of Capital."[119] The reference in a footnote is given to *The Times*. In another speech twenty years later, Gladstone (again, as quoted by Marx) said that "this intoxicating augmentation of wealth and power . . . entirely confined to classes of property . . . must be of indirect benefit to the labouring population."[120] The reference is given to the *Morning Star*. When that quotation was, as explained below, questioned, Marx produced a fuller citation of Gladstone's 1863 speech from *The Times*:

> That is the state of the case as regards the wealth of this country. I must say for one, I should look almost with apprehension and with pain upon this intoxicating augmentation of wealth and power, *if it were my belief* that it was confined to classes who are in easy circumstances. This takes no cognizance at all of the condition of the labouring population. The augmentation I have described and which is founded, I think, upon accurate returns, is an augmentation entirely confined to classes possessed of property.[121]

The last sentence of this passage, however, did not actually appear in *The Hansard*, the official journal of parliamentary debates. Marx thought that it had been deliberately omitted there because it was embarrassing for the chancellor, and was accurately reported by the *Morning Star* and *The Times* because they went to press before the official transcript had been checked and (as Marx believed) revised.

A German professor, Lujo Brentano (writing anonymously) accused Marx of intentionally misquoting Gladstone, whose complex circumlocution (as we can easily note) certainly made misinterpretation possible. Brentano argued that Gladstone, in his concluding sentence above, did not state that the augmentation of wealth was confined to the upper classes, implying that his own (Gladstone's) apprehension was *not* justified.[122] This complicated matter of citations and counter-citations, the clarity of which was not helped by the back-and-forth between the original speech in English and Marx's German translations, continued for years. The debate included, after Marx's death, the intervention of a Trinity College professor from Cambridge (supporting Brentano) and Eleanor Marx, Karl Marx's daughter, supporting her father. It was—to us now, perhaps somewhat surprisingly—considered of sufficient import to be discussed at length in Engels's preface to the fourth edition of *Das Kapital* (in German). But it does show how, at times, both Marx and his opponents would treat empirical matters of income distribution seriously.

CHAPTER FIVE

Vilfredo Pareto: From Classes to Individuals

As Michael McLure writes in his excellent editorial notes to Vilfredo Pareto's *Manual of Political Economy,* Pareto was "born in Paris in the momentous year that was 1848 from a self-exiled Italian patriot, who presumably absorbed and instilled in his son the shrewd concretism of Cavour and the religious-like sense of duty of Mazzini."[1] Thus in the heady days of the 1848 revolution and its immediate aftermath lived three thinkers in close geographical (although no other) proximity: Alexis de Tocqueville, then forty-three years of age, who briefly in 1849 became the French minister of foreign affairs; Karl Marx, then thirty years old, editing and writing for the *Rheinische Zeitung* and soon to be re-expelled from France; and Vilfredo Pareto, born in the midst of the revolution. Pareto's parents were affluent (his father was a marquis) and, throughout his life, Pareto lived in very comfortable circumstances (if somewhat unusual ones in his later years, when he shared his villa with dozens of cats). The regions in which he spent his life (Switzerland, Northern Italy, and Southern France) made up, at the time, probably the richest part of Europe.

Pareto, like many other intellectuals before and since, charted an intellectual course that went from attraction to the liberal ideas of democracy and free trade to rejection of them and adoption, in their place, of a stern realism often bordering on misanthropy, misogyny, and xenophobia. His jaded view of a world ruled mostly by force brought his thinking close to fascist celebration of violence. Mussolini named him—we ignore how little the post was desired—a senator of the Kingdom of Italy only a few months before his death. Like Marx, he was buried in a small ceremony, attended by few.

Although the Fascist Party's claim of Pareto as their own was to a large extent a fabrication—an attempt to co-opt the reputation of a famous social scientist to serve their own cause (especially after his death, when he could not contradict them)—some parts of Pareto's view of the world were more than tangentially related to fascist ideology.[2] But he was not a racist.[3] He did not believe that any race or civilization was superior to another.[4]

When it comes to his attitude toward socialism, it began with a seemingly positive view in his youth and turned to implacable opposition. That opposition was as peculiar as was Pareto. He believed that class struggle summarized the history of the modern world rather well:

> The class struggle, to which Marx has specifically drawn attention, is a real factor, the tokens of which are to be found on every page of history. But the struggle is not confined only to two classes: the proletariat and the capitalist; it occurs between an infinite number of groups with different interests, and above all between the elites contending for power.[5]

He also praised Marx's historical materialism:

> The theory of historical materialism, of the economic interpretation of history, was a notable scientific advancement in social theory, for it serves to elucidate the contingent character of certain phenomena such as morals and religion, to which many authorities ascribed . . . an absolute character.[6]

Pareto thought that socialism was likely to win, but not because it was intrinsically good, economically efficient, or desirable. Rather, he believed the reverse: socialism was likely to win because it commanded the allegiance of a class of fighters ready to destroy the bourgeois order, and willing to sacrifice themselves in the way early Christians did:

> If the "bourgeois" were being animated by the same spirit of abnegation and sacrifice for their class as the socialists are for theirs, socialism would be far from being as menacing as it actually is. The presence in its ranks [among the socialists] of the new elite is attested precisely by the moral qualities displayed by its adepts and which have enabled them to emerge victorious from the bitter test of numerous persecutions.[7]

It is not by accident that Georges Sorel was the only socialist writer whom Pareto esteemed, with whom he maintained amicable correspondence, and whom, even in disagreement, he did not cover with insults and snide remarks—as, in a different context, he did Edgeworth and Marshall.

Pareto's negative view of socialism shaped his early work and influenced his interpretation of income distributions in rich countries. In his first book-length study, *Les systèmes socialistes* (1902), the first topic he takes up is the distribution curve of wealth. He writes that it "probably depends on the distribution of physiological and psychological characteristics [*caractères*] of human beings," which drive the choices they make and the obstacles they face. In any case, while the specific individuals and their positions might be constantly shifting, the basic shape of the social pyramid doesn't change much (*"cette forme ne change guère"*). It seems as if "socialist systems" cannot change it either, no matter how hard they try.[8]

Pareto was by training a civil engineer, and before working as an academic economist he designed railroad systems and was a manager in an ironworks. So he had some hands-on experience of how industrial systems work. His engineering and mathematical skills served him well in the study of economics when he was called by Léon Walras to continue the tradition of strong mathematical economics embedded in general equilibrium. He succeeded Walras as chair of political economy at the University of Lausanne in 1893, when he was forty-five.

Pareto's life is interesting also in the sense that, while he did not move around very much, except within the rich triangle of France, Switzerland, and Italy, he did have a broader experience of the world than other academic economists who were his contemporaries (such as Pigou and Walras).[9] After working, as just noted, in the "real world," he ran unsuccessfully for a political office in 1882 and, after being disappointed by both his electoral failure and even more by Italian politics, he also faced a personally difficult experience when his first wife, Alessandrina Bakunina (a distant relative of the Russian anarchist Mikhail Bakunin), ran off with the household's cook.

Commentators explaining Pareto's philosophy tend to dwell on his personal traits and experiences more than they do with other authors, probably too much. Yet these disappointments may have darkened his frame of mind, contributing to an affect that often seems intended to make readers uncomfortable about facing the truths Pareto is laying in front of them. Raymond Aron, in his review of famous sociologists, notes that Pareto is always difficult to teach to students. This is because one of Pareto's major points is that everything being taught is false, since knowing the truth is harmful to a society; for sufficient cohesion to keep societies together, people must believe in Platonic myths (or, in today's phrase, the "big lie"). Professors must teach falsehoods that they know to be such. "This, it seems to me, is the living heart of Paretian thought," Aron writes, "and this is why Pareto will always remain apart among professors and sociologists. It is almost intolerable to the mind, at least to a teacher, to admit that truth in itself can be harmful."[10]

Pareto was that very unusual breed: a conservative with anti-religious feelings. I think he was basically a nihilist. But that might be a good philosophy to have in an age of globalization, whether his or ours: atomistic individuals, caring only about their own gain and loss, not believing in any community or religious ties, and regarding (as Pareto did) all religions, grand social theories, and the like as fairy tales. Far from what Pareto called "logico-experimental" theories, religion peddled "theories transcending experience."[11] And yet he, chastened by reality and being of somber disposition, believed that no ruling class could justify its power without resorting to such fictions. So we cannot have a society without fairy tales, and yet we know that all fairy tales are false.

Again, however, there is an excessive tendency among sociologists and economists to over-psychoanalyze Pareto and to seek in his life's disappointments the explanation for his acerbic, combative, contemptuous style and even his theories. Werner Stark, for example, sees Pareto's work as imbued with misanthropy, which Stark ascribes to the cruel disappointments noted above: election losses on his first (and only) foray into politics, and abandonment by his wife. "Perhaps," Stark writes, "one can most quickly unravel the enigma of Pareto's personality by saying that his was the psychology of a disappointed lover."[12] Schumpeter also engages in a psychological study of Pareto: "He was a man of . . . passions of the kind that effectively preclude a man from seeing more than one side of a political issue or, for that matter, of a civilization. This disposition was reinforced rather than mitigated by his classic education that made the ancient world as familiar to him as were his own Italy and France—the rest of the world just [barely] existed for him."[13] Franz Borkenau writes: "the creative power of [Pareto] seems to reach exactly as far as his hatreds. And to vanish as soon as they are exhausted."[14] Even Aron does it, although in a more subtle way: "My experience in the course of expounding Pareto's thought convinced me that it creates a certain malaise both in the person who expounds it and in the person who listens. I once mentioned this common malaise to an Italian friend, and he replied: 'Pareto's thought is not designed for young people, it means the most to mature people who are beginning to be rather disgusted with the way of the world.'"[15]

An obvious point needs to be made: whether Pareto's theory owes much or nothing to his life, it stands and falls, like the theory of any other social scientist, on its own merits. While knowing something of the backgrounds and lives of social scientists is without doubt helpful for understanding their writings, it cannot be used to reject or accept the writings. Pareto himself might have delighted in the special attention paid to his psyche: he would have said that his theories, uncomfortable to accept and to teach (as Aron attests), cry out for any explanation that would let them be discounted as products of a disturbed mind. We need to reject his ideas to continue believing in falsehood, Pareto would have exulted. In this misplaced focus on his life, he would ironically have seen yet more proof of the correctness of his views.

Pareto at times revels in that particular kind of contradiction by which, he would claim, certain things, while being true or even *because* they are true, cannot be said and cannot be allowed to affect social opinion. He uses Socrates as an example, arguing that Socrates was not wrong but all too right—or rather, right in a way that undermined society. While fully accepting in words the Athenian attitude toward religion, Socrates insidiously instilled doubts in his disciples and stimulated disbelief by asking people to rationally explain their beliefs. Socrates, Pareto reminds us, obeyed the Athenian laws: instead of leaving the city and escaping the death penalty, he decided to stay and accept the judgment passed on him. The rulers who resented Socrates's teachings were right: they clearly saw the potential for social instability coming from them.[16] In some sense, perhaps, Pareto saw himself in a similar role: his teachings were socially disturbing precisely because they were true, and they could not be taught for that reason. He was just lucky to have lived in a society that was too decadent, too self-assured, or too democratic to make him drink poison.

Inequality in France at the Turn of the Century

For Pareto, apart from ancient Greece and Rome, "the world" meant France and Italy, countries where he was raised, studied, worked, and attempted to start a political career, and in whose languages he wrote. Switzerland, where he lived the second part of his life, was a place whose statistical data he used, but it lacked the size, political importance, and social effervescence to be the equal of the other two.

To understand Pareto's views on inequality it is important to see how inequality was evolving during his life, especially in France.

Studying our authors' writings against the backdrop of the evolving inequality of their societies, we gradually notice a change. When Quesnay was writing, practically no information on inequality in France existed save a few anecdotes. One's inferences about inequality were based on what one observed, was told, or read about in a few volumes at most (which, again, lacked much empirical substantiation). But moving toward the present, the situation improves: data were much more available in Ricardo's and especially in Marx's time than a century before. With Pareto we advance to a real-time awareness of inequality which, while not equal to what exists today, is closer to our own time than to Quesnay's. While Pareto did not have all the data about contemporary France and Italy that we have now, he had a fair share, and would, as we shall see below, make ample use of data in his studies and in his speculations about the future evolution of inequality.

Like his contemporaries in France and Italy, Pareto was well aware that he was living through a politically pregnant period, full of turmoil and conflict among conservative, liberal, radical, Marxist, and anarchist ideas. This was much more the case on the continent, where the anarchist and Marxist movements grew deeper roots, than in Great Britain.

Wealth inequality in France was both very high and rising (Figure 5.1). Even if, at its peak around the turn of the century, the percentage of the nation's wealth controlled by the top one percent of its population was lower than in the United Kingdom (55 to 56 percent versus about 70 percent; compare Figures 4.1 and 5.1), it was extremely high. It was more than twice in 1900 what it is today (the share was around 25 percent in 2012).[17] Probably, it was comparable to the top one percent's wealth share at the time of the French Revolution.

According to Morrisson and Snyder, the *income* share of the top decile was 56 percent before the French Revolution, and between 41 and 48 percent a century later.[18] This allows Thomas Piketty to

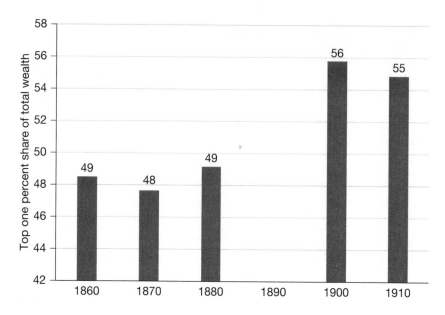

Figure 5.1. Top one percent share in total wealth, France 1860–1910

Data sources: World Inequality Database; Bertrand Grabinti, Jonathan Goupille-Lambert, and Thomas Piketty, "Income Inequality in France: Evidence from Distributional National Accounts (DINA)," WID.world Working Paper 2017/4.

describe an inequality curve that begins at a very high level before the Revolution, drops rather abruptly in the early part of the nineteenth century, then rises steadily from 1830 until around the turn of the century, the time of Pareto's writing, when it reaches a high plateau.[19] Therefore, inequality in France around 1890 to 1900 was greater than at the time of Louis-Napoléon Bonaparte, whose regime, as we know from Marx's writings on the revolutions in 1848 and the Paris Commune in 1871 (discussed in Chapter 4), was one of oligarchic rule. There was a great irony in that the Third Republic, established after France's defeat in the Franco-Prussian War and the overthrow of the Empire, stood, on paper, for a return to the principles of the French Revolution, but in reality was a regime of little-restrained capitalist rule. It formally ended with monarchies and aristocracies, but the nominal equality in the civic sphere coincided with high and rising inequality in income and wealth in the economic sphere.

Piketty highlights the period of the Third Republic precisely because of that combination of civic equality and economic inequality, which strongly resembles current capitalist societies. He reviews what was then called *la question sociale*, the problem of an increasingly displaced and destitute working class in industrializing France. He devotes special attention to Paul Leroy-Beaulieu, an eminent French economist at the end of the nineteenth century. Piketty's charge is that Leroy-Beaulieu argues in "bad faith" (*mauvaise foi*) when, without offering any data to support the claim, he declares that inequality in France is getting less severe.[20] Leroy-Beaulieu wrote: "Disparities of wealth and, above all, of income, are less than is thought, and these disparities are on the decline. . . . We are emerging from what I have called 'the chaotic period of large-scale industry,' the period of transformation, of suffering, of improvisation."[21] While his argument emphasized the (true) fact that real wages increased in the second half of the nineteenth century, Leroy-Beaulieu failed to acknowledge what he certainly knew—that this change implied nothing about the evolution of inequality. Leroy-Beaulieu repeatedly showed real wages increasing as if this alone were proof of income disparity between the rich and the poor decreasing. As Piketty writes, "he intentionally lets an ambiguity hover [*planer*]" between the two—the real income improvement he could honestly show and the reduction of inequality he could not.[22]

Leroy-Beaulieu's most important book on inequality, *Essay on the Distribution of Wealth and on the Tendency to Less Inequality of Condition* [*Essai sur la répartition des richesses et sur la tendence à une moindre inégalité des conditions*], was published in 1881. Pareto was aware of it.[23] To understand why Leroy-Beaulieu might argue in bad faith, it is important to contextualize his work and thus also Pareto's. Leroy-Beaulieu's book was written in the midst of heightened class tensions, more frequent strikes, rising political polarization, and increasingly important socialist and anarchist movements. It was also written amid a prevailing sentiment, felt deeply by Pareto, that liberal and capitalist interests were too weak, the bourgeoisie yielded too easily, and society was overwhelmed by the number and dedication of socialist activists. Both Leroy-Beaulieu and Pareto perceived a clash of interests and values in which socialists were winning because of their ability to rouse the masses and gain support in political and intellectual circles, and their readiness to confront bourgeois "hegemony" with their own form of worker hegemony.

Similar to how Marx saw his own work—as pushing forward proletarian interests—Pareto saw himself as fighting a rearguard action against those interests. Thus both Marx and Pareto were influenced in their work by their perceptions of the contemporary political environment and their views on the probable future evolution of society. But this was no less true, we should note, for other economists discussed in this book. The fear of economic stagnation, were the Corn Laws maintained, drove Ricardo to write his *Principles*.[24] Quesnay's desire for a powerful agricultural kingdom led him to describe, using *Le tableau économique,* the much richer France that could exist if his advice were followed, and then to proffer his policy ideas.[25] Inevitably in these authors we find a connection between what they believed were desirable economic and political changes and their own work. This clearly does not disqualify their works (after all, this book is devoted to discussing them); it only suggests that a "neutral" social science or "pure" scientific inquiry is not within our reach. To a much greater extent than in natural sciences, work in social sciences will always be influenced by its author's time and space.

Pareto's Law and "Circulation of the Elites" as Applied to Socialism

Pareto's contributions to economics, as well as his contributions to sociology, are many. But two of them interest us here: his work on income inequality and his famed "Pareto's law." While earlier economists were primarily, or even solely, interested in functional income distribution, which then resolved itself into interpersonal income inequality, Pareto was the first to look at interpersonal inequality as such. This reflected a wider change by which the focus of political economy moved from studies of class and society to analyses of individual income, consumption, satisfaction, and *ophelimity* (a term Pareto invented, preferring it to *utility*). Classes were no longer at the center of attention; individuals were.

This shift of interest toward interpersonal distribution of income was, in Pareto's case, also due to two factors, one political, the other personal. The political factor was the introduction of direct taxation in many Western European countries and cities. Taxes paid and income on which they were assessed provided the data to reveal how the incomes of individuals (or more accurately, taxpaying households) were distributed. The personal factor was that Pareto was mathematically minded and skilled, and such data were obviously attractive to him.

There was yet a third factor, which will be taken up later, having to do with how deeply comforting his findings were to Pareto. They implied, as he interpreted them, that income distribution was all but dictated by a law of nature (*la loi naturelle*), akin to the distributions seen in the weights and heights of human beings. And in that case, they could not be altered by economic policy or other changes introduced to a social system—such as the replacement of capitalism with socialism.[26] In a somewhat rambling paragraph, perhaps not fully thought through (and only part of which is translated here), Pareto makes this very argument:

> We have shown that the income distribution curve had a remarkable stability; it changes very little when the circumstances of time and place in which it is observed change a lot. . . . This probably has its origin in the distribution of psychological features of people and also in the fact that the proportion in which capitals are combined cannot be random [*quelconques*]. Suppose that, an income distribution curve being given, one expropriates all people with income above a certain limit; it would seem that the distribution of income should be changed for a long time. One can admit that the inequality of the physical and mental features of

people would eventually lead to income inequality, but that would require at least some generations. In reality, another effect will take place much more rapidly and tend to reestablish the disturbed equilibrium. . . . The total sum of mobile capital will suffer a reduction: thereby the proportions of capital will change, and production will, in consequence, be reduced. . . . The fall of productivity will be followed by a general reduction of incomes. . . . The entire lower part of the curve drops down, and consequently the curve itself ends up by taking a form very similar to what it had before.[27]

In Chapter 4 we saw that Marx used English fiscal data from the second half of the nineteenth century. In the last years of the nineteenth century, Pareto would make use of data for other places, structured almost identically, with tranches of taxable income and the number of people falling within each tranche. These included a number of German states (Wurttemberg, Bremen, Hamburg, Schaumbourg-Lippe, and Saxony-Weimar-Eisenach) and the Swiss cantons of Zurich and Ur.[28] In another publication, he presented data from England, Italian cities, Prussia, Saxony, and Basel.[29] These were the data sets he used to derive what would become known as "Pareto's law."[30] He spent two years poring over the data and concluding, through various steps, that incomes were distributed according to a regular pattern, whereby the number of recipients having at least a given threshold income decreased by a regular proportion as the threshold was raised. In other words, if there were p recipients with incomes higher than y, then with the new and higher income threshold of y plus 10 percent, the number of recipients would decrease by a certain fixed percentage (say, by 15 percent). That percentage remained unchanged as the threshold was gradually increased further and further. (This is also called a fractile distribution, because the relative relationships are maintained throughout.) The simplest way to write the relationship is $ln p = A - \alpha\, ln y$, where α is a constant, p is the number of people having income y or more, and A is the overall size of the population. (If income takes some minimal value, then everybody's income must be above it, which would be the entire population *A*.)* The value of *α*, Pareto claimed, did not vary by much among the diverse countries and cities for which he had data. We can imagine *α*, which later became known as the "Pareto constant" or "Pareto coefficient," to be a guillotine that cuts, always by a constant percentage, the number of people as the income threshold is raised. On a double-log chart (with both horizontal and vertical axes expressed in logarithms), as shown in Figure 5.2 and taken directly from Pareto, the relationship is a straight line with a slope representing *α* , the guillotine. (*La courbe de la répartition de la richesse*.)[31] In Figure 5.2, the slopes for England and Italian cities are the same. The minimum income is likewise the same for both. The higher cutoff points for England on the vertical and horizontal axes reflect, respectively, the greater population of England and the greater incomes of the rich there—but the key finding is the similarity (or is it identity?) of the slopes of the two lines.

Why was this finding so comforting for Pareto? It showed that the distribution of incomes was broadly the same in countries that were quite different.[†] And therefore Pareto could posit that there must be some fundamental tendency of incomes in a society to group themselves in a certain way. As he put it in 1896, "We find ourselves here in the presence of a natural law." (*Nous nous trouvons ici en présence d'une loi naturelle*.)[32] That income distributions could not be determined by institutions became clear because England and Italy, with their quite different institutions, had the same shape of income distribution. And neither could the distributions be determined by economic development, because the levels of that, too, were different. There must therefore be some other reason: "the tendency of incomes to be distributed in one particular way could largely depend on human nature."[33] If this were the case, socialist attempts to transform society

---

* The relationship can be directly transformed into a power law distribution:
$$p = \frac{A^*}{y^\alpha}.$$

[†] As Pareto himself realized, this was true only for top incomes, since only the rich were subject to direct taxation.

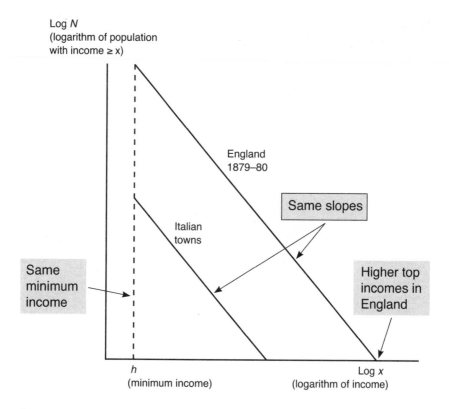

Figure 5.2. Pareto income distributions

and eliminate inequality would be doomed to fail; they would amount to no more than empirically unfounded dreams. Inequality under socialism would be the same, Pareto argued, as under capitalism. Only the ruling elite would be different.

Pareto's finding thus had important implications for his sociological theory, and for what he thought about the conflicts between, on one side, capitalism and liberalism, and on the other side, socialism and statism. Pareto's sociological theory of the "circulation of the elites" was reinforced by his finding of a fundamentally stable distribution of incomes (regardless of political institutions). This meant that, while the type of ruling elite, its origin, and its characteristics might vary, the underlying distribution of wealth and income could not be affected. In his sociological writings, Pareto insisted on the role of the elites, and provided a whole taxonomy of the elites. But probably the most important feature of this discussion was the distinction between two types of elites, which Pareto described using language from Machiavelli: some elites, the "lions," use force to impose their rule, while others, the "foxes," use guile, cunning, and propaganda.[34]

Still, whatever the means by which the elites exercise their rule, if there is an immutable distribution of income, then they are incapable of changing it. It is only a question of who the new elite will be—will they be lions or foxes?—and not how income or wealth will be apportioned. The findings that gave rise to "Pareto's law" justified for many a shift in emphasis away from classes and toward the elites' competition for power. It also aligned quite well with Pareto's stern view of political competition—that it was not driven by competing values and sincere beliefs but mostly by the competing players' interests.*

In Pareto's view, then, even if the new socialist elite came to power (an ascent Pareto feared but thought inevitable), it would be unable to change income distribution. And thus Pareto must have thought that he undercut one of the most important claims being made by socialist parties in Europe at the turn of the twentieth century—that they would be able to change the distribution in favor of the poor and reduce inequality. In his view, none of that was possible. The only thing that was possible was that the new bureaucratic elite would replace the effete and decadent bourgeois elite. But this would leave income and wealth inequalities unaltered.

Some writers insist that Pareto's blindness to differences, his insistence on the sameness of income distributions across time and space, was due to a worldview generally ascendant at the time. Werner Stark calls it "pan-mechanicism." In fundamental contrast to a "pan-organismic" philosophy, it sees social phenomena moving

---

* Pareto did, however, believe it was impossible for leaders to be entirely cynical and to fully disbelieve what they were teaching. They were bound to believe in their own propaganda, at least in part.

in a fully predictable and mechanical way, and commits "the error of believing that everything is the same everywhere: that everything is, as it must always be."[35] While, without doubt, Pareto's work is characterized by excessively mechanical and taxonomical writing, another explanation for his infatuation with an immutable income distribution makes more sense: rather than a methodological preference, it appealed because it seemed to confirm his theory of the circulation of the elites, and to deny the possibility of improvement under socialism.

There is a further element. Pareto insisted that change in "inequality" (as we shall see, he really meant poverty) could come only through change in real income. He came to this conclusion by defining an index of inequality, measuring it as the ratio of the number of people below a certain income level (say, close to the poverty line) to the number of people above that level.[36] Then he argued that, without growth, it was impossible to reduce the number of people below the poverty line (the numerator in his inequality fraction) and thus to reduce inequality. Redistribution, in effect, could not change things if the distribution curve was immutable. In short, Pareto confounded poverty reduction and inequality reduction. It is clear, however, and surely it was clear to somebody as mathematically minded as Pareto, that this *tour de main* was performed by fixing the distribution *a priori* and by defining the index of relative inequality so as to coincide with poverty. Having done that, taxation of the rich or even elimination of private property was, by definition, incapable of producing a lasting change in income distribution.

In fact, one of the major implications of Pareto's view that income distribution is fixed within a very narrow range was precisely to take away the possibility of an improvement in the position of the poor through redistribution. The socialists were thus hemmed in from two directions: the theory of the elites allowed them merely to be a replacement for the bourgeoisie, and Pareto's law told them that all their attempts to lower inequality were doomed. What then was the point of socialism except to bring a new elite to power? The situation must have been dispiriting for many socialists. But perhaps not to those who thought to ask an essential question: Was Pareto's law really a "law"?

Pareto's Law, Pareto's "Law," or No Law at All?

Few economic terms have been subject to greater misunderstanding than the "Pareto law of income distribution" and the "Pareto constant." The misunderstanding of the former has to do with the fixity or immutability of income distribution. Pareto's own writings, without doubt, lead the reader to believe that his results imply exactly that. Here are some of many citations one could make to support this interpretation: "statistics reveal that the curve. . . . varies very little in time and space: different nations have very similar curves. There is thus a remarkable stability in the shape of this curve."[37] "Every attempt to artificially change the distribution of income will face the tendency of incomes to get distributed in the form of an arrow. Left to itself, the society would return to that original distribution."[38] "Statistics reveal that the curve . . . varies very little in time and space; different nations at different times have very similar curves."[39]

The claim of distribution's fixity is based on the finding that the Pareto coefficient, in most studied cases, remains in a range between 1.5 and 2.[40] But this implies substantial variation in the share received by the top 10 percent, from 46 percent of the overall income (if $\alpha = 1.5$) to 32 percent (if $\alpha = 2$). It is not clear if such a difference can be considered small or big. Using current country data (for year 2018), this is equivalent to the difference in the top decile share between Namibia (extremely high inequality) and Turkey (moderate inequality). It covers the range that includes about forty countries in the world. So, the range that appeared to Pareto to be small (with α's of 1.5 and 2 being thought almost equivalent) is clearly not so.

Pareto thought that the data coming from societies very far from Western Europe geographically, socially, and historically, such as pre-conquest Peru or the Roman Empire, displayed the same distributions. That further reinforced the feeling Pareto wanted to convey—that an "iron law" of income distribution applies, not only valid for the developed European states of the nineteenth century but also holding under vastly different constellations of political power and vastly different institutions. "I do not consider impossible that the distribution of income in those societies was similar to the distribution observed in our societies," he writes, even as he allows that, pending access to more data, "I am perfectly willing to admit that my opinion could be wrong."[41]

Thus, if one were to take Pareto's statements literally and have a jury decide, in a legalistic fashion, whether he can be shown to have insisted on his hypothesis of immutability of income distribution through time and place, it would be very difficult to convict him of such a generalization. The reason is that most of Pareto's writings do contain caveats that in one way or another qualify his main assertions.

Caveats are added, too, to his discussion of income distribution under socialism. When he was particularly dejected by Edgeworth's reluctance to credit him with the originality or discovery of the new law, and thus probably felt closer to Sorel, Pareto wrote to his life-long friend Maffeo Pantaleoni: "I pointed out myself to Mr. Sorel the objection that a socialist might make to my curve, that it is a curve valid only for a capitalist society."[42] While at many points in Les systèmes socialistes he writes of the impossibility of distribution being altered by a socialist society, he qualifies that view in the Manual by stating that we do not know whether such distributional change might be possible.[43] One can therefore question to what extent Pareto was being honest in discussing the law of income distribution he unveiled. There is a constant tension in his writing between very clear statements that the distribution cannot be changed and quasi-legalistic wordings that water these down with careful caveats. The qualifiers are never sufficiently numerous or strong, however, to overturn the prior suggestion of the immutability of distribution.

The second confusion, which is perhaps even more important than the confusion over whether Pareto really claimed to have discovered an immutable law of income distribution, has to do with the meaning of what became known as the Pareto constant (α), or what we have called here the "guillotine." It is now very well known that this "constant" applies only to the top of income distributions, and that even there it is not a constant but a variable. The fact that α applies only to the top of income distributions was clear already to Pareto: he knew that he had data only for the relatively rich people who were subject to income taxation, and in the *Manual* he mentions, when he draws the curve of the whole distribution, that the part of the curve to which the coefficient applies is only a range at the top of the distribution.[44] This is something we know well today. If we draw the logarithm of income on the horizontal axis against the logarithm of inverse cumulative distribution on the vertical axis (that is, exactly the same relationship as in Figure 5.2), and do it across the *entire* distribution, we typically get a curve resembling the one in Figure 5.3. No single straight line could be meaningfully fitted over that curve. But if we truncate it, taking only the top of the distribution, then fitting a single straight line begins to make more sense—although even there (as we shall see next) the slope of the line will depend upon where along the top of distribution we focus (that is, where we make our truncation).

We know nowadays not only that the Pareto "constant" changes from one distribution to another (that it is not fixed, regardless of the place and time) but also that, within the same distribution, the coefficient takes different values depending on what portion of income distribution we consider—depending, that is, on whether we look at the top 5 percent of recipients or the top 10 percent, or any other percent. In other words, if we take a given distribution, and then draw the line that best expresses the change in the number of people with incomes above a certain threshold, that line (or more exactly, its slope) will vary depending on where we start "cutting" the distribution. Figure 5.4 shows α's for three income distributions (in the United States, Germany, and Spain, all in 2008), with α calculated at different parts of the distribution. The graph begins with the eightieth percentile of the distribution (meaning that the Pareto

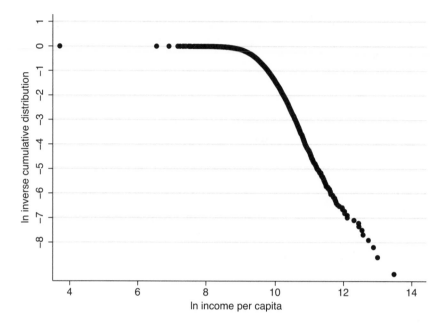

Figure 5.3 Empirical Pareto relationship in an actual income distribution
Note: Calculated from micro data for Germany (2008).
Data source: LIS Cross-National Data Center.

relationship is calculated for the top twenty percentiles); from there, it moves to the eighty-first percentile, calculating the Pareto relationship for the top nineteen percentiles, and so on. It continues like that all the way to the ninety-ninth percentile, calculating at the end the relationship for the top two percentiles. If distributions were truly Paretian or fractile (even for the top 20 percent, that is, since we already know they could not be for the entire distribution), the coefficient would be the same regardless of the portion of the distribution we chose. But obviously the coefficient is not the same: for the United States, it increases (in absolute amount) throughout, implying that the guillotine becomes ever sharper and the top of the distribution ever thinner. In the case of Germany, α at first moves as in the United States, but after the ninety-third percentile the evolution is exactly the opposite: the slope becomes smaller (in absolute amount),

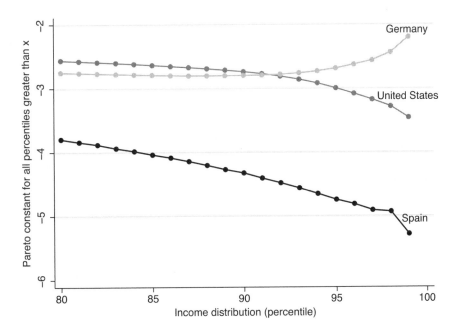

Figure 5.4. The Pareto coefficient as calculated for different countries and at different parts of income distributions

Note: Calculated from micro data for United States (2008), Spain (2008), and Germany (2008).

Data source: LIS Cross-National Data Center.

implying greater thickness at the top than in the United States. The Spanish α remains for the entire distribution greater in absolute amount than in the other two countries, and moreover keeps on increasing as one moves toward the top. This indicates that the number of high-income recipients in Spain is whittled down pretty quickly.

The very idea of immutability of the distribution is contradicted by the fact that the coefficient, which supposedly reflects the immutability of the distribution, is variable *within* any given distribution.[45] In fact, if Pareto's statement in its strong form were true, all three curves shown here would collapse to only one α value. This is obviously far from being the case.

If we take the Pareto coefficient from the equation above and first write it (as we should) with a subscript for the time and place of the distributions where it applies (say, the United States, year 2008), and then add a subscript to indicate the range of the income distribution where it applies (say, the top 10 percent), then it becomes immediately clear that we are not at all talking about something that is invariant between the distributions. Thus, claiming constancy of the entire distribution based on a *coefficient that varies*—and varies not only in time and space but across a given income distribution—becomes absurd.

The variation of the Pareto coefficient between distributions is something that was obvious even to Pareto's contemporaries, and it has grown ever clearer since. Even Pareto himself had two dozen distributions with coefficients that would be considered, despite Pareto's assertions to the contrary, different (and statistically significantly so). Even more destructive of the idea of immutability is that, as we have seen, the very "constant" changes in function of the place in the distribution where it is calculated. The "law" vanishes altogether.

There is yet another confusion which has continued until very recently. It has to do with the very sharp, or gradual, way the guillotine operates, and with synthetic measures of inequality like the Gini coefficient. The relationship between the Pareto and Gini coefficients is straightforward: the higher the absolute value of the constant, the lower the Gini.* This is not fully intuitive, however. The higher value of the Pareto coefficient means that the guillotine works more strongly and that the number of people with incomes above any given level decreases sharply. That means, ultimately, that there are very few people at the very top (others having been quickly whittled down), and also—and here is where our intuition fails us—that income inequality should be greater. But the opposite is true. Synthetic measures of inequality take into account everybody's income and compare it (as in Gini) to the income of everybody else (two persons at a time), or compare it to the mean (like different Theil indexes). If most of the population is at the

---

* The formula is $G = \dfrac{1}{2\alpha - 1}$, where G stands for Gini and α is the Pareto coefficient.

same or similar income level, synthetic inequality measures tend to be low, despite the fact that there are only very few people at the top. Thus, a very sharp guillotine, or the very high absolute value of a, implies a *low* degree of inequality. Thicker upper tails of income distribution are therefore associated with higher synthetic measures of inequality.[46]

Pareto's Contributions

It would be wrong to conclude from this chapter's critique of Pareto's findings that his contributions were small. They were important in several ways. Pareto defined the first power law, which is used in many instances and not only for distributions of income and wealth but also for distributions of cities by population, for sizes of floods, for numbers of publications by author, and even for numbers of Twitter followers. Pareto's power law is used heuristically in income and wealth distributions today, when the need arises to estimate the extreme top of the distribution but the data are lacking—perhaps because the rich do not participate in surveys or incomes are underreported to fiscal authorities. In such cases, we can assume that the Pareto "constant" holds for the top five percent or the top one percent, or whatever top portion of the distribution seems reasonable. Frank Cowell gives an example where extending the Pareto line beyond the recorded tax data enabled tax authorities to conclude that there must be some individuals with unreported extremely high incomes. It turned out to be true.[47] Or take the recent example of corruption cases in China, where estimates of amounts involved in bribery or embezzlement situations were officially recorded at the time of conviction (Figure 5.5).[48] The two same values for corruption at the very top suggest some truncation (meaning that very large amounts were just assumed away), and the extension of the Pareto line past the recorded corruption suggests that there might have been several cases of even greater embezzlement. Continuing uses like these of Pareto's work stand as testimony to his enduring contribution to the study of income inequality.

Another important aspect of Pareto's work is that he very clearly rejected normal or symmetrical distributions as valid for income and

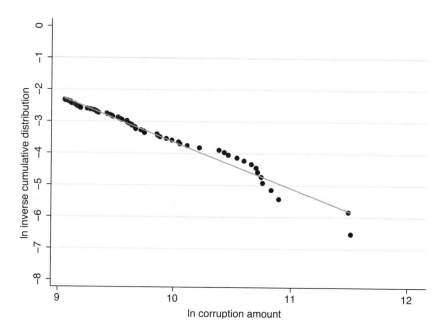

Figure 5.5. Pareto line drawn across the highest amounts of corruption in China

Note: The data refer to the top decile (by amount of bribery or embezzlement) of the cases of corruption, as reported by government judiciary authorities.

Data source: Li Yang, Branko Milanovic, and Yaoqi Lin, "Anti-Corruption Campaign in China: An Empirical Investigation," Stone Center on Socio-Economic Inequality Working Paper 64, April 2023.

wealth. Although the distribution of income and wealth was not studied in a statistical sense before Pareto, there had been an implicit assumption (made probably by extending Adolphe Quetelet's work and reasoning) that the distribution of income would approximate the distribution of other physical or innate characteristics, like weight or height—in other words, that it would be Gaussian. The idea was dispelled by Pareto. We have never gone back to thinking of income distributions as symmetrical.*

---

* One seemingly obvious reason that it cannot be symmetrical is because the bottom of income distribution must have a minimal level of income, or otherwise people would not be able to survive; and, on the other extreme, the right-hand side

Fundamentally in agreement with his theory of the circulation of elites, Pareto did not believe that income distribution was amenable to change. To put it in stronger terms, Pareto did not think that income distribution would change under different social arrangements or that it would change with greater average wealth or economic development. This marked a contrast between income distribution and other phenomena, including marriage rates, population growth, and mortality rates, all of which did, as Pareto forcefully argued in the *Manual,* change with development.[49] It may seem somewhat paradoxical that Pareto assigned to income distribution an immutability which he was (rightly) ready to deny to a number of other social phenomena. It is impossible to say to what extent he was attracted to that conclusion by the data—which indeed could have led one astray—and to what extent he was guided by prior beliefs he hoped to see fully confirmed by the data. It is ironic that Pareto, who endlessly insisted on the logico-experimental method that in principle would be impervious to subjective feelings or preferences, might have been duped at that very point—the same one where he saw many others commit mistakes.

Simon Kuznets would, about a half century after Pareto, go precisely in the direction Pareto refused to take: he would argue that income inequality changes in a regular and predictable fashion with development or increased wealth of society. Rich societies, Kuznets would hold, have different distributions than poor societies.

In any survey of prominent economists' approaches to income inequality and how they have evolved over time, Pareto's position must be acknowledged as quite important. He was the first to have moved fully to the study of interpersonal income inequality, and also the first to critically consider what income inequality under socialism might look like. He brought up a topic that was addressed only indirectly by Marx, as seen in Chapter 4, and then asked a crucial

---

of the distribution is unlimited because there is no ceiling to income. This is, of course, very different from other phenomena, where there are natural limits.

question: Would state ownership of the means of production reduce income inequality?

Pareto also set studies of income inequality on their inductive path. Today all such studies are driven by the availability of data and our attempts to make sense of them, and, if possible, to uncover economic laws that govern inequality. He was thus the first to ask the question point blank: Does income inequality move according to some regularity as social institutions or incomes of society change? For him, the answer was in the negative, and we know by now that he was wrong. But the question was important to ask.

CHAPTER SIX

Simon Kuznets: Inequality during Modernization

Simon Kuznets was arguably (with the other contender being John Maynard Keynes) the most important economist of the twentieth century.[1] He laid the foundations of the two most important areas in economics. First, his early work on national accounts in the 1930s and 1940s helped define the national economic aggregates that have become the indispensable basis for monitoring economic growth and changes in people's welfare. Even as his definition of the national product was adopted by the United Nations (with additional contributions by Richard Stone, James Meade, and others later) and become a standard implemented in all countries of the world, he also articulated the very doubts about the treatment of some parts of national accounts that are increasingly voiced today and might guide future revisions of national aggregates. Second, through his work in the 1950s and 1960s, with which we are concerned here, Kuznets influenced our view of the forces that create and shape income distribution.

Thus, we can credit Kuznets with not only a measure of aggregate welfare (national income) but also an approach to its distribution across households. Those more statistically minded might say he helped define the first and second moments of income distribution: its mean (national income per capita) and its distribution (standard deviation of income across households). Even if his work in the area of income distribution is not as widely accepted today as his definitions of various national account concepts, what would become known as the Kuznets hypothesis, a theory about the evolution of inequality over time, is still very much present in economics.

Before turning to that hypothesis, which was Kuznets's most important contribution regarding income distribution, we should acknowledge his three other seminal pieces of work in the same domain: his empirical study of global inequality, which was the first of its kind; his statement of the maximin principle (or difference principle), which is most associated with John Rawls but had its beginnings, chronologically, in Kuznets's writings; and his groundbreaking discussion of the trade-off between equity and efficiency.

In a 1954 paper, Kuznets produced the first empirical estimates of global income distribution, focusing on three points in time: 1894–1895, 1938, and 1949.[2] Due to the lack of data on income distributions within nations, these were global distributions of people ranked not by their individual incomes but by the average incomes of their countries. This is what I have defined as a "Concept 2" approach to global inequality, to distinguish it from the "true" approach that properly captures personal income variances within nations.[3] Even the data on average national incomes were sparse at the time of Kuznets's writing, so he first produced a Concept 2 distribution only for advanced economies, which represented about 30 percent of the world population in all the years he analyzed. Then he complemented that with a Concept 2 global distribution for 1949, and a much more hypothetical distribution for 1894–1895. For the advanced part of the world, Kuznets's calculations show an increase in the Gini coefficient from 28 points in 1894–1895 to 36–37 points in 1938—thus, an income divergence among the rich. For the world in 1949, Kuznets used UN-provided average income data for seventy countries, and by assumption filled the populations of non-advanced countries into the lower end of the income distribution. He estimated the share of the top 6 percent (which represents approximately the population of the United States, the richest country in both years) to have been almost 28 percent in 1894–1895 and 42 percent in 1949.[4] Thus, population-weighted international inequality increased significantly between the end of the nineteenth century and the middle of the twentieth.

We can repeat these calculations today using better information, now that we have data on GDP per capita from the Maddison Project. We find the share of total global income held by the top 6 percent (again, a group equivalent in the size to the US population) to be 24 percent in 1894–1895 and 31 percent in 1949.[5] The second percentage is much lower than Kuznets thought because of the much greater coverage of GDP data for 1949 that we have now compared with what Kuznets had. But both his idea of creating a world distribution of income and his calculation of the share held by the top of that distribution were new, and the results were the best that could be produced at the time.

In 1963, Kuznets posed the question of instrumental justification of high inequality: Is inequality always good for growth, or are there conditions under which redistribution from high-income groups to those on the bottom might accelerate economic growth?[6] This can also be seen as an application of the maximin principle, by which higher inequality can be justified only if it leads to greater economic growth and, crucially, to higher incomes for the poor. In his usual way, which makes his writings often not among the easiest to read or even to understand, Kuznets answered the question in conditional terms. But this was the explanation he favored: "Would lowering the high incomes, while possibly depressing the contribution of these groups, be more than offset by the contribution of these released resources to other uses by other income groups; and thus on net balance would the change mean a significant positive contribution to economic growth? If the answer is in the affirmative, then some components of the high-income brackets are unwarranted from the standpoint of economic growth."[7] Note that Kuznets accepts here that constraining the ability of the rich to add to their incomes might make them work less than they would otherwise, and thus result in lower overall income, but he thinks that the incentive effect of enabling higher income earning by the poor could more than offset that loss. Kuznets does not question the positive role of incentive of higher income; he questions whether the greatest gain can be realized through provision of such an incentive to the rich or to the poor.

Kuznets thought that every income distribution should be judged by three criteria: adequacy, equity, and efficiency.[8] *Adequacy* is ensuring that even the poorest have an income level consonant with local customs and the society's level of economic development. *Equity* is absence of discrimination, whether it is discrimination in terms of current incomes (as, for example, in racial or gender wage gaps) or in future possibilities (constraining what we now call equality of opportunity). *Efficiency* is achievement of high growth rates.

When it comes to interactions among the three, Kuznets envisages all possibilities. In some cases, pushing for equity too hard, as in full egalitarianism, would have detrimental effects on the growth rate, and also reduce adequacy—that is, egalitarianism might produce poverty. But in other cases, the very achievement of higher growth rates requires greater equity, be it because a significant part of the population is otherwise socially excluded and not allowed to contribute to overall betterment, or because it leads to the fragmentation of society and political instability. Finally, pushing too strongly for adequacy (that is, for reduction in poverty) might reduce incentives, diminish growth rate, and even reduce the value of equity, since presumably people would be rewarded regardless of their efforts, just to reduce poverty. It was a more complex view of the world than a simple tradeoff between equality and growth.

As these examples of Kuznets's thinking show, his contributions to economics go far beyond the main ones for which he is remembered. Questions he raised, in some cases for the first time, remain with us and continue to be debated seventy years hence. He achieved that through the rare combination of his extremely careful data work and deep thinking (motivated, I think, by his empirical work) about the fundamental issues posed by, and reflected in, any society's income distribution.

Inequality in the United States around the Mid-twentieth Century

The period during which Kuznets developed his view of income distribution was a very special, and probably unique, period in American economic history. At the end of World War II, the United States was not only the incontestable victor and the sole power in possession of atomic weapons, it was also by far the world's richest country (in total and in terms of income per capita). The experience of the war left Germany devastated, the western parts of the Soviet Union largely destroyed in terms of both human and physical capital, Great Britain exhausted, and China, Korea, and Japan, for various reasons, in situations of abject poverty. But in the United States income increased tremendously. Much of the increase during the war was due to military production, and the necessary postwar conversion to a consumer focus led to a short recession in 1947. Enormous new industrial capacities had been built, however, and the United States in the early 1950s, with just 6 percent of the world's population, produced more than a third of the world's output.[9] This level of relative economic power of a single nation was unprecedented and has not been repeated since, nor is it likely to be repeated in the foreseeable future.

On top of that, the United States became a more class-open society, thanks to New Deal policies before the War, the GI Bill after the war, and the decrease (some would call it a dramatic one) in income inequality from the mid-1930s to the mid-1950s. The full extent of the decrease (which Kuznets played an important role in calculating) is contested.[10] Yet there is little doubt that a decrease in inequality did happen and that it was large. Despite continued racial discrimination, the United States in the 1950s was a much more economically egalitarian society than twenty years before. The postwar income equalization occurred not only through much more accessible public education (with public universities springing up across the country and attracting thousands of new students) and greater demand for labor (driven by fast economic growth) but also through policy measures that limited highest incomes. Personal taxes were, at times, thought almost confiscatory: for the highest income recipients, the marginal tax rate was in excess of 90 percent throughout most of the 1950s.[11] Such severe taxation has not been repeated since.

Figure 6.1 illustrates American inequality and economic growth over the long term. What is noticeable in the period of concern here is the sharp increase in inequality during the Great Depression, principally on account of high unemployment, followed by the long slide extending to 1957. A Gini coefficient that in 1933 exceeded 50 fell to only 34 in 1957. Such huge declines are extremely rare and almost never encountered short of revolutions. But revolutions tend to produce declines in real incomes, while in this case US real per-capita income more than doubled, from about $8,000 in 1933 to $17,500 in 1957.[12] This remarkable triple development—the unprecedented global power of the United States, the large increases in real per-capita income, and the equally large leveling of income differences—is something we must keep in mind to understand the intellectual climate in which Kuznets developed his thinking about the evolution of income distribution.

In such an atmosphere, perhaps it was natural to believe that the US experience presaged what could be the general experience of advanced capitalist countries: greater social mobility, the end of class-based societies, lower income and wealth inequality, and permanently high rates of growth. To understand Kuznets and his generally optimistic outlook on the future of income distribution, it is therefore important to place him in the right historical context—one wholly different from the context experienced by Marx and Pareto. Marx's medium-term pessimism was cultivated amid the stagnant or only slowly increasing real wages in England of the mid-nineteenth century (a prevailing condition overturned around the time Marx published the first volume of *Capital*).[13] Pareto wrote in the febrile atmosphere of strikes, anarchist agitation, and a seemingly imminent European socialist revolution. To both writers, the picture looked bleak—even if Marx could rejoice at such bleakness since it made the possibility of capitalism's overthrow more real. In contrast to them, Kuznets, working amid US prosperity and significantly lower inequality than a generation

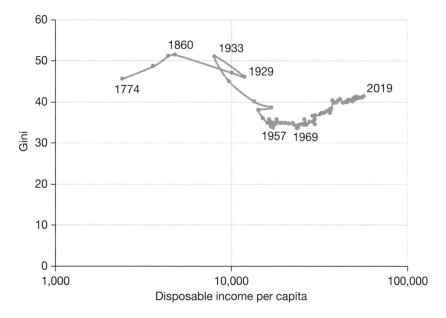

Figure 6.1. Long-run inequality in the United States, 1774–2019

Note: Horizontal axis in log 1990 international dollars (Maddison).

Data sources: for 1774 to 1870: Peter Lindert and Jeffrey Williamson, *"Unequal Gains: American Growth and Inequality since 1700"* (Princeton University Press, 2016), 38, 115; for 1929 to 1947: Eugene Smolensky and Robert Plotnik, "Inequality and Poverty in the United States, 1900–1990," Graduate School of Public Policy, University of California, 1992, figure 2; for 1929: Daniel B. Radner and John C. Hinricks, "Size Distribution of Income in 1964, 1970, and 1971," *Survey of Current Business,* 54 (1974): 19–31, table 10, 27; for 1935, 1941, and 1946: Selma Goldsmith, George Jaszi, Hyman Kaitz, and Maurice Liebenberg, "Size Distribution of Income since the Mid-thirties," *Review of Economics and Statistics* 36 no. 1 (1954): 1–36, 7fn4; for 1944 to 1945 and 1947 to 2019: US Census Bureau, *Income, Poverty and Health Insurance in the United States: 2009,* September 2010, Table A.2: 40–43. For more recent years, subsequent equivalent publications from the US Census Bureau for 1947 to 1988: Arthur F. Jones Jr. and Daniel H. Weinberg, "Change in the Income Inequality for Families: 1947–1998," in *The Changing Shape of the Nation's Income Distribution: 1947–1998,* US Census Report Number P60-204, June 2000.

before, could realistically, and not only as a millennial project, envisage a much richer and more equal society.

The Kuznets Hypothesis Defined

As income increases, inequality at first goes up and then declines. This could be the briefest exposition of the Kuznets hypothesis that was timidly enounced in 1955, based on only a handful of observations. That hypothesis would go on to have a life of its own, which continues today almost seventy years after its unveiling. Kuznets defined it at the outset as follows:

> One might . . . assume a long swing in the inequality characterizing the secular income structure: widening in the early phases of economic growth when the transition from the pre-industrial to the industrial civilization was most rapid; becoming stabilized for a while; and then narrowing in the later phases.[14]

In a later publication, he reiterated the pattern, with additional explanation:

> It seems plausible to assume that in the process of growth, the earlier periods are characterized by . . . forces that may have widened the inequality . . . for a while because of the rapid growth of the non-A [non-agricultural] sector and wider inequality within it. It is even more plausible to argue that the recent narrowing in income inequality observed in the developed countries was due to a combination of the narrowing inter-sectoral inequalities in product per worker [between agriculture and manufacturing], the decline in the share of property incomes in total incomes of households, and the institutional changes that reflect decisions concerning social security and full employment.[15]

The idea was simple, but nobody had expressed it before. Kuznets started from the position that incomes in preindustrial societies were relatively equal. That proposition might not be true, and certainly was not true for societies with large inequality in landholdings, but we can assume (although it is never made explicit in Kuznets's writings) that he had in mind an agricultural society approximating New England, composed of landowning peasantry.[16] That Kuznets had the United States primarily in mind can be guessed from two statements he makes in quick succession. First, he writes that "the urban income inequalities might be assumed to be far wider than those for the agricultural population which was organized in relatively *small individual enterprises.*" Second, he argues that this high urban inequality "would be particularly so during the periods when industrialization and urbanization were proceeding apace and the urban population was being swelled, and fairly rapidly, by immigrants—either from the country's agricultural areas or *from abroad*. Under these conditions, the urban population would run the full gamut from low-income positions of recent entrants to the economic peaks of the established top-income groups."[17] Both statements represent a stylized version of US economic history in the latter part of the nineteenth century and the first two decades of the twentieth century. But Kuznets's objective was much broader than to give a capsule version of US economic history. He thought the regularities he observed had a much wider field of application.

Starting from the premise of a rural society with limited inequality, the impacts of industrialization and urbanization would be twofold. First, higher productivity in the non-agricultural sector would cause workers from agriculture to emigrate to cities. There they would receive wages higher than their previous incomes in rural areas. That would be the first source of rising inequality: the gap in average incomes between the city and the countryside. Second, as industrialization proceeded, it would create new jobs that were much more diverse—both in their productivity and in the wages they paid—than the jobs that had existed in villages. The urban areas would thus display rising inequality, and since the urban areas were becoming more populous (ever drawing on rural labor), this more unequal sector of the economy would expand, and drive overall inequality up. In short, society would move from initial homogeneity in income toward heterogeneity, due to differences in mean incomes between urban and rural areas and the expansion of the more heterogeneous (non-agricultural and urbanized) part of the economy.

Peter Lindert and Jeffrey Williamson published the first comprehensive study of US inequality, tracking it from the time of US independence to the turn of the twenty-first century. They pass judgment on three Kuznetsian mechanisms: the increase in the real wage gap between urban and rural workers; the increase in the gap between urban and rural overall income; and the effect of rising urbanization (with its assumed greater inequality of incomes in cities) on overall inequality. As Lindert and Williamson put it, "the urban transition was certainly dramatic enough to give Kuznets's hypothesis a chance to shine. And shine it does on all three counts."[18] Between 1800 and 1860, the difference between urban and rural wages increased in the United States from a practically nonexistent 1 percent to 27 percent; in the South, the gap increased from 8 percent to 28 percent. In terms of overall incomes, US urban incomes in 1860 were 35 percent higher than rural incomes. Finally, in 1860 (the year for which, as Lindert and Williamson note, inequality data are best), US urban Gini was 58.5 points and rural Gini 48 points.

Table 6.1 summarizes Lindert and Williamson's estimates of US inequality and growth from 1774 to 1929. Over that period, US average income quintupled, with growth rates in most years exceeding Kuznets's own requirement for the setup of modern economic growth (at least one percent per capita annually). Inequality peaked around the 1860s, and remained near that high plateau until the 1930s. After that, inequality began its long decline (this was "the great leveling"). If we look at inequality in terms of the top one percent share, then the rise of inequality continued up to the First World War, after which it stabilized. By either indicator, therefore, inequality behaved as Kuznets averred. The only question is whether US inequality peaked in the last decades of the nineteenth century or in the first decade of the twentieth century.

Table 6.1   Inequality and Mean Income in the United States, 1774–1929

	Inequality		Income
	Gini	Top one percent share	GDP per capita (Maddison Project)
1774	44.1		2419
1800	~40		2545
1850	48.7		3632
1860	51.1		4402
1870	51.1	9.8	4803
1910		17.8	9637
1913		18.0	10108
1920		14.5	10153
1929	49.0	18.4	11954

Data sources: For Gini and top one percent share: Lindert and Williamson, *Unequal Gains,* 18, 115–16, 154, 173. Inequality estimates include all households (including slaves before 1870). Inequality in 1800 is approximated based on Lindert and Williamson statement that it was lower than in 1774 (95). For GDP per capita: Maddison Project, 2020 version.

The mechanism charted by Kuznets is simple and magisterial. With little more than a thumbnail sketch, we can already see the similarities between his model and the experience of many societies, and grasp a hypothesis about the evolution of inequality as society develops. It is clear that, in Kuznets's view, inequality responds to structural change in the economy—although, in later empirical studies, structural change was replaced, for reasons of econometric convenience, by an increase in GDP per capita. It is also clear from the model that the increase in inequality has a natural limit. The rural-urban gap is at its maximum when the society is divided into two groups of equal size (assuming given wage rates in the two sectors), but once most of the county has become urbanized, the contribution of the gap will be small. We can see this very clearly in almost all fully urbanized countries. In the United States, for example, no matter how large the gap, the tiny share of the rural population (less than 2 percent) ensures that the gap itself cannot affect overall US inequality much. The situation is different in China, given its still relatively low degree of urbanization; it has followed the course charted by Kuznets and the emergence of a rural-urban gap has been a key contributor to its increasing overall inequality.

This first (rising) portion of the Kuznets curve is also often associated with Arthur Lewis's 1954 model of growth with unlimited supplies of labor.[19] Kuznets's model, too, can be seen as one of urban areas (or the manufacturing sector) "sucking up" rural labor, at an unchanged wage rate, until the supply of new labor simply runs out. At that point, all the action moves to the cities, where capitalists, facing a supply constraint, become obliged to operate under conditions of rising real wages. Thus, Kuznets's model can be seen as a version of Lewis's. Lewis did not, however, see a growing divergence between urban and rural wages (one of the key requirements for Kuznets-type movement). His belief was that Marx's "reserve army of labor" would always see to it that such divergence did not happen.[20]

What happens after inequality reaches a very high level? According to Kuznets (as is clear from his comments quoted above), when the economy's total income becomes relatively high, three new forces are set in motion. First, the difference in productivity between the non-agricultural and agricultural sectors diminishes, thus reducing the urban-rural wage gap. Second, because the society, being richer, has more capital, the greater abundance of capital drives the rate of return on capital lower and thus reduces the relative incomes of the rich. And third, greater societal wealth allows the society to introduce old-age pensions, unemployment and accident insurance, and other social programs that further blunt the forces of inequality.

Thus, the downward portion of the Kuznets curve also looks very reasonable. Note that, in effect, the main force acting on this side of the curve is the greater wealth accumulated during the previous period of rising inequality. As well as allowing more generous social spending, this greater wealth lowers the rate of return on capital, which reduces the incomes of the rich. Indeed, greater social spending and pro-labor legislation has been the experience of Western European economies, not only in Kuznets's time but also earlier. Limits were placed on working days and hours, factory legislation was introduced in the second half of the nineteenth century in England, and social insurance was enacted in Bismarck's Germany. As for the lower returns to capital, Kuznets's prediction echoed previous ones from Smith and Marx, who both, as we have seen, expected gradual decreases in the rate of profit and, by implication, decreases in inequality.

Kuznets's model is intuitive, and easily understood, but more complex than it seems at first. It features five variables that all change over time: the share of the urban population, the level of rural inequality, the level of urban inequality, the mean rural income, and the mean urban income. The interaction of these variables generates two principal country-level variables—mean income and inequality— also varying over time. But the change occurring in these variables is not all that determines the type of Kuznets curve they produce; their levels (for example, the initial level of rural inequality, and so on) matter, too. Obviously, the speed of urban transition also matters, and so does the size of the gap between urban and rural incomes. Kuznets in his 1955 paper thus devotes considerable effort to presenting various numerical examples of the process and discussing under what assumptions the steepness of the increase in inequality (in the first portion of the curve) may be the greatest, or how quickly inequality might decline. It is clear that the possibilities are almost infinite. The key thing is that, based on Kuznets's three assumptions— rising urbanization, higher mean income in urban areas, and higher inequality in urban areas (but with a peak, after which it decreases)— we can generate over time a parabolic movement in inequality measures and rising overall mean income.[21] We thus link urbanization and structural transformation with modern growth, and can additionally derive an estimate of how the fruits of that modern growth will be distributed among citizens. It is hard to think of another economic model that answers such hugely important questions so, well, *economically*.

Figure 6.2 depicts one example, using the Theil index instead of Gini because Theil is exactly decomposable into its "between" component (inequality due to the urban-rural gap) and its "within"

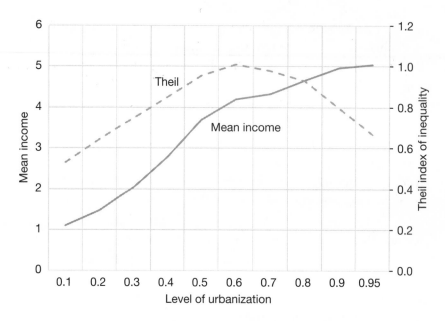

Figure 6.2. Mean income and inequality in a simple Kuznets model

Note: Calculations based on various assumptions consistent with Kuznets's hypothesis.

component (inequality due to the sum of rural and urban inequalities). Here, we assume that the urban-rural income gap and urban inequality both rise until 70 percent of the population has transferred to the urban areas, after which point both decline. For simplicity, we keep rural inequality constant (and lower than urban inequality throughout, of course). These are simple, reasonable, and not particularly demanding assumptions. They readily generate an inverted U-shaped curve of inequality, and they produce an overall mean income that is at first rising very fast and then decelerating. This example, which took me about half an hour to create, highlights the flexibility of Kuznets's approach, but also its power: by changing the numbers in a spreadsheet (much easier to do today than in Kuznets's days, when the results for each iteration had to be calculated by hand), we can vary the results, but as long as we stick to the three key assumptions, the shape of the curve will be the same.

The Kuznets hypothesis represented a very stylized picture of the evolution of income inequality; it was a mix of, as Kuznets said, "perhaps 5 per cent empirical information and 95 per cent speculation, some of it possibly tainted by wishful thinking."[22] In his original formulation of it, Kuznets cited the supporting experience of only six countries: the UK, the United States, and Germany, with their fragmentary long-term data going back to the nineteenth century, and India, Sri Lanka, and the Philippines, with one observation each from the early 1950s. Yet the appeal of the hypothesis was manifold: it provided an empirically testable story regarding the evolution of income distribution as economies develop; it maintained the "conversation" with classical writers in allowing for a "tendency of the rate of profit to fall"; and it broadly fitted patterns observed in the rising industrial powers. Moreover, it seemed that this pattern might be repeated among the developing countries, including Japan, Turkey, Brazil, and South Korea, as they followed the path charted by more advanced Western countries. It was an explanation of economic history and a forecast of the movement of inequality in the future. Its weakest point was its assumption of relatively equal distribution predating the industrial takeoff. But, as we have seen, in some cases even that assumption could be defended.

The hypothesis did have a precursor, although not from economics. When Alexis de Tocqueville published his *Memoir on Pauperism* in 1835, 120 years before Kuznets enounced his hypothesis, he made the same point:

> If one looks closely at what has happened to the world since the beginning of societies, it is easy to see that equality is prevalent only at the historical poles of civilization. Savages are equal because they are equally weak and ignorant. Very civilized men can all become equal because they all have at their disposal similar means of attaining comfort and happiness. Between these two extremes is found inequality of conditions, wealth, knowledge—the power of the few, the poverty, ignorance, and weakness of all the rest.[23]

It is very unlikely that Kuznets knew of the *Memoir,* which was not included in Tocqueville's collected works published in French in the 1860s.[24] Its first English translation was published only in 1968. But we might not be wrong to think of the Kuznets hypothesis as the Tocqueville-Kuznets hypothesis. Nevertheless I shall continue to follow the conventional approach in this chapter and refer to the hypothesis, curve, and inverted U curve discussed here as Kuznets's.

The Curve That Was Defined Too Early?

The Kuznets hypothesis attracted enormous attention not only for the reasons just explained, but also because its formulation coincided with the period when more detailed data on income distribution were first becoming available from tax sources and, increasingly, from the household surveys that began to be fielded in the 1960s. Kuznets himself, as mentioned, broke new ground with his work on income distribution in the United States in the late 1940s and early 1950s; in a 1953 publication he showed a significant reduction in US inequality in the years leading up to and during World War II.[25] That led economist Arthur Burns to proclaim an American "inequality revolution." Since the end of the 1920s, Burns argued, the United States had made a rapid transformation from a high level of income inequality and was progressing toward what would constitute full equality:

> If we now compare 1929 and 1946, we find that the share going to the top 5 per cent group declined 16 points. Had perfect equality of incomes been attained in 1946 the share would have dropped from 34 to 5 per cent, that is, by 29 points. In other words, the income share of the top 5 per cent stratum dropped 16 points out of a maximum possible drop of 29 points; so that, on the basis of this yardstick, we may be said to have traveled in a bare two decades over half the distance separating the 1929 distribution from a perfectly egalitarian distribution.[26]

Shifting the focus to the top one percent, Burns added that the results there were even more striking: the United States had traveled two-thirds of the distance from the 1929 situation to absolute income equality. Between these American developments and, as the 1950s unfolded, similar developments in western Europe, there almost appeared to be an economic law by which lower inequality came with higher incomes. For those working in the new area of development economics, the implication was that developing countries could be expected to traverse the same path as the developed, so that after a phase when growth pushed inequality upward, there would be a turning point, and inequality would then begin to decrease. Two interesting observations can be made about this take on the Kuznets hypothesis: first, in a new way, it repeated the Marxist argument that more developed countries, further along on the path to development, reveal that path to those who follow; and second, it encouraged a form of complacency among development economists, leading many to think that it was sufficient to tend to growth, because growth (that is, higher income level) would in turn take care of inequality. The latter view took hold strongly among economists, whether their focus was on developed or developing countries, and might have contributed to the neglect of income distribution studies between the 1960s and the end of the century. Chapter 7 will explore this possibility.

It became enormously popular in the 1970s and 1980s to test the Kuznets hypothesis with available data.[27] But while the hypothesis, as originally formulated, clearly had to do with how inequality changed in an individual country as it proceeded along the path from underdevelopment to becoming developed, the long-term data required to test the theory were unavailable in the 1970s. Therefore, those who worked on the Kuznets hypothesis relied either on a mix of pooled time-series and cross-sectional data, or entirely on cross-sectional data.[28] The strict implication of using such data—to put it in Kuznets's framework—was that every single country would have to display the Kuznets curve in exactly the same fashion. This obviously stretched credulity. Suppose that both Brazil and Sweden follow the Kuznets curve. At a given time in the 1970s they would be at different income positions (with Sweden more to the right in a chart such as Figure 6.2), and the underlying curves that Brazil and Sweden were "traveling" on might be quite different in their heights (Gini coefficients, plotted on the vertical axis) even if both looked like an inverted U. Therefore, putting all the Gini numbers together might result in something that resembled the Kuznets relationship, as indeed most of the regressions found the required signs on the coefficients of income per capita and squared income per capita, but the goodness of the fit would probably be very low. One such relationship, where no additional control variables are used, is displayed in Figure 6.3. Using data spanning almost half a century, it shows that, while the quadratic relationship between income level and inequality can be discerned, the R-squared is very low (here only 0.12)—so low that the data points look more like a random blur than a distribution belonging to one specific relationship.

Many have tried to solve this problem by introducing controls whose function was, as just implied, to adjust for countries' idiosyncrasies while maintaining the test of the hypothesis of an inverted U. In such regressions, one would expect coefficients on log income and log income squared to be of the correct sign (the first positive, the second negative), while other control variables would make the model more realistic and improve the R-squared.* For example, Williamson and Higgins introduced openness to trade and age structure of the population; Milanovic introduced the extent of trade unionization and the share of state sector employment; Ahluwalia and, later, Kaelble and Thomas introduced the socialist dummy variable (socialist countries were expected to display lower

---

*This was the Kuznets hypothesis's "weak" formulation; the "strong" formulation would be the one in which income alone mattered. Note, however, that Kuznets's strict formulation did not see inequality changing with income but with the structure of the economy (industrialization and urbanization). The structure of the economy was more difficult to approximate with a single variable, and less available internationally, and was replaced (in my opinion, reasonably) by real percapita income.

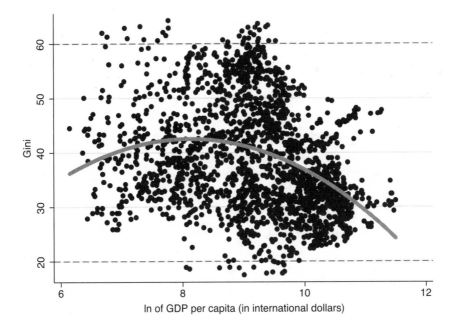

Figure 6.3. Relationship between GDP per capita and inequality, 1970–2014
(pooled cross-sectional and time-series data)

Note: Each dot represents a country/year with its GDP per capita in 2011
international dollars (in logs) and Gini coefficient of disposable income (expressed
in percentages). The thick line is based on the regression of Gini on log income.
The two horizontal dotted lines show the approximate lower and upper bounds of
the Gini coefficient.

Data sources: "All the Ginis" data set, World Bank, World Development Indicators,
Washington, DC.

inequality).[29] Anand and Kanbur argued that the standard quadratic
functional form used to test the hypothesis was wrong.[30] In something
akin to a holy grail quest, economists sought to discover the turning
point of the Kuznets curve—the income level at which inequality begins to decrease. This proved elusive, and impossible to establish.
Many of these adjustments made sense for the reason just explained:
they were ways to distinguish between the underlying characteristics
of the countries while allowing each to follow its own inverted U. On
the other hand, some were only the kinds of adjustments scientists
resort to when attempting to prop up a "degenerating program" of

research, to use Imre Lakatos's term—new assumptions added to extend the life of an increasingly dubious hypothesis.[31]

It was also argued that the peak of inequality found in cross-sectional studies around the middling level of income was an artifact of the data. More unequal Latin American countries just happened also to be at the middle level of income.[32] But suppose that Latin America were as rich as the West. Given that its "original" or underlying inequality was greater (for reasons having to do with history), would that not move the peak of the inverted U curve too much to the right to coincide with the most developed countries? In that case, there would be no inverted U-shaped curve.

The *coup de grâce* for the Kuznets hypothesis came, however, from a different direction. In the early 1980s, the advanced economies of the United States and Western Europe entered a decades-long inequality upswing—a trend that could not at all be reconciled with Kuznets's original formulation. Kuznets had defined his hypothesis in a way that left no doubt: rich countries had to remain at a point of relatively low inequality. Their inequality levels could not go up. Indeed, there was nothing at all in Kuznets's writings that would allow for inequality to increase after sufficient economic maturity had been reached. Already limping along as a "degenerating" paradigm, the Kuznets hypothesis seemed to many, with these incompatible developments, beyond saving. Yet, the declarations of its death might have been premature.

A Possible Revival

Ironically, at the same time that real-world inconsistencies with the Kuznets hypothesis were becoming obvious, new support came in the unexpected form of better data. Kuznets had always presented his story as one that holds for a given country over time, but since long-term studies were unavailable, those attempting to test the hypothesis had been using cross-sectional data. In the early 2000s, many more long-term estimates of inequality (like the one for the United States shown in Figure 6.1) became available. Over such

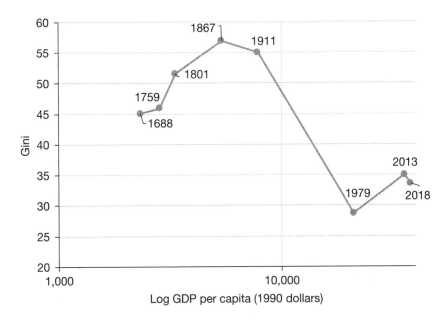

Figure 6.4. Long-run Kuznets curve for England/United Kingdom 1688–2018

Data sources: From 1759 to 1911: calculated from social tables produced by
Gregory King (1688), Joseph Massie (1759), Patrick Colquhoun (1801), Dudley
Baxter (1867), and Arthur L. Bowley (1911), as reworked by Peter H. Lindert and
Jeffrey G. Williamson, "Revising England's Social Tables 1688–1812, *Explorations
in Economic History* 19 (1982): 385–408; from 1979: LIS Cross-National Data
Center; Maddison Project Database in 1990 international dollars.

long time periods, the essential contours of the Kuznets curve,
whether one looked at American or German data (as displayed in
Figure 4.3) or British or Chinese data (displayed in Figures 6.4 and
6.5), seemed to hold. Instead of one Kuznets curve, however, there
might be two, successive in time. The British data, like the American
data, show a second upswing beginning in the early 1980s, and
even the hint of a second downward portion from approximately
2015. China, whose industrialization lags behind the West and includes, in addition to the usual Kuznets-type transformation, the
transformation from a socialist to a mostly capitalist economy, ex-
hibits a very sharp upward portion of the Kuznets curve. This portion comes to an end around 2010 as the supply of cheap rural

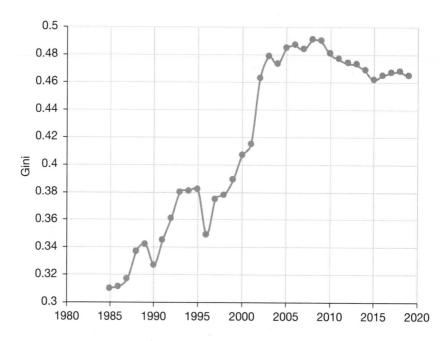

Figure 6.5. Kuznets curve for China, 1985–2019

Data sources: For 1985 to 2002: Ximing Wu and Jeffrey Perloff, "China's Distribution and Inequality," *Review of Economics and Statistics* 87:4 (2005): 763–775. For 2003 to 2019: National Bureau of Statistics.

labor wanes, the skills premium decreases, and more extensive social programs spread to rural areas. In the latest decade, China has
clearly seemed to be engaged in a downward portion of a Kuznets
curve. Its aging population and thus increasing demand for social
transfers, another element mentioned by Kuznets, also plays a role.

Additional strong historical evidence in favor of the curve came
with data on Western European nations before and during the Industrial Revolution. Jan Luiten van Zanden, for example, was able
to describe a "super Kuznets curve" that began in early modern
Europe around 1500; he charted the inverted U shape it took over
the next two centuries.[33] In my own work, I have previously argued
that such historical, wave-like changes are similar to Malthusian cycles (although broader in their causal factors, since they can be triggered by developments such as gold inflows, epidemics, and wars).[34]

But as they occurred against the backdrop of an unchanged historical mean income, the Kuznets waves could be seen only if plotted against time, and not against GDP per capita. In the latter case, the data points would appear only as a blur of dots against a more or less fixed GDP per capita on the horizontal axis.

I have also argued elsewhere that the Kuznets curve could be logically extended to all periods of rapid technological change where a growing sector and its impact on the composition of the labor force would push inequality up.[35] Thus, the increase of inequality in Western countries in the 1980s and 1990s could be seen as just another Kuznets wave, not dissimilar to the one Kuznets described at mid-century. Substitute service-sector employment for manufacturing employment, and manufacturing employment for agricultural employment, and one gets a new version of how the transfer of labor to an inherently more productive and diverse sector offering a greater variety of wage rates (in this case, the service sector) explains the increase in inequality. The forces that would overturn this development are not as clear as in the original case, but one could argue that with passage of time and increased competition there might be a dissipation of the high rents accruing to the companies and company owners who lead the technological change. This would put a damper on further increases in inequality. As in Kuznets's own presentation, political demands for higher social transfers and higher taxation to finance them would stop inequality from rising. Or even reduce it.

Thus, the Kuznets hypothesis was kept alive by the timely arrival of long-term evidence to support it, and by the replacement of a single Kuznets curve with a potentially unlimited number of Kuznets waves driven by technological revolutions. Despite its ups and downs, the Kuznets hypothesis is still with us.

Kuznets's Contributions

Several very important contributions were made by Simon Kuznets. For the first time in the history of economics, his hypothesis clearly linked movements in income inequality to structural transformations of economies (or to rising mean income as a proxy). This marked a sharp break from Pareto's view that income inequality remained at a fixed level under all socioeconomic systems and would thus be unaffected by structural transformation.

As we have seen, all classical authors—and Smith and Marx in particular—did perceive that income inequality evolved in response to structural changes, but none of them had defined the linkage clearly. Their thoughts on the matter have to be pieced together from dispersed mentions. Yet, for both Smith and Marx, the rate of return on invested capital was likely to decrease as capital became more abundant and capitalists increasingly competed with each other. As for wages, Smith believed they would tend to go up, while Marx was more circumspect. Writing a century later than Marx, Kuznets could see clearly that real wages do rise in the process of development, and, unlike Marx, he believed the capital share would go down. It is, in fact, remarkable that Smith, Marx, and Kuznets do agree on the likely evolution of factoral payments: wages going up, the rate of profit going down.

The great contributions of the Kuznets hypothesis were its more explicit statement of what changes in inequality could be expected in times of structural change, and its fairly plausible identification of the mechanism involved—a mechanism that isn't as simple as variations in factor incomes (wages versus profits) but also involves changes in urbanization, the age structure of the population, the demand for social protection, and more. The introduction of these additional elements might at first glance seem like a "kitchen sink" approach, throwing together every plausible factor—and this was a problem with some early testing of the Kuznets hypothesis. It is, however, possible to limit the number of additional elements to ones that are consistent with Kuznets's original, minimalist spirit (for example, the decline in the capital share, and an aging population, with its greater demand for social transfers), so that the hypothesis remains well defined and sufficiently specific.

The greater specificity of the link Kuznets described between structural change and inequality level enabled empirical testing of the hypothesis and made it subject to falsifiability. Its success was not, as we have seen, always guaranteed, and the Kuznets hypothesis engendered a fair amount of controversy and even rejection, especially as inequality in most developed countries moved, from the 1980s, unmistakably upward. Nor could that movement be easily dismissed as unrepresentative, since it involved practically all OECD countries and lasted for at least three and perhaps even four decades. Growing dissatisfaction with the explanatory power of the Kuznets curve led to broader skepticism that any theory linking inequality to structural changes in the economy could be developed. Note, for example, that Tony Atkinson, writing in 1997, and Peter Lindert, in 2000, refer only to "episodes" of rising and decreasing inequality, without attributing them to general laws.[36] This is a point of view still shared by many economists. But, as I will argue in the Epilogue, a model can remain useful even if measured changes do not always obey its predictions. By reformulating the Kuznets hypothesis, devoting closer attention to Marx's predictions, and making use of Piketty's novel approach from *Capital in the Twenty-First Century,* we gain new and powerful lenses for examining inequality—these three paradigms all give useful structure to our thinking.

While Kuznets's approach differed decisively from Pareto's, there are similarities in the fates of their theories. Neither Pareto's nor Kuznets's view came out unscathed from empirical testing, and neither can be accepted fully in its original form. But both are still very much present in today's work on inequality. Pareto's contribution is more obvious in the methods used in work on income distribution. Kuznets's contribution endures in our understanding of the evolution of inequality in countries like Brazil and China, and even in the advanced economies (although not everyone shares this point of view). Their contributions remain, in their different forms, and they will live on, albeit possibly in yet another modified fashion.

Locality and Universality in All Authors Studied Here

As we conclude our consideration of Kuznets and prepare to move on from "the giants," it is worth reemphasizing how profoundly these towering figures were influenced by their social contexts. Their work mirrored the conditions not only of their times but of the places where they were born, lived, traveled, and worked. Quesnay was interested almost exclusively in the wealth of France. His class structure, and the income distribution that went with it, is an embellished copy of the French situation in the second half of the eighteenth century. Smith's *Wealth of Nations* is, in many parts, a summary of British (or indeed even Scottish) economic developments. Ricardo's case is the most extreme: his entire book was written as a treatise on contemporary British laws. Marx took Britain explicitly as his "capitalist paragon," even if at times he regretted not having chosen the United States, or at least not having taken it more seriously. For Pareto, it was France and Italy that mattered above all. And Kuznets's theory, especially as it posits low inequality in preindustrial societies, was closely patterned after American experience.

At the same time, however, each of them did have in mind the broader world, and sought to develop theories with universal validity. Quesnay was laying down the rules of how, in general, nations become rich; his aspiration to universalism is shown by his readiness to propose Chinese (or what he thought were Chinese) solutions for a country as historically and geographically different from China as France. Smith called his magnum opus *The Wealth of Nations,* also showcasing the forces that, in his view, would make *nations* prosper; he did not call it "How Britain Became Rich." Marx's universal objectives were quite obvious, not least because he was a social activist equally at ease in France and Belgium as in Germany and England, and was the founder of "The International" (again, not a title that was randomly chosen). His work faced, like Smith's before him, the problem of applicability to the rest of the world. This was especially evident in Marx's case because his theories became accepted by dedicated followers in every corner of the world and had to be modified to suit local conditions. Pareto's universality shows up, paradoxically, in his denial that differences in history or social systems could produce differences in income distribution. Finally, Kuznets's approach, conceived with rich countries in mind, endured because it was transplanted into development economics, where it was able to survive a prolonged deep-freeze period for inequality studies in neoclassical economics and more generally in developed capitalist economies. (That period, which would begin soon after Kuznets's main contributions, is the topic of Chapter 7.) All our authors thus combined their national focus, and even very local interests, with much broader pretensions—and indeed their broader claims resonated with many, and won them millions of readers and followers around the world.

Kuznets's celebrated essay, presented in 1955 as his presidential address to the American Economic Association, ends with the following injunction:

> If we are to deal adequately with processes of economic growth, processes of long-term change in which the very technological, demographic, and social frameworks are also changing—and in ways that decidedly affect the operation of economic forces proper—it is inevitable that we venture into fields beyond those recognized in recent decades as the province of economics proper. For the study of the economic growth of nations, it is imperative that we become more familiar with findings in those related social disciplines that can help us understand population growth patterns, the nature and forces in technological change, the factors that determine the characteristics and trends in political institutions, and generally patterns of behavior of human beings—partly as a biological species, partly as social animals. Effective work in this field necessarily calls for a shift from market economics to political and social economy.[37]

As we shall see in Chapter 7, this recommendation went unheeded. The next fifty years did not produce individual economists who had the breadth of vision of the six economists we have studied so far. To the contrary, we might say that economics as a field stagnated or even regressed, at least in its understanding of income distribution under modern capitalism. That this happened despite remarkable progress in the availability of data, new techniques of data manipulation, and greater computer power is rather stunning, and requires an explanation. To find it, we can look in three directions: the geopolitics of the Cold War era, the turn taken in economics toward the abstract, and the funding of research by the rich (who, following their own interests, were not particularly inclined to support income inequality studies).

CHAPTER SEVEN

The Long Eclipse of Inequality Studies during the Cold War

For a line of work on inequality to be meaningful—to meet the standard stated in the Prologue of being an integrative study of income distribution—it needs to have three features. First, it needs a narrative of what drives inequality and what are (in its author's view) the most important factors or forces behind it. In other words, it needs to start with a politically or economically motivating story. In all the classical works reviewed here we find such motivating stories. Second, in line with that story, the author needs to develop a theory. Theory does not need to be expressed in mathematics, and often is not—not even by more contemporary authors such as Kuznets—but it does have to have an outline of the relationships between relevant variables. Third, there must be empirical "verification" of the theoretical and narrative claims. Empirics were often lacking in work by classical authors simply because they did not have the required data. But today, such data are an indispensable part of a successful approach to inequality. It is with these three elements in mind that I will now consider how income distribution was studied in socialist and capitalist economies in the period ranging (approximately) from the mid-1960s to 1990.

I have to begin with some historical background. Development of income distribution studies between the two world wars primarily followed the vicissitudes of politics, and was influenced only secondarily by those of economics. The politics of the time were extraordinarily tumultuous, with successful revolutions in Russia and China, failed revolutions in Germany and Hungary, dissolution of five empires, the beginnings of anticolonial struggles in China, India, Vietnam, and Indonesia, and the rise of fascism in Europe and Japan. Although the destruction of property and lives among the belligerents during the Great War had increased poverty and created new inequalities, no systematic studies of income distribution were produced. In fact, there was a marked decline of interest in such topics. To today's observer, it seems that everything between 1918 and 1937–1939 happened too quickly, with one crisis being succeeded by another. Hyperinflation was followed by the Depression, the Depression by nativist policies, nativist policies by the War, and there was little time to do much work on anything related to new inequalities—except in Soviet Russia, where class and hence inequality issues were studied more thoroughly and, in due course, had important and violent political consequences.

Elsewhere, even Keynes, whose famous introductory paragraphs in *The Economic Consequences of the Peace* clearly showed that he was not unaware of the importance of income inequality for the sustainability of societies, assigned almost no role to inequality in his 1936 *General Theory*.[1] As the most obvious place for it in the Keynesian system, there could have been a discussion of its affecting the aggregate marginal propensity to consume, and hence determining the multiplier and the effect of a given increase in government spending—yet even there, inequality was ignored. Indeed, Keynes made the assumption of an unchanged income distribution throughout—for convenience, treating inequality and the aggregate propensity to consume as fixed or at least as parameters. It was left to Hans Staehle to point out a year after the *General Theory*, in a very nice article using German data, how much wage distribution varies and how this in turn affects the marginal propensity to consume.[2] In retrospect, one of the justifications for ignoring income distribution came (and continued to come after World War II) from a general acceptance of what had been termed Bowley's Law, a massively overgeneralized conclusion based on a single empirical study of one country. Arthur Bowley had calculated factor shares in Great

Britain during the early years of the twentieth century and found them approximately stable.[3] This research gave rise to an assumption that factor shares were invariant over the long run.* And if factoral income distribution does not change, the story continued, then personal income distribution must also be close to constant.[4]

We see here a beginning of an explanation of the eclipse of income distribution studies after the Second World War, and the broader point on which this chapter shall insist: whenever the class division is supposed either to be fixed or not to matter, interpersonal income distribution studies fall into a desuetude. There is no logical reason why this should be so; factoral income distribution can be stable while changes occur in the distributions of both wage incomes and incomes from property (and household formation, linking the two). Yet, while this is formally true, we will see that the effect of minimizing class importance, or wishful thinking that classes had ceased to exist, was to cripple, marginalize. and make superfluous studies of income distribution. We found this among the authors of the nineteenth and early twentieth century and will find it again among those of the second half of the twentieth century. When class analysis and the role of capital incomes are ignored, studies of income distribution are, too.

This is exactly what happened after the Second World War, when the competition between communism and capitalism pushed economics, on both sides, into service of the ruling ideologies' political ends. Both camps shared the belief that, within their own systems, classes were the thing of the past, class divisions no longer existed, and work on income distribution was all but irrelevant. There was, they thought, not much to study.

In a simple table, reproduced below, Martin Bronfenbrenner nicely summarizes three leading positions on distribution problems. Both the capitalists (or neoclassicals) and the Marxists believe that, once the right background institutions are in place (in the capitalists'

---

*Recall from Chapter 4 that, in fact, factor shares varied significantly in England during the nineteenth century, and Marx considered a decreasing labor share to be a central feature of developed capitalism.

Table 7.1   Three Leading Positions on Distributional Problems

	Importance of distribution	Desirable property share	Desirable wage differentiation
Capitalist [neoclassical]	Minor	Finite	Large
Social-democratic	Major	Infinitesimal [small]	Small
Communist [Marxist]	Minor	Infinitesimal	Large

Source: Martin Bronfenbrenner, *Income Distribution Theory* (Chicago: Aldine-Atherton, 1971), table 1.1, 6, with modifications by Milanovic in brackets.

case, a free market and the inviolability of property; in the Marxists' case, abolition of private ownership), there is no reason to worry about high wage differentiation or to consider income distribution a major issue.[5] A disappearance of work on these topics is exactly what happened during the Cold War under both systems.

In the next section, we will explore how this belief was driven in socialist countries by an effective elimination of the traditional Ricardian or Marxian capitalist class, which had derived its income from ownership of property. This meant that all incomes were the product of labor and, since (according to this view) the background institutions now made exploitation impossible, such labor incomes as existed were justified. Additionally, the differences between incomes were small and not worthy of investigation.

The elimination of class-based analysis thus eliminated concern with income distribution. It is true that, in the place of the old classes, a new class structure was erected, as will be argued below, but discussion of this reality was not something that communist authorities were willing to endorse or even condone. Thus, a combination of factors both "objective" (the elimination of the traditional property-owning class) and "subjective" (a political dictatorship committed to the idea of a classless society and seeing studies of inequality as a possible ideological weapon against it) put an end to any serious research into income inequality in socialist economies.

Not much different was the situation in the West. There, too, "objective" factors exerted influence on what economics research was favored, and downplayed the importance of income distribution. Economics as a discipline saw its center of gravity shift from the class-divided Europe to the much more class-fluid United States, and the most influential American economists did not see class structure in the same way it was seen in Europe by classical economists, or as it appeared in older societies like China, India, the Middle East, and the historically unequal Latin America. The American Dream, where everyone could dream of wealth regardless of their background, had been part of the country's ideology since its founding. It was, however, more forcefully promulgated during the Cold War to diminish the appeal of Marxism, to render irrelevant the Soviet claim of having eliminated classes, and to disprove the characterization of capitalist societies as irredeemably class-divided and unequal. In other words, so long as the socialist camp claimed to have abolished class divisions, the American camp had to claim the same thing—that classes did not matter in their own countries. Here, too, economists were discouraged from undertaking income distribution studies by the combination of an "objective" factor (less salient class division in the United States) and a "subjective" one (an ideology unreceptive to evidence of such divisions even where they existed, such as in racial discrimination).

The discipline of economics, to the extent that its evolution can be considered independent of the political influences noted above, also became inimical to the study of inequality. The dominant approach of general equilibrium analysis concerned itself with the determination of relative prices of final outputs and factors of production. Incomes of participants in an economy are, according to the neoclassics, by definition equal to the product of factor prices (equal to their marginal products) and the quantities of endowments of capital and labor with which they enter the economic process. But these quantities of endowments themselves are outside the ambit of general equilibrium analysis. Whether endowments, and principally property, were acquired through previous market transactions, pillage, exploitation, inheritance, monopoly, or whatever other means was not the subject of economics as the science of relative prices. Pareto optimum, which is simply a validation of the current holding of assets by whoever holds them, is a perfect complement to that theory.[6] Neoclassics had almost nothing to say about what Marx called "the primitive accumulation" and what Smith saw as property acquired through political influence, monopoly, and plunder (see Chapter 2). In economics, links with the classics had been severed.

This methodological preference pulled the rug out from under class analysis, since owners of labor power and owners of capital were formally seen as equivalent agents who just differed in the factors of production they owned. Economics became the science of the present, slightly related to the future through saving and investment decisions, but fully disconnected from the past. This attempt to introduce formal equivalency between the two factors of production—one requiring constant work effort to yield an income, and the other demanding no work of its owner to yield a return—was well captured by Milton and Rose Friedman's quip, "to each according to what he and the instruments he owns produce."[7] It turned the classical (and especially Marxist) distinction between the two factors of production and classes on its head. Using the same language, in a semi-mocking way, it claimed that classes did not exist in any meaningful fashion—it was just that people owned different assets. This approach no longer saw the distribution as taking place among individuals; instead, it was among individuals and objects (capital). It failed to recognize that the marginal productivity of capital is a technical matter, and that capital yields an income to its owner only when there is a "social contract" or economic system in place that enables owners of tools (including capital) to collect the products of the tools they own. Surely, labor endowment did not yield any income to the slave— because the system did not recognize the self-appropriation of the fruits yielded by that endowment. The social relations underpinning capitalism were entirely ignored.

The neoclassical approach sought to "naturalize" relations of production. That is, it treated relations of production not as specific to a certain way of organizing production and certain stage of development, but as the only possible, "natural" order of things. There was, strictly speaking, no capitalism either. The effect of this naturalization, which denied the relevance of the social relations people enter into in the processes of production and distribution, was to efface class structure and make the study of income distribution superfluous.

Thus, researchers in communist and capitalist countries similarly lived and worked in what we can call the Cold War economics period. Political imperatives intersected with the "objectively" diminished visibility of traditional classes to deny relevance to any integrative work on income distribution.

Systems of Nonprivate Ownership of Capital: Inequality in the Socialist Market Economy

One of Marx's most important insights concerns the historical character of the "normal" (or long-run equilibrium) price. In the Marxist literature, this is generally discussed under the heading of the transformation problem, where the normal (labor-value) prices in a market economy based on small-scale commodity production are, as the economy evolves, transformed into new normal (capitalist) prices, the "prices of production." Prices of production differ from prices based only on labor inputs because of the ability of capital to move from one sector to another, which leads to the equalization of the rates of profit across sectors. This is different from value formation in petty-commodity production, where capital is largely immobile and where rates of return, even in equilibrium, vary across sectors. Under the latter conditions, the long-run equilibrium price is equal to the "socially necessary" quantity of labor. But under capitalism, the normal price must include the same rate of return in both capital-intensive and labor-intensive sectors. Since the total labor input in capital-intensive sectors is, by definition, relatively small, prices of production in such sectors will be higher than their labor values; the opposite, of course, holds for labor-intensive sectors.

A similar transformation problem exists when an economy transforms from capitalist to socialist, assuming that socialism remains a commodity-producing system—that is, a system where products are "commodities" and not only "use values." As the best example of such a transformation, consider the worker-managed economy that existed in Yugoslavia. The objective function of a labor-managed enterprise is *maximization of output per worker,* as opposed to a capitalist firm's maximization of profit. Assuming that a company pays a user charge on capital that is "socially" owned (or, to simplify, owned by the state and being used by the company), the average wage per unit of type i labor employed in company j becomes

$$W_{ij} = p_j q_j - r K_j$$

where p_j and q_j are, respectively, the price and the quantity of output produced by company j, r is an economywide rate of return or user charge on capital, and K_j is the amount of capital controlled by the company. It should be noted that, in a worker-owned company, wage has to be subscripted by both the type of labor and the type of company, because workers within each company receive a greater or lesser return due to company-specific characteristics. Additional income may be due to a company's extra productivity, monopoly status, or other rent-like powers it enjoys that are not swept away by a capital user charge (and alternatively a company would see negative impact on wages if it lacked such advantages). Thus, identical workers will be paid differently depending on the sectors and companies employing them. It was well known in socialist Yugoslavia, and documented in the voluminous literature on market socialism, that workers in more capital-intensive sectors of production were better paid than workers in labor-intensive sectors.[8] Clearly, not all of the advantages of higher capital intensity were "mopped up" by the capital user charge. Working in a sector or company that had some monopoly power was even better. The key point is that, unlike in capitalism, where extra income from, say, monopoly power would translate into extra profits, here it boosted workers' wages. Therefore, identical workers in different sectors, or even in different companies within the same sector, were paid different wages. This was because the residual income claimants under market socialism are workers—while, under capitalism, they are the owners of capital.*

For income distribution, the implication of the difference in the residual claimant is twofold. First, everything else being the same, wages for a given type of labor will be more diversified under market socialism than under capitalism. Second, since there is no private appropriation of return to capital, that source of inequality will disappear. Because the ownership of capital in capitalist societies is always very skewed, the absence of private appropriation of return to capital is an element of significant importance for the reduction of inequality. In fact, one part of the return to either capital or management that was not fully taken by the state through the user charge would, under market socialism, emerge in the form of labor income—and this would be received by many people—while in capitalism it would be included in capital income and be received by few (rich) people.

This example highlights the fact that, under different socioeconomic systems, the difference in where the locus of entrepreneurship lies, whether capital is mobile across sectors or not, or whether the return from capital is received by capitalists or by the state, drives differences in "normal" or long-run equilibrium prices and in interpersonal income distributions. This is why, even at the most abstract level, we expect that income distribution under market socialism will not be the same as under capitalism—not merely as measured by an overall indicator like the Gini coefficient, but also regarding the individuals receiving high, middle, or low incomes. Workers' wages

---

* One could rationalize this difference in wages for the same labor by arguing that the wage rate in a socialist market economy is composed of two components: wage proper, and a management bonus that is greater in better-run companies. And since workers are managers, they should receive it. The argument is weakened, however, by the fact that the extra component varies not only in function of quality of management but also in function of monopoly power and capital intensity of production.

for a given type of labor should be *more* unequally distributed in market socialism than in capitalism, while overall inequality, thanks to nonprivate appropriation of capital income, may be *less*. And, obviously, some social classes (like capitalists) may be very small or not exist at all.

Systems of State Ownership of Capital: Inequality in the Planned Economy

Income distribution in planned economies was also driven by simple rules that reflected the nature of the system. It is at times argued that income distribution in a planned system is shaped by "voluntaristic" or ideological elements. On a very general level, this is true. One should not, however, emphasize such elements to the point of overlooking more important systemic causes. Income distribution in planned economies was not simply a reflection of communist ideology, but objectively determined by the main characteristics of the system (state ownership of capital) and requirements for its functioning—or, to put it in Marxist terms, for its "expanded reproduction."

As already mentioned, the marginalization (or all but elimination) of private ownership of capital is an inequality-reducing force, given that in capitalist economies the productive wealth (and hence, return from capital) is very unequally distributed. In a socialist society with state-owned capital, by contrast, we might imagine a situation in which everyone gets the same amount of capital income. In reality, however, planned economies were hierarchical or even class-based societies where the return from state-owned capital was not equally shared; one's income increased as one moved up the state and party hierarchy. The state and party hierarchy played, in fact, a role similar to that of a capitalist hierarchy (the latter, of course, determined by the amount of capital a person owned). In principle, a planned economy differs from a socialist market economy in that workers performing a given type of labor are paid equally regardless of which specific companies or sectors employ them. This is, of course, a description at a very high level of abstraction. There were, in fact, significant wage differences across sectors and republics in the USSR and other planned economies.[9] Intersectoral differences were the products, however, of discrete policy decisions to stimulate particular sectors of the economy (for example, in the well-known case of the mining sector in Poland) or to encourage a certain geographical distribution of production. The USSR pursued the latter objective when, to attract labor to harsh and sparsely populated Siberia, it paid workers of the same skill level higher wages there than elsewhere in the republic. But the point is that, unlike under market socialism, there are no systemic reasons in a planned economy for wages to vary within the same labor type.

There was, however, an ideological preference to eliminate the distinction between intellectual and manual labor, and thus to reduce the gap between wages of nonmanual and manual workers. This was true in both types of socialist economies. The returns to skill or education were less than under capitalism.[10] Given that the topic has been so thoroughly studied, it will suffice to offer just two illustrations here. Table 7.2 compares the wages of skilled and unskilled workers in a single country (Yugoslavia) under capitalism and early socialism. Table 7.3 shows a similar comparison pitting several European capitalist economies against three Central European socialist countries and the USSR. It is notable that, in the latter comparison, the socialist country with the *highest* nonmanual-to-manual wage ratio was still less unequal than the capitalist country with the *lowest* nonmanual-to-manual ratio. The two systems did not overlap at all. Table 7.3 also shows the ratio of managers' average wages to the average wages of all employed people, and again, the ratio is generally smaller under socialism.

When we compare skilled and unskilled wages in capitalist and socialist economies, we should not forget that free public education under socialism meant that, even without an ideological preference to improve the relative position of low-skilled workers, the compensatory differential between high-skilled and low-skilled workers had to be less.[11] The lower skill premium observed under

Table 7.2 Relative Wages in Yugoslavia under Capitalism and Early Socialism

Year	1938	1951
Low-skilled workers	1	1
Skilled workers	3.30	1.35
State administration (all employees)	1.66	1.03
White-collar employees (outside state administration)	2.00	1.10

Note: Low-skilled wage = 1.

Data source: Branko Horvat, *Ekonomska Teorija Planske Privrede* [Economic Theory of a Planned Economy] (Belgrade: Kultura, 1961), 162.

Table 7.3 Relative Wages in European Capitalist and Socialist Economies

	Ratio of average nonmanual wage to average manual wage in industry	Ratio of average manager wage to average wage of all employed
Capitalist economies		
Belgium	1.49	1.84
Denmark	1.30	
France	1.70	2.36
West Germany	1.38	1.42
UK	1.18	1.64
Range	*1.18–1.70*	*1.42–2.36*
Socialist economies		
Hungary	1.13	1.50
Poland	1.05	1.30
East Germany	1.05	
USSR	1.05	
Range	*1.05–1.13*	*1.3–1.5*

Note: Data for capitalist economies are for 1978; data for socialist economies are for 1980.

Data sources: Combines data from Dominique Redor, *Wage Inequalities in East and West,* trans. Rosemarie Bourgault (Cambridge: Cambridge University Press, 1992), tables 3.4 (61) and 3.10 (71).

socialism, in other words, should not be fully ascribed to ideological preferences.[12]

Finally, with regard to government redistribution, it is true that direct taxation and social transfers were relatively high in planned socialist economies (Table 7.4), but two points should be made. First, social transfers were determined by household demographics and

Table 7.4 Composition of Gross Income in Socialist, Capitalist, and Developing
Economies, 1980s (unweighted average; gross income = 100)

	Socialist economies	Capitalist economies	Developing economies
Primary income	77	85	90
Labor income	63	64	35
Self-employment income	13	14	48
Property income	1	5	6
Occupational (private) pensions	0	2	0
Social transfers	19	14	3
Pensions	13	12	2
Child benefits	4	1	1
Other cash transfers	2	1	0
Other income	5	1	7
Gross income	100	100	100
Total taxes	34	38	*n.a.*
Direct taxes	3	20	n.a.
Payroll tax (employee)	7	5	n.a.
Payroll tax (employer)	24	13	n.a.
GDP per capita in $PPP thousands (around year 1988)	5.5	14.0	1.8

Note: See source for underlying data citations. All averages are unweighted. Socialist
economies are Czechoslovakia, USSR, Bulgaria, Hungary, Yugoslavia, and Poland. Capitalist
economies are Australia, Canada, France, West Germany, Israel, New Zealand, Norway,
Spain, Sweden, the United Kingdom, and the United States. Developing economies are Cote
d'Ivoire, Ghana, Jordan, Peru, Madagascar, and Vietnam.

Data source: Milanovic, "Income, Inequality, and Poverty during the Transition from
Planned to Market Economy," table 2.3, 14.

not much by assessments of contributions or needs. And second, direct taxation was proportional—that is, it was a flat tax imposed almost solely on labor incomes. (Since capital incomes were minimal, taxing them highly or not would not have made much difference.) This made social transfers less redistributive than under mature capitalism with disbursements based on needs—for example, unemployment benefits, social pension, welfare payments (see Figure 7.1). The redistributory element of direct taxes was much less important in socialism because taxes were broadly proportional to income. In fact, it is striking how small a role direct taxes played in equalizing incomes, and likewise how little they figured in the public imaginary. (See Table 7.4.) This was also because they were withdrawn at source (automatically contributed by enterprises as they paid wages) and thus "hidden" from contributors who mostly thought of wages and incomes in net terms.[13]

We can now write a simplified equation for disposable per-capita income y_i in socialist planned economies as follows:

$$y_i = w_{is} + \alpha_i \bar{k} + b_i(d_i) - \bar{tw}_{is}$$

where w_{is} is the wage of person i at skill level s (which for simplicity may be assumed to take only two values, for skilled and unskilled labor); α_i is a hierarchical coefficient that increases with one's position in a state and party structure; $\bar{k}$ is country-average return from state-owned capital (which we can take to be equal to total non-labor income minus the amount used for gross investment, divided by the size of the population); b_i is the amount of social transfers, which depends on the demographic characteristics of the person or household (d_i); and $\bar{tw}_{is}$ is a given (flat) tax rate applied to labor income only. It becomes evident that income inequality will vary largely in function of the hierarchical coefficient α_i, which plays here the same role that capital ownership does under capitalism. All other conditions being the same, the more hierarchical the planned economy, the greater the overall interpersonal inequality—the best example of which is probably the Stalinist economy of the 1930s. There is, in effect, only one additional element to α_i that can play a significant role in income distribution: the skill premium. But as already indicated, the skill premium tended to be small in socialist economies. And as Figure 7.1 shows, social cash transfers could not influence distribution much, either, because they were demographically determined and thus rather flat across income distribution. They might have had an equalizing role in less developed socialist economies, as in Central Asia, where large and (per-capita) poor households benefited from child allowances, but in more developed economies with small households their redistributive role was small. Finally,

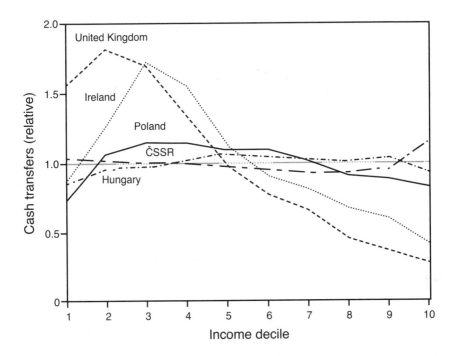

Figure 7.1. Distribution of social cash transfers by income decile

Note: The graph shows the amount of per capita social transfers across the ten deciles of income distribution. Equal per capita distribution = 1. ČSSR = Czechoslovak Socialist Republic.

Reformatted from Branko Milanovic, *Income, Inequality, and Poverty during the Transition from Planned to Market Economy* (Washington, DC: World Bank, 1998), fig. 2.1, 17.

taxes depended on wage income and, being proportional, did not affect overall inequality.

The equation can be understood to cover only monetized incomes; thus, three important sources of income that it disregards should be added: nonmonetized own production, which was important for rural households and which in some parts of the socialist world was sizeable; consumption subsidies, which were egalitarian in that they heavily subsidized food, energy, and other essential goods; and specific nonmarket advantages, which were enjoyed by the top of the state and party hierarchy (the *nomenklatura*). These last took the forms of access to scarce goods, state-provided apartments and houses, subsidized vacations, and the like, and can be included in our hierarchical coefficient α_i, making it greater.[14]

It is difficult, based on such a generalized approach, to say whether there would necessarily be less inequality under socialism than under mature capitalism, given the latter's needs-based social transfers and progressive taxation. Socialism, even theoretically, had an ambivalent attitude toward economic equality. The objective of socialism has been the abolition of classes, and thus of hired wage-labor, rather than the abolition of income inequality. (And neither was that the goal of communism, although for different reasons.) As Engels wrote, "the real content of the proletarian demand for equality is the demand for the *abolition of classes*. Any demand for equality which goes beyond that necessarily passes into absurdity."[15] And as he explained elsewhere, even more emphatically:

> "The elimination of all social and political inequality," rather than "the abolition of all class distinctions," is similarly a most dubious expression. As between one country, one province and even one place and another, living conditions will always evince a *certain* inequality which may be reduced to a minimum but never wholly eliminated. The living conditions of Alpine dwellers will always be different from those of the plainsmen. The concept of a socialist society as a realm of *equality is* a one-sided French concept deriving from the old "liberty, equality, fraternity," a concept which was justified in that, in its own time and place, it signified a *phase of development,* but which, like all the one-sided ideas of earlier socialist schools, ought now to be superseded, since they produce nothing but mental confusion, and more accurate ways of presenting the matter have been discovered.[16]

High income differentials were not therefore something to be too concerned about once the "just" institutions (making up a classless society) were achieved. The logic there is identical to that of libertarians or market fundamentalists: for libertarians, once there is a fully market-based system, income can be acquired only by providing valuable gods and services to others, and hence inequality is immaterial.* Or, as Hayek thought, with the rules-based system, speaking of "just" distribution is meaningless: "In a free society in which the position of the different individuals and groups is not the result of anybody's design—or could, within such a society, be altered in accordance with a generally applicable principle—the differences in reward simply cannot meaningfully be described as just or unjust."[17] Neither communists nor libertarians ask, however, if inequality might in turn undermine the institutions each side holds dear.[18]

Typically, inequality under socialism was less than under capitalism—so significantly that many cross-country studies in the 1970s and 1980s applied a "socialist variable" to adjust their regression analyses (while controlling for income levels and other characteristics).[19] Socialism's lower inequality was due to its lower skill premiums, much lower incomes from property, and broad-based consumption subsidies. It is, of course, doubtful that the hierarchical coefficient a_i implied inequality as high as that resulting from capitalism's unequal distribution of property, but in some periods (such as the 1930s era of high Stalinism in the USSR) it was undoubtedly elevated by in-kind advantages enjoyed by the elite and "payments in envelopes" made to people under various circumstances.[20] It is a real problem that, for that period, we have little empirical evidence. Yet some evidence of strikingly unequal consumption available to different strata, and collected from official sources, is reported by R. W. Davies; for example, five hundred delegates at the September 1932

---

* Income inequality in socialism is theoretically complex. Once classes and private capital ownership are abolished, all differences stem from labor and thus are not condemned as they reflect varying skills and effort. Still, the mechanisms set in motion by communist revolution (free education and health care, and a reduced skilled-to-unskilled wage ratio) reduce the differences. Even theoretically, then, Marxists could expect less wage difference under socialism—while not being in principle against it.

Communist Party plenum were allocated, for the two weeks of the plenum, 1.33 kilograms of meat per person daily, while the highest individual meat ration for ordinary citizens was 3 kilograms per *month*.[21] Inequality in wage distribution, as reported by the official statistics, increased between 1928 and 1934 (although it was still less than in 1914, before the war).[22]

Leveling, which under the Russian term of *uravnilovka* became synonymous with excessive egalitarianism, was criticized for stunting incentives and making workers lazy and uninterested in improving their skills.[23] In 1931, Stalin addressed a group of industrial managers and took up the question of what was causing high turnover in their workforces. According to him, the question mattered because too much mobility of workers undermined productivity and adoption of new technologies. The reasons, he said, were various:

> The cause is the wrong structure of wages, the wrong wage scales, the "Leftist" practice of wage equalisation. In a number of factories wage scales are drawn up in such a way as to practically wipe out the difference between skilled and unskilled labour, between heavy and light work. The consequence of wage equalisation is that the unskilled worker lacks the incentive to become a skilled worker and is thus deprived of the prospect of advancement; as a result he feels himself a "visitor" in the factory, working only temporarily so as to "earn a little money" and then go off to "try his luck" in some other place. The consequence . . . is that the skilled worker is obliged to go from factory to factory until he finds one where his skill is properly appreciated.[24]

Inequality became much lower in the Soviet Union after the period of "high Stalinism," and was always rather low in other socialist countries.[25] The fact, nevertheless, is that membership in a state and party bureaucratic hierarchy played the same role in socialist systems (in terms of income distribution) that ownership of capital

Table 7.5 Perceptions of the Class Nature of the Socialist System

Income level (per capita)	The social system is:		
	(1) Class-based (%)	(2) Not class-based (%)	(3) Ratio (1)/(2)
Under 500 dinars	44	32	1.38
501–1,000	39	32	1.22
1,001–1,500	39	39	1.00
1,501–2,000	40	40	1.00
Over 2,000	27	52	0.52
Members of the LCY	32	51	0.63
Nonmembers	40	28	1.43

Note: Respondents were asked, "Does our [Yugoslav] society contain different social classes?" The numbers responding "do not know" are not shown here. Note that only urban dwellers were surveyed. LCY is the League of Communists of Yugoslavia.

Data source: Miloslav Janićijević, "Klasna svest i društvena struktura" [Class consciousness and social structure], in *Društveni slojevi i društvena svest* [Social groups and social consciousness], ed., Mihailo Popović, Silvano Bolčić, Vesna Pešić, Milosav Janićijević, and Dragomir Pantić (Beograd: Centar za sociološka istraživanja, 1977), 214–215.

played in capitalist systems.[26] From that realization, it is only one step further to argue that, functionally, socialist societies were class-based, even if the dominant class was selected and ruled differently, and, importantly, was unable to transfer most of its acquired advantages across generations.* Miloslav Janićijević reported in 1977 a finding that was not surprising. The higher one's position in the state hierarchy—as a member of the Communist Party and in terms of income level—the more likely one was to believe that society was classless (see Table 7.5, column 3). Only 27 percent of those in the top income group believed that the system was class-based, versus 44 percent of those in the poorest group. The ideas justifying the existing system were most popular among those who benefited from it.

* Of course, there were exceptions—such as North Korea, which created the first communist monarchy. Even in China, the importance of "princelings" and inheritance of connections (if not wealth) from parents was important. This was not the case in the European socialist economies.

Looking at income formation and income distribution enables us to circumvent laborious ideological studies that in the past attempted to define the exact class nature of socialist economies, and distinguish between social classes (undesirable) and social layers or social strata (acceptable).[27] That still remains a task for sociologists, but economists can treat bureaucratic income hierarchies as similar to capitalist hierarchies. As Branko Horvat put it, "while the capitalist participates in the distribution of the social surplus value in proportion to his capital, the bureaucrat participates in proportion to his status in the hierarchy of power."[28]

A note on China. The situation in China during its socialist period was different from the situations in the USSR and in Eastern European countries. While in both of those, the "sought-after" outcome of the revolution was the abolition of classes and treatment of everybody as a state worker, and departures from this "ideal" type (for example, privately owned agriculture) were treated as temporary anomalies, the Chinese revolution formally maintained the existence of clear social classes. They were the workers, the peasants, and importantly, the petty bourgeoisie (small owners) and the "patriotic capitalists." These four classes were defined in Mao Zedong's 1949 speech "On the People's Democratic Dictatorship."[29] They are represented on the Chinese flag by the four smaller stars surrounding the big star (standing for the Communist Party). Until the early 1960s, former capitalist owners who were not considered counterrevolutionaries and whose property was not confiscated were entitled to a yearly payment of a dividend, ranging from one to six percent of the estimated value of nationalized assets.[30] This allowance, at least formally, for the existence of a class structure meant that studies of income distribution could in principle connect functional and interpersonal income distributions.[31] Such research was undertaken in China, however, only in a very timid fashion; the data sources necessary for such work were only developing with the creation of a centralized statistical system in the 1950s, and probably it was also true that political pressures discouraged it.[32] Chinese statistics, like Soviet data, were focused on rural versus urban differences; in China, even household incomes were surveyed separately for the two areas and were unified in a single, national survey only in 2013.

On the other hand, China, especially during the period of the Cultural Revolution, provided one of the most egalitarian examples ever: earnings of its manual and nonmanual workers were generally equalized, and in many cases, manual workers' earnings exceeded nonmanual workers'. As Henry Phelps Brown documented, the attempt to "create a new man," who would work regardless of incentives, resulted in unusual pay schemes.[33] A scheme of rewards applied in Beijing in the mid-1960s, around the time of the Cultural Revolution, included a feature by which all men were paid according to the average number of units produced by men, and all women were paid according to the average number of goods produced by women. Thus, a gender gap in pay was intentionally introduced. But since all individuals of a given gender were paid the same, there was no material incentive for anyone to work harder and produce more. Phelps Brown explains the reasoning:

> This story brings out what to Western observers may seem a contradiction in Chinese pay structure: if it is right and proper to pay a man more than a woman because the man being stronger produces more, why should not a man who exerts himself and produces more than another man likewise be paid more? To the Chinese the answer is simply that the latter differential appeals to self-interest whereas the former cannot. Strangely but intelligibly, the Chinese treat payment in proportion to the amount of work done as a self-evident principle of natural justice while differences in that amount are not within the worker's own control, but as mischievous when they are.[34]

The anti-incentive pay structure was thus the very opposite of the Taylorism of the Stalinist piecework reward structure, where wages were proportional to individual output and the obvious incentive was to produce more. The anti-incentive approach was in line with

Marx's view of income distribution in communism, where labor would be undertaken out of personal interest and for pleasure ("self-realization") rather than for pay, and where earnings would be distributed according to "needs." While the earnings in the Chinese example here were not determined by needs (within the groups, men or women, there must have been some whose needs were greater than the average), the first part of Marx's desideratum—namely, that work not be undertaken in response to material incentive—was satisfied.

China in its socialist phase thus provides an unusual combination of egalitarian extremism and formal preservation of class society.

Three socialist equalities. Having just considered wage formation under the conditions of the Chinese Cultural Revolution—one of the most radical egalitarian experiments in history—we might see this as a fitting point at which to move into questions of ideology, and specifically to contrast the three (broadly speaking) concepts of equality advanced by different varieties of socialism: social-democracy, traditional Marxism, and Marxism with Maoist characteristics.

Social-democratic equality is the best known and the easiest to explain. Most of its authors were steeped in British utilitarianism, Fabianism, and trade union activities. This concept of equality begins with the acceptance of capitalist relations of production and a class division of society. This is a very important point of contrast with the traditional Marxist approach. Within a capitalist society, social democracy attempts to reduce the importance of what John Roemer refers to as "circumstances" (for example, parental wealth and inheritance, gender, and race) to one's lifetime income, and to tolerate only those inequalities that stem from differences in effort, "episodic luck," and investment performance (and, regarding the latter, only if the invested funds were acquired through savings, not by inheritance).[35] Desirable under this approach are any interventions that have the effects of making education more accessible to all, increasing the bargaining power of labor vis-à-vis capital, or promoting progressive taxation and thereby reducing inequality. These interventions, as we know, have been core to the political and social activities of trade unions, left-wing parties, and various fraternal associations for more than a century in developed capitalist economies.

This is not, however, the Marxist concept of equality. For Marx and his followers, the all-important equality is the one that abolishes social classes and ends private ownership of capital. The fundamental inequality is, in Marx's view, in-built in the very essence of capitalist relations of production: owners of capital hire laborers and appropriate the surplus value. If, out of the surplus value, a larger share accrued to workers, Marxists would welcome that, but they would not regard that as their political goal, or even as a point of great importance. As Shlomo Avineri has argued (see Chapter 4), the kinds of activities trade unions engage in are seen by Marx only as training grounds—preparing people for a future when relations of cooperation among workers will extend to the entire society. Equality is, in Marx's view, the normal condition in a world where social classes have been abolished. But, in the first stage of that future system of socialism, it is not fundamentally wrong to allow significant differences in wages if they result from differences in effort and thus individual choice. To be sure, no Marxist believed that such income differences could be as great as the differences under capitalism, because other tools set in motion by the revolution (free health and education and low skill premiums) would naturally tend to reduce them. Indeed, as we have seen empirically, the differences were not high. There was no private ownership of capital, which in all capitalist societies (including today's social democracies) was extremely concentrated; there was no significant inheritance; and education was free and accessible to all. Yet, and this is a point on which one must insist, equalization of economic outcomes was not an objective *per se*. It was something that would naturally stem from a society without a capitalist class, not something that would need special striving for once classes were abolished. Thus, theoretically, socialism was consistent with relatively high income inequality.

The third socialist concept of equality is the one exemplified by the Cultural Revolution. While the Marxist and social-democratic concepts accept the role of incentives—that is, of pay variations that motivate workers and create inequality—the Maoist approach was exactly the reverse. Socialism in this view is a system where work should be undertaken out of social obligations, the desire to help others, altruism, love of one's country, and so forth—not in response to material incentives. Consequently, during the Cultural Revolution, all incomes had to be equalized. The fact that the Chinese accepted gender-based pay inequality in this era additionally highlights the uniqueness of the approach. By rewarding a circumstance associated with higher productivity (gender, favoring men over women) rather than recognizing variations in individual effort, it stood in direct contrast to John Roemer's principle of equality of opportunity.

We thus see three very different views on what constitutes real equality espoused by the three (broadly speaking) left-wing ideologies. This is important to highlight in today's left-wing environment, with its prevailing, almost unquestionable, convergence on just one approach: accepting private ownership of the means of production, and working to reduce those income inequalities that are due to "circumstances." This might be the most efficient and the most common approach, but it is not ideologically the only valid one.

Paucity of Income Inequality Studies under Socialism

Income inequality studies under socialism were beset by a multitude of problems, and ultimately produced very little of value. For scholars today, these efforts elicit only an antiquarian interest, similar to the interest now taken in historical studies of inequality. In fact, working with Soviet data on income distribution, even during the heyday of socialism (that is, in real time), was a bit like working with historical Roman or Byzantine data. One had access only to some individual data points and anecdotes. With little in the way of systematized information being published by government offices or researchers, one was left to draw connections between disparate data points. One could reach seemingly reasonable conclusions—yet, quite different and equally reasonable conclusions could also be imagined. One always worked in a statistical "fog."

For convenience, we can group the many factors hampering the study of income inequality under socialism into four big categories: ideological pressures; obsessions with data secrecy under authoritarian (and, before 1953, totalitarian) regimes, which were also not above data falsification; the lack of good methodological frameworks for studying income distribution; and the absence of compelling political narratives regarding inequality. I shall consider them in turn.

Ideological pressures. As we have seen in the previous chapters, most of the historical work on inequality was structured around social classes. Even if one studied interpersonal inequality without reference to social classes, as Pareto did, elites were very much present in his sociological work. It was only with Kuznets and the dominance of the American school in economics that both classes and elites disappeared. It took until the early twenty-first century for the elite, restyled as the top one percent, to reappear.

Socialism, meanwhile, as the antechamber to the classless society, had abolished the traditional class structure. Nationalization of land in 1917, and then of the most important industrial enterprises in 1918, put an end to the capitalist class in the Soviet Union: one could not be a capitalist if one had no property.[36] Only in the countryside (in the USSR) did class structure remain. Spontaneous takeovers of large estates created widespread small holdings, essentially as happened in France after the 1789 revolution. There were, however, better-off peasants who either already owned larger parcels of land (the landholding "modernization" or "capitalization" of Russia had begun with the Stolypin reforms in 1906) or bought land from other peasants after the revolution. These were the so-called kulaks. It is therefore understandable that, as early as the 1920s, the class structure of the Soviet society seemed very simple: on one side, there were state-sector workers, who included practically everyone in the urban areas (even government and party bureaucrats) and, on the other,

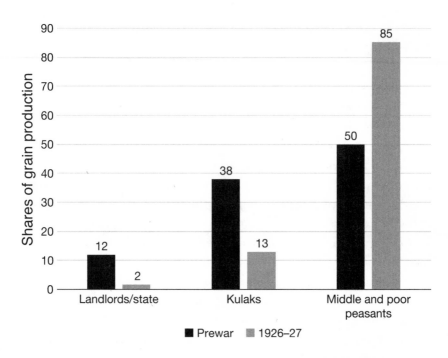

Figure 7.2. Class structure in Soviet agriculture before World War I and before collectivization

Data source: Joseph V. Stalin "On the Grain Front: Talk to Students of the Institute of Red Professors, the Communist Academy, and the Sverdlov University, 28 May 1928," *Voprosy Leninizma* (Moscow: Partiinoe izdatel'stvo, 1933). In English, https://www .marxists.org/reference/archive/stalin/works/1928/may/28.htm.

there were rural areas where there was some class differentiation. It was to the latter that the Bolsheviks directed their attention. Stalin in 1928, on the eve of collectivization, presented data on the class structure in the countryside based on shares in the production of grain (Figure 7.2). The share of poor and middle peasants was much greater than before the revolution, reflecting the "parcelization" of the land into many small holdings. The state's share was minimal, much smaller than the landlords' share before World War I.[37]

When collectivization began in 1928, its explicit objective was to transform both the ordinary and poor peasants into state workers, and to dispossess the kulaks (who were in many cases only so-called kulaks, that is, not really wealthy). Collectivization entirely swept away any class distinction. It could indeed be claimed, as Stalin's constitution in 1936 did, that antagonistic classes had ceased to exist in the Soviet Union.[38] There was only one class, the working class. Whether employed in manufacturing, services, government, transport, or agriculture, all worked for the state; formally, everyone's social position was the same.

The gap between urban and rural incomes remained, however. Early Soviet household surveys (almost all of which have since been lost) focused on it, and within the urban areas these surveys distinguished between manual and nonmanual workers. But it was understood that these were classifications of convenience and did not reflect actual class (or antagonistic) relations. Thus, the fact that ideology did not recognize the possibility of classes under socialism (except for a few capitalist residuals), and the fact that the changes that were accomplished in the Soviet Union by the late 1930s were broadly in agreement with what Marxist ideology implied, limited the ability to study inequality in the Soviet society with the tools that existed. This is true independent of the totalitarian controls that were imposed on such studies (to which we turn next).

In Eastern Europe, after Stalin's death, the situation was different. In Poland and Yugoslavia, most agriculture remained in private hands, and in all countries a small private sector existed in services and ancillary activities (very seldom in industry). Although the private sector was hamstrung both by the restricted list of activities in which it could engage and by the number of employees it could hire—and never produced more than 20 percent of the country's value-added—some remnants of the traditional class structure were preserved.[39] This, and also the thaw after Khrushchev's "secret speech" in 1956, made the study of income distribution possible and more meaningful. In Eastern Europe, household surveys were introduced in the early 1960s (approximately at the same time as in the West) and, when the authorities permitted, they were used as key sources for research on income inequality. Social scientists like Ivan

Szelény and Branko Horvat began writing more seriously about the class structure of socialist societies (or, as Horvat called them, "etatistic" societies), where the bureaucracy took on the role of the overthrown capitalist class.[40] And thus the ideas of Pareto—even if those participating in the debate never showed much interest in or sympathy with him—were vindicated.[41]

Authoritarian obsession with data secrecy. Authoritarian, and up to 1953 totalitarian, political systems made research of inequality of income and wealth very difficult and, in some cases, impossible. To some extent, "objective" conditions made it challenging to use the common tools of inequality studies, but the decisive constraints were political ones. Often the relevant data were not collected. When they were collected, they were treated as confidential or secret and not released to the researchers or the public.[42] Even if crumbs of such data made their way into researchers' hands, it was dangerous to publish any finding that contradicted official ideology or displeased an important leader. Information on the stagnation of rural incomes in the Soviet Union was always regarded as not only a veiled critique of collectivization but a critique of those in charge of agriculture (which, incidentally, was the least desirable portfolio in the Soviet government or in the Politburo). Thus, the possible use of information in internecine political fights further limited what was safe to publish.

The political constraints operated throughout the system: it was not only the researchers who had to fear how their work might be interpreted; their bosses were also fearful that its publication might throw negative light on units they managed and cause them to be demoted. It was much safer for the producers of data (working in statistical offices) not to release any data, or not even to collect data. Throughout the entire structure necessary for work to be done on inequality, there was a strong, inherent incentive to release, publish, and discuss as little as possible. It seldom happened—and in many countries never happened—that someone was demoted or jailed for inaction. The same could not be said for action. Anyone acquainted with the first principles of economics can guess that, in countries where information is scarce or intentionally made scarce, the political value of any piece of information is high. Its use in these authoritarian systems was thus much more politicized than in democracies.

In the end, one wonders why data collection exercises, such as household surveys that barely saw the light of the day, were undertaken at all. A common answer is that they afforded better insight to the leadership, or politically reliable individuals, into what was really happening. But this could not have been true for household surveys since, to the best of my knowledge, they were never seriously used by any communist government. A better explanation might be that there was some desire to *appear* to have information amid the typical inertia and bureaucratic tendency to treat everything as secret. Two contradictory impulses caused, on the one hand, information to be collected, and on the other hand, that information to be hidden as confidential and never used by authorities or researchers. The net result was a waste of time and energy.[43]

Essentially the same, secretive attitude toward data was maintained in the USSR almost until the end of the regime and dissolution of the country. The surveys nevertheless continued throughout the years. The data were collected in individual republics and sent to Moscow to the State Committee for Statistics (*Goskomstat*), which was the only authorized "processor" and user of the combined data. Data summaries for specific republics were then returned to those republics—under a "top secret" label—showing some dozen fractiles of the population with their average incomes, but in a display format that made the data utterly unusable. It was difficult to see what exactly was so secret in that information.[44] (Of course, if one could have had the data, for example, for ten years, one could have charted the evolution of real income and its distribution, and such charts might have been embarrassing to the authorities.)

There was an additional issue in the Soviet Union that remained until the end, and that was present to some extent in Eastern Europe, as well. This had to do with the historic origin of household surveys.[45] Originally, they were supposed to monitor the living conditions of the "standard" or average industrial worker relative to those of the average farmer (or conditions in cities relative to those in the countryside), and also to monitor the average living conditions of manual workers relative to nonmanual workers or pensioners. The surveys focused on what was representative or average for a given group (say, for the urban industrial workers, focusing on the living conditions of a household of two parents, both employed in the state sector, with two children, living in an average-size apartment), rather than considering conditions across the group's whole distribution, which would also include the extremes. To the extent that studying any type of inequality was an objective, it was merely this mean-against-the-mean type of inequality (which is technically called horizontal inequality, to distinguish it from the vertical inequality that includes the entire distribution). By truncating the extremes, surveys misrepresented the situation, underestimating inequality. Emphasizing the representative household or individual is the same approach as used by neoclassical economics and it is, despite its more sophisticated appearance in the latter case, similarly inadequate for the study of inequality (as will be further argued below).

Lack of good methodological frameworks. It is by now obvious that the difficulties of comprehending the social structure of new socialist societies, the lack of data, the secretiveness, and the clear discouragement (or worse) of undertaking such studies produced an intellectual void in which no methodological framework to study inequality could be developed. To study socialist societies as class societies was both difficult from the Marxist point of view, and extremely dangerous to one's welfare. Purely empirical studies (like ones being done, as we shall see, in the West) were often impossible to undertake because of lack of data. Things evolved from the late 1950s onward; in Poland, Hungary, Yugoslavia, and Czechoslovakia, empirical work on income distribution was conducted, papers were published, and, in some cases, even microdata could be obtained. But this work, under the best of circumstances, did not rise above sterile empiricism (which also characterized studies of income distribution in capitalist countries), was not anchored to any methodological framework, was unable to study (or uninterested in studying) drivers of inequality systemically, was voiceless on the evolution of inequality that can be expected in the future, and was fearful of mentioning social classes. In sum, it merely produced rows of numbers and ratios. This was the best that the students of inequality in socialist countries during the Cold War era could hope to achieve.

Absence of compelling political narrative. As noted in the Prologue, a good study of income distribution needs to have a compelling narrative, a solid theoretical foundation, and abundant empirics. We have already seen that, most of the time, access to data was difficult under socialism, and empirical studies were limited to a few countries and time periods. The theoretical or methodological foundation was quasi-nonexistent because the social structure was new and "objectively" difficult to analyze. The absence of opportunities to freely exchange opinions and writings on the topic also inhibited development of such a theoretical framework. When researchers are not allowed to write what they think, or to criticize, or to exchange their writings with others, in this area as in any other, development is stunted. All of this contributed to a situation where no compelling narrative regarding income distribution in socialism was developed.

By contrast, compelling political narratives were developed on the subject of authoritarianism, by dissident voices in Eastern Europe and the Soviet Union, and by political scientists in capitalist countries. It may be that the political issues were seen by many people as more important, or that dissident scholars were more keen to develop that area than economists were to dwell on income distribution, or that analysis of political issues was less dependent on data. It could be that studying income distribution suffered from a peculiar handicap: for those opposing the system, the topic was much less attractive than parts of economics that dealt with incentives and efficiency (and where socialism could have been easily shown to be inferior to capitalism), while for the defenders of the system, the topic was "unreliable" since the data might show truths different from what was supposed to be happening. Thus neither the *contra* nor the *pro* side found much to gain from studying income distribution.

In the last decade of the communist regimes' existence, empirical works on income distribution became much more common.[46] The data became more easily available, researchers were freer to write what they wanted, and the discussion picked up. The involvement of eminent Western researchers with much more experience in empirical work helped. Anthony Atkinson and John Micklewright published an almost encyclopedic review of income distributions in Poland, Czechoslovakia, Hungary, and the USSR.[47] It included results from numerous household and earning surveys going back to the mid-1950s, and devoted extensive discussion to inequality in earnings, redistribution via taxes and social transfers, informal incomes, and the like. At every step of the analysis, results were compared with those from the UK, a country on which Atkinson has particularly focused, and this yielded additional insights into both similarities and differences between income distributions under communism and capitalism. Particularly important, given that many Soviet household surveys were lost by negligence, was their book's data annex, which runs to almost 150 pages and presents in tabulated form the income and earning distributions of the four countries as well as many inequality statistics. The work, however, displayed the weakness already mentioned of entirely sidestepping the political and social developments that produced the distributions so expertly surveyed. These were societies that had experienced de-Stalinization, swings between pro-market reforms and economic tightening, the Prague Spring, the 1970 and 1980 strikes in Poland, and more—yet all go unmentioned in the book, and their relationships with income inequality go unexplored. The same absence of political narrative and methodological framework characterizes my own 1998 book documenting income changes during the process of transition.[48] To be clear, the topic of that book was distribution not under socialism (except in one chapter) but in the early post-socialist period, but still its approach was identical to the one used by Atkinson and Micklewright, and earlier by Harold Lydall: sheer empiricism and nothing else.[49]

Sociological and political analyses of communist regimes thus never managed to be integrated with the empirical work on income distribution. They continued to exist in two distinct spheres. Probably more time (during which open discussion would be possible) was needed to bring them together. But the decay of the regimes proceeded faster than anyone expected and overtook the ability of researchers to provide a more comprehensive view of socialist societies. We thus end up in the somewhat paradoxical situation that, today, socialist societies—which are practically contemporary societies—have to be studied with techniques belonging to economic history. The gap is so wide between the determinants of present-day income distribution in the formerly socialist countries and the determinants of their income distributions under socialism, that the very recent past has to be approached almost as a different age. This also affects the attention paid to such studies, because they are viewed almost as interpretations of "antiquity" without much relevance to capitalist economies of today. Researchers who studied socialist economies tended to switch to studying these countries' "transitional" and capitalist income distributions—or they simply grew old and died.

A series of constraints made original work on inequality under socialism, as we have seen, very difficult. By the time these constraints disappeared, the entire system had crumbled. And studying it changed from being important for policy and ideology to being a matter of historical record. Whether we ever achieve a satisfactory understanding of how politics and economics interacted in socialism, and what impact they had on distribution of income among citizens, will depend on young researchers' readiness to do archival work and to study a topic that does not seem very promising for their careers.[50]

Income Inequality Studies under Advanced Capitalism

It is an invidious task to write about inequality studies during the peak rule of the neoclassical paradigm in the West, from around mid-1960 to 1990. This is true for two reasons. First, the quantity of writing, most only tangentially referring to inequality, is enormous and no single individual can read it all, absorb it, and do it justice. What follows is not a literature review but a discussion of some works that, in my view, reflect the spirit of the times or were important to the future development of income distribution studies. There is a strong subjective element in the choices.

Second, most writings, with the exception of a few that maintained tenuous links with classical economics, are without much importance to the intellectual history of the discipline. It is an arid area we are trying to survey here. One is reminded of Kolakowski's judgment of the enormous production of Marxist quasi-philosophical literature in the Soviet Union—that most of it could be safely pulped.[51] Just as those Soviet philosophical books were written by party hacks, much of what is considered to be the neoclassical literature on inequality was written by what Marx called "hired prize-fighters."[52]

For many, including students, these were wasted years.

Reasons for Disintegration

There are several reasons for the disintegration of inequality studies in the West in the period we cover here. But in each area we have to distinguish the negative developments from the positive ones—the works that maintained the conversation with classical economics and ultimately enabled the flourishing of income distribution studies around the turn of the century and in the first decades of the twenty-first century. Without them, no bridge would have been built and the discontinuity would have been much greater.

"Objective" factors. The period after the Second World War until the mid-1970s was characterized in the West by unusually high growth rates, the emergence of the welfare state, greater social mobility, a decrease in the capital share of income, and a reduction in interpersonal income inequality. All five factors, but especially the last two, "objectively" reduced interest in income distribution studies because they suggested that class distinctions were a thing of the past,

that the power of capital was waning, and that Western societies would continue their travel toward a rich, high-growth, and classless future. There was some wishful thinking in such a view; the real world, fraught with strikes, unemployment, and inflation, was not so rosy. Even so, the new situation was a huge improvement over the prewar class conflicts, which had escalated to street battles (in Weimar Germany), the rise of fascism in Italy, and civil war in Spain. This much more placid political landscape, with its high growth rates, lulled many economists into a comfortable belief that "a rising tide lifts all boats." It is indeed remarkable to see, in the dominant economic literature of the period, how widely such beliefs were held. The dissenters were few, and they were shunted aside.

Economic theory. The second reason for the disintegration of inequality studies has to do with the type of economic theory that became dominant in the West after World War II, and more specifically, general equilibrium analysis. With its main, or even sole, focus on price formation, it leaves out class structure and the endowments of capital or skills with which individuals come to the market. Wealth acquisition takes place offstage. Neoclassical economics' use of a representative agent further eliminates considerations of inequality; it does so by definition, since to talk of income distribution and inequality we must have multiple and diverse "agents." Thus, the mathematically complex models of general equilibrium were only very distant relations of real-world phenomena. It is ironic that this arid region of theory became, for a while, the leading trend in economics. Its founder, Lèon Walras, thought of *pure* economics as a theoretical aid in understanding political economy and wrote two accompanying treatises on social economics and applied political economy.[53] Both were all but ignored in favor of his more abstract and mathematical approach.

What saved theories of income distribution from complete disappearance were parts of economics, some couched in neoclassical garb, that maintained the relationship with the past work in political economy. Keynesian economics played an important role here, and this mostly through its use of the marginal propensity to consume.

This was perhaps unexpected, because Keynes himself did not make an explicit link between changes in income distribution and changes in the aggregate propensity to consume. Why Keynes did not do so—when it seemed obvious that government policies, such as those advocated by him, would affect income distribution and in turn the aggregate propensity to consume—can perhaps be explained by his careful avoidance of taking the side of under-consumptionists. He often came close to their position, but seemed fearful that he might for that "sin" be consigned, together with them, to the "underworld of economics." Kalecki, meanwhile, did link income distribution and consumption, but only in passing at the end of an article mainly concerned with monopolistic competition and the increasing capital share associated with it.[54] When one allows, however, that distribution affects the aggregate propensity to consume, and when one posits (as Kaldor did in 1956) a classical saving function where workers consume all they earn and only capitalists save, the class structure of society reemerges.[55]

That type of work, often done as part of the growth economics popular in the 1960s and 1970s, naturally led to multiple class differentiations and to the early visions of heterogeneous agents (households that differ in terms of their ownership of capital and labor, and may as a result exhibit different behaviors and face different ranges of possible options).[56] Although it was better than what preceded it, the defect of such work was that, as a rule, it avoided dealing with institutions, power, and politics. For that reason it failed, as will be discussed below, to create integrative studies of income distribution.[57]

There are two types of purported income inequality studies that made, I think, minimal contributions. The first were the stochastic models of income distribution that assumed certain relations (say, the ratio between wages at different bureaucratic levels: the wage at level n would be n^2 times greater than the wage at level 1, and so forth), and described certain behaviors of individuals without providing any compelling evidence for the claims. Having done so, these studies, by the manipulation of parameters, then simulated an income distribution that mimicked the observable lognormal or, at the top, Pareto distribution.[58] The authors pretended that, by doing so, they explained income distribution. They did nothing of the kind. They simply took a black box of individual and social behavior, endowed it with some constants and parameters, and provided an imitation of actual distributions—unaware that the number of similarly weakly motivated black boxes and parameters that could also produce lognormal or Pareto distributions is infinite. Such studies would have been wholly dismissed as juvenile exercises were it not for their attractiveness to some parts of the economics profession inclined to believe that they provided deeper insights into the forces shaping income distributions, or even that they rooted inequality in human nature.

The second type of income inequality studies making minimal contributions are the neo-Ricardian studies that often have "distribution" in their titles but seem determined in their use of extraordinary abstract methodologies to out-Ricardo Ricardo.[59] Their single contribution to the study of real income distributions is to highlight the important, but already well-known, facts that there is a trade-off between wages and profit, and the exact position on that trade-off may be determined exogenously by the relative power of workers versus employers. Other than this general observation about the factor shares, there is nothing a student of income distribution can find in such works.

Subfields. The breakup of economics into many subfields, where inequality is a derivative phenomenon, also helped pave the way for the dissolution of inequality studies. International trade, for example, deals with inequality, but only with inequality of wages and only wages in industries affected by trade. The debate about the role that trade with China played in US wage evolution, and the debate regarding the increase in the skill premium, are the best known recent examples. Issues of racial and gender discrimination also often involve wage inequalities. But there, too, the focus is only on one aspect of inequality, and often a somewhat misleading one, since such studies frequently assimilate inequality into the unexplained difference in mean earnings between the races or genders in question, while ignoring the distribution of earnings—that is, the inequality—within each group of recipients.

In many such studies, inequality of one type or another is discussed, but it would be very wrong to mistake a collection of incidental studies of inequality for a theory of income distribution.

Politics and right-wing funding of research. Another reason for the dissolution can be found in the implicit and sometimes outright political pressures that made the topic of inequality "undesirable"— and unhelpful to authors hoping to climb normal ladders in their academic careers or to have social or political influence. That pressure was most intense in the United States during the brief period of McCarthyism, which led to the purge of Marxist economists from top universities in the 1950s. The pressure continued afterward in softer and more sophisticated forms. Class-based analysis (or "class warfare," as it was called by opponents) was not generally welcome. Many of these pressures were not "spontaneous," nor did they arise solely from the political sphere. Business interests constantly nurtured, through financial contributions to institutions and to individuals, the types of analysis that minimized or set aside distributional concerns. There is a long history of such "interference," beginning with the Chambers of Commerce that generously funded the Mont Pèlerin Society, founded in 1947.[60] In 1968, the Swedish Central Bank endowed the Nobel Memorial Prize in Economics and gained influence in the selection of laureates.[61] "Dark money" was infamously used by billionaires to transform economic departments and think tanks in ways they consider desirable.[62] The libertarian Cato Institute was founded in 1977 in Washington, DC. In the early 1980s, I attended several lectures in its modest offices in a townhouse near Dupont Circle. Less than a decade later, it would boast one of Washington's most glittering and large buildings, not far from the US Congress, having benefited from the generous funding of the Koch brothers.

Contributions of rich individuals and foundations to neoclassical or conservative economic think tanks and departments have become even more frequent in the post-Reagan decades as billionaires have proliferated. A direct line can be drawn from control over the development of economics as a science to "generated" public opinions on economic issues and on to policy decisions that serve the interests of the rich. This trend has only accelerated in recent years, but since they extend beyond the scope of this book, I will not discuss it further. The intent is to highlight a chain that has been successfully forged, the first link of which is the funding of economic departments and individual researchers (viz., the producers of knowledge), as nicely illustrated in the film *Inside Job*.[63] The second link is the funding of the think tanks that play a key role in translating arcane research into more broadly understandable forms. And the third link is the media that "feed" this knowledge to the public and are owned by the same people who provide the research funding in the first place (for example, Jeff Bezos and the *Washington Post*; Mike Bloomberg and *Bloomberg News*; and Laurene Powell Jobs, Steve Jobs's widow, and *The Atlantic*). The right-wing financiers have thus built an integrated system of knowledge creation, divulgation, and policy influence.

Arrayed against all this ideological political pressure and billionaire money were the various countervailing forces that exist in a democracy (and are absent in authoritarian systems). There were individuals who managed to resist political pressures or the lure of money; there were others who were sufficiently rich to pursue their preferred work; there were university departments possessed of academic integrity; finally, there were individuals and organizations (like social-democratic and other left-wing parties and their foundations, and trade unions) that tried to counterbalance the pressure of the wealthy business elites. It is inevitable that, under capitalism, such countervailing forces would be weaker. High income inequality—that is, greater economic power of the rich—ensures greater influence for the policies that are pro-inequality, pro-business, or that aim to sideline income distribution topics. This is simply because the rich have (by definition) more money, and more to lose from policies that would curtail their wealth. They thus have both more wherewithal and more incentive to fight for what is good for them. The "intellectual hegemony" in unequal capitalist societies will always be exerted by the rich. It is naive to expect a change in that regard—unless, against all odds, radical egalitarianism succeeds in breaking through. In most cases, such breakthroughs have occurred only through political revolutions.

This particular type of neoclassical economics, supported by political exigencies and underwritten by billionaires' money, might be labeled "Cold War economics." It is a term that reveals the true nature and objectives of the enterprise more accurately than the conventional labels of "neoclassical" and "mainstream" economics. A version of neoclassical economics may have been at its intellectual core, but its success was due to the extra-academic pressures of money and politics.

Empiricism. The fourth reason for the diminished importance of income distribution, empiricism, is not in itself a negative phenomenon; combined with better theory and a political narrative, it is indispensable for integrative studies of income distribution. But empiricism alone, bereft of support of political analysis, presents a very limited and, at times, biased picture of reality. The purely and solely empirical studies (of which there were many) did not much advance our understanding of modern capitalism. The neoclassical-based work that was, however, also open to class and income distinctions (such as Joseph Stiglitz's 1969 paper, and the empirical work undertaken by Anthony Atkinson, Harold Lydall, Lee Soltow, Henry Phelps Brown, Jan Pen, and several others) did provide the ingredients necessary for the theory-empirics-politics synthesis that would bring income distribution studies back in from the cold. Empiricism combined with good theory can do wonders, but empiricism alone never makes for great economics or great social science.[64]

Critique of the Neoclassical Approach to Income Distribution

To understand the Cold War economics reflected in studies of inequality in the 1970s and 1980s, it may be best to begin with a personal reminiscence about the methodological approach taken by two books published in English at almost the same time, in 1974 and 1975. The decade of the 1970s was the period of my greatest excitement for work on inequality—and also my greatest disappointment in it.

Samir Amin opened my eyes to the enormous chasm in income between rich countries and the "third world," and to the historic origins of that gap.[65] Amin's early work (about which more will be said below) is remarkable for its holism, so absent from neoclassical economics. It is not sufficient to present empirical evidence (which Amin did present in abundance for Egypt, the Maghreb, and a number of sub-Saharan African countries); that evidence must be situated in its historical context, as Amin and the dependency theorists did. The next step is to study, based on that view of the world, whether and why inequality would persist, and how it would evolve. Amin thought that the capitalist catchup was impossible because the system governing relations between the metropolis and the periphery was structured in such a way as to permanently discriminate against the periphery. While that part of Amin's and the dependency theorists' reasoning was not borne out by the facts (one can, by now, list several countries that have moved from the periphery to the core), the great lesson that I learned in the 1970s was that it was important to look at income inequality empirically and historically, and not simply as an assemblage of numbers or a series of equations.

My greatest intellectual disappointment, on the other hand, came courtesy of neoclassical economics, which lacked *both* the elements I found so attractive in Amin. It was with great anticipation that I went to a library to get Alan Blinder's *Towards an Economic Theory of Income Distribution*, published in 1975, the title of which promised so much.[66] It is possible that I expected too much—perhaps a revelation or an explanation of how different theories hang together. What I found in Blinder's book was a theoretical treatise full of rather meaningless equations, where everybody was an agent optimizing over an infinite time horizon with full knowledge of what the future would bring, including their own income. Gian Singh Sahota, in a review of income distribution theories published in 1977, appears to have shared this disappointment. With a touch of irony, he carefully lists Blinder's assumptions:

> All of the following variables of the model are exogeneous and are *known* to the individual with *certainty* at the beginning of his or her economic life: the rate of interest; the length of economic life; inherited material wealth and education up to about 18 years of age implying an exogenously given wage at that age; the trend rate of growth of real wage; and tastes which are related neither to wealth nor income. There are seven taste parameters assumed as "givens": subjective time discount, relative weights attached to consumption, leisure, and bequests; and the speed of the decline of marginal utilities of consumption, leisure and bequests.[67]

It is often said, in their defense, that the very abstract methods used by neoclassicals should not be criticized for their unrealistic assumptions, because abstract methods are just parables: they tell the story by extracting the most salient and important elements. There is some truth in this—but not too much. The problem with Blinder's approach, and with similar neoclassical work, is not just that the assumptions are unrealistic, and certainly have nothing to do with the living experience of 99 percent of the world population. Much worse is that, by seeing the world as populated by interchangeable "agents," neoclassical analysis ignores the real differences in people's endowments and their scopes of possible action. The range of decisions faced by daily wage workers, who do not know whether they will have a job the next day or the next week, is not only much more limited than the range of decisions that a rich capitalist has, but the very optimization process is different: the acceptable risk is different, the discount of future earnings is different, the time horizon is shorter. Practically all the parameters that Blinder uses to "homogenize" people are in truth heterogeneous across different classes of individuals. And within classes, too, they change with individual circumstances that change in (rather obviously) unforeseeable ways.

Furthermore, such an approach ignores the essence of income inequality: power structures. The relationship between an employer and an employee is not merely a numerical relationship expressed by the gap between their incomes; it is also the difference in power that is so clearly present in Smith's and Marx's analyses of capitalist production. One commands people, another is being commanded. One makes policy changes, another learns about them. As Sebastian Conrad rightly notes, the failure to note power structures misleadingly "confers agency on everyone who is involved in exchange and [economic] interactions."[68] To avoid this error, inequality work must situate the theoretical and empirical analysis in its historical context. This is not something, however, that Blinder even tries to do: his world is an alien, abstract world that relates to life on Earth about as much as the theories that astrobiologists have developed about life on Mars.

Blinder's work failed on all three dimensions of what constitutes a good income distribution study: it contained no historical or other narrative, it had no theory that corresponded with reality, and it contained no useful numbers. The vacuity of Blinder's work (which is representative of neoclassical Cold War economics more generally) is equal to those empty Soviet descriptions of income inequality under socialism: neither had anything useful to tell us about historical determinants of inequality, class structure, discrimination, income gaps, or anything else from real life.

Other examples. Paul Samuelson's *Economics* was an immensely influential textbook worldwide.[69] It also stands as evidence of this inability to integrate income distribution studies within the neoclassical paradigm. While issues of factor shares—determinations of wages and profits—are given lots of space, over a hundred pages spanning six chapters, they are never "unified" into an income distribution. We thus learn in detail how wages are determined, see the relationship between entrepreneurship and profit, and the like, but we never put these factor returns together, combining wages, interest, profits, rent, and so on, to find out how they form household total income, or to discover how such total income is distributed, or to see what political and social forces influence it, or to understand how that distribution influences society and its politics. Inequality is studied on two pages of a book that runs to over nine hundred pages, in one of the last chapters that, revealingly, opens with "Humanity does not live by GNP alone."[70] Clearly, according to Samuelson, inequality is to be considered as one of these addendums to economics which, while not entirely irrelevant, need only be mentioned at the end—in the way that, on American TV news programs, anchors turn in the last minutes of their broadcast to some common-interest story on which they comment in a faux-relaxed fashion.

In an influential book, Charles F. Ferguson dedicates *one* out of more than four hundred pages to the topic of distribution, after paradoxically highlighting it in the book's title. This is done in a short section, moreover, that establishes that factor shares are constant under a given type of technological progress.[71] Another fitting illustration of this trend is that, until the 1990s, the premier system for classifying economic papers and books according to their subject matter, maintained by the *Journal of Economic Literature,* did not even provide a code for economic inequality. In keeping with that, Nobel laureate Robert Lucas, president of the American Economic Association, stated that "of the tendencies that are harmful to sound economics, the most seductive, and . . . the most poisonous, is to focus on questions of distribution." He was able to implement his priorities: very few students of economics learned anything about income distribution.[72]

The political and ideological pressure *not* to see the existence of inequality in developed countries, and especially in the United States, relegated the entire topic of inequality studies to the field of development economics. "If one types in the key words 'income distribution' to the *EconLit* database 1969/1995," Tony Atkinson observed in 1997, "then one comes up with 4,549 entries. (In contrast, 'international trade' generates twice as many entries.) But if one examines these, one discovers that a large proportion deal with development economics."[73] This is, indeed, where a student of economics would have found out that there was such a topic as inequality, and that there were tools to study it. (The Lorenz curve and the Gini coefficient were typically introduced only in textbooks focused on development.) This is also where Kuznets's theory was taught. It appeared that, if the evolution of inequality was charted over time (*pari passu* with economic development), the Kuznets hypothesis really applied only to developing economies. Thomas Piketty is thus correct in arguing that the Kuznets hypothesis was used during the Cold War as a justification for ignoring inequalities (in both developed and developing countries) because it allowed everyone to pretend that growth alone would take care of them.[74] Even more important is to notice that the very concern with inequality was applied only to the developing nations. Inequality, many proponents of the Cold War economics thought, really did not matter in the rich world.

There were, fortunately, better and more serious studies that tried to present a broader and less biased view of income distribution, even as they used a neoclassical marginalist framework as their key theoretical workhorse. I have in mind here Bronfenbrenner's *Income Distribution Theory* and Jan Pen's *Income Distribution,* both published in the early 1970s.[75] In these books, wages and profit are determined through marginal pricing of inputs. Yet in their considerations of factor incomes, both authors note other forces at work: returns to capital are affected by monopoly and concentration of economic power; labor incomes are affected by trade unions, collective bargaining, inflation, monopsonies, and even unfair pricing of raw materials from the developing world. Both discuss Ricardo's and Marx's approaches, and Bronfenbrenner also considers the under-consumptionists (Sismondi, Hobson, even Marx) and the link they proposed between income inequality and macroeconomic cycles. He also complains about the lack of interest in income distribution and the "dormancy" of the topic in contemporary American academia. Both Bronfenbrenner and Pen introduce income policies (popular in the early 1970s as a way to combat inflation), taxation, and the welfare state. Although not fully convincingly, each tries to move from neoclassical factor pricing to personal income distribution. Both books point to the increases in labor shares in postwar Western Europe and the United States as a rebuttal of Marx (whose analysis, as seen in Chapter 4, predicted that labor share would go down), and both devote substantial space to Keynesian and Kaleckian macroeconomic theories of factoral income distribution. Even if macro theories of factoral income distribution were operating at a very high level of abstraction (with Kaldor's approach, making the labor share directly dependent on the savings decisions of capitalists, perhaps best illustrating their remoteness from reality), they still maintained intercourse with classical economics and class differences.

Bronfenbrenner and Pen were both very good writers. Their books are imbued with a mild sense of irony and especially entertaining in their scathing attacks on economists of whom they disapprove. For Pen these include Kaldor and Kalecki, who are criticized several times, albeit rather unfairly (although at least some of Kalecki's lesser-known papers are thus brought to readers' attention). Pen also, somewhat bizarrely, takes aim at Marcuse and the New Left. The scorn he expresses for Marcuse's pronouncements on work and leisure choices, "repressive tolerance," the role of advertisement, and so on is perhaps justifiable; the error here is in giving the New Left authors, whose work has but scant relevance to income distribution studies, too much attention.

One important work of that period—not written in such an engaging way or much cited today, but a book that raised issues that have remained with us for decades—was James Meade's *The Just Economy*.[76] It deals with income inequality statically and dynamically, and thus introduces the topics of intergenerational transmission of advantages (and disadvantages), endowments, and assortative mating. Meade also tries to bridge the (methodological) gap between functional and personal income distributions and emphasizes, much more than other authors, the contribution of capital incomes to total inequality. This leads him to advocate workers' ownership as a way to broaden ownership of financial assets, and thus to break the quasi-automatic relationship between rising capital share and higher interpersonal inequality.

Bronfenbrenner, Pen, and Meade mark the few exceptions I know to the mainstream neoclassical approach to income distribution. Otherwise, how can we characterize the work done in that era? Perhaps by saying that, during a century marked by two world wars, communist revolutions over the globe, immense destruction of property and "human capital," confiscations, nationalizations, hyperinflation, unemployment, and forced labor, neoclassical economists chose to focus on models of infinitely-lived agents with guaranteed rules of bequeath, with full knowledge of all future states of the world, including future decisions of all other "agents"—in short, that they posited a world that, from now until an indefinite future, was fully certain and known as such by all participants. It was almost as if they wanted their model world to look as different as possible from the world where people lived.

Three Types of Inequality Studies under Capitalism

Reflecting on the three elements of meaningful inequality studies—political or social narrative, plus theory, plus empirics—we come now to the question of how the inequality work done in Western economies during the Cold War measures up. In short, none of these three requirements was satisfied.

There were three types of inequality work in Western countries during the period we consider here, roughly from the mid-1960s to 1990: purely empirical work, purely theoretical work, and incidental (or accidental) inequality work.

Purely empirical studies. As explained in the Prologue, empirical studies are not of interest to us if they do not represent or are not driven by some underlying theoretical framework. Almost all of the empirical works done during the period of Cold War were lacking that framework, and we can hence ignore them. This book is *not* a review of empirics.

It is useful, however, to briefly illustrate such studies using the work of their most important practitioner, Tony Atkinson. Atkinson was an English professor and a student of mathematics who later became interested in economics and more specifically in income distribution, the area where he made important contributions. He was a follower of the very strict English utilitarian tradition. This is best seen in the well-known 1970 paper in which he introduced a new measure of inequality, entirely based on the idea of loss of utility brought about by unequal distribution.[77] The loss of utility stems from the fact that people with higher incomes enjoy lower utility from a marginal dollar than people with lower incomes. Hence, any departure from perfect equality must entail loss of overall utility, assuming that all individuals have the same concave utility functions—meaning that, for all of them, marginal utility of consumption or income diminishes in the same way that consumption or income increase. (The sameness of utility functions is a huge and unverifiable assumption.) Atkinson's paper is an extension of Hugh Dalton's 1920 work, which basically opened up all the venues that Atkinson later explored.[78] To be clear, Atkinson never denied the importance of Dalton's work; indeed, he wrote (with Andrea Brandolini) a very important preface to the republication of Dalton's paper in 2015.[79] That part of Atkinson's work is methodological, deals with the methods of measuring inequality, and is not of primary interest for this book.

Most of Atkinson's work was on the empirics of inequality, and because he was at first and for a long time interested only in the UK, his early work gives a sense of insularity and parochialism. Later he began working with François Bourguignon on France, and eventually did a very important volume on Eastern Europe with John Micklewright.[80] Toward the end of his life Atkinson worked on income distribution data produced by British colonial authorities, relating to many African colonies in the first half of the twentieth century.

The distinguishing feature of Atkinson's work is its unrelenting empiricism, without intrusion of politics. His work is extremely valuable for improving our knowledge about the changes in income and wealth distributions over time, often over very long periods, but it does not deal with the politics, political economy, or structural forces that drove these changes. Even when momentous changes in tax rates are mentioned and discussed as factors that have an obvious impact on income distribution, these tax changes themselves are treated entirely as exogeneous events. There is no historical or political discussion or analysis: no strikes, no political parties, no class interests. A couple of examples of such studies are Atkinson's impressive papers on British wealth inequality (cited in Chapter 4) and on the top of the UK income distribution from 1799 until the 2010s.[81] The latter paper covers, in minute detail, various tax schedules, tax rates, and published numbers of tax units, but it does not contain a single sentence on the political or social background against which these changes were occurring.[82] Surely, one wonders, tax changes responded to some political events: changes in government, expanded franchise, wars, workers' parties, various Factory Acts, strikes, agitation of the suffragettes, the repeal of the Corn Laws, the power of aristocracy. None of that is even mentioned. It would appear that policy takes place in a political vacuum.

It is important, however, to credit Atkinson with the realization that studies of inequality would be greatly advanced by much better incorporation of inequality in capital incomes. This area was almost entirely neglected by the Cold War economics with its emphasis, especially in the US, on wage inequality and the skill premium. Atkinson's two review articles (published in 1994 and 1997) are very important in this respect, and may be even taken as watershed events dividing Cold War economics from the new, much less politically inhibited, studies of inequality that followed.[83] Whether Atkinson meant to send this message or not we do not know, but once capital-income inequality is paid attention to and fully integrated in a study of inequality, political dimensions become inevitable.

Similar, solely empirical work was done for a number of countries. It would be both tedious and unnecessary to list examples; the largest number of them would focus on the United States. But one could go on to cite literally hundreds of similar papers for Western European and Latin American countries, and (somewhat fewer) for Eastern European countries. My own work from the 1980s and 1990s belongs to this category. Asia, with the exception of India, was much less studied. Even Japan has attracted scant attention (significantly less than many small Western European countries), in part because of the Japanese government's long-standing policy of restricting access to micro data. Africa, not surprisingly, has been almost entirely ignored, both by Western and African researchers. For African countries, often the only studies that existed were done as part of the normal economic work of the World Bank. There was a glaring lack of studies for the Middle East, which paradoxically coexisted with the development of the Middle Eastern and Maghreb countries' abilities to collect the data. The disconnect there between data collection and data analysis was similar to the disconnect in socialist countries, discussed above.

What is the overall value of such empirical works? They are valuable in revealing trends in income inequality and perhaps even helping us to better understand them. But their greatest *potential* value lies in their power to empirically assess the validity of theories, or more broadly, the validity of different approaches to studying inequality.* If they failed, it is because of their uber-empiricism and absence of connection with theories. Atkinson, for example, could speak (as mentioned in Chapter 6) only of "episodes" of changes in income distribution, each of them apparently obeying its own rules. This meant ultimately giving up on any more general understanding of the forces shaping income distribution, whether they were structural, political, or demographic.

Conversely, in the area of economic growth, long-term empirical studies extending over several decades or in some cases over a couple of centuries were crucial in stimulating discussions of such key topics as the origin and causes of the Industrial Revolution, the "great divergence" between northwestern Europe and China, the petering out of Soviet growth, and more. In these cases, empirical work gave an entirely new impetus to economic history. This was not the case in the area of income distribution.

---

*I am using the term *approach* to indicate that not every comprehensive study of income distribution ought to have a strict micro-based *theory*. Yet it must have some prior hypotheses for which it is using empirics to tease them out or to check them. It cannot run numbers blindly.

Purely theoretical studies. The second strain of income distribution work was made up of purely theoretical studies.* I have already discussed the obstacles that neoclassical theoretical economics presents to any serious work on income distribution, and there is no need to repeat them. But there is another angle from which neoclassical work can be considered, too. It can be defended by making recourse to Ricardo's simplifications and abstractions. And in a way, with its austere modeling, neoclassical economics does represent a continuation of the abstract approach initiated by Ricardo. The differences between Ricardo's abstractions and those of neoclassical economics, however, are greater than their similarities. Ricardo's model is, if anything, too concrete, in the sense that it was designed for a specific historical circumstance. The main actors or classes in that model are easily recognizable: landlords who benefit from duties on corn, industrialists who lose by having to pay workers more, and workers whose real wage is more or less the same anyway. But the world presented by neoclassical economics is not the world of classes, or any groups of recognizable people confronting each other as groups; it is a world of individuals who each, like so many parallel lines, exist simultaneously but never confront each other. It

---

* In an excellent survey, Sahota examines seven types of income distribution theories: ability theories, stochastic theories, individual choice theories, human capital theories, educational inequality theories, inheritance theory, and life-cycle theory. Gian Singh Sahota, "Theories of Personal Income Distribution: A Survey," *Journal of Economic Literature* 16, no. 1 (1978): 1–55. I have already mentioned the significant inadequacy of the stochastic theories. Ability theories and individual choice theories both downplay or ignore the role of society in influencing inequalities and are clearly apologetic (as well as having low explanatory power). So-called educational inequality theories hardly qualify as *theory* of income distribution; they are merely observations that educational inequalities, which themselves are due to social inequalities (that remain unexplored), explain a part of overall income inequality. The most developed, in my opinion, are the human capital theories, the obvious heirs to the classical (Smith and Marx) approach to explaining wage differences. The disadvantage of these, however, is that they deal with only one part of total income, and their authors have not evinced much interest in building more comprehensive theory that would go past wage determination. Combining human capital theory with inheritance theory would make lots of sense. But the inheritance theory has remained woefully underdeveloped.

is a mock-up world that consciously avoids all political and social entanglements.

The neoclassical model-world thus departs from the Ricardian world in at least three respects: it ignores conflict and contradictions between classes, it does not map to any historically recognizable episode, and it pretends to be universal. Inequality descends from its role where it either influenced or was influenced by growth to a role where it does not matter because it does not change, or where it is studied in a peripheral manner, in connection with different subtopics ("the incidental studies of inequality," reviewed below).

Both empirical and theoretical studies lacked what may be called a dynamic element. They did cover long slices of time (especially the empirical studies), but since they did not capture the political or structural elements driving income distributions, the empirical studies of inequality remained exactly that—empirical studies of past episodes. This absence of underlying political framework hampered theoretical studies, too, because their ideas of the future were just teleological unfoldings of their premises. These were purely mathematical exercises, where the conclusions were already contained in the way the problem was postulated. As Atkinson commented, in a guarded way, about one such paper (the Stiglitz article discussed just below), the "result depends on the assumptions."[84]

We can thus see that, of the three components that inequality studies should ideally have, purely empirical and purely theoretical studies each offered only one. Theoretical work seldom went into the search of empirical verification, and empirical work had no theoretical backing. And neither strand had any political or social view of the world. Absence of politics, which is in reality absence of the idea of how society is organized, implied the absence of a dynamic element: inability to say anything about the future evolution of income distribution.

As noted above, however, a connection to the classical tradition, and hence to the relevance of income distribution, was sustained. It happened through an unlikely tool introduced by Keynes: marginal propensity to consume. This theory states that the marginal propensity to consume varies with income—and some have argued it even varies with wealth.[85] And once that idea is accepted, it leaves open a back door through which we can introduce differentiation of income by class, the role of inequality in aggregate demand and business cycle, and ultimately a class structure, in what is essentially a macro model.

It is therefore not surprising that one of the attempts of the Chicago school to undermine the relevance of income redistribution was to claim that the marginal propensity to consume (out of long-term or "permanent" income) is constant across the entire income distribution. The construct of the "permanent" income, and the set of parameters contained in the constant that links consumption to permanent income,[86] can be varied at will so that consumption always remains proportional to "permanent" income. It is thus unfalsifiable. (This is especially the case for the "portmanteau" variable that is not observable and can vary in time for the same individual.) The problem of the permanent income hypothesis being unfalsifiable does not concern us here as such; the point is to flag it as a reaction by conservative economists against an intrusion of inequality into the macro sphere.

A conjunction of Keynesian economics and neoclassical economics thus left a door ajar for inequality studies. This is best seen in Joseph Stiglitz's influential 1969 paper that used perfectly "respectable" neoclassical economics, including explicit references to the theory of marginal productivity and to "human capital," and yet opened the way to more serious studies of income inequality.[87] Stiglitz began with a simple definition of personal income (y_i) which consists of the same wage (w) for all, and the same rate of return (r) applied to different amounts of capital or wealth that individuals own (c_i).

$$y_i = w + rc_i$$

Interestingly, the only difference between people is the quantity of assets they own—a clear class distinction—and not their different wages (at least not in the first sketch of the model). Stiglitz then assumed a constant marginal savings rate m (equal to 1 *minus* marginal propensity to consume).

$$s_i = b + m \, (w + rc_i)$$

Change in wealth is by definition savings over the original wealth (s/c), which thus becomes

$$\frac{\dot{c}_i}{c_i} = \frac{b + m(w + rc_i)}{c_i} = \frac{b + mw}{c_i} + mr$$

where the first term denotes savings out of wages and the second term denotes savings out of capital income (with b being some minimal amount of savings, a savings constant). To get to the change in inequality of wealth between two individuals (or classes) such that $y_j > y_i$, we look at the difference in the rates of growth of their wealth. It is equal to

$$\frac{\dot{c}_j}{c_j} - \frac{\dot{c}_i}{c_i} = (b + mw)\left(\frac{1}{c_j} - \frac{1}{c_i}\right) < 0$$

and thus inequality in wealth under such simple condition has to go down. We are not much interested here in the result that obviously derives from the assumption that the wages of the two classes and savings out of wages are the same; in consequence, savings of the poor and the rich differ less than their capital endowments, and thus wealth of the poor increases faster than the wealth of the rich.[88] What is important in Stiglitz's model is not the conclusion (which does not have much to do with the real world) but that this simple model (re-)introduced classes through the difference in capital endowments—and then added wage differences (Stiglitz did this in the second part of his paper), and then differences in the saving propensities between individuals, and finally differences in savings from capital and labor incomes.

A simple, two-class situation (rich versus poor; labor income versus capital income) already gives us four marginal propensities to save (and consume). In addition, one can introduce the differentiation between the rates of return—allowing, for example, the richer person or class to enjoy a higher rate of return on assets than the poorer.[89] Furthermore, nothing limits us to looking at only two individuals or classes: we can introduce many, and we can also, to make things more realistic, have many individuals with zero (or even negative) assets.[90] In other words, everything in the original equation can be made person-specific: wage, average and marginal propensity to save, the rate of return on assets, and endowment of assets. We have thus introduced income distribution, a reality, through the neoclassical door that was cracked open. But that opening was for a long time left unexplored for lack of broadening Stiglitz's conceptual apparatus and filling it in with data. And even with that done, to accomplish something more, institutional and political analyses were needed to introduce taxation and social transfers and to better reflect Western societies deeply polarized with regard to ownership of capital.

Theory versus reality. In contrast to the neoclassical papers' imaginary world of non-differentiated individuals, the United States and all other advanced capitalist economies remained deeply divided along class lines, even during a period of fast economic growth and shrinking inequality. The share of financial assets owned by the richest 10 percent was, for each individual asset class, around 90 percent even in years such as 1983, when US income and wealth inequalities were historically low (Figure 7.3). If we sum up all financial assets, we see that the level of concentration was even greater. For directly and indirectly owned equity (that is, equity owned through mutual and pension funds), the share of the top decile hovered above 90 percent. It is therefore no exaggeration to say that the United States (in terms of its financial wealth) was owned by one-tenth of its citizens.[91] And even these numbers are likely to be underestimates, because private equity holdings tend to be undervalued in such studies (the shares of unincorporated companies held by investors are usually undervalued relative to the market valuation determined once the companies go public), and such holdings are highly concentrated among the wealthy.[92]

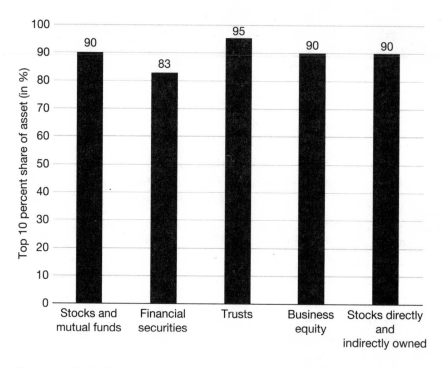

Figure 7.3. Top decile's share of various financial assets (United States, year 1983)

Note: Stocks directly and indirectly owned include individual equity and stocks owned through mutual funds, trusts, IRAs, Keogh plans, 401(k) plans, and other retirement accounts.

Data source: Edward N. Wolff, "Household Wealth Trends in the United States, 1962 to 2016: Has Middle Class Wealth Recovered?" NBER Working Paper 24085, November 2017, table 10.

Annual incomes from capital, which are, of course, the product of such unequal asset holdings, remained so highly concentrated that the Gini coefficient of capital income was in most Western countries around 0.9 in the early 1980s, the earliest period for which we have consistent and country-comparable data. This is about twice the inequality of labor incomes (see Figure 7.4). These numbers grew even more extreme after the end of the period we study here, in the run-up to the 2008 global financial crisis. A Gini of 0.9 is equivalent to the inequality that would obtain if 90 percent of the population had zero capital income, and all income from capital were equally shared

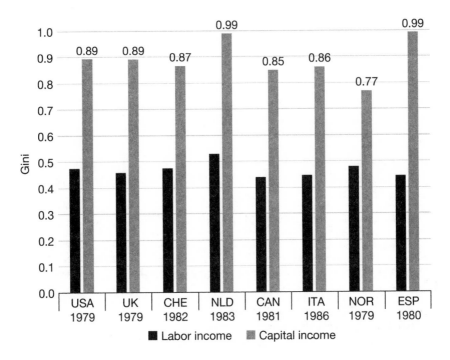

Figure 7.4. Gini coefficients of capital and labor incomes in Western countries, around 1980

Data source: Calculated from LIS Cross-National Data Center.

among those in the top decile. In the real world, obviously, the bottom 90 percent did have some capital income, and income within the top decile was heavily skewed toward the richest among them. But the 90–10 approximation is not far off the mark—and this extreme inequality in wealth (and income from wealth) is clearly incompatible with the neoclassical economists' vision of an almost classless society.

If we include housing wealth, too, which is the main type of wealth held by the middle class, the concentration of wealth indeed declined after the Second World War, and it never came close to the extravagant values of the early twentieth century.[93] But it nevertheless remained extremely high: in the United States, the one percent share oscillated around 30 percent, and the top decile's share around

Table 7.6   American Perceptions of Three Keys to Personal Success

	"Please show for each of these how important you think it is for getting ahead in life . . ." (% responding "essential/very important" to these factors)		
	Having well-educated parents	Coming from a wealthy family	Knowing the right people
Average (US public)	50	31	46
Top one percent	24	1	21
Gap in perception (percentage points)	+26	+30	+25

Data sources: Author's calculations based on data in Leslie McCall, "Political and Policy Responses to Problems of Inequality and Opportunity: Past, Present, and Future" in Irwin Kirsch and Henry Braun, eds., *The Dynamics of Opportunity in America: Evidence and Perspectives* (New York: Springer, 2016): 415–442, figure 12.3. McCall's source for the average was the 2010 US General Social Survey; her source for the top one percent was an (unpublished) 2011 "Survey of Economically Successful Americans" led by Fay Lomax Cook, Benjamin I. Page, and Rachel Moskowitz, Northwestern University. (Note the limited sample of the latter, a pilot study collecting data from 104 successful individuals living in four selected neighborhoods in the Chicago area.)

70 percent. There was no significant change in these shares from 1950 to 1990.[94] Meanwhile, between a fifth and a third of Western populations had zero or negative net wealth, even using the same comprehensive definition of wealth.[95]

Much as we saw in socialist economies, the myths of classlessness encouraged by the system tend to be much more believed by the rich than by the rest of the population. As Table 7.6 shows, there are enormous gaps between the US top one percent and average Americans in their perceptions of how important parental education, family wealth, and knowing the right people are to getting ahead. The responses of the rich imply a conviction that their own success was fully deserved and that society offers everyone the same chance to prosper. It is not surprising that studies taking a critical stance toward that belief would seldom find favor with the rich and powerful.

Willful unreality. Lined up against such elementary and well-known facts, the kind of theoretical model of an economy that has all participants owning both human and financial capital, saving part of their income, optimizing their investment strategies, and bequeathing their assets to their descendants feels purely imaginary. The distance between reality and what is implied by such models quickly becomes apparent. Is it true that the range of options faced by the poor and the rich does not fundamentally differ, that the process of optimization is the same for both, that Bill Gates and a homeless person behave alike economically and are just like any two agents optimizing within constraints, and that economists need make no acknowledgment of their differences in power, ability to survive without a positive income, and economic influence over others? In that case, a class society as we normally understand that term does not exist.

It is important to realize that the criticism here is not the common one that takes neoclassical (Cold War) economics to task mainly for the lack of realism of its assumptions. That critique is too simple and too mild. The critique here does not deal with the simplification of reality, but with its falsification. The criticism is not that assumptions are unrealistic, but that assumptions are designed to obfuscate reality. As Keynes wrote: "[o]ur criticism of the accepted classical theory of economics has consisted not so much in finding logical flaws in its analysis as in pointing out that its tacit assumptions are seldom or never satisfied, with the result that it cannot solve the economic problems of the actual world."[96] It is not a criticism of obliviousness to reality; it is a claim that models were chosen to present the reality in a way that agreed with the ideological postulates of the authors. Neoclassical economics thus combined two opposite vices: simplistic assumptions, and exceedingly complex mathematical models.

The most positive thing that can be said for such theoretical studies is that they approximated the behavior and the choices faced by the top 5 or 10 percent of the population in the richest capitalist countries—in other words, about one percent of the world's population. Marx observed that social sciences in class societies tend to reflect the views and interests of the dominant class, and it is in that light that the mismatch between theoretical work and reality is understandable.[97]

Incidental studies of inequality. The last strain of work consists of incidental studies of inequality. Here, the objective is not to study inequality as such, but to study how various changes in economic life affect some types of inequality. The most popular approach was to study the skill premium and whether its increase was driven by technological progress or by international trade. Many such analyses were done for the United States. Incidental studies did possess a framework (in the production function or the theory of international trade) and did have the data. So they had two of the three elements specified above as necessary for good work on income distribution. They even had somewhat of a political foundation because of social differentiation between high-skilled and low-skilled workers.

Their main problem was that they focused on just one source of income: labor. Certainly, labor is quantitatively the largest source, but focusing on it alone leaves out the most important sources of income for both the top and the bottom of the income distribution: property incomes and social transfers, respectively. Their work can therefore be said to deal only with the middle of the income distribution. But even that is too generous. In wage studies, wage earners are by definition the units of analysis. These wage earners are not randomly mating, however, and it is the family that is the primary unit through which inequality in incomes impacts the way of life of individuals and their chances of social mobility. That inevitable flaw affected the ability of wage studies to really address income distribution.[98]

Additionally, wage studies leave out large chunks of what makes inequality: they leave out "income without work" which comes from property (dividends, interest, rents), capital gains and losses, and the entire system of redistribution through direct taxation and government cash and in-kind transfers (for example, Social Security benefits and SNAP, formerly known as food stamps, in the United States). They also leave out self-employment income, home consumption (that is, personally produced and consumed goods and services), and imputed income from housing—all items of crucial importance in middle-income countries. Wage inequality studies are of even lesser relevance for poor countries, where formal wages typically represent just a third (or less) of total income (see Table 7.4).

The very high wages at the top of the wage pyramid that are received by company board members, CEOs, workers in wealth management funds, and so forth cannot at all be integrated in, or explained by, the skills-driven framework. They are the products of different forms of monopoly power. And while the inability of wage studies to deal with the top of the distribution might not have been as obvious in the 1980s (simply because such wages were not as high then as they have since become), the problem was already evident.[99]

In other words, wage inequality studies deal with the distribution of income from one factor of production (labor) among wage earners—which is indeed important—but ignores everything else: the other factors of production, capital and land, which because of their concentration among the rich are often the most important determinant of inequality; the entire system of government redistribution; self-employment income and home consumption; family formation; and, finally (and ironically, in terms of their topic of study), the highest wages.

But the principal problem is that they miss why we care about inequality in the first place. Inequality is created and reproduced at the level of the household, not at the level of individual wage earner. It is total household income, adjusted for the number of individuals, that makes families rich, poor, or middle class, and causes them to embrace corresponding social values. The socialization is done within households, not within individual wage earners (whatever that could possibly mean). It is through the processes of mating, household formation, and through combining of multiple sources of income that rich and poor households, and social classes, are created—and that, most importantly, opportunities are differentiated at birth, allowing for the reproduction of social inequities.

We study inequality because we care about social classes and their ability to transmit advantages across generations and create self-sustaining "aristocracies." The concern with returns to schooling is surely one of the issues, but far from the most important. People who care about inequality are as concerned about social factors that make access to education uneven as about the fact that the returns to schooling may go up.

Wage inequality studies belong to the area of labor economics, which is an important, but subsidiary, field to inequality studies. Their position is similar to that of studies of wages as affected by trade. The latter belong to trade economics, not to inequality studies.

Most income distribution economists do agree on this. Lindert and Williamson write: "Caring about economic inequality means caring about how unequally people consume resources over their lifetimes. Even if data constraints force us to study annual incomes rather than life-cycle incomes, Kuznets pleaded for measurement per *household member.*"[100] Tony Atkinson, in his 1975 book *The Economics of Inequality,* did not include Tinbergen's wage inequality work at all.[101] He just ignored it. Later Atkinson wrote: "It is indeed striking how much the recent discussion has focused exclusively on wage differentials and not asked whether such differences are associated with [income] inequality."[102] Rawls likewise thought that while inequality has to be limited both in terms of capital and labor incomes, the key concern ought to be with inequality of overall income and household-driven reproduction of such inequality.

In conclusion, conflating studies of wages, whether from a labor or trade economics perspective, with studies of inequality is not only inaccurate. It displays a profound incomprehension of why we care about inequality and what the real objective of such work is: figuring out the fundamental determinants of class structure and its effects on politics, behavior and values, and transmission of such characteristics across generations.[103]

Other incidental inequality studies were even more limited in importance, and never came close to wage inequality studies. They dealt with topics such as effects of remittances on income distribution, the effects of various social transfers and taxes, inequalities observable in female employment, and more. These are not unimportant topics per se but they offer nothing like the desired comprehensiveness of income distribution studies. Such studies always looked at *marginal* changes in distribution brought about by changes in some types of income or outside parameters. They were, by their very construction, unable to say anything about the overall distribution, much less about the forces that shaped it, and about its future evolution.

Therefore, all three strains of inequality work that developed between the mid-1960s and the 1990s in Western countries fell short of what desirable and useful studies of income distribution should have done. They fell victim to the Cold War, an unfortunate abstract turn in economics, the desire to present an embellished picture of reality, and, not least important, funding of research by the rich.

Linking Between-Nation and Within-Nation Inequalities

It is only the neo-Marxist or heterodox approaches that have broken new ground in the work on inequality in the period of the Cold War.[104] They have done it through a research program that had North-South inequality, rather than inequality within nations, as its main concern. The concern was with "unequal exchange" (transfer of the Southern surplus to the North) and arrested development of the South because of rich countries' economic dominance or imperialism. At first glance, neither of these topics seemed to have much to do with inequality as such. A deeper look reveals this is not true. By looking at the world as a whole, and by drawing an important—in the authors' view, crucial—distinction between the core (or the North) and the periphery (or the South), these approaches have opened up the agenda of research on inter-country inequality, a topic that was hitherto dormant or nonexistent. All authors reviewed so far in this book (with the exception of Kuznets) focused only on within-nation inequalities in the most developed capitalist countries. The entire area of between-nation inequalities was unexplored.

The lack of interest in inter-national inequalities can be explained by the fact that, until the early nineteenth century, these gaps were relatively small. They were not, however, nonexistent. As shown in Chapter 2, they did not go unnoticed by Adam Smith. Smith's

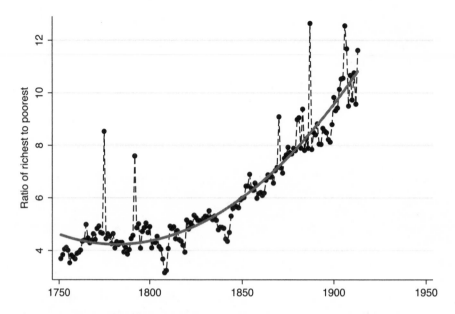

Figure 7.5. Ratio of GDP per capita of the richest to the poorest country in the world, 1750–1914

Note: Not all countries' data for all years are available, which explains some of the spikes (for example, if a very poor country is introduced in the sample). The dashed line is the actual maximum/minimum ratio; the thick line is based on a regression against time.

Data source: Calculated from Maddison Project Database 2020.

stadial theory of development may be interpreted as a way to explain the gap. Yet, income differences between the Western (European and North American) countries and the rest of the world became more obvious and more studied with the expansion of European colonialism and imperialism. The Maddison Project's 2020 data show that the per-capita gap between the richest and the poorest country in the world has steadily risen throughout the nineteenth century, from about 4 to 1 in the beginning of the century to 12 to 1 just before World War I. In Figure 7.5, some of the spikes in the individual years are due to the changing sample of countries, but the trend shown by the thick line is unmistakable.

By the time Marx was writing, that difference was so obvious that it began to affect economics as studied in the metropolis. Marx was, as we have seen, ambivalent toward British imperialism in India: he saw it both as a progressive force in breaking the traditional and backward village structure of India, and as a sign of aggressive global capitalism. In addition, Marxists were soon confronting the question (even before the Russian revolution) of whether less developed countries could move to socialism without being "condemned" to suffer the primitive accumulation of capital, the dispossession of peasantry, and the class divisions that had accompanied the rise of capitalism in Britain and northern Europe.[105]

It is therefore not surprising that the issues of global or more exactly, international, inequalities were studied much more by economists who had an interest in or affinity with Marx than by the others.* When neoclassical economists during the "eclipse" era cared to look at huge inequalities that have opened up in the world, they saw them either through the prism of comparative advantage and trade alone, or, later when the growth models became more popular, through the tendency of mean country incomes to converge. On both grounds, they expected higher growth rates in poor countries to eventually cancel out the gap. They never showed any inclination to look at *inequalities* between rich and poor countries in a systematic fashion or within a global framework. It is only the dependency or system-theory economists who, as Peer Vries, who is otherwise critical of them, writes, obliged the rest of the economics profession to focus on the divergence of incomes between the West and the rest:

> Whatever its exact tenability, the dependency approach in any case forced mainstream economists and others to think about the striking phenomenon that in the nineteenth and twentieth centuries an overall increase in economic *divergence* emerged in the

---

*I use the term "global" for income differences between all citizens of the world (that is, the unit of analysis is the individual) and the term "inter-national" or "international" for differences in mean incomes between countries.

global economy accompanied by an overall increase in trade contacts.[106]

Marxists, of course, did precisely that, beginning with Lenin, Bukharin, Rosa Luxemburg, and M. N. Roy in the early twentieth century. But their work was concerned with capitalism as a socioeconomic formation in its "late" stage. They did not scrutinize inequality between countries, but rather presupposed it—and, in Luxemburg's case, argued (as seen in Chapter 4) that this inequality was a way for metropolitan capitalism to surmount its own difficulties and escape from the domestically falling rate of profit.

After the Second World War and independence of most African and Asian nations, the North-South inequality became an important topic. Neo-Marxists (I have mostly in mind dependency theorists) looked at it, not unlike how neoclassical economists did, through the lens of trade first. Arghiri Emmanuel argued in 1972 that the trade between rich and poor countries implied a transfer of value (that is, of unpaid labor) from the poor to the rich. Poor countries with historically lower wages, and higher rates of surplus value, transfer some labor to rich countries for free.[107] In other words, the production prices of poor countries' products are lower than their labor values, and the production prices of rich countries' products are greater than their labor values. Emmanuel's work was couched in Marxist terms (transformation of values into prices of production) and transposed Marx's analysis from the national level to the world level. Emmanuel's approach was expanded, amended, and criticized. Around the same time, Samir Amin published *L'accumulation à l'échelle mondiale* (*Accumulation on a World Scale*), which also begins with the theory of international trade, but then deepens the discussion of dependency by focusing on the transformation of relations of production and income distribution in the periphery, to make them compatible with unequal structural relations between the North and the South.[108] Thus the North-South structural inequality influenced class inequality in the countries of the periphery (and even perhaps determined it, in one possible reading of Amin). It was, if one may term it such, a "global political" theory of national income distribution:

> It is the nature of political relations between the foreign capital, local business bourgeoisie, the privileged layers of the salaried class, and the administrative bureaucracy which, in the last resort, determine distribution of incomes.[109]

Amin's interest in domestic inequality thus proceeded from his concern with international inequality. He provided a series of social tables for Egypt and the Maghreb countries from the second half of the nineteenth century to around 1960, and remarkably detailed (for the time) analyses of income distributions in several sub-Saharan African countries. One such social table for Egypt, in the year 1950, is shown in Figure 7.6. (For comparison, see the social table for England in 1759, in Chapter 2, and for France in 1831, in Chapter 4.) The class differences are enormous. Landless peasants are more than half of the total population, and their average per-capita income is just one-tenth of the mean income; on the other end of the distribution is the urban bourgeoisie, accounting for less than one percent of the total population, but with an average per-capita income that is about twenty-five times the mean.[110] In figures like this, where social classes are ordered on the horizontal axis according to their income level, we are used to seeing a strong negative relationship: as the social class becomes smaller, its relative income is higher. The Egypt example is just an extreme case of such regularity: its Gini coefficient, even without taking into account the intra-class inequality, is extraordinarily high at almost 77 points. This excessive inequality, presided over by a tiny and rich "comprador" bourgeoisie, was, according to the dependency doctrine, both a consequence of world inequalities and a condition for their maintenance.

Whether any given version of unequal trade or dependency was true or not is not of great interest to us.[111] What matters here is that the works of the dependency theorists addressed two issues that broadened the scope of inequality studies. First, they highlighted

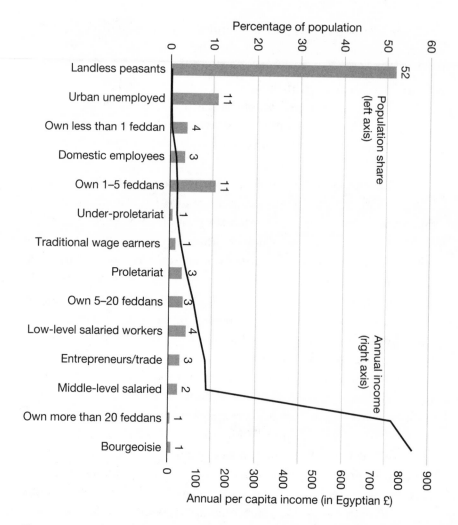

Figure 7.6. Population shares and relative incomes by social class in Egypt, around 1950

Note: Classes are ranked from the poorest to the richest. Population shares in percent are shown by the bars. Annual per-capita income is shown by the line. "Feddan" is a measure of land area equal to 0.42 hectares.

Data sources: Samir Amin, *L'accumulation à l'échelle mondiale*, vol. 1 (Paris: Editions Antrhopos, 1970), 445; Hassan Riad, *L'Égypte nassérienne* (Paris: Editions de Minuit, 1964).

unequal development in the world and thereby brought the topic of inter-national inequality in. Second, they argued that such inter-national inequality was structural in nature ("the rules of the game" being skewed in favor of rich countries) and created domestically, in poor countries, an income distribution that ensured the continuation of a subaltern role for the South. There are two aspects of inequality that were thus linked: the between-nation inequality that produced a specific type of domestic class structure, and the domestic inequality that in turn perpetuated the gap between rich and poor countries. It was in the interest of the ruling classes in the South that the South should remain underdeveloped. Dependency theorists therefore introduced an entirely new point of view, seeing within-national and inter-national inequalities as interdependent. As Anthony Brewer summed this up (using a term popularized by André Gunder Frank):

> The "development of underdevelopment" occurs because the world capitalist system is characterized by a metropolis-satellite structure. The metropolis exploits the satellite, surplus is concentrated in the metropolis, and the satellite is cut off from potential investment funds, so its growth is slowed down. More important, the satellite is reduced to a state of dependence which creates a local ruling class with an interest in perpetuating under-development, a "lumpen bourgeoisie" which follows a "policy of underdevelopment."[112]

This was not a link that was seen previously, although one could argue that *any* trade theory establishes an implicit link between trade and domestic class structure (as, for example, we saw with Ricardo's in Chapter 3). By doing this on the global level, neo-Marxists created an entirely new field. That field would naturally lead to global inequality studies, where the global level would be considered a new "normal" level at which to look at inequalities.

For this reason, the neo-Marxist studies during the Cold War provided the only important methodological breakthrough of that period in the way we visualize or study inequality. As mentioned before, they did it not while being focused on inequality as the key topic but rather while discussing difficulties of development in the global South, trade, and modern imperialism.

In terms of our three components, dependency theory certainly had a very clear political narrative and a developed theoretical framework. Its empirics were its weakest point. It tended to deal in broad historical generalizations, making very selective use of data (one could easily accuse the main dependency theorists of cherry-picking), and it ultimately failed to account for the fact that some underdeveloped countries—even if, until now, few—were able to break through the barrier of the uneven North-South relationship and attain higher levels of development. Its Achilles' heel was indeed its weak empirical basis, despite a seeming plethora of references to many parts of the world and historical developments. But looking more closely at them, one finds that such examples are often used in a purely rhetorical fashion—to make a point—and seldom based on serious data work. This is certainly the case in Samir Amin's and André Gunder Frank's later works, with their broad-brush historical discussions—in contrast to earlier works by both that took the empirical part much more seriously. (As mentioned, Amin had contributed important original work on Egypt, the Maghreb, and sub-Saharan Africa.) Neo-Marxist theories failed precisely in the area where they seemed superficially strong: in the empirical part which, in principle, they highlighted but in reality treated rather cursorily, especially when contrasted with the work done at the same time in economic history. This is unfortunate because a more sustained effort to do empirical work on income distributions in the Third World countries was long overdue. These countries were all but ignored by metropolitan neoclassical economists, and contributions by economists from the less developed countries were, due to lack of interest and training, sparse. Neo-Marxist approaches thus possessed a "natural" advantage, but they failed to capitalize on it.

Epilogue: The New Beginning

Inequality studies exploded in the first decades of the twenty-first century, and there were several objective, or external, reasons for this. The straitjacket of classlessness and "rational agents" imposed by Cold War economics was broken. Research was becoming freer just as income inequality, which had been rising for thirty years, was becoming more obvious. The world was leaving an era when rich Wall Street bankers celebrated the "Great Moderator" Alan Greenspan—who served nearly a decade as Fed Chair (1987–1996) through three administrations, Reagan, Bush Senior, and Clinton— even to the extent of spending thousands of dollars for portraits of him to adorn their Martha's Vineyard and Cape Cod homes.[1] But at the same time, the US middle class was struggling and the minimum wage had fallen lower (on a price-adjusted basis) than its level in 1968. Middle-class income stagnation was covered up by the ease of borrowing (because the rich had increasing amounts of free financial capital in search of "placements") and by the ease of home-buying— always a dream of middle-class living—even for those lacking steady jobs or much money for down payments. Consumption by the middle classes in America thus rose, suggesting a moderate prosperity, while underlying real incomes stagnated.

The financial crisis of 2007–2008 uncovered this disparity between the movements in income and consumption. Loans had to be repaid and mortgages serviced, and there was simply no income with which to do this. Many people lost their homes to repossession by banks.[2] Interest on credit card and other debt could not be endlessly rolled over. In short, the middle classes in the United States and elsewhere in the rich world realized that what they had taken for prosperity in the past thirty tears had been a mirage. But the prosperity of the top earners (especially the "one percent" singled out by protests) was not a mirage. This fraction of the population did well indeed. Figure E.1 shows the growth incidence curve for the United States, displaying cumulative real income gains at different points of US income distribution between 1986 and 2007. Incomes of 85 percent of the population increased at an almost identical rate of 20 percent over twenty years (representing an average growth rate of less than a one percent per annum). But, looking at the top 15 percent of the population over that same period, we see that each richer percentile enjoyed a rate of growth higher than the last. For the top one percent, real cumulative growth was 90 percent, or four-and-a-half times greater than for most people in America. On top of this, it seemed to many of the "cheated" poor and middle classes that it was the rich, the main beneficiaries of US growth, who had caused the crisis with their reckless lending. And in the end, not only had top earners' incomes risen much faster during the two decades, and not only had they fueled the crisis, they were even spared its consequences thanks to taxpayers' contributions to the bailouts of the banks.

It was all suddenly recognized as unfair. And it was this realization at the time of the crisis, I think, that brought the topic of inequality—which had only been hovering in the background—to the forefront of people's consciousness. The crisis legitimized the topic. Even the term *inequality*, formerly invoked only with some reticence and trepidation, began to be used widely and openly.

This resurgence of popular concern with income distribution—spurred, as we have just seen, by "objective" developments—was further reinforced by the remarkable research on income inequality published around the same time. The true relationship between such studies and the sudden interest in income distribution is difficult to gauge, but probably they reinforced each other. Had general interest in inequality remained at its previous (low) level, this new wave of

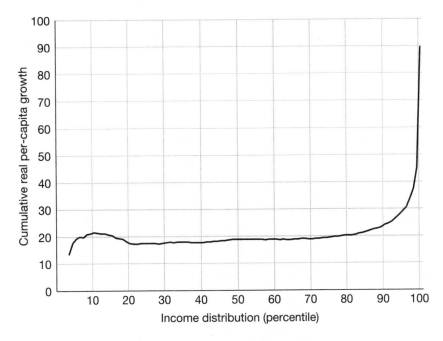

Figure E.1. Percentage increase in real per-capita after-tax income at different points of US income distribution (cumulative growth 1986–2007)

Data sources: Calculated from LIS Cross-National Data in Luxembourg; Current Population Survey (CPS), US Census Bureau.

inequality studies might have languished in obscurity. Instead, they became international bestsellers.

There are three remarkable developments in the work on inequality that, I believe, are most likely to have enduring impact on the economics profession and social scientists, at least for another half century. All three originated during the heady period of the early 2000s. They are, first, Thomas Piketty's work on long-term trends of inequality in rich countries, aptly summarized in his $r > g$ formula (stating that the rate of profit in an economy is greater than its rate of growth); second, the creation of dynamic social tables, which extend the knowledge of income distribution to times for which neither fiscal data nor household income surveys exist; and third, the introduction of *global* inequality studies as a new area of research.

Each of these trends is now only at the beginning of what I expect to be many tumultuous and successful developments in the decades to come. Each deserves, as this book comes to its close, some paragraphs of explanation.

Piketty's contribution. In 2014, the English-language version of Thomas Piketty's *Capital in the Twenty-First Century* became a huge international bestseller.[3] Probably it had the highest first-year sales of any economics book ever. While this is remarkable, it does not tell the full story. Many books have become bestsellers only to be soon forgotten. But this is unlikely to be the case here, both because Piketty has gone on to expand the agenda of his work in several promising directions, and because he proposed a new way of looking at inequality—a new theory of inequality whose importance stands independent of the book's appeal to a wide audience. For both reasons, future economists will probably regard *Capital in the Twenty-First Century* as the most influential book since Keynes's *General Theory* was published in 1936.[4]

Piketty originally studied inequality in France from the nineteenth century onward (the focus of his earlier book, *Top Incomes in France in the Twentieth Century*), and later extended this work to the United States, Germany, and the UK. He developed what may be called a "political theory of income distribution."[5] According to it, capitalism, left to itself, generates ever-increasing inequality because the returns to capital, received mostly by the rich, consistently exceed the growth of mean income—a tendency Piketty sums up as $r > g$. This inexorable increase in inequality is interrupted or reversed only by external events, such as economic crises, wars, periods of hyperinflation, and political decisions (for example, tax increases). I will not repeat the advantages and disadvantages of this theory that I have discussed elsewhere.[6] What is important here is to acknowledge that Piketty's work represented a new view, pregnant with many implications, and thus, not surprisingly, it has generated an enormous empirical and theoretical literature.

Moreover, Piketty has tried like very few before him to integrate theories of production and distribution. As return to capital (which he believes has historically been stable, at around 5 percent per year) exceeds the rate of growth of the economy, which stands as a proxy for the growth of income of an average person, inequality increases: in effect, capitalists who are at the top of income distribution receive an increase in income of r percent which is greater than the rate of income growth of the average person (g), and the gap between the rich and the middle class rises. Capitalists also use part (or all) of their capital income to invest, and thus the ratio of the stock of capital to GDP (Piketty's β) increases. But as β becomes greater and production more capital-intensive, the share of capital income in total GDP (Piketty's α) increases as well—which, given that capital belongs mostly to the rich, further exacerbates income inequality. There is thus a vicious circle of ever-rising inequality. Of course, if greater capital intensity were associated with reduction of the rate of return (that is, if r were trending down), the capital share α would not rise. But Piketty rejects this by pointing to the relative fixity of return to capital through history.*

We have thus re-encountered in Piketty some of Marx's ideas, but in very different packaging. Like Marx, Piketty thinks that the capital share will tend to rise, but he rejects Marx's prediction of a decline in the rate of return to capital. It is then clear, if capital intensity of production rises forever and r does not decrease, that the system will eventually move to an unsustainable situation where the entire income is received by capital owners. This does not happen, however, because "preventive checks"—wars and periods of hyperinflation—destroy capital, whether physically or by spoliating creditors. Once capital stock is reduced by such a check, capitalists go back to their Sisyphean task of reconquering their ruling position. Short of wars and other calamities, they would succeed—but taxation of wealth and of high incomes can also slow them down.

---

*In terms of the production function, a quasi-fixity of r despite an increase in the K/L ratio requires high elasticity of substitution (greater than unity) between capital and labor. That is, rising quantity of capital does not sufficiently depress (or in Piketty's extreme case does not depress at all) the rate of return and capitalists' share in total income increases.

By outlining this dynamic, Piketty has thus proposed an entirely new and compelling argument that peaceful development of capitalism leads to the breakdown of the system—not because the profit rate crashes to zero and capitalists give up investing (as Marx would have it), but for the very opposite reason that capitalists tend to end up in possession of a society's entire output and that is a socially unsustainable situation. In Marx's view, capitalists (as a class) fail because they are not too successful; in Piketty's view, they fail because they are too successful. In Marx's view, capitalists, through competition against each other, diminish the cost of production and reduce profits. To use Keynes's expression, they ultimately cause the euthanasia of the rentier. In Piketty's contrary view, capitalists are extraordinary successful. They keep on accumulating more and more capital, but the rate of return on that more abundant capital somehow does not decrease. In the end, they would own everything. But that must provoke a revolution, whether by pitchforks or by extraordinary taxation.

Piketty's success has been that, for the first time since Kuznets, economists have been presented with an alternative theory of the forces that determine income distribution. If one surveys the landscape today, we have on offer three theories of income distribution in capitalism. First, there is Marx's theory, by which increasing concentration of ownership of capital and decreasing rate of profit ultimately lead to the death of capitalism through zero investments. Second, we have Kuznets's hypothesis of a wave of rising and then decreasing inequality—or as I have argued, successive waves.[7] Such waves consist of a first phase driven by technological revolutions (the rise), followed by a second phase (the decline) featuring dissipation of technological rents, a greater abundance of capital reducing the rate of return, and greater demand for social transfers and thus higher taxation. And third, now, there is Piketty's theory of unfettered capitalism that, left to its own devices, maintains an unchanged rate of return and sees the top earners' share of capital income increasing to the point that it threatens to swallow the entire output of the society, and only a political response can prevent such an outcome.

It is therefore not surprising that Piketty puts such strong emphasis on the politics of redistribution, and (as in his subsequent book, *Capital and Ideology*) on ideologies that either justify high inequality or try to limit it.[8]

We are thus in the remarkable position today of having access both to an infinitely greater quantity of data on inequality, and to three relatively clear theories of change of inequality under capitalism that can be empirically tested.

Social tables. The second remarkable development in the first two decades of the twenty-first century is the exploitation of historical and archival sources which, of course, had been around for a long time but were brought to light thanks to new abilities to digitalize and process large amounts of data using computers. This launched the investigation of social structures, and thus inequalities, in many countries where the data on occupational incomes and estimates of incomes of various social classes were preserved and could be located. Such work is rapidly expanding. While Piketty's work (based on fiscal data) shed light on developments in the twentieth century—that is, in the years since advanced countries introduced personal taxation—social tables enable us to dig much deeper, back to the Commercial Revolution, the Middle Ages, and even earlier.

To appreciate the importance of social tables, one must know that many countries still do not have fiscal or tax data, and when they do, the data refer only to the top of the income distribution since the rich are the only people subject to direct taxation. Only such data are displayed in the standard information on tax payments. For everybody else, direct taxes are withheld at source (that is, automatically deducted from wages)—or, as is true for many people in poor countries, not assessed at all. For example, only 7 percent of households in India pay direct taxes that are listed in fiscal tabulations, and less than one percent do so in Russia and China. For these countries today, the only complete data come from household surveys and, for the past, from social tables—if the latter can be constructed.

There are several remarkable developments in the use of dynamic social tables. (I apply the term "dynamic" to social tables that are equally or similarly structured in terms of classes or occupational categories, each for a given year, and that are then linked by including additional information on the evolution of wages, capital incomes, and the like.) Peter Lindert and Jeffrey Williamson were the pioneers in using and harmonizing English/British social tables, starting with Gregory King's famous 1688 table. They also created the first social tables for the United States (1774–1870), mentioned in Chapter 7. They have thus produced the first integrated, long-run study of income distribution in the United States.[9] More recently, Robert Allen has standardized English/British social tables, and compressed their multiple and variegated social classes into only a few key classes.[10] (I have used them, together with Lindert and Williamson's reworking of the English social tables, in Chapters 2 through 4.) Similar social tables were created for France (see Morrisson and Snyder's table in Chapter 4).[11] And, very importantly, the recent works by Javier Rodriguez Weber (for Chile, 1850–2009), Diego Castañeda and Erik Bengtsson (for Mexico, 1895–1940), and Maria Gómes León and Herman de Jong (for Germany and the United Kingdom, 1900–1950) have produced extremely valuable long-run income distributions for these countries.[12] Filip Novokmet did the same for Czechoslovakia, Poland, and Bulgaria.[13] And likewise, Mikołaj Malinowski and Jan Luiten van Zanden pushed our knowledge of pre-capitalist inequality much further than only a decade ago for Poland.[14] Philipp Erfurth has contributed similar knowledge for pre-unification Prussia, and for Bavaria just prior to the 1848 revolution.[15] These studies open up the economic and social histories of the countries they study and provide invaluable sources of hypotheses and data for other economists, sociologists, and political scientists.

There is, in my opinion, no doubt that more of such dynamic social tables, produced at ever smaller time intervals and covering an increasing number of countries, will transform our knowledge of pre-capitalist and early-capitalist economies and will enable us to see social structures in such societies in ways not possible before. Particularly promising in this area is additional work on China (with its plentiful and unused archival sources), Japan, the Ottoman Empire, and Russia.

This work combines empirical research with extended time horizons, and also introduces political and social components. It shows how we can integrate studies of inequality, politics, and political economy; in other words, it treats inequality as embedded in society.

Global inequality. The third very promising development is work on global inequality. Doing such research empirically is impossible as long as most countries do not field regular household surveys (which are the best, or only, detailed source of information for entire national distributions), and if price levels in different countries cannot be compared. Both of these empirical obstacles, however, have been overcome in the past thirty years. The first problem was solved when China and the Soviet Union, and then the post-Soviet countries, began to share data from household surveys, and many African countries began to conduct regular surveys. At this point, there are nationally representative household surveys covering more than 90 percent of the world's population and approximately 95 percent of world's economic output.* Not all countries produce surveys annually, but researchers can work with relatively close benchmark years (say, a benchmark year every three or five years), and use all available surveys that fall within those time windows. This is entirely different from the situation in the 1980s, when data from China, the Soviet republics, and much of Africa were nonexistent or unavailable.

Meanwhile, the second obstacle has been largely overcome by the ever-broadening scope and more accurate information provided by the International Comparison Program, which allows us to compare countries' price levels and thus assess real living standards across the

---

* It should be mentioned, however, that countries that do not conduct or do not publish household income surveys tend to be poor or in the midst of civil wars. Thus, approximately the poorest 10 percent of the world's population is not included in our statistics. This obviously imparts a downward bias to estimates of both global inequality and global poverty.

world.[16] This will be even further improved when more within-country price information becomes available, so that (for example) researchers will be able to distinguish price levels in different parts of China (and thus establish more accurate estimates of real welfare). Currently, Chinese and Indian price levels distinguish between rural and urban areas only, and for all other countries only a single average countrywide price level is used to adjust nominal incomes.

The empirical work, however important, is only the first necessary step toward what will hopefully become a global history as seen and reflected in global income distribution. For it is clear that global income data contain in them the entire narratives of the Great Divergence, colonization, enslavement, decolonization, successful and failed growth episodes, and economic and political rise and fall of nations. Such histories are all, for obvious reasons, reflected in incomes that people in different parts of the world command. Examining the data from large countries enables us to see, for example, how the declines in Chinese per-capita incomes during the Great Leap Forward and Cultural Revolution added to China's contribution to global inequality (by making the Chinese population poorer) and pushed global Gini up by almost two points, an enormous amount. Or how, since the early 1980s, China's fast growth drove global inequality down, especially—for a given rate of per-capita growth—when China was a relatively poor country.[17] With that period at its end now that Chinese average income exceeds global mean income, other engines of global inequality reduction, perhaps India and Africa, may take over.

The narrative of global inequality, of the reshuffling of income positions among different nations and classes, remains to be teased out from the data. But the data, and some first attempts to devise such a global narrative, are already there. It is encouraging to see new books highlighting the narrative of global income distribution as part of the social sciences more broadly and not only of economics.[18] Ideally, the empirical work on global income distribution will be combined with the broad global narratives that characterized the Annales school, and the work of Fernand Braudel and Paul

Bairoch in particular, and indeed of the world's systems theorists.[19] This is why, in the previous chapter, I emphasized the vital, neo-Marxist linkage between (systemic) inter-country inequality and within-national inequalities.

In the work that I have in mind here, I envisage a complete integration of three levels of understanding: first, the *between-country inequality* that influences the power relations of countries (including political and economic domination, colonization, and the like); second, the *within-county inequality* that may in turn be seen, as the dependency theorists saw it, as both determined by and facilitating the maintenance of uneven international power relationships (although it also responds to domestic class and other cleavages); and third, the *global inequality* among citizens of the world, where all of these perspectives are refracted.

We must also allow for the potential that the forces of globalization will create a global elite and that the displacement of, say, some rich Americans by some rich Chinese from their top places in the global income distribution may not have much of a political effect on either between- or within-country inequality, because the global top layer may operate at a level apart from nation-states. If we anticipate, as we should, that the current globalization will produce the first global elite, then social scientists must prepare to engage with new questions. What would the advent of such a global elite (or even a global middle class, if it were created) imply for international relations? For democracy? For corruption and taxation? These would be entirely new questions that the traditional social science, which has always taken the nation-state as the unit at which most of the political and social competition and developments took place, did not study. Nor envisage—or even imagine.

NOTES

Prologue

1. Heinz D. Kurz, "Will the MEGA 2 Edition Be a Watershed in Interpreting Marx?" *European Journal of the History of Economic Thought* 25, no. 5 (2018): 783–807.

2. Joseph A. Schumpeter, *History of Economic Analysis,* ed. Elizabeth Boody Schumpeter (Oxford: Oxford University Press, 1954; repr. 1980); Mark Blaug, *Economic Theory in Retrospect* (Homewood, IL: R. D. Irwin, 1962).

3. Leszek Kolakowski, *Main Currents of Marxism,* trans. P. S. Falla, 3 vols. (Oxford: Clarendon Press, 1978).

4. Robert Heilbroner, *The Worldly Philosophers: The Lives, Times, and Ideas of the Great Economic Thinkers,* 7th ed. (New York: Touchstone, 1999).

5. See John Rawls, *A Theory of Justice* (Cambridge, MA: Belknap Press of Harvard University Press, 1971), 53–59.

6. See, for example, Amartya Sen, *On Economic Inequality* (Oxford: Clarendon Press, 1973).

7. Shlomo Avineri, *The Social and Political Thought of Karl Marx* (Cambridge: The University Press, 1968). Avineri writes that Marx "never believed that trade union activity as such could remake the world, since it could not change the structure of society or the quality of human labor under the conditions of capital" (121). He also explains that the concept of the workers' association "does not have a narrowly political, nor a trade union significance: it is a real constructive effort to create the social texture of future human relations" (142).

8. Karl Marx, "Postface to the Second Edition," *Capital,* vol. I, trans. Ben Fowkes, intro. by Ernest Mandel (London: Penguin, 1976), 99.

9. For comparisons of European wealth inequalities, see World Wealth and Income Database, https://wid.world; and Daniel Waldenström, "Wealth and History: An Update," IFN Working Paper No. 1411, Research Institute of Industrial Economics, Stockholm, October 14, 2021, https://www.ifn.se/media/442pkvuk/wp1411.pdf.

10. "Notwithstanding of these superior advantages it is not likely that slavery should ever be abolished, and it was owning to some peculiar circumstances that it has been abolished in the small corner of the world in which we live. In the democratic government it is hardly possible that it ever should [be abolished], as the legislators are here persons who are each masters of slavers; they therefore will never incline to part with so valuable a part of their property." Adam Smith, "Report of 1762–63," *Lectures on Jurisprudence,* ed. R. L. Meek, D. D. Raphael, and P. G. Stein (Oxford: Clarendon Press, 1978; repr. Indianapolis: Liberty Classics, 1982), 186.

11. "A fight for the continuance of the Union is a fight against the continuance of the slavocracy—that in this contest the highest form of popular self-government till now realized

is giving battle to the meanest and most shameless form of man's enslavement in the annals of history. . . . Such a war [is] so distinguished by the vastness of its dimensions and the greatness of its ends, from the groundless, wanton and diminutive wars Europe has passed through since 1849." Karl Marx, "The London Times and Lord Palmerston," *New York Tribune,* November 7, 1861, in Karl Marx, *Dispatches for the New York Tribune: Selected Journalism of Karl Marx* (London: Penguin, 2007).

12. Regarding the expansion of the line of research of Marx beyond the Western confines, Anderson argues, against the dominant view, that Marx's last decade was not barren but rather very active, with his work directed precisely in that new direction that the dominant Marx scholarship has tended to undervalue. Keith B. Anderson, *Marx at the Margins: On Nationalism, Ethnicity and Non-Western Societies,* enl. ed. (Chicago: University of Chicago Press, 2016).

13. As far as we know, Quesnay and Smith never sat down together to discuss their ideas *tête-à-tête.*

14. Vilfredo Pareto, *Les systèmes socialistes* (Paris: V. Giard and E. Brière, 1902).

15. Georges Weulersse, *Le mouvement physiocratique en France (de 1750 à 1770),* 2 vols. (Paris: F. Alcan, 1910), 85. My translation.

16. Adam Smith, *The Wealth of Nations, Books I–IV,* edited with notes and marginal summary by Edwin Cannan, preface by Alan B. Krueger (New York: Bantam Classics, 2003), based on 5th ed. as edited and annotated by Edwin Cannan in 1904. On rent: "I shall conclude this very long chapter," Book I, 335; on financial manipulations: Book II; on customs rules: Book IV.

17. Adam Smith, *The Theory of Moral Sentiments* (1759; London: Alex. Murray, 1872).

18. Schumpeter's complaint about Ricardo is worth quoting more fully: "The comprehensive vision of the universal interdependence of all the elements of the economic system that haunted [Johann Heinrich von] Thünen probably never cost Ricardo as much as an hour's sleep. His interest was in the clear-cut result of direct, practical significance. In order to get this he cut that general system to pieces, bundled up as large parts of it as possible, and put them in cold storage—so that as many things as possible should be frozen and 'given.' He then piled one simplifying assumption upon another until, having really settled everything by these assumptions, he was left with only a few aggregative variables between which, given these assumptions, he set up simple one-way relations so that, in the end, the desired results emerged almost as tautologies. . . . The habit of applying results of this character to the solution of practical problems we shall call the Ricardian Vice." Schumpeter, *History of Economic Analysis,* 472–473.

19. David Ricardo, *The Principles of Political Economy and Taxation,* intro. by F. W. Kolthammer (London: J. M. Dent and Sons, 1911; repr. New York: Dover, 2004).

20. David Ricardo to James Mill, September 29, 1818, in *The Works of David Ricardo,* ed. Piero Sraffa, vol. 7, *Letters 1816–1818* (Cambridge: University Press for the Royal Economic Society, 1952), 305. Also, David Ricardo to James Mill, November 8, 1818, "I cannot be blind to my utter inability of putting my thoughts on paper with any degree of order, clearness, or precision. I am astonished at my own deficiency, for this is a talent which every one around me possesses in a superior degree to myself" (7:327).

21. Commenting on Ricardo's "On Machinery" essay, Marx writes: "This section which Ricardo added to his third edition bears witness to his *bonne foi* which so essentially distinguishes him from vulgar economists." Karl Marx, *Theories of Surplus Value,* in Karl Marx and Frederick Engels, *Collected Works,* vol. 32: *Karl Marx Economic Works, 1861–1863* (New York: International Publishers, 1989), 181.

22. Martin Milligan, "Translator's Note on Terminology," in Karl Marx, *The Economic and Philosophic Manuscripts of 1844* (New York: Prometheus Books, 1988).

23. Karl Marx, *The Eighteenth Brumaire of Louis Napoleon,* trans. Daniel De Leon (New York: International Publishing, 1897), 47.

24. Karl Marx, "The Elections in England—Tories and Whigs," *New York Tribune,* August 21, 1852, in Marx, *Dispatches for the New York Tribune* (London: Penguin, 2007), 103.

25. Benedetto Croce, *Historical Materialism and the Economics of Karl Marx,* trans. C. M. Meredith (New York: Macmillan, 1914), 49.

26. Kurz, "Will the MEGA 2 Edition Be a Watershed?"

27. This causes one to wonder how many important writings may be languishing in archives or personal libraries, unlikely ever to be published and widely read.

28. In an obituary essay on his mentor Alfred Marshall, Keynes wrote: "The master-economist must possess a rare combination of gifts. . . . He must be mathematician, historian, statesman, philosopher—in some degree. He must understand symbols and speak in words. He must contemplate the particular, in terms of the general, and touch abstract and concrete in the same flight of thought. He must study the present in the light of the past for the purposes of the future. No part of man's nature or his institutions must be entirely outside his regard. He must be purposeful and disinterested in a simultaneous mood, as aloof and incorruptible as an artist, yet sometimes as near to earth as a politician." John Maynard Keynes, "Alfred Marshall" (1924), in *The Collected Writings of John Maynard Keynes,* vol. 10: *Essays in Biography* (London: Macmillan for the Royal Economic Society, 1972; repr. Cambridge: Cambridge University Press, 2013), 173–174.

1. François Quesnay

1. According to Weulersse, Quesnay is likely to have invented the term because of his love of Greek and composite words. Georges Weulersse, *Le mouvement physiocratique en France (de 1750 à 1770),* 2 vols. (Paris: F. Alcan, 1910), 1:128. François Quesnay, *Physiocratie, ou Constitution naturelle du gouvernement le plus avantageux au genre humain,* ed. Pierre-Samuel Dupont de Nemours, 6 vols. (Yverdon, 1768).

2. As Quesnay writes: "This science [political economy] is not confused . . . with the trivial and specious science of finance operations whose subject matter is only the money stock of the nation and the monetary movements resulting from traffic in money, in which credit, the rate of interest, and so on, as in the case of gambling, bring about nothing but a sterile circulation which only in exceptional circumstances can be of any benefit. It is in a knowledge of the true sources of wealth, and the means of increasing and perpetuating them, that the science of economic administration of a kingdom consists." *Tableau économique,* Maxime 24, extract from the *Royal Economic Maximes of M. de Sully, Third Edition of Tableau Économique,* in François Quesnay, *Quesnay's Tableau économique,* ed., with new material, translations, and notes by Marguerite Kuczynski and Ronald L. Meek (London: MacMillan for the Royal Economic Society and the American Economic Association, 1972), 21.

3. Romuald Dupuy, Pierre Le Masne, and Philippe Roman, "From the Accounts of *Philosophie rurale* to the Physiocratic Tableau: François Quesnay as Precursor of National Accounting," *Journal of the History of Economic Thought* 42, no. 4 (2020): 457–481.

4. Gianni Vaggi writes: "The fact that physiocratic analysis stresses opposing class interests and the contrasting aspects of economic and political structures must be regarded as one of its major merits." Later, however, it would become a political embarrassment for the physiocrats when the aristocracy refused to see this as a simple intellectual exercise. Gianni Vaggi, *The Economics of François Quesnay* (Durham, NC: Duke University Press, 1987), 187.

5. For estimates of French inequality and mean income, see Branko Milanovic, "The Level and Distribution of Income in Mid-18th Century France, According to François Quesnay," *Journal of the History of Economic Thought* 37, no. 1 (2015): 17–37, Table 4. The estimates come from François Quesnay, "Les rapports des dépenses entre elles" (1763),

in Quesnay, *Physiocratie,* ed. Jean Cartelier, 149–207 (Paris: Flammarion, 2008); Achille-Nicolas Isnard, *Traité des richesses* (Lausanne: F. Grasset, 1871); Jean-Claude Toutain, *Le produit intérieur brut de la France de 1789 à 1982* (Paris: Institut de sciences mathématiques et économiques appliquées, 1987); and Christian Morrisson and Wayne Snyder, "The Income Inequality of France in Historical Perspective," *European Review of Economic History* 4 (2000): 59–83. The estimate for England and Wales is based on Joseph Massie's social table from 1759, as revised in Peter H. Lindert and Jeffrey G. Williamson, "Revising England's Social Tables, 1688–1812," *Explorations in Economic History* 19, no. 4 (1982): 385–408.

6. Morrisson and Snyder, "Income Inequality of France in Historical Perspective." In today's France, the share of the top decile is some 32 to 33 percent. See Piketty, *Le capital au XXIe siècle* (Paris: Seuil, 2013), 429.

7. At the peak of British wealth inequality around 1900, it was estimated that the top decile owned around 70 percent of national wealth. Facundo Alvaredo, Anthony B. Atkinson, and Salvatore Morelli, "Top Wealth Shares in the UK over More Than a Century, *INET Oxford Working Paper,* No. 2017–01 (2016); Peter Lindert, "Unequal British Wealth since 1867," *Journal of Political Economy* 94, no. 6 (1986): 1127–1162.

8. Branko Milanovic, Peter Lindert, and Jeffrey Williamson, "Pre-industrial Inequality," *Economic Journal* 121, no. 1 (2011): 255–272.

9. Milanovic, "Level and Distribution of Income," table 4.

10. Branko Milanovic "Towards an Explanation of Inequality in Pre-modern Societies: The Role of Colonies, Urbanization, and High Population Density," *Economic History Review* 71, no. 4 (2018): 1029–1047, figure 3.

11. Milanovic, "Level and Distribution of Income," table 4.

12. Calculation based on Massie's social table for England, year 1759, in Milanovic, "Level and Distribution of Income," 33.

13. Maddison Project Database, version 2020, https://www.rug.nl/ggdc/historicaldevelop ment/maddison/releases/maddison-project-database-2020?lang=en.

14. Quesnay, "Les rapports des dépenses entre elles" (1763).

15. François-René de Chateaubriand, *Memoires d'outre-tombe,* vol. 2, *Livres 13–24* (Paris: Garnier frères, 1898; Garnier: Livre de poche, 2011), bk. 13:32–33. My translation.

16. Arthur Young, *Arthur Young's Travels in France during the Years 1787, 1788, and 1789,* ed. with intro. and notes by Miss Betham-Edwards (London: G. Bell and Sons, 1900), entry for September 19, 1788.

17. For an excellent discussion, see Gertrude Himmelfarb's "Introduction" in Alexis de Tocqueville, *Memoir on Pauperism,* trans. Seymour Drescher (Chicago: Ivan R. Dee, 1997). Drescher translation originally published New York: Harper and Row, 1968.

18. This point comes out even more strongly in Tocqueville, *Sécond memoire sur le paupérisme* (1837): "Men who are thus violently forced out from the cultivation of the land seek a refuge in manufacturing. The industrial class does not expand simply in a natural and gradual way following the needs of industry, but does so suddenly and artificially driven by the poverty of the agricultural class." Available through "Les classiques des sciences sociales" collection, Université de Québec à Chicoutimi, http://classiques.uqac.ca/classiques /De_tocqueville_alexis/memoire_pauperisme_2/memoire_pauperisme_2.html. My translation.

19. Friedrich Engels, *The Condition of the Working Class in England* (London: Penguin Classics, 2009).

20. According to Mirabeau, "The science of economics is the study and demonstration of the laws of nature relating to the sustenance and multiplication of the human race. The universal . . . knowledge of these laws is therefore the indispensable basis, and the necessary means of the happiness of all." Mirabeau, "Suite de la seizième lettre de M. B. à M***," *Éphémérides du citoyen,* 2 (1769) : 1–67, 13. My translation.

21. François Quesnay, "Maximes générales du gouvernement économique d'un royaume agricole" (1767), in Quesnay, *Physiocratie*, ed. Jean Cartelier (Paris: Flammarion, 2008), 243.

22. For an excellent discussion of this institution of the imperial government, see Charles Hucker, *The Censorial System of Ming China* (Stanford: Stanford University Press, 1966). The Ming dynasty ended in 1636, but the system continued unchanged under the Qing, who ruled China when Quesnay was writing.

23. Toynbee compares China and France, claiming that France has played a role within Europe similar to China's role within Asia, in the sense that France was culturally the most influential country in Europe, with other countries either imitating or looking up to it. Arnold Toynbee, "Looking Back Fifty Years," in *The Impact of the Russian Revolution*, ed. Toynbee (Oxford: Oxford University Press, 1967), 14.

24. Charles Montesquieu, *The Spirit of Laws,* Book VIII, 21 (Cambridge: Cambridge University Press, 1989). Quesnay devotes an entire chapter, entitled "Defects Attributed to the Government of China," to rebutting, point-by-point, Montesquieu's claims of arbitrary despotism. His opening salvo is that "M. de Montesquieu has above all ventured many conjectures, which he has put forward with so much skill that one could regard them as so many specious sophisms against this government." François Quesnay, *Le Despotisme de la Chine* (1767), in *Œuvres économiques et philosophiques de F. Quesnay,* 563–660 (Paris: Peelman, 1888), https://www.chineancienne.fr/17e-18e-s/quesnay-despotisme-de-la-chine/. My translation.

25. Alexis de Tocqueville, *The Old Régime and the French Revolution,* trans. Stuart Gilbert (Garden City, NY: Doubleday Anchor Books, 1955), 162.

26. Tocqueville, *The Old Régime,* 163–164.

27. François Quesnay, "Du commerce" (1766), in Quesnay, *Physiocratie*, ed. Jean Cartelier (Paris: Flammarion, 2008), fn 304–305. My translation).

28. Quesnay, "Les rapports des dépenses entre elles" (1763). The Quesnay work also appears in V. R. de Mirabeau, *Philosophie rurale*, 3 vols. (Amsterdam: Chex les Libraries Associés, 1763).

29. Weulersse, *Le mouvement physiocratique en France (de 1750 à 1770),* 2 vols. (Paris: F. Alcan, 1910), 85. My translation.

30. The expression comes from Friedrich Melchior Grimm, cited in Weulersse, *Le mouvement physiocratique,* 85.

31. Quesnay, "Les rapports des dépenses entre elles" (1763).

32. Vaggi, *Economics of François Quesnay,* 140–143.

33. *Maximes Générales,* quoted in Vaggi, *Economics of François Quesnay,* 141.

34. Mirabeau, who was more outspoken in his support of tenant-farmers than Quesnay, ended up being imprisoned for a week and banished to his estate for two months. Vaggi, *Economics of François Quesnay,* 143, based on Weulersse, *Le mouvement physiocratique.*

35. Weulersse, *Le mouvement physiocratique.* 540.

36. An interesting question (although it does not directly concern us here) is whether Quesnay believed that only agriculture was sufficiently productive to yield a surplus, or whether his model is "fitted" in such a manner (due to the relations of exchange assumed between the sectors) that only agriculture *appears* productive. Jean Cartelier in an excellent preface argues the latter. Cartelier, "Preface," in Quesnay, *Physiocratie*, ed. Jean Cartelier (Paris: Flammarion, 2008). But this explanation seems anachronistic. Quesnay did not think in terms of multisectoral or Sraffian models but simply observed that most, or even all, of propriétaires' incomes came from tax assessments on agricultural production. It fundamentally does not matter whether he thought that agriculture was intrinsically more productive or took the social relations as he experienced them as given.

37. Marx wrote: "The capitalists [in the physiocratic system] are only capitalists in the interest of the landowner, just as political economy in its later development would have them be capitalists only in the interest of the working class." Karl Marx, *Theories of Surplus Value*, in Karl Marx and Frederick Engels, *Collected Works*, vol. 32, *Marx: 1861–1863* (New York: International Publishers, 1989), 53.

38. Isaac Ilyich Rubin, *A History of Economic Thought*, trans. Donald Filtzer and Miloš Samardžija (London: Ink Links, 1979). Originally published in Russian in 1929.

39. Quesnay, "Maximes générales du gouvernement économique d'un royaume agricole," (1767), 265. My translation.

2. Adam Smith

1. It is impossible to establish the precedence: Adam Ferguson, John Millar, and Anne Robert Jacques Turgot proposed similar stadial theories at around the same time.

2. Smith never discussed how the advancing, stationary, or declining states of society should be related to the stadial theory of history. It could be that, within each development stage, some societies go forward and others do not. Would the advancing societies in the feudal stage move to become commercial societies? We just do not know, and Smith does not tell us.

3. Page references for Books I–IV are to Adam Smith, *The Wealth of Nations*, edited with notes and marginal summary by Edwin Cannan, preface by Alan B. Krueger (New York: Bantam Classics, 2003), based on 5th ed. as edited and annotated by Edwin Cannan in 1904. Page references for Book V are to Adam Smith, *Of the Revenue of the Sovereign or Commonwealth (Book V of The Wealth of Nations, 1776)*, ed. D. N. Deluna (Altoona, AL: Owlworks/Archangul Foundation, 2009).

4. Smith, *Wealth of Nations*, Book II, ch. 3, 436.

5. For example, regarding financial regulation Smith writes: "But those exertions of natural liberty of a few individuals [creators of Ponzi-like financial schemes], which might endanger the security of the whole society, are, and ought to be, restrained by the laws of all governments; of the most free as well as of the most despotical." Smith, *Wealth of Nations*, Book II, ch. 2, 414.

6. The passage comes to us via Smith's contemporary Dugald Stewart, who later quoted selections from "a short manuscript drawn up by Mr. Smith in the year 1755, and presented by him to a society of which he was then a member." Dugald Stewart, "Account of the Life and Writings of Adam Smith, LLD, from the transactions of the Royal Society of Edinburgh, read by Mr. Stewart, January 21 and March 18, 1793," in *The Glasgow Edition of the Works and Correspondence of Adam Smith*, vol. 3, *Essays on Philosophical Subjects*, ed. W. P. D. Wightman, J. C. Bryce, and I. S. Ross, 269–332 (London: Cadell, 1811; Oxford: Oxford University Press, 1980).

7. Smith, *Wealth of Nations*, Book II, ch. 3, 442.

8. The impression of going backward economically, which Smith ascribes to many in France, was not, in his opinion, accurate for that country, but was especially an opinion "which nobody can possibly entertain with regard to Scotland who sees the country now, and who saw it twenty or thirty years ago." Smith, *Wealth of Nations*, Book I, ch. 9, 127.

9. Smith, *Of the Revenue (Book V of The Wealth of Nations)*, ch. 7, 813–814.

10. Marvin Brown argues that Smith accepted slavery in economic life while rejecting it as a moral philosopher. Marvin T. Brown, "Free Enterprise and Economics of Slavery," *Real-world Economics Review* 52 (2010): 28–39, http://www.paecon.net/PAEReview/issue52 /Brown52.pdf. This is consistent with my view that *The Theory of Moral Sentiments* and *The Wealth of Nations* were written to explain two different aspects of our lives: life within an organic community and commercial life.

11. Smith, *Of the Revenue (Book V of The Wealth of Nations)*, ch. 3, 243.

12. Smith, *Wealth of Nations*, Book I, ch. 11, 276.

13. Smith, *Wealth of Nations*, Book I, ch. 8, 102.

14. Maddison Project Database, version 2020 by Jutta Bolt and Jan Luiten van Zanden, Groningen Growth and Development Center, Faculty of Economics and Business, University of Groningen, https://www.rug.nl/ggdc/historicaldevelopment/maddison/releases/maddison -project-database-2020?lang=en.

15. It is also possible that I have placed Poland in a higher category than Smith would. While Poland is always used (as is Portugal) as an example of the least developed European countries, it seemed to me to be placed implicitly above Asian countries. But Smith does not make the comparison directly.

16. Karl Marx, *A Contribution to the Critique of Political Economy*, trans. S. W. Ry-azanskaya (Moscow: Progress, first written in 1859), Note C: Theories of the Medium of Circulation and of Money.

17. Even based on Dennis C. Rasmussen, *The Infidel and the Professor: David Hume, Adam Smith, and the Friendship That Shaped Modern Thought* (Princeton, NJ: Princeton University Press, 2017), where the hypothesized friendship between Hume and Smith is the point of the title and extensively explored in the text, one might think that the friendship was not fully reciprocated by Smith. Without entering into a more specialist dispute about their relationship, I would venture the impression that Smith often avoided Hume, and wrote to him mostly when he needed a recommendation for himself or one of his students. Smith's lack of engagement with Hume's incessant invitations can also be interpreted in a way Rasmussen does not mention: it could be that Smith found his friend somewhat annoying and, rather than offer excuse after excuse for not getting together, simply chose to keep quiet.

18. The "they" here refers to a group he had just called a "sect of men of letters," clearly the physiocrats. Smith, *Of the Revenue (Book V of The Wealth of Nations)*, ch. 2, 113.

19. According to Cannan, "it is plain that Smith acquired the idea of the necessity of a scheme of distribution from the physiocrats." Edwin Cannan, "Introduction," in Adam Smith, *Lectures on Justice, Police, Revenues, and Arms, Delivered in the University of Glasgow by Adam Smith; Reported by a Student in 1763*, ed. Edwin Cannan (Oxford: Clarendon Press, 1896), xxxi. Quoted in Maurice Dobb, *Theories of Value and Distribution since Adam Smith: Ideology and Economic Theory* (Cambridge: Cambridge University Press, 1973), 56n. However, a draft of Smith's Edinburgh lectures from the 1750s, discovered only in the 1930s, implies, if generously interpreted, that the influence of physiocrats might have been less. Schumpeter, while noting Smith's ungenerous treatment of other authors, including Mandeville and Quesnay (184), writes that he "almost certainly did not fully grasp the importance of the *tableau économique*." Joseph A. Schumpeter, *History of Economic Analysis*, edited from manuscript by Elizabeth Boody Schumpeter (Oxford: Oxford University Press, 1954; repr. 1980), 232.

20. Stewart, "Account of the Life and Writings of Adam Smith," 329–330.

21. Johnson is quoted in his biographer's private papers: James Boswell, *Boswell: The Ominous Years, 1774–1776*, ed. Charles Ryskamp and Frederick A. Pottle (New York: McGraw-Hill, 1963). His "as dull a dog" is from Boswell's journal entry of April 13, 1776, on 337; "most disagreeable fellow" from Boswell's journal entry of March 17, 1776, on 264.

22. Wesley Mitchell, *Types of Economic Theory: From Mercantilism to Institution-alism*, vol. 1, edited with an introduction by Joseph Dorfman (New York: Augustus M. Kelley, 1967), 136.

23. As Smith himself would have enjoined us to do: "and he [a person] must be rich or poor according to the quantity of labor which he can command." Smith, *Wealth of Nations*, Book I, ch. 5, 133.

24. I am grateful to David Wootton for guidance on Adam Smith's probate and wealth.

25. Stewart, "Account of the Life and Writings of Adam Smith," 326.

26. The library was not actually small, and might explain a part of the gap. According to the most recent inventory, Adam Smith owned about two thousand books. Daniel B. Klein and Andrew G. Humphries, "Foreword and Supplement to 'Adam Smith's Library: General Check-List and Index,'" *Econ Journal Watch* 16, no. 2 (2019): 374–383. Some eighteen hundred books were listed by an earlier inventory. Hiroshi Mizuta, *Adam Smith's Library* (London: Cambridge University Press, 1967). Books are added by Klein and Humphries based on being owned by the University of Edinburgh and bearing Adam Smith's bookplate.

27. Massie's and other historical English and British social tables were recently reworked to create a series of class-consistent social tables (that is, with the same classes maintained throughout). Robert C. Allen, "Class Structure and Inequality during the Industrial Revolution: Lessons from England's Social Tables, 1688–1867," *Economic History Review* 72, no. 1 (2019): 88–125. I am mostly using Allen's version of the tables here. Massie's original table is much more detailed than Allen's reworking of it: it contains close to sixty groupings, from the highest-titled class No. 1 (there are twelve such high-titled classes) down to vagrants, estimating the average income of each class. Joseph Massie, *A Computation of the Money That Hath Been Exorbitantly Raised Upon the People of Great Britain by the Sugar-Planters, in One Year, from January 1759 to January 1760,* broadside, January 10, 1760, London, Kress Collection no. 9612.12, Baker Library Special Collections, Harvard Business School.

28. Allen, "Class Structure and Inequality." "Workers" are defined as "the manufacturing workforce, the building trades, miners, labourers and outservants, soldiers, seamen, domestic servants, and farm servants" (98).

29. Peter Lindert and Jeffrey Williamson, "Reinterpreting Britain's Social Tables 1688–1911," *Explorations in Economic History* 20 (1983): 94–109; Branko Milanovic, Peter Lindert, and Jeffrey Williamson, "Pre-industrial Inequality," *Economic Journal* 121, no. 1 (2011): 255–272; Allen, "Class Structure and Inequality."

30. Mitchell, *Types of Economic Theory,* 287.

31. Smith writes: "In every society the price of every commodity finally resolves itself into some one or other, or all of these three parts [wages, profit and rent] and in every improved society, all three enter . . . as component parts, into the price of the far greater part of commodities." Smith, *Wealth of Nations,* Book I, ch. 6, 71.

32. The first quote is from an early draft of *The Wealth of Nations,* composed prior to Smith's trip to France. Jerry Evensky, *Adam Smith's* Wealth of Nations: *A Reader's Guide* (Cambridge: Cambridge University Press, 2013), 33; Tony Aspromourgos, "'Universal Opulence': Adam Smith on Technical Progress and Real Wages," *European Journal of the History of Economic Thought* 17, no. 5 (2010): 1169–1182, 1176. The second quote is from Smith, *Wealth of Nations,* Book I, ch. 8, 111.

33. For the same interpretation, see David Wootton, *Power, Pleasure, and Profit: Insatiable Appetites from Machiavelli to Madison* (Cambridge, MA: Harvard University Press, 2018), 174: "Another view concedes that the two works [*The Theory of Moral Sentiments* and *The Wealth of Nations*] do not fit quite so nicely together, for one is about how we ought to behave toward our family, friends, and neighbors (who evoke our benevolent feelings), and the other about how we should interact with strangers we meet in the marketplace (to whom we owe no particular duty of care—caveat emptor is an attitude we can legitimately adopt to strangers, but not to family, friends, and neighbors)."

34. Amartya Sen, "Adam Smith and the Contemporary World," *Erasmus Journal of Philosophy and Economics* 3, no. 1 (2010): 50–67; Amartya Sen, *The Idea of Justice* (Cambridge, MA: Belknap Press of Harvard University Press, 2009); Amartya Sen, "Uses and Abuses of Adam Smith," *History of Political Economy* 43, no. 2 (2011): 257–271; George J. Stigler, "Smith's Travels on the Ship of State," *History of Political Economy* 3, no. 2 (1971): 265–277.

35. Sen, "Uses and Abuses of Adam Smith," 267. Sen quotes Adam Smith, *Lectures on Jurisprudence,* ed. R. L. Meek, D. D. Raphael, and P. G. Stein (Oxford: Clarendon Press, 1978; repr. Indianapolis: Liberty Classics, 1982), 104.

36. There is an earlier mention of the invisible hand in Smith's treatise on astronomy, but that does not concern us here.

37. Adam Smith, *The Theory of Moral Sentiments* (1759; London: Alex. Murray, 1872), Part IV.i.10.

38. Consider two different positions. In one, each of ten people owns land of equal size, and each person earns 10 units. In the other position, one person has all the land and all the income, leaving everybody else with nothing—but then this rich person spends 90 units hiring the others to provide him with goods and services so that their incomes become ten. The two positions are not equivalent. In the second, to reach the presumed equality, we compare *incomes* of the poor (10) with net *savings* of the rich (100 minus 90). To see the full absurdity of that "equality," suppose that the rich man spent his *entire* income on goods and services, so that his net after those purchases was zero. Would it then make sense to claim he was actually poor?

39. Smith, *Theory of Moral Sentiments,* Part IV.i.10.

40. While acknowledging that God (by whatever appellation) plays a much more important role in *The Theory of Moral Sentiments* than in *The Wealth of Nations,* Rasmussen tends to minimize the deistic element in the former by insisting that Smith's several, rather modest, revisions made in the last edition "tempered some of his claims on behalf of religion." Overall, Rasmussen considers Smith to be a "deist of some kind" and a "skeptical deist." Rasmussen, *The Infidel and the Professor,* 233, 15–16.

41. The theistic element appears also in Smith's strong rejection of Mandeville's "pernicious system." Smith, *Theory of Moral Sentiments,* Part VII.ii.98, 273.

42. Nirad C. Chaudhuri, *Thy Hand, Great Anarch! India: 1921–1952* (New Delhi: Vintage/Ebury div. Random House, 1987), 130.

43. To clarify, this duality does not, in my opinion, arise because of the different times when the two books were written. (As has been pointed out many times, *The Theory of Moral Sentiments* was revised by Smith after *The Wealth of Nations* had already been published, so there cannot be a "Young Smith" and an "Old Smith" in the way that there is a "Young Marx" and an "Old Marx.") Rather, it arises because the two books deal with different topics and reflect the different social positions we have in our lives.

44. Thorstein Veblen, *The Theory of the Leisure Class: An Economic Study of Institutions,* intro. by C. Wright Mills (New York: Macmillan, Mentor Book, 1953).

45. Smith, *Wealth of Nations,* Book III, ch. 2.

46. Smith, *Wealth of Nations,* Book III, ch. 2.

47. Smith, *Wealth of Nations,* Book IV, ch. 5, 682–683.

48. Smith, *Wealth of Nations,* Book I, ch. 10.

49. Smith, *Wealth of Nations,* Book IV, ch. 7, 807.

50. Smith, *Wealth of Nations,* Book IV, ch. 7, 722.

51. Smith, *Wealth of Nations,* Book III, ch. 3, 513.

52. Smith, *Wealth of Nations,* Book IV, ch. 2, 592.

53. Smith, *Wealth of Nations,* Book III, ch. 2.

54. Smith asks: "Have the exorbitant profits of the merchants of Cadiz and Lisbon augmented the capital of Spain and Portugal? Have they alleviated the poverty, have they promoted the industry of those two beggarly countries?" Smith, *Wealth of Nations,* Book IV, ch. 7, 779.

55. Smith, *Wealth of Nations,* Book I, ch. 11, 109.

56. Smith, *Wealth of Nations,* Book I, ch. 9.

57. Smith, *Lectures on Jurisprudence,* A, vi, 33–34.

58. J. Cunningham, *An Essay on Trade and Commerce* (London: printed for S. Hooper, 1770), 266–267, quoted in Mitchell, *Types of Economic Theory*, 115.

59. Smith, *Of the Revenue (Book V of The Wealth of Nations)*, ch. 2, 157.

60. "The real value of the landlord's share, his real command of the labor of other people, not only rises with the real value of the produce, but the proportion of his share to the whole produce rises with it." Smith, *Wealth of Nations*, Book I, ch. 11, 335.

61. Smith, *Wealth of Nations*, Book I, ch. 11.

62. The rate of interest simply mimics what happens to the rate of profit because it depends on it: "as the usual market rate of interest varies in any country, we may be assured that the ordinary profits of stock must vary with it, must sink as it sinks, and rise as it rises." Smith, *Wealth of Nations*, Book I, ch. 9, 123.

63. Smith, *Wealth of Nations*, Book IV, ch. 3, 624.

64. Smith, *Wealth of Nations*, Book I, ch. 11.

65. Smith, *Wealth of Nations*, Book I, ch. 9.

66. Smith writes: "It is not the actual greatness of national wealth but its continual increase which occasions a rise in the wages of labor. It is not accordingly in the richest countries but in the most thriving or in those which are growing rich the fastest that the wages of labor are highest." Smith, *Wealth of Nations*, Book I, ch. 8, 99. Also: "The proportion between the real recompence of labour in different countries, it must be remembered, is naturally regulated, not by their actual wealth or poverty, but by their advancing, stationary, or declining condition." Smith, *Wealth of Nations*, Book I, ch. 11, 258.

67. Smith, *Of the Revenue (Book V of The Wealth of Nations)*, ch. 3, 234. Ordinary people in North American colonies have, according to Smith, higher wages than in England, while slaves "are in a worse condition than the poorest people either in Scotland or Ireland." This view is confirmed by Peter Lindert and Jeffrey Williamson, *Unequal Gains: American Growth and Inequality since 1700* (Princeton, NJ: Princeton University Press, 2016), Figure 2.2 and the discussion around it, 40.

68. Smith writes: "The most detestable of all employments, that of public executioner, is, in proportion to the quantity of work done, better paid than any common trade whatever." Smith, *Wealth of Nations*, Book I, ch. 10, 140.

69. Smith writes that "in the same society or neighborhood, the average or ordinary rates of profit in the different employments of stock should be more nearly upon a level than the pecuniary wages of the different sorts of labor." Smith, *Wealth of Nations*, Book I, ch. 10, 154.

70. Smith, *Wealth of Nations*, Book I, ch. 10, 196–197.

71. Smith writes that, "though the interest of the laborer is strictly connected with that of the society, he is incapable either of comprehending that interest, or of understanding its connection with his own." Smith, *Wealth of Nations*, Book I, ch. 11, 337.

72. Smith, *Wealth of Nations*, Book I, ch. 11, 339.

73. Smith, *Wealth of Nations*, Book I, ch. 11, 339.

74. Smith, *Wealth of Nations*, Book I, ch. 7, 176.

75. Smith, *Wealth of Nations*, Book IV, ch. 3, 621.

3. The Ricardian Windfall

1. De Quincey's use of the familiar phrase (from John 19:5, for "Behold the man") is described in a short biographical sketch by Baudelaire: "Heureusement, l'économie politique lui restait, comme un amusement. Bien qu'elle doive être considérée comme une science, c'est-à-dire comme un tout organique, cependent quelques-unes de ses parties integrantes en peuvent être detachées et considerées isolement. Sa femme lui lisait de temps à autre les debats du

parlement ou les nouveautes de la librairie en la matière d'économie politique; mais pour un literateur profond et érudit, c'etait là une triste nourriture; pour quiconque a manié la logique, ce sont les rogations de l'ésprit humain. Un ami d'Edimbourg cependant lui envoya en 1819 un livre de Ricardo, et avant d'avoir achever le premier chapitre, il s'écriait, 'voilà l'homme.'" Charles Baudelaire, *Les paradis artificiels* (Paris: Poulet-Malassis et de Broise, 1860; Paris: Editions Gallimard, Livre de Poche, 1964), 193. David Ricardo, *The Principles of Political Economy and Taxation*, 3rd ed, with intro. by F. W. Kolthammer (London: J. M. Dent and Sons, 1911 [Everyman's Library]; repr. New York: Dover, 2004). First edition: London: John Murray, 1817; 3rd edition: London, John Murray, 1821.

2. Jean-Baptiste Say, *A Treatise On Political Economy; or the Production, Distribution, and Consumption of Wealth*, 5th American ed., trans. from 4th French ed., by C. R. Prinsep (Philadelphia: Grigg and Elliott, 1832), xlvii.

3. Joseph A. Schumpeter, *History of Economic Analysis,* edited from manuscript by Elizabeth Boody Schumpeter (Oxford University Press, 1954; repr. 1980), 472–473.

4. See Arnold Heertje, "The Dutch and Portuguese-Jewish Background of David Ricardo," *European Journal of the History of Economic Thought* 11, no. 2 (2004): 281–294.

5. This is clear from Ricardo's correspondence: "As for myself, I have all my . . . money invested in Stock; and this is as great an advantage as ever I expect or wish to make by a rise. I have been a considerable gainer by the loan; . . . and I have every reason to be well contented." David Ricardo to Thomas Malthus, June 27, 1815, in Ricardo, *The Works and Correspondence of David Ricardo*, ed. Pierro Sraffa with the collaboration of M. H. Dobb, vol. 6, *Letters, 1810–1815* (Cambridge: University Press for the Royal Economic Society, 1952), 233. (Hereafter *Works and Correspondence of David Ricardo*). Ricardo was also a shareholder of the Bank of England.

6. Ricardo's words are paraphrased as a recalled anecdote in Henry Vethake, "The Distinctive Provinces of the Political Philosopher and the Statesman," *Merchants' Magazine and Commercial Review*, January 1840, 109–110, quoted in Wesley Mitchell, *Types of Economic Theory: From Mercantilism to Institutionalism*, vol. 1, ed. with an introduction by Joseph Dorfman (New York: Augustus M. Kelley, 1967), 265.

7. George Soros, "Fallibility, Reflexivity, and the Human Uncertainty Principle," *Journal of Economic Methodology* 20, no. 4 (2013), 309–329.

8. The wages of skilled laborers in London in 1806 ranged between three and four shillings per day. Robert C. Allen, "Real Wages Once More: A Response to Judy Stephenson," *Economic History Review* 72, no. 2 (2019): 738–754, 743. If we use the average (3s 6d), which was also a bricklayer's and mason's wage, and assume 250 days of work, this yields almost £44 annually. An alternative could be to use Colquhoun's social table for 1801, which gives the average worker's family income as £55. Peter Lindert and Jeffrey Williamson, "Revising England's Social Tables 1688–1911," *Explorations in Economic History* 19, no. 4 (1982): 385–408, 400. Assuming that there are some families (more exactly, one-fifth) with two wage earners, this yields an annual income per worker also of around £44. Ricardo's wealth of £615,000 therefore equals the annual wages of about fourteen thousand skilled workers.

9. We can compare Ricardo's wealth with the wealth of a fictional character: Mr. Darcy from *Pride and Prejudice,* whose wealth Jane Austen judiciously expressed in realistic terms. Even if the story is set about a decade before Ricardo's death, the nominal amounts from the two periods are quite comparable. Mr. Darcy's wealth, which would put him also securely among the top one percent in Colquhoun's English 1801 social table, was 200,000 pounds, and thus less than half of Ricardo's wealth.

10. Mitchell, *Types of Economic Theory,* 1: 313–314.

11. Schumpeter wrote: "Ricardo is the only economist whom Marx treated as a master. . . . he learned his theory from Ricardo. But much more important is the objective

fact that Marx used the Ricardian apparatus; . . . problems presented to him in the forms that Ricardo had given to them." Schumpeter, *History of Economic Analysis,* 390.

12. On the Ricardian socialists, Marx's comment is very apt: "Since the . . . real development . . . unfolded . . . the contradiction between the growing wealth of the English 'nation' and the growing misery of the workers, and since moreover these contradictions are given a *theoretically* compelling . . . expression in the Ricardian theory, . . . it was natural for those thinkers who rallied to the side of the proletariat to seize on this contradiction, for which they found the theoretical ground already prepared." Karl Marx, *Theories of Surplus Value,* in Karl Marx and Frederick Engels, *Collected Works,* vol. 32: *Marx: 1861–1863* (New York: International Publishers, 1989), 395. Emphasis in original.

13. Maddison Project data come from Stephen Broadberry, Bruce M. S. Campbell, Alexander Klein, Mark Overton, and Bas van Leeuwen, *British Economic Growth 1270–1870: An Output-Based Approach* (Cambridge: Cambridge University Press, 2015).

14. Modern growth, according to Simon Kuznets, implies a per-capita growth rate of 2 percent per year. Simon Kuznets, *Economic Growth of Nations: Total Output and Production Structure* (Cambridge, MA: Belknap Press of Harvard University Press, 1971), 10–27. Traditional growth rate was below 0.2 percent per year. English growth in the second half of the nineteenth century was therefore at least twice as high as the traditional growth.

15. This is obtained from an estimated 6.0 million people living in England in 1750, and 8.3 million people according to the 1801 census. Census of Great Britain, 1801, *Abstract of the Answers and Returns: Enumeration: Part I: England* (Lake Hanlard: Greater Turnstile, 1802). The implied growth rate is 0.7 percent per year.

16. Ricardo's *Principles of Political Economy and Taxation* (1817) was preceded by two years by his *An Essay on the Influence of a Low Price of Corn on the Profits of Stock, Shewing the Inexpediency of Restrictions on Importation* (London: John Murray, 1815), where arguments are made that are very similar to those in *Principles* but much less developed. The two perhaps most important points of *Principles*—that the distribution and the rate of growth are determined by the cost of producing the marginal unit of food, and that, to prevent economic stagnation, imports of food have to be generally free—are, as the title of the *Essay on the Influence of a Low Price* shows, already contained there.

17. Peter Lindert, "Unequal British Wealth since 1867," *Journal of Political Economy* 94, no. 6 (1986): 1127–1162, 1154.

18. Ricardo, *Principles of Political Economy and Taxation,* ch. V, 57.

19. Marx, *Theories of Surplus Value,* in *Collected Works,* 32:243–244. Emphasis in original.

20. Marx, *Theories of Surplus Value,* in *Collected Works,* 32:348. Emphasis in original.

21. Ricardo, *Principles of Political Economy and Taxation,* ch. XXXII, 276n1.

22. Ricardo, *Principles of Political Economy and Taxation,* ch. VII, 77.

23. David Ricardo to Thomas Malthus, October 11, 1816, in *Works and Correspondence of David Ricardo,* vol. 7, *Letters, 1816–1818,* 78.

24. David Ricardo, "An Essay on Profits (and the Rent of Land)," in *Works and Correspondence of David Ricardo,* vol. 4, *Pamphlets and Papers, 1809–1811,* 18, quoted in Maurice Dobb, *Theories of Value and Distribution since Adam Smith: Ideology and Economic Theory* (Cambridge: Cambridge University Press, 1973), 72.

25. Ricardo, *Principles of Political Economy and Taxation,* ch. XXI, 197 (my emphasis); and *Principles,* ch. XXI, 193.

26. Kenneth Pomeranz, *The Great Divergence: China, Europe, and the Making of the Modern World Economy* (Princeton: Princeton University Press, 2000). "Ghost" acreage, the additional land that the country would need to produce the food that it derives from sources outside its borders, was introduced in Georg Borgstrom, *The Hungry Planet: The Modern*

World at the Edge of Famine, rev. ed. (New York: Collier, 1967). See also Peer Vries, *Escaping Poverty: The Origins of Modern Economic Growth* (Vienna: V&R Unipress, 2013), 290–298.

27. As Offer puts it: "Agricultural protection was sacrificed in 1846 in order to cheapen food, but this carried an obligation to make the oceans safe [for Britain]." Avner Offer, *The First World War: An Agrarian Interpretation* (Oxford: Clarendon Press, 1989), 218.

28. In the chapter on wages, Ricardo accepts the possibility of a difference in real wages among countries, and also recognizes that what is considered subsistence may be socially determined; "habits and customs" play a role: "It is not to be understood that the natural price of labour, estimated even in food and necessaries, is absolutely fixed and constant. It varies at different times in the same country, and very materially differs in different countries. . . . An English labourer would consider his wages under their natural rate, and too scanty to support a family, if they enabled him to purchase no other food than potatoes, and to live in no better habitation than a mud cabin; yet those moderate demands of nature are often deemed sufficient in countries where 'man's life is cheap' and his wants easily satisfied." Ricardo, *Principles of Political Economy and Taxation,* ch. V, 54–55. The view that wages are differentiated temporally (within a given country) and geographically (between countries) was held by Smith, Ricardo, and Marx. But often, for their short- to medium-term analyses, they assumed that wages—at whatever real level they may be—were fixed.

29. Ricardo, *Principles of Political Economy and Taxation,* ch. XVI, 146–148.

30. As is often the case with Ricardo, matters do get more complicated than the initial, strongly stated point suggests. Chapter XVI begins with the statement that the cost of a tax on wages is entirely borne by the employer. Ricardo then goes on to write that taxes, in general, and no less so wage taxes, are often wastefully used. Thus, less of the purchasing power transferred to the government will return to the manufacturer, and the manufacturer's income and investment will diminish. Because demand for labor depends on the capital stock (or on its rate of increase), demand for labor will slow down, and laborers can in the end lose some of their income, even if they have not originally paid the tax. Ricardo, *Principles of Political Economy and Taxation,* ch. XVI, 145.

31. See especially Ricardo, *Principles of Political Economy and Taxation,* ch. V. "It is a truth which admits not a doubt that the comforts and well-being of the poor cannot be permanently secured without some regard on their part, or some effort on the part of the legislature, to regulate the increase in their numbers, and to render less frequent among them early and improvident marriages" (61).

32. The point is nicely illustrated in Dobb, *Theories of Value and Distribution,* 87fn.

33. Ricardo, *An Essay on the Influence of a Low Price,* 5.

34. Ricardo, *Principles of Political Economy and Taxation,* ch. XXI, 193n1.

35. During his travels in Holland in 1822, and comparing the state of the country then with what he remembered from his youth, Ricardo was strongly impressed by the progress and economic prosperity of the country: "The towns of Flanders and particularly of Holland give certain indications of great opulence. The harbours are crowded with ships—the warehouses appear to be full of goods, and the houses are of the first order, and withal kept so clean and neat as to leave no doubt of the opulence of their inhabitants." Ricardo, "Journal of a Tour of a Continent," in *The Works and Correspondence of David Ricardo,* vol. 10, *Biographical Miscellany,* 197.

36. Robert C. Allen, "Class Structure and Inequality during the Industrial Revolution: Lessons from England's Social Tables, 1688–1867," *Economic History Review* 72, no. 1 (2019): 88–125.

37. Ricardo, *Principles of Political Economy and Taxation,* ch. VI, 68n1.

38. In Ricardo's numerical example nominal wages change by about 3 percent (up when the price of corn increases, down when it decreases), which is less than the nominal change in the

price of corn in each direction (6 to 7 percent). The assumption is that wages are regulated not only by the price of corn, but also by other goods whose prices are assumed fixed. This is said in one of Ricardo's long letters to Hutches Trower in 1820, written three years after the publication of the *Principles*: "Corn [price] rises because it is more difficult to produce it. In consequence of the rise of this prime necessity, [price of] labor rises also but not in the same degree in which corn rises." David Ricardo to Hutches Trower, September 15, 1820, in *Letters of David Ricardo to Hutches Trower and Others, 1811–1823*, ed. James Bonar and J. H. Hollander (Oxford: Clarendon Press, 1899; repr. Elibron Classics, 2006), 120.

39. Arthur Okun, *Equality and Efficiency: The Big Trade-off*, rev. and expanded ed., foreword by Lawrence Summers (Washington, DC: Brookings Institution Press, 2015).

40. The effect of the repeal of the Corn Laws was consistent with what Ricardo expected: workers and capitalists gained in real terms, landlords lost, and overall income inequality shrank. Douglas A. Irwin and Maksym G. Chepeliev, "The Economic Consequences of Sir Robert Peel: A Quantitative Assessment of the Repeal of the Corn Laws," Working Paper 28142, National Bureau of Economic Research, Cambridge MA, November 2020, rev. January 2021.

4. Karl Marx

1. Leszek Kolakowski, *Main Currents of Marxism*, trans. P. S. Falla, 3 vols. (Oxford: Clarendon Press, 1978).

2. Michael Heinrich, *Karl Marx and the Birth of Modern Society*, trans. Alexander Locasio (New York: Monthly Review Press, 2019).

3. Heinrich, *Karl Marx*, 144.

4. Heinrich, *Karl Marx*, 56.

5. The estimate was made by Gerd Callesen, historian and editor of the Marx-Engels-Gesamtausgabe (MEGA), in "A Scholarly MEGA Enterprise," *Brood & Rozen* [Bread & Roses: Journal for the History of Social Movements] 7, no. 4 (2002), 79; quoted in Keith B. Anderson, *Marx at the Margins: On Nationalism, Ethnicity and Non-Western Societies*, enl. ed. (Chicago: University of Chicago Press, 2016), 255n9, and see 277n8, 279n25.

6. Michael Heinrich is more specific. He believes that the conversion of Heinrich and Henriette Marx took place sometime between April 3, 1819, and December 31, 1819. Heinrich, *Karl Marx*, 64.

7. There are two remaining legal documents written by Heinrich Marx. One of them, written in 1815 and sent to the Prussian Governor General, was in favor of rescinding French anti-Jewish legislation from 1808. No answer has been preserved, and the legislation was maintained. Heinrich, *Karl Marx*, 59–61.

8. The date of Karl Marx's baptism, together with other children, is not contested: it was 1824.

9. "Indeed, there is not a single indication that Jewish holidays were celebrated in Karl Marx's family or that the children had a Jewish upbringing. . . . It is just as unlikely that Protestant Christianity, to which the family had converted, played an especially large role in Karl Marx's upbringing." Heinrich, *Karl Marx*, 112.

10. This point is stressed in Heinrich, *Karl Marx*, 288.

11. Heinrich, *Karl Marx*, 78.

12. Heinrich, *Karl Marx*, 78.

13. Moritz Kuhn, Moritz Schularick, and Ulrike Steins, "Income, Wealth and Inequality in America, 1949–2013," *Journal of Political Economy* 128, no. 9 (2020): 3469–3519, Figure 5, 18.

14. Dudley R. Baxter, *National Income: The United Kingdom* (London: MacMillan and Co., 1868); Robert Allen, "Class Structure and Inequality during the Industrial Revolution: Lessons from England's Social Tables 1688–1867," *Economic History Review* 72, no. 1 (2019): 88–125, tables 1 and 3.

15. Gregory Clark, "The Condition of the Working Class in England, 1209–2004," *Journal of Political Economy* 113, no. 6 (2005): 1307–1340; and Charles Feinstein, "Pessimism Perpetuated: Real Wages and the Standard of Living in Britain during and after the Industrial Revolution," *Journal of Economic History* 58, no. 3 (1998): 625–658.

16. Friedrich Engels to Karl Marx, October 7, 1858, cited in Roman Rosdolsky, *The Making of Marx's 'Capital,'* trans. Pete Burgess (London: Pluto Press, 1977), 312fn. For the full letter, see Friedrich Engels to Karl Marx, October 7, 1858, Karl Marx and Frederick Engels, *Collected Works*, vol. 40, *Marx and Engels: 1856–1859* (New York: International Publishers, 1975), 381. The idea that the high standard of living of British workers is achieved at the expense of low wages and high rate of exploitation in India appeared as early as Marx's *Poverty of Philosophy*, published in 1847. See Shlomo Avineri, *The Social and Political Thought of Karl Marx* (Cambridge: The University Press, 1968), 168.

17. Engels writes: "The truth is this: during the period of England's industrial monopoly the English working-class have, to a certain extent, shared in the benefits of the monopoly. These benefits were very unequally parceled out amongst them; the privileged minority pocketed most, but even the great mass had, at least, a temporary share now and then." Friedrich Engels, "England in 1845 and in 1885," *Commonweal*, March 1885, 12–14.

18. Karl Marx, *Capital*, vol. I, trans. Ben Fowkes, intro. by Ernest Mandel (London: Penguin, 1976), ch. 25, 803–807.

19. The relative prices of basic goods have indeed tended to rise faster than the prices of luxuries. Philippe T. Hoffman, David Jacks, Patricia A. Levin, and Peter H. Lindert, "Real Inequality in Europe since 1500," *Journal of Economic History* 62, no. 2 (2002): 322–355.

20. Robert Allen, "Capital Accumulation, Technological Change and the Distribution of Income during the British Industrial Revolution," Discussion Paper no. 239, Department of Economics, University of Oxford, June 2005, https://ora.ox.ac.uk/objects/uuid:ee5e13de-74db-44ce-adca-9f760e5fe266.

21. Karl Marx, *The Class Struggles in France (1848–50)*, ed. C. P. Dutt, intro. by F. Engels (London: Martin Lawrence, 1895).

22. Charlotte Bartels, Felix Kersting, and Nikolaus Wolf, "Testing Marx: Income Inequality, Concentration, and Socialism in Late 19th Century Germany," Working Paper 32, Stone Center on Socio-economic Inequality, Graduate Center, City University of New York, March 2021, https://stonecenter.gc.cuny.edu/research/testing-marx-income-inequality-concentration-and-socialism-in-late-19th-century-germany/.

23. John Stuart Mill writes: "The laws and conditions of the production of wealth partake of the character of physical truths. There is nothing optional or arbitrary in them. Whatever mankind produce, must be produced in the modes, and under the conditions, imposed by the constitution of external things, and by the inherent properties of their own bodily and mental structure. . . . It is not so with the distribution of wealth. That is a matter of human institution solely. The things once there, mankind, individually or collectively, can do with them as they like. . . . The distribution of wealth, therefore, depends on the laws and customs of society. The rules by which it is determined, are what the opinions and feelings of the ruling portion of the community make them, and are very different in different ages and countries; and might be still more different, if mankind so chose." John Stuart Mill, *Principles of Political Economy*, Book II, ch. 1, "Of Property."

24. Karl Marx, *Capital*, vol. III, trans. David Fernbach, intro. by Ernest Mandel (London: Penguin: 1978), ch. 51, 1018.

25. Marx, *Capital,* vol. III, ch. 51, 1018 and 1022.

26. Karl Marx, "Critique of the Gotha Program," part I (1875), in Karl Marx and Friedrich Engels, *Selected Works in Three Volumes,* vol. 3 (Moscow: Progress, 1970), 13–30.

27. Eli Cook, "Historicizing Piketty: The Fall and Rise of Inequality Economics," in *Histories of Global Inequalities,* ed. by Christian Olaf Christiansen and Steven Jensen, 35–57 (Cham, Switzerland: Palgrave McMillan, 2019), 46–47, 55.

28. As discussed in the next chapter, this was also Pareto's view, reflected in his distinction between the "optimum for a community" (commonly referred to as the Pareto optimum), and the "optimum of a community." The latter allows that the deterioration in positions of some individuals may be acceptable for the achievement of some social "good." But the decision on that belongs to politicians, not to economists.

29. Karl Marx, *Grundrisse,* trans. with a foreword by Martin Nicolaus (London: Pelican, 1973), 81–110.

30. Marx, *Critique of the Gotha Program,* Part I.

31. The point is nicely discussed in Engels, "Supplement and Addendum to Volume 3 of *Capital,*" Marx, *Capital,* vol. III, 1027–1047.

32. Marx, *Value, Price and Profit,* quoted in Allen W. Wood, "Marx on Equality," in Wood, *The Free Development of Each: Studies on Freedom, Right, and Ethics in Classical German Philosophy* (Oxford: Oxford University Press, 2014), 255.

33. Wood, "Marx on Equality," 255.

34. Friedrich Engels to August Bebel, March 18–28, 1875, Marx, *Critique of the Gotha Program.*

35. Under socialism, too, Marx angrily noted, workers will not receive the full value of their product ("proceeds of labor") because deductions will have to be made for capital depreciation, investments, government administration, workers' insurance against accidents and natural calamities, and more. These deductions, however, and the decisions about their imposition will be made by worker-controlled government, not by individual capitalists. Marx, *Critique of the Gotha Program,* Part I.

36. As we have seen above, this is the point at which Ricardo's *stationary state* kicks in. The term appears in David Ricardo, *The Principles of Political Economy and Taxation,* 3rd ed., intro. by F. W. Kolthammer (London: J. M. Dent and Sons, 1911; repr. New York: Dover, 2004), ch. V, 63.

37. One of the best examples, I think, of the rate of surplus value is from Chinese economic history. As shown in the example, all payments were made *in natura,* and there was no "interference" of capital's contribution to the value added. Jacques Gernet gives the following example. Temporarily enslaved workers in Hongzhou in the mid-thirteenth century were paid eight bushels of wheat per month, or about 0.3 bushels per day (assuming that they worked six out of every seven days). Any worker who, however, did *not* work for a day, was supposed to compensate the owner by 1.5 bushels of wheat (and more in high season). Jacques Gernet, *Daily Life in China: On the Eve of Mongol Invasion, 1250–1276,* trans. H. M. Wright (Palo Alto, CA: Stanford University Press, 1962). The compensation amount thus gives the net gain to the owner from the work of the worker. The rate of surplus value can be easily calculated as 1.5 (surplus) divided by 0.3 (wage) = 5.

38. Karl Marx, *The Eighteenth Brumaire of Louis Napoleon,* trans. Daniel De Leon (New York: International Publishing, 1897), 119.

39. These issues, and especially the length of the workday, are discussed *in extenso* in Marx, *Capital,* vol. I, ch. 10. They can be also philosophically related to Marx's view that real wealth consists of free time: "but free time, disposable time is wealth itself, partly for the enjoyment of the product, partly for free activity which—unlike labor—is not determined by a compelling extraneous purpose which must be fulfilled." Karl Marx, *Theories of Surplus*

Value, in Karl Marx and Frederick Engels, *Collected Works*, vol. 32: *Marx: 1861–1863* (New York: International Publishers, 1989), 391.

40. Marx, *Capital*, vol. I, ch. 23, 716. Even if the original source of alienation lies in the division of labor, and especially the division between manual and mental labor. Like Adam Smith and Adam Ferguson, with whose views Marx was familiar, Marx believed that the division of labor fosters unidimensional interest and ignorance in workers and has negative sociological effects. For Smith and Ferguson, see Ronald Hamowy, "Adam Smith, Adam Ferguson, and the Division of Labor," *Economica* n.s. 35, no. 139 (1968): 249–259.

41. Marx, *Capital*, vol. III, ch. 48, 953.

42. Leszek Kolakowski, *Main Currents of Marxism*, vol. 1: *The Founders*, trans. P. S. Falla (Oxford: Clarendon Press, 1978), 356.

43. Karl Marx, *Class Struggles in France*, 113. The financial bourgeoisie invests in companies' and government bonds. Its income therefore comes from profits—in the first case (companies' bonds) directly so, and in the second case (government bonds) indirectly, as the taxes raised to pay interest on bonds are assessed on profits.

44. Marx, *The Eighteenth Brumaire*, 26.

45. Marx, *Class Struggles in France*.

46. Karl Marx to Pavel Vassilyevich Annenkov, December 28, 1846, in Karl Marx, *The Letters of Karl Marx*, selected, trans., notes by Saul K. Padover (Englewood Cliffs, NJ: Prentice-Hall, 1979), 53.

47. Or, more accurately, their own particular class interest is at the same time universal.

48. Chateaubriand writes that the French "n'aiment point la liberté; l'égalité seule est leur idôle" ("do not like liberty at all; equality is their only idol"). Chateaubriand, *Mémoires d'outre-tombe*, vol. 2: *Livres 13–24* (Paris: Garnier frères, 1898; Garnier: Livre de poche, 2011), 727. Tocqueville similarly asks, with unequal property "remaining the only obstacle to equality among men, and seemingly its only obvious sign, wasn't it necessary . . . that it should be abolished in its turn, or at least that the idea of abolishing it came to the mind of those who did not enjoy it?" Alexis de Tocqueville, *Souvenirs*, preface by Fernand Braudel, postface by J. P. Meyer (Paris: Gallimard, 1978), 130. My translation.

49. The first quotation is from Marx, *Class Struggles in France*, 71. The second quotation is from Marx, *Capital*, vol. III, ch. 47, 949.

50. Marx, *The Eighteenth Brumaire*, 78.

51. Michał Kalecki, "Political Aspects of Full Employment," *Political Quarterly* 14, no. 4 (1943): 322–330. Axel Leijonhufvud, "Capitalism and the Factory System," in *Economic as a Process: Essays in the New Institutional Economics*, ed. R. N. Langlois, 203–223 (New York: Cambridge University Press, 1986).

52. Marx, *Class Struggles in France*, 50.

53. Marx, *The Eighteenth Brumaire*, 45.

54. Christian Morrisson and Wayne Snyder, "The Income Inequality of France in Historical Perspective," *European Review of Economic History* 4 (2000): 59–83.

55. Tocqueville, *Souvenirs*, 146. My translation.

56. Croce writes that "*Das Kapital* is without doubt an abstract investigation; the capitalist society studied by Marx, is not this or that society, historically existing, in France or in England, nor the modern society of the most civilised nations, that of Western Europe and America. It is an ideal and formal society, deduced from certain hypotheses." Benedetto Croce, *Historical Materialism and the Economics of Karl Marx*, trans. C. M. Meredith (New York: Macmillan, 1914), 50.

57. Marx expressed this in an 1847 lecture as follows: "What, then, is the cost of production of labour-power? It is the cost required for the maintenance of the labourer as a labourer, and for his education and training as a labourer . . . the shorter the time required for

training up to a particular sort of work, the smaller is the cost of production of the worker, the lower is the price of his labour-power, his wages." Karl Marx, *Wage Labor and Capital*, trans. J. L. Joynes, introduction by Frederick Engels (Chicago: C. H. Kerr, 1891), ch. 3.

58. Ferdinand Lasalle, "the iron law of wages." Marx, although perhaps (as was his habit) periodically annoyed with Lassalle, writes: "it is well known that nothing of the 'iron law of wages' belongs to Lassalle except the word 'iron,' which is borrowed from Goethe's "great, eternal iron laws,'" Marx, *Critique of the Gotha Program*, Section 2.

59. Rosdolsky, *The Making of Marx's 'Capital.'* Ernest Mandel, *Traité d'économie marxiste*, vol. 1: *Collection 10/18* (Paris : Julliard, 1962). According to Rosdolsky, the only reference that could be interpreted in that sense is in *The Communist Manifesto*, which was a programmatic and political document written by Marx and Engels when Marx was under thirty years old, before he even studied political economy (300). The same view is shared by Avineri, *Social and Political Thought of Karl Marx*, 121.

60. See Ernest Mandel, "Introduction," in Karl Marx, *Capital*, vol. I, 73.

61. This point, however, is not incontestable. It could be that more expensive labor is paired with more productive jobs precisely because it is more expensive to produce. Note also the following difference with the neoclassical economics. In the neoclassical paradigm, technological progress tends to increase productivity of highly skilled labor, which in turn increases its wage. Responding to the wage increase, potential workers increase their demand for the types of education conducive to high-skill jobs. This makes such education more expensive. In the Marxist framework, education may be considered a monopoly of the rich, who erect barriers to entry in the form of high education costs. To recoup these costs, skilled wages need to be high. Such workers are then used only in high-productivity jobs. In other words, it is not that the high productivity of skilled workers is in the driver's seat, but rather that the most expensive education is paired with highly productive jobs.

62. Marx, *Capital*, vol. I, ch. 7, 305.

63. "The improved dexterity of a workman may be considered in the same light as a machine or instrument of trade which facilitates and abridges labor, and which, though it costs a certain expense, replaces that expense with a profit." Adam Smith, *The Wealth of Nations, Books I–IV*, edited with notes and marginal summary by Edwin Cannan, preface by Alan B. Krueger (New York: Bantam Classics, 2003), based on 5th ed. as edited and annotated by Edwin Cannan in 1904, Book II, ch. 1, 358.

64. Jacob Mincer, "Investment in Human Capital and Personal Income Distribution," *Journal of Political Economy* 66, no. 4 (1958): 281–302.

65. Marx, *Theories of Surplus Value*, Part II, quoted in Mandel, "Introduction," in Marx, *Capital*, vol. I, 67n.

66. Marx, *Capital*, vol. I, ch. 22, 702–703.

67. See Marx, *Grundrisse*, 398ff.

68. Karl Marx, *Grundrisse*, trans. with a foreword by Martin Nicolaus (London: Pelican, 1973), 398, emphasis in original.

69. This is, of course, true even if necessary labor time does not go up. It is simply that greater productivity within the same labor time will increase the number of goods and services that workers can buy with their wages.

70. Marx, *Capital*, vol. I, ch. 7, 275.

71. Marx, *Capital*, vol. III, ch. 50, 999.

72. Marx, *Capital*, vol. I, ch. 22.

73. Allen, "Capital Accumulation."

74. Marx, *Wage Labor and Capital*, ch. 5.

75. Marx, *Wage Labor and Capital*, ch. 5.

76. Avineri, *Social and Political Thought of Karl Marx*, 79.

77. See Rosdolsky, *The Making of Marx's 'Capital,'* 294.

78. Note that in the neoclassical production function, K is not a stock but a flow of capital services, again conventionally defined over a year. Joan Robinson insisted that Marx's c should be written as C for the stock of machines and raw materials, and c for the annual expense of both. One can obviously do that, but the problem disappears if we assume the annual turnover of capital. Joan Robinson, *An Essay on Marxian Economics* (New York: St Martin's Press, 1942).

79. Strictly speaking, Marx distinguishes between the technical composition of capital (how many there are actual machines per worker) from the value composition of capital (how much c per unit of v). The discrepancy between the two arises when increased technical composition improves productivity in the production of wage goods and may thus reduce v (while of course keeping the real wage expressed in terms of physical wage goods unchanged). The price changes can also reduce the value of machines used and reduce c as well. But in the definition of the organic composition of capital, Marx assumes that prices are given so that the organic composition moves up or down the same way as technical composition of capital. This allows us to speak of rising organic composition of capital as equivalent to the greater capital (machine) intensity of production. See also a very nice discussion in Guillermo Escudé, *Karl Marx's Theory of Capitalism: Exposition, Critique, and Appraisal* (Moldova: Lambert Academic Publishing, 2021), 400–402.

80. Marx's definition of capital as including advanced wages follows Quesnay's (as discussed in Chapter I).

81. "Necessary time" to produce wage goods may be reduced thanks to higher productivity in the wage-goods sector, leaving the real wage (expressed in terms of goods that a worker can purchase) unchanged while the rate of surplus value increases. We may thus simultaneously have an increase in the real wage and a decrease in the labor share.

82. This particular mechanism was behind Piketty's well-known $r > g$. If more capital-intensive processes of production do not affect the rate of return (that is, r remains more or less constant), then the share of capital must increase. This, in turn, implies elasticity of substitution between capital and labor greater than unity.

83. Marx, *Capital*, vol. III, ch. 13–15.

84. The terms "tendential fall in the rate of profit" and "the tendency of the profit rate to fall" will be used interchangeably as they indeed are in the English-language Marxist literature.

85. Marx, *Theories of Surplus Value*, 73.

86. A constant elasticity of substitution (CES) production function, with the elasticity of substitution greater than 1, will produce, in the case of an increased capital-to-labor ratio (that is, Marx's greater organic composition of capital), exactly the "desired" outcomes: a decline in the marginal productivity of capital, and an increasing capital share. Even a Cobb-Douglas production function will produce a diminished marginal product of capital—that is, the narrow version of Marx's "law."

87. Michael Heinrich, "Crisis Theory, the Law of the Tendency of the Profit Rate to Fall, and Marx's Studies in the 1870s," *Monthly Review* 64, no. 11 (2013): 15–31.

88. Paul Sweezy, *Theory of Capitalist Development* (London: D. Dobson, 1946) quoted in Rosdolsky *The Making of Marx's 'Capital,'* 495. The last seven words read in the original "decrease in the proportion of variable to total capital." For simplicity and consistency with the rest of the analysis here, they can be re-expressed as an increase in the organic composition of capital.

89. In Heinrich's words, "the increase in the rate of surplus-value as a result of an increase in productivity is not one of the 'counteracting factors,' but is rather one of the conditions under which the law as such is supposed to be derived." Heinrich, "Crisis Theory, the Law of the Profit Rate to Fall, and Marx's Studies in the 1870s," *Monthly Review* 64, no. 11 (2013): 15–31.

90. Indeed in Germany, which is perhaps an extreme example, the annual number of hours of work was reduced from 2,400 in 1950 to less than 1,400 in 2014. Data from "Average Annual Work Hours, 1950–2014," Clockify, Palo Alto, CA, https://clockify.me/working-hours.

91. For a more detailed discussion and the summary of earlier contributions, see Samuel Hollander, *The Economics of Karl Marx: Analysis and Application* (New York: Cambridge University Press, 2008), ch. 4. Hollander very carefully shows that the value relationships in (1) can move very differently from technical relationships depending on where technological progress is faster. If it is faster in wage-goods' production and real wage is assumed fixed, s/v can increase by even more than c/v, and thus overturn the tendency of the profit rate to fall. In the long run, however, s/v cannot approach infinity, while c/v can. This was, Hollander explains, Marx's view, as well.

92. William Stanley Jevons, *The Theory of Political Economy,* ed. R. D. Colison Black (1871; London: Pelican, 1970), 245–246.

93. We assume that wage income is entirely consumed.

94. By "random," I mean that the actual rates of profit will have a distribution around the mean profit rate (which in this case is assumed to be close to zero). So, some profit rates will be positive, and some may even be very high.

95. This is a point made, with his usual clarity, by Ricardo: "for no one accumulates but with a view to make his accumulation productive, and it is only when so employed that it operates on profits. . . . The [tenant-]farmer and manufacturer can no more live without profit, than the labourer without wages. Their motive for accumulation will diminish with every diminution of profit, and will cease altogether when their profits are so low as not to afford them an adequate compensation for their trouble, and the risk which they must necessarily encounter in employing their capital productively." Ricardo, *Principles of Political Economy and Taxation,* 73.

96. Note, incidentally, that if the profit rate is zero, Marx's values and prices of production coincide. Also, in the Sraffian system, where the fundamental relationship is $\dfrac{1}{w} = \dfrac{R'}{R' - \pi}$ where R' = maximum rate of profit such that wage = 0, the fact that $\pi = 0$ results in the entire product being purchased by the expended wages. In other words, the "labor commanded" is equal to the labor expended.

97. Marx, *Capital,* vol. III, ch. 14.

98. Engels held a similar view. Thus in 1850 he writes: "We have had many of these revulsions [crises] happily overcome hitherto by the opening of new markets (China 1842), or the better exploiting of the old ones . . . But there is limit to this too. There are no new markets to be opened now." Friedrich Engels, "Social Revolution and Proletarian Ascendance, Say We," *Democratic Review,* March 1850, quoted in Kolakowski, *Main Currents of Marxism,* 1: 300.

99. There is a difference between concentration and centralization of capital. Concentration is increased inequality in the process of expanded reproduction and accumulation of capital; centralization is increased inequality under the given total income or wealth. Thus, Marx writes, it is thanks to centralization of capital through joint-stock companies that large enough capital was created to build railroads: "the world would still be without railways if it had had to wait until accumulation had got a few individual capitals far enough to be adequate for the construction of a railway." Marx, *Capital,* vol. I, ch. 25, 780.

100. Marx, *Capital,* vol. I, ch. 25, 777.

101. For example, "Along with the constantly diminishing number of the magnates of capital, who usurp and monopolise all advantages of this process of transformation, grows the mass of misery, oppression, slavery, degradation, exploitation." Marx, *Capital,* vol. I, ch. 32, 929.

102. The topic of concentration of ownership and monopolization was later used quite extensively in Marxist literature starting with Karl Kautsky, *The Economic Doctrines of Karl Marx,* trans. H. J. Stenning (London: A. and C. Black, 1925), originally published in 1886; Rudolf Hilferding, *Finance Capital,* ed. with intro. by Tom Bottomore, from translations by

Morris Watnick and Sam Gordon (London: Routledge and Kegan Paul, 1981), originally published in 1910; and Paul A. Baran and Paul Sweezy, *Monopoly Capital* (New York: Monthly Review Press, 1966).

103. Branko Milanovic *Capitalism, Alone* (Cambridge, MA: Belknap Press of Harvard University Press, 2019); Yonatan Berman and Branko Milanovic, "Homoploutia: Top Labor and Capital Incomes in the United States, 1950–2020," Working Paper No. 28, Stone Center on Socio-Economic Inequality, Graduate Center, City University of New York, December 2020, https://stonecenter.gc.cuny.edu/research/homoploutia-top-labor-and-capital-incomes-in-the-united-states-1950-2020/. Marco Ranaldi and Branko Milanovic, "Capitalist Systems and Income Inequality," *Journal of Comparative Economics* 50, no. 1 (2022): 20–32.

104. Marx, *Capital,* vol. III, ch. 30, 615.

105. Marx, *Capital,* vol. II, trans. David Fernbach (London: Penguin: 1978), 486–487, emphasis in original.

106. Ernest Mandel, "Introduction," in Karl Marx, *Capital,* vol. II.

107. As shown by Rosdolsky, *The Making of Marx's 'Capital,'* 464ff, 492. The same conclusion was reached by Sergei Bulgakov and Henryk Grosman more than a century ago.

108. Strictly speaking, the income of a capitalist is $\pi\,(c+v)$ where $c+v$ is the amount of capital owned. It is possible, and even likely, that as total capital increases, total profits increase, while the rate of profit declines. For simplicity, however, we take π as representative of capitalists' incomes (as it stands both for the ability of capital to reproduce itself and for the relative power of the capitalist class). Likewise, we take the average wage per unit of work as representative of workers' income. The latter is also a simplification because the number of hours of work can vary.

109. Robinson, *An Essay on Marxian Economics,* 42–43.

110. Marx, *Capital,* trans. Samuel Moore and Edward Aveling (Moscow: Progress Publishers, 1887), ch. 15, sec. 9. The translation by Ben Fowkes in *Capital,* vol. 1, 617–618 is slightly different ("We have seen, too, how this contradiction [between the technical basis of large-scale industry and social relations] bursts forth without restraint in the ceaseless human sacrifices required from the working class, in the reckless squandering of labour-powers."

111. Marx, *Capital,* vol. I, ch. 25, 790.

112. Marx, *Capital,* vol. I, ch. 25, 818.

113. Marx, *Capital,* vol. I, ch. 32, 929.

114. "It follows therefore that in proportion as capital accumulates, the situation of the worker, *be his payment high or low,* must grow worse. . . . Accumulation of wealth at one pole is . . . at the same time accumulation of misery, torment of labour, slavery, ignorance, brutalization and moral degradation at the opposite pole." Marx, *Capital,* vol. I, ch. 25, 799; emphasis added. Note, however, that even in this bleak statement, Marx allows for the increase in the real wage; workers' deteriorating position may be due to the decrease in the labor share.

115. Different scenarios are (unintentionally) presented by Friedrich Engels, "Appendix," in Karl Marx, *Wage Labour and Capital,* trans. J. L. Joynes (1891; Vancouver, BC: George Whitehead, 1991). The 1891 pamphlet is a revision by Engels of Marx's 1847 lecture to the German Workingmen's Club. After opening up the possibility that workers' per-capita incomes may increase, noting that "the share falling to the working class (calculated per head) either rises slowly and inconsistently . . . and at times it may even fall" (58–59), Engels then goes on to assert in a much more politically potent paragraph that "the cleavage of society into a small, extremely rich class, and a great, non-possessing class of wage-workers, causes this society to suffocate from its own superabundance, whereas the great majority of its members are hardly, or not at all, protected against extreme want" (59). We thus have, in two adjacent paragraphs, two very different visions of future workers' income and income inequality.

116. I am grateful to Pepijn Brandon, Anton Jäger, and Jan Luiten van Zanden for very useful comments on the implications of more than one single scenario in Marx.

117. There are also similar data from England and Wales for 1864, as well as the data sets from Ireland for the same two years. Marx, *Capital,* vol. 1, ch. 25.

118. Vilfredo Pareto, "La courbe de la repartition de la richesse," Université de Lausanne, Recueil publié par la Faculté de Droit à l'occasion de l'Exposition nationale suisse, Genève, 1896.

119. Marx, *Capital,* vol. I, ch. 25, 805.

120. Marx, *Capital,* vol. I, ch. 25, 806.

121. Marx's letter published in *Volksstaat,* June 1, 1872, quoted in Frederick Engels, "Editor's Preface," Karl Marx, *Capital,* vol. I, ed. Frederick Engels, trans. S. Moore and E. Aveling, rev. by Ernest Untermann according to the 4th German (1890) ed. (New York: Charles H. Kerr, Modern Library, 1906).

122. Lujo Brentano (anonymously), "How Karl Marx Quotes," *Concordia* 10, March 7, 1872. *Concordia* was the organ of the German Manufacturers' Association.

5. Vilfredo Pareto

1. Michael McLure, "Editor's Notes," in Vilfredo Pareto, *Manual of Political Economy: A Critical and Variorum Edition,* ed. Aldo Montesano, Alberto Zanni, Luigino Bruni, John S. Chipman, and Michael McLure (Oxford: Oxford University Press, 2014), 615. Original Italian edition: Vilfredo Pareto, *Manuale di economia politica* (Milan: Società Editrice Libraria, 1906).

2. See Raymond Aron, "Paretian Politics," in *Pareto and Mosca,* ed. James H. Meisel (Englewood Cliffs, NJ: Prentice-Hall, 1965), 115-120.

3. Pareto rails against racism, in fact: "The thing would seem incredible if it were not true—but there are those among these fierce believers in Holy Equality who hold that Jesus died to redeem all men (and they call them 'brethren in Christ'), and who give their mite to missionaries to go and convert people in Africa and Asia, yet who refuse to worship their God in an American church to which a Negro is admitted." Vilfredo Pareto, *Selections from His Treatise* (New York: T. Y. Crowell, 1965), 73.

4. Pareto scoffs: "If the Negroes were stronger than the Europeans, Europe would be partitioned by the Negroes and not Africa by the Europeans. The 'right' claimed by people who bestow on themselves the title of 'civilized' to conquer other peoples whom it pleases them to call 'uncivilized,' is altogether ridiculous, or rather, this right is nothing other than force." Vilfredo Pareto, *Sociological Writings,* selected by Samuel E. Finer, trans. Derick Mirfin (New York: Frederick A. Praeger, 1966), 136.

5. Pareto, *Sociological Writings,* 140.

6. Pareto, *Sociological Writings,* 213.

7. Pareto, *Sociological Writings,* 138.

8. Vilfredo Pareto, *Les Systèmes Socialistes: Cours professé à l'Université de Lausanne,* 2 vols. (Paris: V. Giard et E. Brière, 1902), 1:7. The beginning of the book contains several strikingly pretentious statements that are supposed to distinguish the kind of economics Pareto likes, the "scientific" kind, as opposed to all others, presumably nonscientific ideologies: "liberal, Christian, Catholic, socialist, etc." (1:2). Just as it would be folly to promote a Catholic or atheistic astronomy, Pareto believes, economics and natural sciences stand on an objective basis of fact, and need no additional qualifier—except, of course, *scientifique.* Such naivete must have been shocking then as it is now.

9. For an excellent biography of Pigou, see Ian Kumekawa, *The First Serious Optimist: A. C. Pigou and the Birth of Welfare Economics* (Princeton, NJ: Princeton University Press, 2017).

10. Raymond Aron, *Main Currents in Sociological Thought,* trans. Richard Howard and Helen Weaver, vol. 2 (1967; London: Pelican, 1970), 177.

11. Vilfredo Pareto, *The Mind and Society*, vol. 1, *Non-Logical Conduct*, ed. Arthur Livingston (New York: Harcourt, Brace, 1935), 9, 231–384.

12. Werner Stark, "In Search of the True Pareto," *British Journal of Sociology* 14, no. 2 (1963): 103–112, 105.

13. Joseph A. Schumpeter, *History of Economic Analysis*, ed. Elizabeth Boody Schumpeter (Oxford: Oxford University Press, 1954, repr. 1980), 860.

14. Franz Borkenau, "A Manifesto of Our Time" (1936), reprinted in *Pareto and Mosca*, ed. James H. Meisel, 109–114 (Englewood Cliffs, NJ: Prentice-Hall, 1965), 113.

15. Aron, *Main Currents in Sociological Thought*, 2:176.

16. Pareto, *Mind and Society*, 1:163n1.

17. Bertrand Garbinti, Jonathan Goupille-Lebret, and Thomas Piketty, "Income Inequality in France, 1900–2014: Evidence from Distributional National Accounts (DINA)," *Journal of Public Economics* 162 (2018): 63–77, Fig. 8, 73.

18. Christian Morrison and Wayne Snyder, "The Income Inequality of France in Historical Perspective," *European Review of Economic History* 4 (2000): 59–83, Tables 2 and 9.

19. Thomas Piketty, *Les hauts revenus en France au xxe siecle: Inegalités et redistribution, 1901–1998* (Paris: Grasset, 2001). Note, however, that Morrisson and Snyder, in "Income Inequality of France," argue that the peak might have been reached around 1860. Their view is explicitly Kuznetsian: inequality increases with industrial development (see Chapter 6). Piketty's view is explicitly anti-Kuznetsian: there is no "spontaneous" change in inequality, and inequality moves in reaction to "big" events like wars and policy decisions such as higher income taxes and taxation of inheritances. Piketty shows conclusively that, across the nineteenth century, inequality widened in France: "les resultats obtenus ne font cependent aucun doute: les dernières estimations disponibles permettent de mettre en évidence un élargissement tendentiel et significatif des inégalites patrinomiales en France au XIXe siècle." Piketty, *Les hauts revenus en France*, 536.

20. Thomas Piketty, *Top Incomes in France in the Twentieth Century: Inequality and Redistribution, 1901–1998*, trans. Seth Ackerman (Cambridge, MA: Harvard University Press, 2018), 497–501.

21. Paul Leroy-Beaulieu, *Essai sur la répartition des richesses et sur la tendance à une moindre inégalité des conditions*, 4th ed., rev. and enl. (Paris: Guillaumin, 1897), vii–viii, quoted in Piketty, *Top Incomes in France*, 498.

22. Piketty, *Les hauts revenus en France*, 537. My translation.

23. Paul Leroy-Beaulieu, *Essai sur la répartition des richesses et sur la tendance à une moindre inégalité des conditions* (Paris: Guillaumin, 1881). Pareto, *Sociological Writings*, 101.

24. David Ricardo, *The Principles of Political Economy and Taxation*, intro. by F. W. Kolthammer (London: J. M. Dent and Sons, 1911; repr. New York: Dover, 2004).

25. François Quesnay, *Quesnay's Tableau Économique*, ed., trans., and notes by Marguerite Kuczynski and Ronald L. Meek (London: MacMillan, 1972).

26. It is somewhat interesting that eugenicists, who were also in some cases Paretians, thought that the distribution of height, weight, intelligence, and, most notoriously, the length of skulls could be altered by conscious state policies, but that income distribution could not. See Terenzio Maccabelli, "Social Anthropology in Economic Literature at the End of the 19th Century: Eugenic and Racial Explanations of Inequality," *American Journal of Economics and Sociology* 67, no. 3 (2008): 481–527.

27. Pareto, *Les Systèmes Socialistes*, 1:158–159. My translation.

28. They are in Vilfredo Pareto, "Aggiunta allo studio sulla curva delle entrate," *Giornale degli economisti*, 2nd series, vol. 14 (January 1897): 15–26.

29. The last five are in Vilfredo Pareto, "La courbe de la répartition de la richesse," in *Recueil publié par la Faculté de Droit, University of Lausanne*, 373–387 (Lausanne: Viret-Genton,

1896), reprinted in Vilfredo Pareto, *Écrits sur la courbe de la répartition de la richesse*, ed. Giovanni Busino (Geneva: Librairie Droz, 1965), 2, 4.

30. In obtaining the data, according to Busino, Pareto was helped by the Swiss Canton of Vaud, where he lived. Giovanni Busino, "Présentation," in Pareto, *Écrits sur la courbe*, x. The data were gathered in 1893 and the first publication was Vilfredo Pareto, "La legge della demanda," *Giornale degli economisti*, 2nd series, vol. 10 (January 1895): 59–68.

31. Pareto, *Écrits sur la courbe*, 1–15.

32. Pareto, *Écrits sur la courbe*, 3.

33. Pareto, *Écrits sur la courbe*, 7. My translation.

34. "So, as a prince is forced to know how to act like a beast, he must learn from the fox and the lion; because the lion is defenceless against traps, and the fox is defenceless against wolves. Therefore one must be a fox in order to recognize traps, and a lion to frighten off wolves." Niccolò Machiavelli, *The Prince*, trans. George Bull (London: Penguin, 1961), 56–57.

35. Stark, "In Search of the True Pareto," 111.

36. Pareto, *Manual of Political Economy*, 197–198.

37. Pareto, *Manual of Political Economy*, 195.

38. Vilfredo Pareto, "La Courbe des Revenus," *Le Monde Économique*, July 25, 1896, 99–100, reprinted in Pareto, *Écrits sur la courbe*, 16–18.

39. Pareto, *Manual of Political Economy*, 195.

40. Vilfredo Pareto, "La répartition des revenus," *Le Monde Économique*, August 28, 1897, 259–261, reprinted in Pareto, *Écrits sur la courbe*, 47.

41. Pareto, "La répartition des revenus," 48. My translation.

42. Vilfredo Pareto to Maffeo Pantaleoni, cited in Busino, "Présentation," in Pareto, *Écrits sur la courbe*, xv. My translation.

43. Pareto, *Manual of Political Economy*, 196.

44. Pareto, *Manual of Political Economy*, 194. The whole curve of income distribution and its "known part" are drawn (Fig. 54, p. 194) in a way that implies that the known part comprises all incomes above the mode of the distribution. Since the mode of the distribution is below the median in asymmetric distributions, Pareto implied that he had data for more than half the population. This seems close to truth. Pareto lists the number of tax units for which he has income data. For Hamburg in 1891, it is 147,000 out of a population of more than 700,000 (21 percent). For Bremen, probably also in 1891, it is 45,000 out of a population of 190,000 (24 percent). In the canton of Zurich, in 1891, it is 81,000 out of a population of 430,000 (19 percent). Pareto, "Aggiunta allo studio sulla curva delle entrate." Using Pareto's own ratio between population and tax units of 2.5 for Saxony in 1886, we can estimate that his fiscal data cover between 50 and 60 percent of the population. Busino, "Présentation," in Pareto, *Écrits sur la courbe*, xiii. Note also that Prussian district-level fiscal data show fairly high coverage (taxpayers/population) until the reforms in 1891, when the fiscal threshold was raised. Charlotte Bartels, Felix Kersting, and Nikolaus Wolf, "Testing Marx: Income Inequality, Concentration, and Socialism in Late 19th Century Germany," Working Paper 32, Stone Center on Socio-economic Inequality, Graduate Center, City University of New York, March 2021, figure D1, 35, https://stonecenter.gc.cuny.edu/research/testing-marx-income-inequality-concentration-and-socialism-in-late-19th-century-germany/.

45. The same point is made in Juliette Fournier, "Generalized Pareto Curves" (PhD diss., Paris School of Economics, 2015).

46. There is yet another unfortunate problem. This is the proliferation of various "Pareto coefficients" that are reformulations of the original α, but—to confuse the reader—retain "Pareto" in their names and add various qualifiers. Atkinson has defined "the inverted Pareto coefficient" $\alpha/(\alpha-1)$, which was known before as the constant β (also known as Van der Wijk's constant), linking the mean value above a given threshold to the level of the threshold.

Anthony B. Atkinson, Thomas Piketty, and Emmanuel Saez, "Top Incomes in the Long Run of History," *Journal of Economic Literature* 49 (2011): 3–71. In fact, in all fractile distributions, for any given threshold, mean income above that threshold will be equal to a constant—in Pareto's case, $\alpha/(\alpha-1)$—times the threshold. There is then "the inverse Pareto coefficient" used by Soltow, which is, more sensibly, defined as simply $1/\alpha$. Lee Soltow, "The Wealth, Income, and Social Class of Men in Large Northern Cities of the United States in 1860," in *The Personal Distribution of Income and Wealth*, ed. James D. Smith (New York: National Bureau of Economic Research, 1975), 235.

47. Frank Cowell, *Measuring Inequality*, 3rd ed. (Oxford: Oxford University Press, 2011).

48. Li Yang, Branko Milanovic, and Yaoqi Lin, "Anti-Corruption Campaign in China: An Empirical Investigation," Stone Center on Socio-Economic Inequality Working Paper 64, April 2023.

49. Pareto, *Manual of Political Economy*, 199–200.

6. Simon Kuznets

1. Simon Kuznets was born in 1901 in the city of Pinsk, then part of the Russian Empire and now in Belarus. During World War I and the Russian civil war, his family was forced by the tsarist government to relocate to Kharkiv, in today's Ukraine. He studied at a gymnasium there and in 1918 entered the Kharkiv Commercial Institute, where studies were often interrupted by war. In 1922, Kuznets emigrated, via Danzig (Gdańsk), to the United States. The only detailed account of his early life can be found in Moshe Syrquin, "Simon Kuznets and Russia: An Uneasy Relationship," in *Russian and Western Economic Thought: Mutual Influences and Transfer of Ideas*, ed. Vladimir Avtonomov and Harald Hagemann (Berlin: Springer, 2022).

2. Simon Kuznets, "Regional Economic Trends and Levels of Living" (1954), reprinted in Kuznets, *Economic Growth and Structure: Selected Essays* (New York: W. W. Norton, 1965).

3. Branko Milanovic, *Worlds Apart: Measuring International and Global Inequality* (Princeton, NJ: Princeton University Press, 2005), 7–11.

4. Kuznets, "Regional Economic Trends," Table 8, 165.

5. My calculations are based on data on GDP per capita from the Maddison Project. I find that the top 6 percent's (that is, the US population's) share of total global income was 24 percent in 1894–1895 and 31 percent in 1949. Maddison Project Database, version 2020 by Jutta Bolt and Jan Luiten van Zanden, Groningen Growth and Development Center, Faculty of Economics and Business, University of Groningen, https://www.rug.nl/ggdc/historicaldevelopment/maddison/releases/maddison-project-database-2020?lang=en.

6. Simon Kuznets, "Inequalities in the Size Distribution of Income" (1963), reprinted in Kuznets, *Economic Growth and Structure: Selected Essays* (New York: W. W. Norton, 1965), 303.

7. Kuznets, "Inequalities in the Size Distribution of Income," 302.

8. Kuznets, "Inequalities in the Size Distribution of Income," 301.

9. My calculations based on World Bank data from World Development Indicators give for 1952 (the first year when China is included in the data) a share of 37 percent. Maddison data, as we have seen above, give 31 percent.

10. For a slightly less optimistic view of the extent of decrease, see Selma Goldsmith, George Jaszi, Hyman Kaitz, and Maurice Liebenberg, "Size Distribution of Income since the Mid-thirties," *Review of Economics and Statistics* 36, no. 1 (1954): 1–36.

11. Piketty, *Le capital au XXIe siècle*, figure 14.1, 805.

12. The data are in real PPP (purchasing power parity) dollars, which adjust for temporal changes in price levels within countries (in addition to differences in countries' price

levels at any given date). My calculations are based on data from the Maddison Project at the University of Groningen (2020 version). Incidentally, this yields for the period 1933–1957 an average per-capita growth rate of 3.3 percent per annum.

13. As discussed in Chapter 4, most of Marx's economic work that was posthumously published by Engels as *Capital,* volumes II and III, was written together with volume I and thus reflects the economic situation as it was known to Marx up to the mid-1860s, including the financial crisis of 1866–1867. The 1870s brought a significant improvement in the position of the English working class and was discussed by Marx and Engels in their correspondence but was never adequately reflected in Marx's own economic research.

14. Simon Kuznets, "Economic Growth and Income Inequality," *American Economic Review* 45 (1955): 1–28, 18.

15. Simon Kuznets, *Modern Economic Growth* (New Haven: Yale University Press, 1966), 217.

16. For support of the assumption of less inequality in preindustrial societies, we may look to findings published some seventy years after Kuznets articulated his original hypothesis. Lindert and Williamson produced the first estimates of inequality for the entire United States, beginning with the thirteen colonies. For 1774, they find a Gini coefficient of 44.1 and a share of 8.5 percent of total income for the top one percent of the population. The northwestern European countries (England and Wales, Holland and the Netherlands) had at that time much higher inequality (a Gini of 57). They conclude: "indeed, there was no documented place on the planet that had a more egalitarian distribution [than the thirteen colonies] in the late eighteenth century" (37). Peter H. Lindert and Jeffrey G. Williamson, *Unequal Gains: American Growth and Inequality since 1700* (Princeton, NJ: Princeton University Press, 2016), 37–39.

17. Kuznets, "Economic Growth and Income Inequality," 16, emphasis added.

18. Lindert and Williamson, *Unequal Gains,* 124.

19. W. Arthur Lewis, "Economic Development with Unlimited Supplies of Labour," *The Manchester School* 22, no. 2 (May 1954): 139–191.

20. These differences are addressed using the example of Mexico's development over the long term in Ingrid Bleynat, Amílcar E. Challú, and Paul Segal, "Inequality, Living Standards, and Growth: Two Centuries of Economic Development in Mexico," *Economic History Review* 74, no. 3 (2021): 584–610. They "argue that [their] findings are explained by a dual economy model incorporating Lewis's assumption of a reserve army of labour and we explain why the decline in inequality predicted by Kuznets has not occurred" (584).

21. "The basic assumptions used throughout are that the per-capita income of sector B [nonagricultural] is always higher than that of sector A [agricultural]; that the proportion of sector A in the total number declines; and that the inequality of the income distribution within sector A may be as wide as that within sector B but not wider. Kuznets, "Economic Growth and Income Inequality," 13.

22. Kuznets, "Economic Growth and Income Inequality," 26.

23. Alexis de Tocqueville, "Memoir on Pauperism" (1835), trans. Seymour Drescher, in Drescher, *Tocqueville and Beaumont on Social Reform* (New York: Harper and Row, 1968), 6.

24. See Gertrude Himmelfarb, "Introduction," in *Alexis de Tocqueville's Memoir on Pauperism,* trans. Seymour Drescher (London: Civitas, 1997), 3.

25. Simon Kuznets, *Shares of Upper Income Groups in Income and Savings* (New York: National Bureau of Economic Research, 1953).

26. Arthur F. Burns, "Looking Forward," in Burns, *Frontiers of Economic Knowledge* (New York: National Bureau of Economic Research, 1954), 136.

27. Felix Paukert, "Income Distribution at Different Levels of Development: A Survey of the Evidence," *International Labour Review* 108 (1973): 97–125; Jacques Lecaillon, Felix

Paukert, Christian Morrisson, and Dimitri Germidis, *Income Distribution and Economic Development: An Analytical Survey* (Geneva: International Labor Office, 1984); Hartmut Kaelble and Mark Thomas, "Introduction," in *Income Distribution in Historical Perspective*, ed. Y. S. Brenner, H. Kaelble, and M. Thomas (New York: Cambridge University Press, 1991); Peter Lindert and Jeffrey Williamson, "Growth, Equality and History," *Explorations in Economic History* 22 (1994): 341–377.

28. It was obvious even then that the real testing should be done for individual countries over a long period of time: "Ideally, such processes should be examined in an explicitly historical context for particular countries." Montek Ahluwalia, "Inequality, Poverty and Development," *Journal of Development Economics* 3 (1976): 307–342, 307.

29. Matthew Higgins and Jeffrey Williamson, "Explaining Inequality the World Round: Cohort Size, Kuznets Curves, and Openness," Working Paper 7224, National Bureau of Economic Research, July 1999. Branko Milanovic, "Determinants of Cross-country Income Inequality: An 'Augmented' Kuznets Hypothesis," in *Equality, Participation, Transition: Essays in Honour of Branko Horvat*, ed. V. Franičević and M. Uvalić, 48–79 (London: Palgrave Macmillan, 2000); Montek Ahluwalia, "Income Distribution and Development: Some Stylized Facts," *American Economic Review* 66, no. 2 (1976): 128–135; Kaelble and Thomas, "Introduction."

30. Sudhir Anand and Ravi Kanbur, "Inequality and Development: A Critique," *Journal of Development Economics* 41 (1993): 19–43.

31. Imre Lakatos, "Falsification and the Methodology of Scientific Research Programmes," in *Criticism and the Growth of Knowledge*, ed. I. Lakatos and A. Musgrave, 91–195. In a strong refutation of the Kuznets hypothesis, Li, Squire, and Zou argue that the Gini variability due to *differences among* countries is much greater than the Gini variability due to *changes within* countries, and consequently that the more important factors driving a country's inequality are idiosyncratic or specific to that country. Hongyi Li, Lyn Squire, and Heng-fu Zou, "Explaining International and Intertemporal Variations in Income Inequality," *Economic Journal* 108, no. 446 (1998): 26–43. The same argument, albeit with less data, was made by Kaelble and Thomas, "Introduction," 32.

32. Higgins and Williamson, "Explaining Inequality the World Round," 11.

33. Jan Luiten van Zanden, "Tracing the Beginning of the Kuznets Curve: Western Europe during the Early Modern Period," *Economic History Review* 48, no. 4 (1995): 1–23.

34. Branko Milanovic, *Global Inequality: A New Approach for the Age of Globalization* (Cambridge, MA: Harvard University Press, 2016), 50.

35. Milanovic, *Global Inequality,* ch. 2.

36. Anthony B. Atkinson, "Bringing Income Distribution in from the Cold," *Economic Journal* 107, no. 441 (1997): 297–321, 300. And Peter Lindert: "It is time to move onto explorations that proceed directly to the task of explaining any episodic movement, without bothering to relate it to the Kuznets Curve." Peter Lindert, "Three Centuries of Inequality in Britain and America," in *Handbook of Income Distribution*, ed. A. B. Atkinson and F. Bourguignon (Amsterdam: Elsevier, 2000), 173.

37. Kuznets, "Economic Growth and Income Inequality," 28.

7. The Long Eclipse of Inequality Studies during the Cold War

1. John Maynard Keynes, *The Economic Consequences of the Peace* (London: Macmillan, 1919); John Maynard Keynes, *The General Theory of Employment, Interest, and Money* (London: Palgrave Macmillan, 1936).

2. Hans Staehle, "Short-Period Variations in the Distribution of Incomes," *Review of Economics and Statistics* 19, no. 3 (1937): 133–143.

3. Arthur L. Bowley, *Wages and Income in the United Kingdom Since 1860* (Cambridge, UK: Cambridge University Press, 1937). Based on Bowley's finding that the share of Great Britain's economic output going to wages had remained stable over time, later economists called it "Bowley's Law."

4. Keynes very significantly contributed to this belief. But the first person who called it a "law," although he later changed his mind, was Michal Kalecki. Hagen M. Krämer, "Bowley's Law: The Diffusion of an Empirical Supposition into Economic Theory," *Cahiers d'économie politique* 61, no. 2 (2011): 19–49.

5. Martin Bronfenbrenner, *Income Distribution Theory* (Chicago: Aldine-Atherton, 1971).

6. Of the Pareto optimum, Offer writes that "its main effect is to provide legitimacy, and protection for the existing distribution of property, however acquired and however unequal." Avner Offer, "Self-interest, Sympathy, and the Invisible Hand: From Adam Smith to Market Liberalism," Oxford Economic and Social History Working Paper 101, Department of Economics, University of Oxford, August 2012.

7. Milton Friedman with the assistance of Rose D. Friedman, *Capitalism and Freedom* (Chicago: University of Chicago Press, 1962), 161–162.

8. For example, Jaroslav Vanek, *The General Theory of Labor-Managed Market Economies* (Ithaca, NY: Cornell University Press, 1970).

9. Anthony Atkinson and John Micklewright, *Economic Transformation in Eastern Europe and the Distribution of Income* (Cambridge: Cambridge University Press, 1992), 99–104.

10. See Dominique Redor, *Wage Inequalities in East and West*, trans. Rosemarie Bourgault (Cambridge: Cambridge University Press, 1992), 61–64; Jan Rutkowski, "High Skills Pay Off: The Changing Wage Structure during Economic Transition in Poland," *Economics of Transition* 4, no. 1 (1996): 89–112; and Richard Jackman and Michal Rutkowski, "Labor Markets: Wages and Employment," in *Labor Markets and Social Policy in Central and Eastern Europe: The Transition and Beyond,* ed. Nicholas Barr (Washington, DC: World Bank; and London: London School of Economics, 1994).

11. Typically, high-skilled labor requires substantially greater education, which costs learners many unpaid hours (reducing the total hours of their active working careers) and might also entail tuition costs. In recognition of this, the observed skill premium is at least in part compensatory (to ensure that the workers choosing the high-skilled path are not penalized in terms of lifetime income). This compensatory part is reduced, obviously, if tuition is zero.

12. This argument does not affect the comparison in Table 7.3 because capitalist countries included there also had free public education. Table 7.3 thus highlights systemic differences.

13. During the "high Stalinism" period, Russia even made wage taxes regressive (with the marginal tax rate *decreasing* with higher wages) to stimulate productivity in the piece-wage-system—a change seen by Mancur Olson as a significant contributor to fast industrialization in the Soviet Union. Mancur Olsen, "Why the Transition from Communism Is So Difficult," *Eastern Economic Journal* 21 (1995): 437–461.

14. In a study that attracted a lot of attention when it was published, Ofer and Vinokur interviewed Soviet émigrés and found that informal payments had made very little difference to overall inequality. Gur Ofer and Aaron Vinokur, "Private Sources of Income of the Soviet Union Households," paper presented at the Second World Congress of Soviet Studies, Garmisch-Partenkirchen, Germany, 1980. Hungarian data similarly find the importance of informal incomes to be less than 10 percent of reported incomes, not out of line with the experience of non-socialist countries. Income inequality moves up when informal incomes are included but very moderately. In the USSR, however, there was a well-known split between the

"core" Slavic republics where informal incomes were relatively small, and the Caucasian republics and Central Asia where they were larger and contributed more to overall inequality. Atkinson and Micklewright, *Economic Transformation in Eastern Europe*, 120–121.

15. Quoted in Allen W. Wood, "Marx on Equality," in Wood, *The Free Development of Each: Studies on Freedom, Right, and Ethics in Classical German Philosophy* (Oxford: Oxford University Press, 2014), 3.

16. Friedrich Engels to August Bebel, March 18–28, 1875, in "Preface," Karl Marx, "Critique of the Gotha Program," part I (1875), in Karl Marx and Friedrich Engels, *Selected Works in Three Volumes* (Moscow: Progress, 1970), 3: 13–30.

17. Friedrich Hayek, *Law, Legislation and Liberty*, vol. 2, *The Mirage of Social Justice* (Chicago: University of Chicago Press, 1978), 70.

18. This point is not often sufficiently appreciated by left-wing thinkers because, having accepted the inevitability of capitalist relations of production, their views naturally tend toward reformism and lower income inequality as an objective in itself.

19. As economists tested the Kuznets curve (as discussed in Chapter 6), it was standard practice to introduce a dummy variable for socialist countries, which was always found to be significant and negative. That is, socialism was associated with less inequality than would otherwise be expected. See, for example, Montek Ahluwalia, "Income Distribution and Development: Some Stylized Facts," *American Economic Review* 66, no. 2 (1976): 128–135; Montek Ahluwalia, "Inequality, Poverty and Development," *Journal of Development Economics* 3 (1976): 307–342; Hartmut Kaelble and Mark Thomas, "Introduction," in *Income Distribution in Historical Perspective*, ed. Y. S. Brenner, H. Kaelble, and M. Thomas (New York: Cambridge University Press, 1991); Branko Milanovic, "Determinants of Cross-country Income Inequality: An 'Augmented' Kuznets Hypothesis," in *Equality, Participation, Transition Essays in Honour of Branko Horvat*, ed. V. Franičević and M. Uvalić, 48–79 (London: Palgrave Macmillan, 2000).

20. Wang Fan-Hsi describes such cash payments occurring as early as the 1920s. When Wang, then a student in Moscow, traveled to Leningrad on an official trip accompanying the German Communist leader Ernst Thaelman, he was paid for each day of that trip the equivalent of his *monthly* student stipend (which in turn was equal to the average worker's wage). Fan-Hsi Wang, *Memoirs of a Chinese Revolutionary 1919–1949*, trans. with introduction by Gregor Benton (Oxford: Oxford University Press, 1980; New York: Columbia University Press, 1991), 101.

21. R.W. Davies, *The Industrialisation of Soviet Russia*, vol. 4, *Crisis and Progress in the Soviet Economy, 1931–1933* (London: Palgrave Macmillan, 1996), 454.

22. Abram Bergson, *The Structure of Soviet Wages: A Study in Socialist Economics* (Cambridge, MA: Harvard University Press, 1946), Table 11, 123.

23. Trotsky evidently believed that excessive leveling was bad for productivity. According to him, "the 'equalizing' character of wages, destroying personal interestedness, became a brake upon the development of the productive forces." Leon Trotsky, *The Revolution Betrayed: What Is the Soviet Union and Where Is It Going?* trans. Max Eastman (Garden City, NY: Doubleday Doran, 1937), 112. Somewhat inconsistently, however, Trotsky in the same book criticized too much emphasis on piecework and the high salaries of Stakhanovite workers, whom he described as a new "workers' aristocracy" (124).

24. Joseph V. Stalin, "New Conditions—New Tasks in Economic Construction: Speech Delivered at a Conference of Business Executives June 23, 1931," in J. V. Stalin, *Works*, vol. 13 (Moscow: Foreign Languages Publishing, 1954), 58–59.

25. For example, in the Soviet Union, the decile ratio of wages of all workers declined from 4.4 in 1956 to 2.86 in 1968 (the minimum point), after which it increased slightly to 3.35 in 1976. Rabkina and Rimashevskaya (1978), cited in Atkinson and Micklewright, *Economic Transformation in Eastern Europe*, Table UE2.

26. The idea of a "new [ruling] class" under socialism predates the actual communist revolutions. Pareto predicted it at the end of the nineteenth century (see Chapter 5). As early as 1923, the manifesto of the Workers' Opposition (a faction within the ruling Bolsheviks that was later liquidated by Stalin) stated: "we are faced with danger of the transformation of the proletarian power into a firmly entrenched clique, which is animated by the common will to keep political and economic power in its hands." E. H. Carr, *A History of Soviet Russia,* vol. 4, *The Interregnum* (New York: Macmillan, 1954), 277. Such expressions multiplied, but, unlike for capital owners under capitalism, the questions of the origin of the power of the new ruling class, and indeed whether it was a class at all, were not agreed upon by all critics.

27. Wesolowski writes that, "although classes (in Marx's sense of that term) disappear in a developed socialist society, there remain social differentiations which may be called social stratification." Włodzimierz Wesołowski, "Social Stratification in Socialist Society (Some Theoretical Problems)," *Polish Sociological Bulletin* 15, no. 1 (1967): 22–34, 24. Originally published in French as Wesołowski, "Les notions de strate et de classe dans la société socialiste," *Sociologie du Travail* 9, no. 2 (1967): 144–164.

28. Branko Horvat, *Ogled o jugoslavenskom društvu* [An essay on Yugoslav society] (Zagreb: Mladost, 1969), 197–198. My translation.

29. Mao Tse-tung, "On the People's Democratic Dictatorship," in commemoration of the 28th anniversary of the Communist Party of China, June 30, 1949, transcription by the Maoist Documentation Project, Marxists.org, https://www.marxists.org/reference/archive/mao/selected-works/volume-4/mswv4_65.htm.

30. Yuan-Li Wu, *The Economy of Communist China: An Introduction* (New York: F. A. Praeger, 1966), 76.

31. The classification remains to this day, including in Chinese household surveys. It was recently used to study the change in the composition of the Chinese "elite" (the richest 5 percent of the population) between 1988 and 2013. Li Yang, Filip Novokmet, and Branko Milanovic, "From Workers to Capitalists in Less Than Two Generations: A Study of Chinese Urban Elite Transformation between 1988 and 2013," *British Journal of Sociology* 72, no. 3 (2021): 478–513.

32. For the development of centralized Chinese statistics, see the excellent Arunabh Ghosh, *Making It Count: Statistics and Statecraft in the Early People's Republic of China* (Princeton: Princeton University Press, 2020).

33. Henry Phelps Brown, *The Inequality of Pay* (Oxford: Oxford University Press, 1977).

34. Phelps Brown, *Inequality of Pay,* 53.

35. John E. Roemer, *Equality of Opportunity* (Cambridge, MA: Harvard University Press, 1998).

36. At first, some of the former owners remained at the managerial positions, but not only was this a short-term compromise, even then their incomes were labor (management) incomes, not property incomes.

37. The rationale for collectivization lay in the alleged (not proved, yet widely believed at the time) lower efficiency of small farms, and the unwillingness of poor and middle peasants to increase production much beyond what was necessary to cover their own needs. (Since industrial production plummeted during Russia's 1917–1922 Civil War, there was nothing for which they could exchange their grain.)

38. Article 1 of the Constitution defines the Soviet Union as "a socialist state of workers and peasants." J. V. Stalin, *Constitution (Fundamental Law) of the Union of Soviet Socialist Republics (1936)* (London: Red Star Press, 1978).

39. One of very few investigations of the private sector in Eastern Europe showed some 20 percent to 25 percent of the private sector share in GDP was the maximum that the system

could tolerate without either turning capitalist or seriously endangering the power of the party/state. Anders Aslund, *Private Enterprise in Eastern Europe: The Non-Agricultural Private Sector in Poland and the GDR, 1945–83* (London: Macmillan, 1985). During the early Chinese liberalization in the 1980s, private-sector companies were limited to eight employees, which, according to some Chinese readings of Marx, was the maximum compatible with absence of exploitation. Yang, Novokmet, and Milanovic, "From Workers to Capitalists in Less Than Two Generations."

40. György Konrád and Ivan Szelényi, *The Intellectuals on the Road to Class Power*, trans. Andrew Arato and Richard E. Allen (New York: Harcourt Brace Jovanovich, 1979); Branko Horvat, *The Political Economy of Socialism: A Marxist Social Theory* (Armonk, NY: M. E. Sharpe, 1983).

41. There were, of course, much earlier statements about the creation of a new ruling class in the Soviet Union. Emma Goldman wrote about the new class already in 1923. Emma Goldman, *My Disillusionment in Russia* (New York: Doubleday, Page, 1923). A number of other, mostly Trotskyist, writers concurred. Probably the first theoretical arguments regarding the class character of the new society were published by Anton Pannekoek and Arturo Labriola. A. Pannekoek, "World Revolution and Communist" (1920), in *Pannekoek and Gorter's Marxism*, trans. D. A. Smart (London: Pluto, 1978); and A. Labriola, *Karl Marx, L'Economiste, Le Socialiste* (Paris: M. Rivière, 1910). Milovan Djilas, in the 1950s, popularized the term "the new class." Milovan Djilas, *The New Class: An Analysis of the Communist System* (New York: Frederick Praeger 1957). But many of these ideas were mere hints or impressionistic descriptions of what the critics observed. They were not laid out in any consistent framework, and even Trotsky himself, despite the ferocious critique of Stalinism, had trouble with the characterization of the Soviet Union as a class society. In fact, Trotsky until his death argued that, despite all, the USSR was a workers' state, even if a degenerate one, and governed by the "ruling stratum," not a ruling class. Trotsky, *The Revolution Betrayed*, ch. 5 and 6, and esp. ch. 9. It was indeed difficult to say differently from the purely Marxist perspective. More developed theoretical arguments had to wait until the 1960s.

42. There was a famous case of a Soviet income distribution published very unexpectedly, in a typical lognormal form, which would normally provide much more information than was usually available. The problem, though, was that the horizontal axis was unlabeled, so one needed to use some creative guesswork to estimate (say) the percentage of workers paid less than a given amount of rubles. The detective work was successfully done by Peter Wiles and Stefan Markowski, "Income Distribution under Communism and Capitalism," *Soviet Studies* (1971): Part I, vol. 22, no. 3: 344–369, Part II, vol. 22, no. 4: 487–511; cited in Atkinson and Micklewright, *Economic Transformation in Eastern Europe*, 42–43.

43. Peter Wiles writes: "They [Communist authorities] clearly dispose of innumerable surveys and a rich store of data, but scarcely any absolute figure has been published." Peter Wiles, *Distribution of Income: East and West* (Amsterdam: North-Holland, 1974), 1. Perhaps "they" theoretically might have disposed of such data, but there is scarcely any evidence that they used them for policy or anything else.

44. I have seen such pieces of information, sent from Goskomstat back to the republics, in the statistical office of Latvia.

45. The Soviet Union was one of the pioneers in the introduction of household surveys. The first surveys of workers' incomes and living conditions took place in the 1920s, were discontinued during high-Stalinism, and then restarted without further interruptions in 1951.

46. It is true even for the Soviet Union. See Natalia Rimashevskaya, ed., *Доходы и потребление населения СССР* [Income and consumption of households of the USSR] (Moscow: Statistika, 1980).

47. Atkinson and Micklewright, *Economic Transformation in Eastern Europe*.

48. Branko Milanovic, *Income, Inequality, and Poverty during the Transition from Planned to Market Economy* (Washington, DC: World Bank, 1998).

49. Atkinson and Micklewright, *Economic Transformation in Eastern Europe;* Harold Lydall, *A Theory of Income Distribution* (Oxford: Clarendon Press, 1980). As in Atkinson and Micklewright, copious data annexes with numerous income distributions are included in Milanovic, *Income, Inequality, and Poverty*. Thus, new researchers, using the data provided in these sources, can start searches for more data relatively easily. It is important to highlight this because so much data collected in the past (especially from the Soviet Union) have been lost due to lack of interest, insufficient financing of archival work, and even technical problems such as incompatibility of older Soviet software with more modern systems. Ironically, despite wondrous technological developments, information saved on paper proved much more durable.

50. An encouraging example is Filip Novokmet's 2017 doctoral dissertation, which gave rise to several published articles. Novokmet studied historical income distributions going back to the pre-communist period of several Eastern European countries. Particularly impressive is Novokmet's integration of economics and politics in studies of long-term inequality in Bulgaria, Poland, and Czechoslovakia. Filip Novokmet, "Between Communism and Capitalism: Essays on the Evolution of Income and Wealth Inequality in Eastern Europe 1890–2015 (Czech Republic, Poland, Bulgaria, Croatia, Slovenia and Russia)," PhD diss., Paris School of Economics, 2017; Filip Novokmet, "The Long-Run Evolution of Inequality in the Czech Lands, 1898–2015," WID.World Working Paper, May 2018, https://wid.world/document/7736/.

51. Leszek Kolakowski, *Main Currents of Marxism,* vol. 1, *The Founders,* trans. P. S. Falla (Oxford: Clarendon Press, 1978).

52. In *Capital,* Marx writes: "In place of disinterested inquirers there stepped hired prize-fighters, in place of genuine scientific research, the bad conscience and evil intent of apologists." Karl Marx, "Afterword to the Second German Edition," *Capital,* vol. I, ed. Frederick Engels, trans. S. Moore and E. Aveling, rev. by Ernest Untermann according to the 4th German (1890) ed. (New York: Charles H. Kerr, Modern Library, 1906).

53. Many economists in addition conflated the abstractness of the theory (which may be useful as a first approximation) with the way the economy really worked. The difference is nicely pointed out by Rawls in his letter to Amartya Sen: "That's like saying general equilibrium theory is partially blind economics. This is something one might reasonably say about an economist but not about the theory, that is, about an economist who thinks general equilibrium theory is all there is to economics and a satisfactory theory of all of economic phenomena." John Rawls to Amartya Sen, July 28, 1981, quoted in Herrade Igersheim, "Rawls and the Economists: The (Im)possible Dialogue," *Revue économique* 73, no. 6 (2023): 1013–1037.

54. Michał Kalecki, "The Determinants of the Distribution of National Income," *Econometrica* 8, no. 2 (1938): 97–112.

55. Nicholas Kaldor, "Alternative Theories of Distribution," *Review of Economic Studies* 23 (1956): 83–100

56. This is a somewhat too charitable interpretation of such models because they often would miss the differences in the scope of socially permissible and possible actions that exist for people at different levels of income distribution, education, race, caste, and gender.

57. The same is true for the so-called macroeconomic models of income distribution that can be dated from Aghion and Bolton. They fall after the time limit of the study here, but they also did not, despite their complexity, bring much new *and* useful. Philippe Aghion and Patrick Bolton, "Distribution and Growth in Models of Imperfect Capital Markets," *European Economic Review* 36 (1992): 603–621.

58. Examples of studies of stochastic models of income distribution include D. G. Champernowne, *The Distribution of Income between Persons* (Cambridge: Cambridge University

Press, 1973); Benoit Mandelbrot, "The Pareto- Lévy Law and the Distribution of Income," *International Economic Review* 1, no. 2 (1960), 79–106; Thomas Mayer, "The Distribution of Ability and Earnings," *Review of Economics and Statistics* 42, no. 2 (1960): 189–195.

59. See, for example, Christopher Bliss, *Capital Theory and the Distribution of Income* (Amsterdam: North-Holland, 1975); Piero Garegnani, "Heterogeneous Capital, the Production Function and the Theory of Distribution," *Review of Economic Studies* 37, no. 3 (1970): 407–436.

60. See Quinn Slobodian, *The Globalists: The End of the Empire and the Birth of Neoliberalism* (Cambridge, MA: Harvard University Press, 2018); and Philip Mirowski, *Never Let a Serious Crisis Go to Waste: How Neoliberalism Survived the Financial Meltdown* (New York: Verso, 2013).

61. For a thorough discussion, see Avner Offer and Gabriel Söderberg, *The Nobel Factor: The Prize in Economics, Social Democracy and the Market Turn* (Princeton: Princeton University Press, 2016).

62. See, for example, Jane Mayer, *Dark Money: The Hidden History of the Billionaires behind the Rise of the Radical Right* (New York: Doubleday, 2016).

63. *Inside Job*, which won the Best Documentary Feature Oscar at the 2011 Academy Awards ceremony, finds the roots of the 2008 global financial crisis in a complex system of corruption. Charles Ferguson, dir., *Inside Job,* Berkeley, CA: Sony Pictures Classics, 2010, DVD.

64. Joseph Stiglitz, "Distribution of Income and Wealth among Individuals," *Econometrica* 37, no. 3 (1969): 382–397.

65. Samir Amin, *Accumulation on the World Scale: A Critique of the Theory of Underdevelopment,* trans. Brian Pearce, 2 vols. (New York: Monthly Review Press, 1974).

66. Alan S. Blinder, *Toward an Economic Theory of Income Distribution* (Cambridge, MA: MIT Press, 1975). Amin's and Blinder's books were both based on their doctoral dissertations. Amin's book was originally published in French in 1970.

67. Gian Singh Sahota, "Personal Income Distribution Theories of the Mid-1970s," *Kyklos* 30, no. 4 (1977): 724–740, 731. Emphasis in original.

68. Sebastian Conrad, *What Is Global History?* (Princeton: Princeton University Press, 2016), 71.

69. Paul Samuelson's *Economics* had an inestimable effect on the schooling of thousands of economists in the United States and around the world. Paul A. Samuelson, *Economics: An Introductory Analysis* (New York: McGraw Hill, 1948). It had an early competitor in Lorie Tarshis's text, but the latter quickly lost out because, among other things, its approach was regarded as too Marxist. Lorie Tarshis, *Elements of Economics: An Introduction to the Theory of Price and Employment* (Boston: Houghton Mifflin, 1947).

70. Paul Samuelson, *Economics,* 10th ed. (New York: McGraw Hill Kogakusha, 1976). And note that Samuelson was hardly alone in this neglect of the topic. Jan Pen complains about the authors of a neoclassical competitor to Samuelson's *Economics,* Richard G. Lipsey and Peter O. Steiner, *Economics* (New York: Harper and Row, 1966), that they devote "*one page of text to distributive shares . . . where they explain that economics really does not yet understand anything about this subject.*" Jan Pen, *Income Distribution: Facts, Theories, Policies* (New York: Praeger, 1971), 23. Emphasis in original.

71. Charles F. Ferguson, *The Neoclassical Theory of Production and Distribution* (London: Cambridge University Press, 1969), 235.

72. "JEL [*Journal of Economic Literature*] Classification System / EconLit Subject Descriptors," American Economic Association, updated February 1, 2022, https://www.aeaweb.org/econlit/jelCodes.php. Robert E. Lucas, "The Industrial Revolution: Past and Future," Annual Report, Federal Reserve Bank of Minneapolis, vol. 18 (May 2004): 5–20, https://www.minneapolisfed.org/article/2004/the-industrial-revolution-past-and-future. Lucas's address

is remarkable in his very accurate description of economic growth and rising (population-weighted and unweighted) between-country inequality from the Industrial Revolution until the end of the twentieth century. But it is also remarkable in his total ignorance of within-national inequalities, and even more surprisingly in his lack of realization that within-national inequality might influence a country's rate of growth (in which Lucas is mainly interested).

73. Atkinson, "Bringing Income Distribution in from the Cold," *Economic Journal* 107, no. 441 (1997): 297-321, 299

74. Piketty allows that Kuznets might simply have been unduly influenced by postwar prosperity, but suspects the economist was not entirely innocent of that pretense: "In order to make sure that everyone understood what was at stake, he took care to remind his listeners that the intent of his optimistic predictions was quite simply to maintain the underdeveloped countries 'within the orbit of the free world.'" In Piketty's judgment, "the magical Kuznets curve theory was formulated in large part for the wrong reasons." Thomas Piketty, *Capital in the Twenty-First Century*, trans. Arthur Goldhammer (Cambridge, MA: Belknap Press of Harvard University Press, 2014), 14, 15. It is, of course, also possible that Kuznets used the qualifier "free" to indicate that his regularity applied only to the capitalist economies of the world, and that those that underwent a socialist revolution might experience a more abrupt decrease in inequality. (See also Chapter 6.)

75. Martin Bronfenbrenner, *Income Distribution Theory* (Chicago: Aldine-Atherton, 1971); Pen, *Income Distribution*.

76. James E. Meade, *The Just Economy* (Boston: G. Allen and Unwin, 1976).

77. Anthony B. Atkinson, "On the Measurement of Inequality," *Journal of Economic Theory* 2, no. 3 (1970): 244-263.

78. Hugh Dalton, "The Measurement of the Inequality of Incomes," *Economic Journal* 30, no. 119 (1920): 348-361; reprinted in *Economic Journal* 125, no. 583 (2015): 221-234.

79. Anthony B. Atkinson and Andrea Brandolini, "Unveiling the Ethics behind Inequality Measurement: Dalton's Contribution to Economics," *Economic Journal* 125, no. 583 (2015): 209-234.

80. Atkinson and Micklewright, *Economic Transformation in Eastern Europe*.

81. Anthony B. Atkinson and A. J. Harrison, *Distribution of Personal Wealth in Britain* (Cambridge: Cambridge University Press, 1978); Anthony B. Atkinson, "Pareto and the Upper Tail of the Income Distribution in the UK: 1799 to the Present," *Economica* 84, no. 334 (2017): 129-156.

82. Regarding the tax schedules, the UK for a long time did not have a tax on unified total income, but rather separate taxes on different types of incomes. For one such example, see Marx's use of tax schedules in Chapter 4.

83. Anthony B. Atkinson, "Seeking to Explain the Distribution of Income," Working Paper 106, Welfare State Programme, London School of Economics, September 1994; and especially Atkinson, "Bringing Income Distribution in from the Cold."

84. Atkinson, "Bringing Income Distribution in from the Cold," 312.

85. See James E. Meade, "Factors Determining the Distribution of Property," in *Income and Wealth Inequality*, ed. Anthony B. Atkinson (Harmondsworth: Penguin, 1973), 298.

86. Various rates of interest, the ratio between labor and capital incomes, and most notably, "the factors symbolized by the portmanteau variable . . . determining the consumer unit's tastes and preferences for consumption versus additions to wealth." Milton Friedman, *A Theory of the Consumption Function* (Princeton: Princeton University Press, 1957), 25.

87. Stiglitz, "Distribution of Income and Wealth among Individuals."

88. The wealth gap is decreasing because both classes have the same wage income, and the rate of savings out of that wage income is assumed to be the same. If wages were

different, or if the saving rates out of wages of the two classes were different, or if savings out of wages were zero, inequality could increase or remain the same.

89. A point mentioned by Meade, "Factors Determining the Distribution of Property," 297.

90. Stiglitz does something similar in his model by allowing the poor to borrow from the rich. Stiglitz, "Distribution of Income and Wealth among Individuals." This mechanism was further developed, empirically and in a much greater theoretical detail, many years later as the explanation for the 2008 financial crisis. Atif Mian, Ludwig Straub, and Amir Sufi, "What Explains the Decline in r*? Rising Income Inequality versus Demographic Shifts," Working Paper 2021-10, Becker Friedman Institute for Economics, University of Chicago, September 2021, https://bfi.uchicago.edu/wp-content/uploads/2021/09/BFI_WP _2021-104.pdf.

91. The shares remained remarkably stable throughout the period between the Second World War and the 2008 global financial crisis. Edward N. Wolff, *A Century of Wealth in America* (Cambridge, MA: Harvard University Press, 2017); Edward N. Wolff, "Household Wealth Trends in the United States, 1962–2016: Has Middle Class Wealth Recovered?" NBER Working Paper 24085, National Bureau of Economic Research, November 2017; Moritz Kuhn, Moritz Schularick, and Ulrike Steins, "Income and Wealth Inequality in America, 1949–2016," *Journal of Political Economy* 128, no. 9 (2020): 3469–3519.

92. For each individual asset class, the top 10 percent of owners are not necessarily the same people. But the evidence based on combined assets indicates that the top 10 percent still owned 90 percent of all financial wealth, and the correlation between the wealthy from one and the wealthy from another asset class is very strong.

93. Daniel Waldenström, "Wealth and History: An Update," IFN Working Paper No. 1411, Research Institute of Industrial Economics, Stockholm, October 14, 2021, https://www .ifn.se/media/442pkvuk/wp1411.pdf.

94. Kuhn, Schularick, and Steins, "Income and Wealth Inequality in America," 3489, Fig. 5B.

95. For the United States: Wolff, *A Century of Wealth in America*, 42, Table 1. For Germany: Markus M. Grabka and Christian Westermeier, "Persistently High Wealth Inequality in Germany," *DIW Economic Bulletin* 4, no. 6 (2014).

96. Keynes, *The General Theory of Employment, Interest, and Money,* 378.

97. "The ideas of the ruling class are, in every age, the ruling ideas; that is, the class which is the dominant material force in society is at the same time its dominant intellectual force. The class which has the means of material production at its disposal, has control at the same time over the means of mental production, so that in consequence the ideas of those who lack the means of mental production, are, in general, subject to it. The dominant ideas are nothing more than the ideal expression of the dominant material relationship." Marx and Engels, "The German Ideology," in Robert C. Tucker, *The Marx–Engels Reader* 2nd ed. (New York: W. W. Norton, 1978), 172.

98. This is true for Tinbergen's work, as well, as he believed both that the skill premium would go down to zero and that income from capital would become minimal. Jan Tinbergen, *Income Distribution: Analysis and Policies* (Amsterdam: North Holland, 1975). Obviously, if the labor share came close to 100 percent of national income, there would not be much use studying distribution of income from capital, or inheritances.

99. I am grateful for this comment to one of the anonymous reviewers who read this book in manuscript.

100. Peter Lindert and Jeffrey Williamson, *Unequal Gains: American Growth and Inequality since 1700* (Princeton: Princeton University Press, 2016), 20, my emphasis.

101. Anthony Barnes Atkinson, *The Economics of Inequality* (Oxford: Clarendon Press, 1975).

102. Atkinson, "Bringing Income Distribution in from the Cold," 311.

103. Last several paragraphs on wage studies are based on Branko Milanovic, "Basic Difference between Wage Inequality and Income Inequality Studies," blog post, Global Inequality blogspot, December 1, 2020, http://glineq.blogspot.com/2020/12/basic-difference-between-wage.html.

104. As mentioned in the Prologue, this is true of structuralist studies, mostly carried out in Latin American countries. As an illustration of the influence of social environment on the types of studies undertaken, Latin American economists were both surrounded by evident class and ethnic cleavages and working in a part of the world that was not as caught up in the Soviet–US conflict as other regions. Latin American authors thus had much greater "freedom" to study income inequality and to question it. In this section, however, I deal principally with dependency theorists—close "cousins" to structuralists but yet a different school. Others with more knowledge of the structuralists might devote more discussion to them than I feel able to.

105. As Trotsky would later sum up the argument, "the privilege of historical backwardness—and such a privilege exists—permits, or rather compels, the adoption of whatever is ready in advance of any specified date, skipping a whole series of intermediate stages." Leon Trotsky, *The History of the Russian Revolution*, trans. Max Eastman (Chicago: Haymarket, 2008), 4.

106. P. H. H. Vries, *Escaping Poverty: The Origins of Modern Economic Growth* (Göttingen: V&R Unipress, 2013), 89. Emphasis in the original.

107. Arghiri Emmanuel, *Unequal Exchange: A Study of the Imperialism of Trade* (New York: Monthly Review Press, 1972).

108. Amin, *Accumulation on the World Scale*.

109. Samir Amin, *Accumulation à l'échelle mondiale* (Paris: Editions 10/18, 1974), 1:464. My translation.

110. In the literature on the top shares that would become popular half a century later, the top one percent income share above one-fifth would be considered an excessive inequality. See, for example, Thomas Piketty, *Capital in the Twenty-First Century*.

111. It was not, in most respects, a "blind alley," as argued in Anthony Brewer, *Marxist Theories of Imperialism: A Critical Survey*, 2nd ed. (London: Routledge, 1990), 198. That blind alley changed our perspective on inequality.

112. Brewer, *Marxist Theories of Imperialism*, 164. For more on what Frank meant by the term, see André Gunder Frank, "The Development of Underdevelopment," *Monthly Review* 18, no. 4 (1966): 17–31.

Epilogue

1. Ben White, "Student Finds a Market for Greenspan Portraits," *Cape Cod Times*, August 16, 2005, https://www.capecodtimes.com/story/business/2005/08/16/student-finds-market-for-greenspan/50902672007/.

2. In 2008, the number of foreclosures in the United States (1.8 percent of all housing units) was thrice as high as in 2006, before the crisis (0.6 percent). See "Minorities, Immigrants, and Home Ownership: Through Boom or Bust, Part 5: Foreclosures in the U.S. in 2008," Pew Research Center Report, May 12, 2009, https://www.pewresearch.org/hispanic/2009/05/12/v-foreclosures-in-the-u-s-in-2008/.

3. Thomas Piketty, *Capital in the Twenty-First Century* (Cambridge, MA: Belknap Press of Harvard University Press, 2014).

4. John Maynard Keynes, *The General Theory of Employment, Interest, and Money* (London: Palgrave Macmillan, 1936).

5. Thomas Piketty, *Top Incomes in France in the Twentieth Century: Inequality and Redistribution, 1901–1998* (Cambridge, MA: Belknap Press of Harvard University Press, 2018).

6. Branko Milanovic, "The Return of 'Patrimonial Capitalism': Review of Thomas Piketty's *Capital in the 21st Century*," *Journal of Economic Literature*, 52, no. 2 (2014): 519–534.

7. Branko Milanovic, *Global Inequality: A New Approach for the Age of Globalization* (Cambridge, MA: Harvard University Press, 2016).

8. Thomas Piketty, *Capital and Ideology* (Cambridge, MA: Belknap Press of Harvard University Press, 2020).

9. Peter Lindert and Jeffrey Williamson, "Reinterpreting Britain's Social Tables 1688–1911," *Explorations in Economic History* 20 (1983): 94–109; Peter Lindert and Jeffrey Williamson, *Unequal Gains: American Growth and Inequality since 1700* (Princeton, NJ: Princeton University Press, 2016).

10. Robert Allen, "Class Structure and Inequality during the Industrial Revolution: Lessons from England's Social Tables, 1688–1867," *Economic History Review* 72, no. 1 (2019): 88–125.

11. Christian Morrisson and Wayne Snyder, "The Income Inequality of France in Historical Perspective," *European Review of Economic History* 4 (2000): 59–83.

12. Javier Rodríguez Weber, *Desarrollo y desigualdad en Chile 1850–2009: Historia de su economía política*, Centro de Investigaciones Diego Barros Arana (Santiago de Chile: Ediciones de la Dirección de Bibliotecas, Archivos y Museos, 2017), https://www.centrobarrosarana .gob.cl/622/articles-75886_archivo_01.pdf; Diego Castañeda Garza and Erik Bengtsson, "Income Inequality in Mexico 1895–1940: Industrialization, Revolution, Institutions," Lund Papers in Economic History, General Issues, no. 2020:212, Department of Economic History, Lund University, 2020, https://lup.lub.lu.se/search/files/77326250/LUPEH_212.pdf; Maria Gómez León and Herman de Jong, "Inequality in Turbulent Times: Income Distribution in Germany and Britain, 1900–50," *Economic History Review* 72, no. 3 (2018): 1073–1098.

13. Filip Novokmet, "Entre communisme et capitalisme: essais sur l'évolution des inégalités des revenues et des patrimoines en Europe de l'Est, 1890–2015" (PhD diss., Paris School of Economics, 2017).

14. Mikołaj Malinowski and Jan Luiten van Zanden, "Income and Its Distribution in Preindustrial Poland," *Cliometrica* 11, no. 3 (2017): 375–404.

15. Philipp Emanuel Erfurth, "Unequal Unification? Income Inequality and Unification in 19th Century Italy and Germany," Working Paper 46, Stone Center on Socio-Economic Inequality, Graduate Center, City University of New York, November 2021, https://stonecenter .gc.cuny.edu/research/unequal-unification-income-inequality-and-unification-in-19th-century -italy-and-germany/.

16. International Comparison Program, Development Data Group, World Bank, https://www .worldbank.org/en/programs/icp.

17. My calculations, based on World Development Indicators databank, World Bank, https://datacatalog.worldbank.org/search/dataset/0037712/World-Development-Indicators.

18. Christian Olaf Christiansen and Steven Jensen, eds., *Histories of Global Inequality: New Perspectives* (Cham, Switzerland: Palgrave Macmillan, 2019).

19. See, for example, Fernand Braudel, *Civilization and Capitalism, 15th–18th Century*, 3 vols., trans. Sian Reynolds (New York: Harper and Row, 1982–1984); Paul Bairoch, *Victoires et déboires*, 3 vols. (Paris: Gallimard, 1997).

ACKNOWLEDGMENTS

This book has been under "preparation" for many years, in some ways perhaps even since my early university studies, when I first read Marx. The preparation continued over the years with Ricardo and Smith, and then, as I became more interested in income distribution, with Pareto and Kuznets. It was around that time that I read Schumpeter's brilliant studies of classical economics, first in his short book *Economic Doctrine and Method: An Historical Sketch,* originally published in 1912, and then in his unfinished and monumental *History of Economic Analysis.* Wesley Mitchell's discussions of Smith and Ricardo were also texts I enjoyed and from which I learned much. Quesnay came a bit later and, as he has done for many readers, provided hours of both frustration and enjoyment.

The history of economic thought is not very much studied today, and unfortunately students seldom read classical authors in their entirety. At most, they are offered selected parts from the most important works, and even these are being squeezed further. It was perhaps to improve this sad state of affairs that I came to the idea of looking at how, from before the French Revolution to the end of the Cold War, history's most influential economists studied income distribution, and what they thought about the forces that create and maintain economic inequality among people.

These issues are discussed throughout the book. There is no need to say more about them here—except possibly to explain my choice of the time span under examination. The beginning date was relatively easy: François Quesnay is in many ways the founder of political economy. He influenced Smith directly and, by extension, Marx. Moreover, his look at income distribution in prerevolutionary France lets us see how inequality appeared to economists working in a society where the social class was not only an economic but also a legal category. The end period is no more arbitrary. The 1990s were a tremendously important decade that witnessed the fall of communism and the end of the Cold War. As I argue in the book, the eclipse of income distribution studies in the second half of the twentieth century, in both socialist and capitalist countries, was due to political elements—notably, the Cold War itself. It was only after the ideological competition of the two systems ended that inequality studies revived, reinvigorated not only by the end of the ideological "prohibition" against looking at social classes and inequality, but also by the rising inequality in most countries of the world. Thus, I think, work on income distribution has a bright future—the subject of the book's Epilogue.

I wrote these chapters during the first year and a half of the COVID-19 pandemic, at first while practically secluded in my house in Washington, DC, and then while I was "free" to move, but not fully. Comments I received while writing reflect this unusual situation. On the one hand, I was able to present my work in progress remotely to audiences in many parts of the world—sessions that certainly would have been more difficult and more costly to organize in person. On the other hand, the fact that each discussion and exchange of comments ended with the Zoom session meant that I lost some exposure to opinions and critiques that could have been more easily shared in person, over a dinner or a beer.

During the conception and the development of the book, I benefited from the always wise advice of Ian Malcolm, the editor of my previous two books with Harvard University Press and the original editor of this one. Ian provided very useful comments on the first draft of the book. He had left the Press by the time the book was nearing its turnover date, but was ably replaced by Grigory Tovbis, whose many comments have been very valuable. I am grateful to Julia Kirby for her excellent and very thorough editing which has improved the quality of the book, and to Anne McGuire for pushing me hard to document, in endnotes and footnotes, many of my statements.

I would especially like to thank two readers for their very careful critiques of the book. The comments they provided are every writer's dream: careful and substantive, but also implementable without major structural adjustments.

Various chapters were kindly read by many friends and colleagues. I have received insightful written comments from all of them, with some of the more committed readers even commenting on three or four chapters. Those who contributed to the book in this way are listed here in alphabetical order: Kevin Anderson, Mihail Arandarenko, Charlotte Bartels, Ingrid Bleynat, Pepijn Brandon, Christian Christiansen, Pascal Combemale, Simon Commander, Angus Deaton, Cedric Durand, Juan Grana, Karen Hoffmaester, Anton Jäger, Max Krahe, Rishabh Kumar, Michael Landesmann, Peter Lindert, Ulysse Lojkine, Boško Mijatović, Filip No-vokmet, Avner Offer, Leandro Prados de la Escosura, Marco Ranaldi, Gérard Roland, Mike Savage, Paul Segal, Bas van Bavel, Jans van t'Klooster, Mattias Vernengo, Isabella Weber, David Wootton, and Stefano Zamagni.

I would also like to thank organizers and participants at the seminars where the chapter on Marx was presented (in chronological order of presentation): University of Massachusetts in Boston, University of Geneva, University of Greenwich, University of Utrecht, Université Libre de Bruxelles, Universidad Nacional de San Martin, Indian Economy Lab, Uppsala University, and Bucknell University. As well as generating many valuable comments, these sessions introduced me to the sources I did not know about, and presented me with different interpretations of Marx. All of this significantly improved the Marx chapter, which was probably the most demanding of the book.

Working at the Graduate Center, City University of New York, and at the Stone Center on Socio-Economic Inequality helped me access many sources I needed. I also benefited from the congenial atmosphere for work and research created by my colleagues at the Stone Center, and especially by its director, Janet Gornick.

INDEX

Page numbers in italics indicate figures, tables, or illustrations.